The Maritime Traditions of the Fishermen of Socotra, Yemen

Julian Jansen van Rensburg

Archaeopress Archaeology

ARCHAEOPRESS PUBLISHING LTD
Gordon House
276 Banbury Road
Oxford OX2 7ED

www.archaeopress.com

ISBN 978 1 78491 482 0
ISBN 978 1 78491 483 7 (e-Pdf)

Cover image: The author consulting with fishermen in Zahaq (Photo: author)

This book is available direct from Archaeopress or from our website www.archaeopress.com

Acknowledgments

This book is the result of a long relationship with Socotra and its fishing communities which began in 2003 when I first visited the island as a neophyte researcher. As many visitors to the island will attest, Socotra holds a strange allure that continues to draw one back time and time again. Personally, this attraction is the result of having the opportunity to share in the lives of the fishermen, who have been overwhelmingly generous throughout my years of constant questioning and for whom I have the utmost respect. My deepest gratitude goes to all of those fishermen who shared their knowledge and experience with me, allowed me to accompany them on their fishing trips and supplied me with endless cups of tea.

I would especially like to thank my Socotri guides Ahmed Abdullah, Abdullah Hazeem and Eisa Abdullah, whose tireless efforts have made it possible for me to gather such a rich corpus of data. I am also extremely grateful to Miranda Morris, who kindly shared her extensive knowledge of Socotra and its people, and helped me in my research both on and off the island. Finally, I would also like to thank Dionisius Agius and John Cooper for their guidance, and Paul Lunde and Kay van Damme for all their help in finding and translating the Portuguese and Dutch texts used in this research.

Acknowledgements

Contents

List of Figures

Notes on transliteration

In this study I have used words in Socotri and the dialectical Arabic spoken on Socotra. These words are distinguished by the insertion of the following notations: (Soc) for Socotri and (Ar) for Arabic. For the transliteration of Arabic text I have adopted the Library of Congress Arabic Transliteration System, which is outlined below. For place names, such as Hadhramaut and Socotra, I have retained their common English spellings to aid in readability. The exceptions to this are the place names of villages and significant landmarks on Socotra, which have been transliterated. I have chosen to transliterate these to demonstrate the similarities between these features and the fishing areas identified by the fishermen interviewed.

Arabic transliteration

Consonants

ء	ʾ	س	s	ل	l
ب	b	ش	sh	م	m
ت	t	ص	ṣ	ن	n
ث	th	ض	ḍ	ه	h
ج	j	ط	ṭ	و	w
ح	ḥ	ظ	ẓ	ي	y
خ	kh	ع	ʿ		
د	d	غ	gh		
ذ	dh	ف	f		
ر	r	ق	q		
ز	z	ك	k		

Vowels

Long vowels		Short vowels	
ا	ā	ـَ	a
و	ū	ـُ	u
ي	ī	ـِ	i
	ō	o	
	ē	e	

Doubled

شّ	iyy (final form, ī)
وُّ	uww (final form, ū)

Diphthongs

يْ	ay
وْ	aw

The Socotri language is an ancient spoken Semitic language that represents one of the six Modern South Arabian (MSA) Languages (Simeone-Senelle 1998: 310). Socotri has a variety of local dialects, which are geographically divided into three main regions, namely the eastern, western and central mountain area (Morris 2002: 8). The Socotri words I have recorded are in the eastern and central dialect. While there have been a number of studies concerning the Socotri language, no formal system of transliteration is available. Consequently, for the transliteration of the Socotri terminology I have used a system followed by Miranda Morris, an ethnographer and linguist, who has spent several years studying the Socotri people and their language. While the majority of symbols used in the transliteration of Socotri are the same as those used in the Library of Congress Arabic Transliteration System, there are several additional symbols used. These are listed below:

/ ə / – A mid-central short vowel that sounds like the first / a / in banana.

/ ˈ / – An accent used to mark stress, written over the vowel of the stressed symbol, for example: e̍ʾeris – An easterly wind.

/ ɛ / – An open-mid front unrounded vowel, or low-mid front unrounded vowel that sounds like the / a / in dare.

/ ʌ / – An open-mid back unrounded vowel, or low-mid back unrounded vowel that sounds like the / u / in cut.

/ š / – Represents the / sh / used in the Library of Congress system for ش.

/ ġ / – Represents the / gh / used in the Library of Congress system for غ.

/ ź / – A lateralized voiced palato-alveolar, which gives a sound peculiar to Socotri and the other MSA Languages.

Glossary

Arabic

A

ᶜarīš – A building of inferior construction, but can also be used to describe a building with a palm-frond roof.
ᶜayn – Eye.
ᶜayn wāḥid – One eye.
Azyab – The North East monsoon.

B

Bāb al-Khayr – Gate of fortune.
Al-baḥr – The sea.
Baḥr al-Hind – The Indian Sea.
Bārija (pl. bawārij) – Pirate ship.
Barrī – A hot wind that blows from the land.

D

Dāᶜwa – Land-use law cases.

F

Futūḥ/ al-futūḥ/ futūḥ al-baḥr – These terms are used to describe an open season, or an open sea, where the sea and weather is calm enough for the fishermen to go fishing, normally during the North East monsoon.

H

Al-Hind – India.
Hindī – An easterly wind.
Hūrī (pl. hawārī) – A dugout log boat.

J

Jebel – Mountain.
Jāhiliyyah – (Lit., A state of ignorance). This is the period before Islam.
Jinn – spirit.

K

Kaᶜal Fīrᶜūn – Pharaoh's testicles.
ḳharīf – Autumn.
Khawr – A small fresh or brackish lake.
Kōs – South West monsoon.

L

Luʾluʾ – Pearl.

M

Miqdāf – A paddle.
Mūsim maṭar – Rainy season.
Muqaddim (pl. muqaddamīn) – Village leader(s).
Muwalladīn – (Lit., born again). A term used to describe the African community. The term is used as a socio-cultural reminder that they are of slave descent and separate from the rest of the Socotri community.

Q

Qāfal – A period when the sea is said to be closed, normally during the South West monsoon.
Qaṭaᶜat – An area.
Quṭn – Imported cotton twist from East Africa.

R

Rabīᶜ – Spring.
Rās – head, also used to refer to a headland.

S

Ṣabb – Seine net.
Ṣayf – Summer.
Sharq – An easterly wind.
Shāsha (pl. shāshāt or shūsh) – A date palm-frond boat.
Shimār – A northerly current.
Shitāʾ – Winter.
Sikūṭ – A southerly current.
Surrāq – Pirates.

W

Wādī – A valley, although this word is also used to refer to a dry riverbed that flows during heavy rains.
Wārra – A motorised vessel.
Watār – Fishing line.
Wazīr – Minister.

Z

Zanj – Land of the Blacks, in reference to the Bantu population of East Africa.

Socotri

A

ᶜa̍brihi – A northerly wind.
ᶜālə – An easterly flowing current.

B

Be̍ᶜelə – The Green sea turtle.
Bɛ̄ – Without/ lacking.
Bɛ̄-dōti – A monsoon period in which no summer rains have occurred.
Bi̍lbil – An oyster shell (Pinctada radiata, and others of this family).

D

Di-ᶜabde̍rihon – A Loggerhead turtle.
D-il-wāšik – Possibly an Olive Ridley turtle.
Ḍi-gīneṭ – Hook shaped.
Di-gyɛ̄me – Those who live below.
Di-ᶜīləhe – A monsoon period that is generally characterised by variable winds and unsettled weather.
Di-ṣa̍ᶜanhen (pl. Di-ṣa̍ᶜanhen) – Those who live above.

Di-tịmərə – Date-palm tree.
Dɔ̄mer – A stormy period characterised by strong winds and high seas.
Dɔ̄ti – A monsoon period that is generally characterised by high humidity, cloudy skies and occasional showers of rain.

E

ẹ̀ʾeris – An easterly wind.
ᶜẹ̀ḳelhe (pl. ᶜaḳālihe) – Fish hook.

F

Fɔ̄tir – The fruiting stalk of a date palm.

G

Gɔ̄diᶜ – Tree trunk.
Gyạ̀ḥś – A period when the skies begin to clear and the winds drop. The period in which the NE winds finally begin to blow steadily.

H

Ḥal idụ̀mhur – A time when the clouds begin to gather and there is a threat of storms.
Ḥfo – A small tree belonging to the Vernonia species.
Ḥfōs – A Sea cucumber.
Ḥorf – South West monsoon.
Hūrī d-mʌ̀ḳədef – A hūrī that is paddled.
Ḥʌ̀ṣihin – Iron.

I

ịʾiśhur – Cotton fibre.
ịʾiśīrə – A cotton bush.
ịkšə – Commiphora ornifolia.

K

ḳārat̩ – A Hawksbill turtle.
ḳdf – To row or stir.
ḳeneᶜịti – The end, tip, or extremity.
ḳẹ̀rḳor – Fish trap.
ḳẹ̀yat̩ – Summer.

L

Lẹ̀ḥe – A westerly flowing current.

M

Mạ̀ᶜadeft – A circular cast net.
Mạ̀ᶜaribo – A westerly wind.
Maḥrif – A friend or acquaintance, but is mostly used to describe a relationship based upon a system of mutual assistance and dependency that operates on different levels and within different groups of society.
Maᶜḳɔ̄mə – A holed stone.
Mẹ̀de – A southerly wind.
Menḳẹ̀yat̩ (Soc) – A monsoon period when the heat becomes very intense and there are no clouds.
Mġēbīya – A hot wind that blows during dɔ̄ti and ḳẹ̀yʌt̩.
Mgịbbə – An area where the sea is deep.
Mịdəher – Current.
Mịnzek – Gaff.
Mịtrer – Croton socotranus, a widespread endemic shrub that grows abundantly on the coastal plains.
Mọ̀gədif – A paddle.
Mọ̀ṣəliḥ – A black-lip pearl shell (Pinctada margaritifera).
Mɛ̄ʾ – Towards or in the direction of, used in connection with mịdəḥer.
Mə̀ḳdif (pl. mḳādif) – An oar or paddle.

N

Nāmilə – Possiby a Leatherback turtle.

R

Rhịy – Headland.
Rɛ̄muš – A raft.

S

Šạ̀ḥaḳ – Shellfish gathering, can also mean a low tide, or when the tide is out.
Sə̀dʌḳ – A sail-powered wooden vessel.
Ṣẹ̀rbihi / ᶜạ̀brihi – A northerly wind.
Ṣerẹ̀bhen – An inter-monsoon period that occurs after the SW Monsoon and before the NE monsoon, it is characterised by the build up and dispersal of clouds, variable winds and the possibility of rain.
Śẹ̀rḥʌ – A sewn boat.
Šhibereh – A ridge, plateau, or escarpment that overlooks the sea.
Śọ̀ʾhor – Fishing line.
Ṣɛ̄reb – Winter.
Šwạ̀r – Calm, in reference to the sea.

T

Ṭịfher (pl. ṭifherịtin) – The operculum of a shell, can also mean a fingernail.

Z

Źʌ̀mdə – Bait.

Part One:
The Study

Chapter 1

Introduction

The Socotra archipelago lies at 11° 50'N 51°17'E, approximately 135 nautical miles (Nm) northeast of Cape Guardafui, Somalia and 205Nm south of Rās Fartaq, Yemen (Figure 1). The archipelago is made up of four main islands, Socotra, ᶜAbd al-Kūri, Samḥa, Darsa and two rocky outcrops Sābūniyah and Kaᶜal Fīrᶜūn. The largest and most important of these islands is Socotra, which measures 135km in length, 42km in width and has a surface area of 3650sq.km, making it one of the largest of the Arabian islands (Edgell 2006: 423). Socotra has approximately 50,000 inhabitants, who are mainly engaged in pastoralism, cultivation and fishing (Morris 2003: 6; Klaus *et al.* 2003; Miller and Morris 2004; Elie 2008). The inhabitants of Socotra may be divided into two areas based upon their geographical location and livelihood, namely: the mountain dwelling pastoralists and the coastal dwelling fishermen and merchants. The highest concentrations of people live in and around the capital of Ḥadiboh, Qalansiyah and several fishing villages along the north coast. These villages are made up of an eclectic ethnic mix of East and North Africans, South Arabians and to a lesser extent Socotri Bedouin. Recently the coastal population has seen a substantial rise in the amount of seasonal immigrants from Yemen. These immigrants mainly work as labourers and merchants and now form the bulk of the coastal population. This influx of seasonal immigrants has brought about substantial changes to the people of Socotra in a number of ways. First, their presence has brought about a marked change in the market for fish, which has transformed fishing from a means of subsistence to one of the most lucrative economic activities on Socotra. This has led many of the interior pastoralists to abandon their cultural disdain and social taboos on fishing and become fishermen (Elie 2004: 74). Secondly, this influx of Arabic speaking immigrants is also leading to a gradual decline in the use of their native Socotri, an ancient spoken Semitic language that represents one of the six Modern South Arabian languages (Simeone-Senelle 1996; Morris 2002). This change to the socio-economic and cultural lives of the inhabitants and the resultant loss of their cultural traditions, practices, knowledge and language

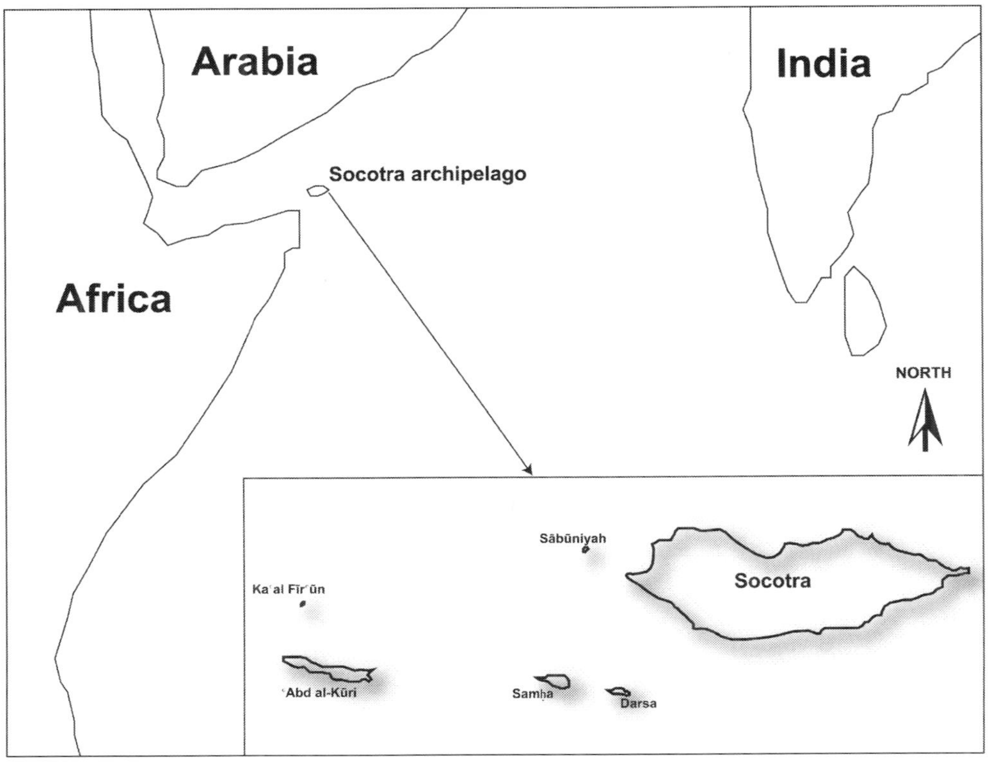

Figure 1. The Socotra archipelago (Drawn: author).

is widely recognised and several studies have been undertaken to document it (Naumkin 1993; Stein 1996; Simeone-Senelle 1996; Morris 2002; Miller and Morris 2004; Jansen van Rensburg 2010). Unfortunately, the majority of these studies have focussed on the interior pastoral inhabitants and few have specifically looked at the fishermen and their cultural traditions, practices and knowledge.

The earliest ethnographic study to specifically address the Socotri fishermen was undertaken in 1967 by the linguist and ethnographer R. B. Serjeant (1992; 1995), who sought to investigate and describe the coastal communities of Socotra as part of a joint military and civilian survey of the island. This study contains a wealth of information concerning the fishermen's cultural traditions, practices and social organisation and provides a corpus of data that has been used in subsequent studies concerning fishermen on Socotra. However, due to the limited amount of time he had available, the difficulties he encountered in travelling around the island and problems with the language spoken, there are several shortcomings in his study (Serjeant 1992: 133). These are mainly to do with the geographical scope of his study, which was limited to a few villages on the north coast, and his reliance on Arabic speaking informants. The next ethnographic study was undertaken between 1970 and 1988, by the Russian ethnographer and linguist Vitaly Naumkin. This work did not focus on the fishermen, but does provide a brief descriptive account of their socio-economic circumstances, fishing practices and the equipment used (Naumkin 1993). This was followed, approximately 20 years later, by another ethnographic description of the inhabitants of Socotra undertaken by the ethnographer Miranda Morris, who also briefly examined the fishermen (Morris 2002). Morris's unpublished study provides a brief, relatively detailed description of the fishermen's cultural traditions and practices, although it is primarily focussed on the transhumant pastoralists of the interior (Morris 2002: 8). While these three ethnographic studies have helped contribute to our understanding of the cultural traditions, practices and knowledge of the fishermen of Socotra, there is still a significant amount of work left to be done. In particular, there is still a great deal we do not understand about the ways in which the diverse ethnic groups involved in fishing have influenced maritime traditions and the adoption and use of fishing equipment in different parts of the island. We also know nothing about the fishermen's fishing areas or methods of navigation. Furthermore, there is comparatively little we understand about the effect of the environment and maritime landscape on regional fishing traditions. This is in spite of the fact that each of the aforementioned studies have emphasised the influence of the environment on fishing practices and have gone so far as to list the characteristics and duration of the different fishing seasons. Due to these gaps in our knowledge, the brevity of these studies into the fishermen and their traditions, and the rapid socio-economic and cultural changes

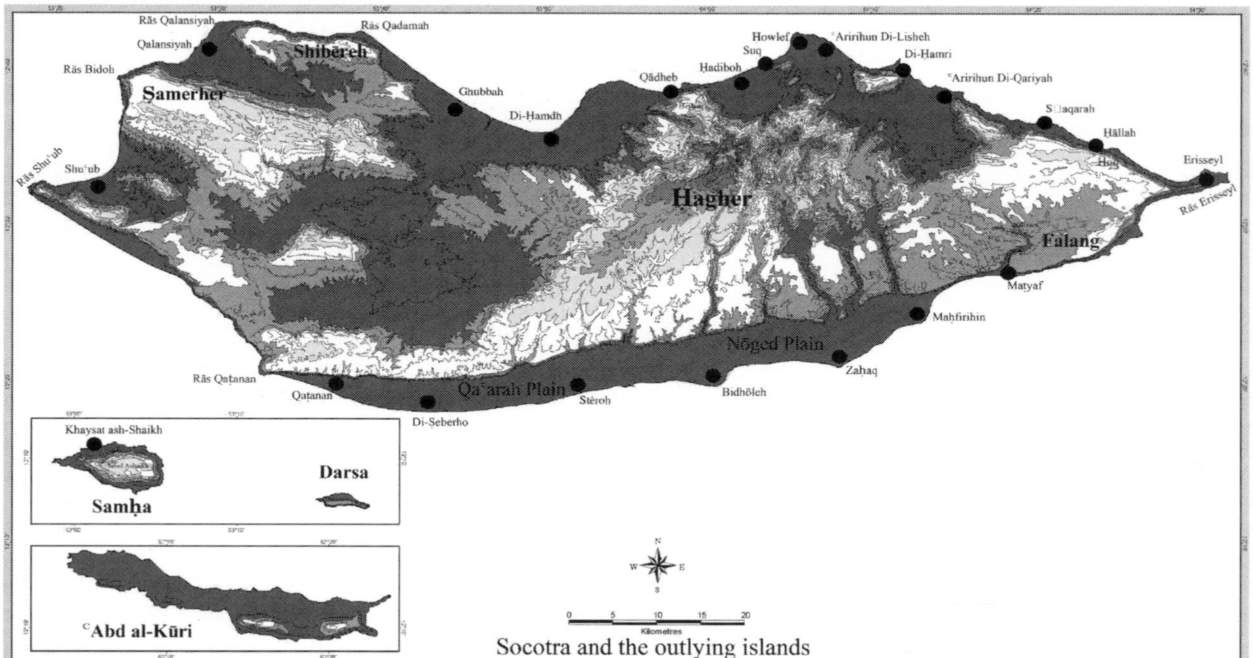

Figure 2. Topographical map of Socotra together with the outlying islands of Samḥa, Darsa and ᶜAbd Al-Kūri; showing the fishing villages around the island of Socotra and Samḥa.

affecting the fishermen's cultural traditions, practices, knowledge and language today, there is a real need for a comprehensive study of the fishing communities on Socotra.

I first identified this lacuna when undertaking research into the fishermen and their traditional vessels, between 2003 and 2007. During this time I was acutely aware of how the modernisation of the fishing industry was causing the loss of many social and cultural traditions. I also recognised the geographical disparities of previous studies, which have favoured the populous fishing villages on the north coast of the island and almost completely ignored those less-established villages in the south. Consequently, when undertaking my current research I sought to address these gaps in our knowledge and undertake a study that would describe and analyse the fishermen's maritime traditions. To avoid the same imbalances of my predecessors I chose to include fishermen from villages along the north and south coast of Socotra and the island of Samḥa. The villages I was able to visit and obtain information from are given in Figure 2.

Research objectives

The research objectives of this study were to analyse the fishermen's maritime traditions and knowledge and to determine how social, environmental and technological influences have shaped them. By maritime traditions I mean those practices that are borne out of the human experience of the sea and the elemental activities and objects of the fishermen's daily life. These encompass both intangible and tangible elements. The intangible refers to the fishermen's perceptions, beliefs, knowledge and language, whilst the tangible or physical elements refer to their fishing equipment and includes vessels and tackle.

In order to realise these aims I adopted a transdisciplinary approach, which allowed me to cross the disciplinary boundaries of ethnography, history, archaeology, meteorology and geography, and present a holistic view of the fishermen and their maritime traditions. The primary research discipline used is ethnography, which forms the bulk of the data. This is complemented by archaeological and historical evidence, which give an insight into the ethnic and cultural background of the fishing communities and provide a temporal framework for this study. The spatial framework rests with the disciplines of meteorology and geography, which are used to contextualise findings at different scales of analysis.

To address the main objectives of this research I posed the following main questions:

1. How have social, environmental and technological influences shaped the maritime traditions of the fishermen of Socotra?
2. How long have the different ethnic groups on Socotra been involved in fishing, and what influence has this had on their maritime traditions?
3. How has the ethnicity of the fishermen influenced social interaction and how has this affected the regional traditions?

Other questions that I will address are:

4. What role does the weather and landscape have in shaping maritime traditions and are there regional differences?
5. How have the technological developments of fishing vessels and equipment been affected by the social, economic and environmental factors on Socotra, and are there any regional differences?

To answer these questions and make sense of the complexities surrounding the adoption and formation of maritime traditions it has been necessary to divide this book into four parts. The first part provides an introduction to the study, reviews the diverse literature available and outlines the theoretical and methodological approaches I have adopted. The second looks at the ethnic diversity of the fishing population in the past and present and their social interaction on land and at sea. The third section outlines the environmental influences affecting the fishermen and analyses the way in which these influences are perceived and what adaptations have been made on a regional level. The fourth and final part describes and interprets the fishing equipment that was, and still is being used on the island and examines how social, economic and environmental influences have affected what and where this equipment is used. With these four parts in place I conclude by looking at how this study can aid in our understanding of the social, cultural and political factors influencing maritime communities and port towns along the Indian Ocean littoral.

Chapter 2

Literature Review

Ethnographic studies of the Socotri fishing communities and their practices have attracted little interest in the research agendas of Socotra, which have been primarily concentrated on documenting the cultural traditions, social transformation and language of the Socotri inhabitants living in the interior. Moreover, those studies interested in the fishermen communities on Socotra have been undertaken by governmental agencies or academics on behalf of governmental organisations, and are mostly descriptive accounts of the fisheries sector. This is clearly seen in the four volumes of the Proceedings of the First International Symposium on Socotra 1996, in which the only reference to these communities are within reports concerning the fisheries sector, which provide little more that quantitative data on the number of fishermen and their catch. Furthermore, none of the ethnographic studies published within these four volumes refer to the social or cultural traditions of Socotra's fishing communities (Dumont 1998; 1999). Consequently, there are many gaps in our understanding of the fishermen's living traditions; the interrelationship between the fishermen's adaptation to and exploitation of the maritime environment and the role played by socio-political and cultural influences. To fully appreciate the extent of this gap this literature review not only examines the ethnographic accounts concerning the fishermen of Socotra, but also scrutinises the historical and archaeological record for information about them. The literature reviewed is divided into three themes: historical, archaeological and ethnographic accounts.

Historical Accounts

> '[Socotra's] history has yet to be written, and must be compiled from references dispersed in a multiplicity of books and records, not so much as in Arabic as in Greek, Latin, Syriac, Portuguese, Dutch, English, French, and even Danish. [Chinese and Indian sources can now also be added to this list]...It will be long before all significant allusions have been collected from chronicles, travel narratives, and the archives of the European trading companies' (Beckingham 1983: 172).

To unravel Socotra's historical narrative from the multitude of historical sources available is exceedingly complex and beyond the remit of my research and this review. Moreover, as studies into the historical narrative of Socotra continue, more and more primary sources are tracked down, which has left many of the earlier studies lacking (Beckingham 1983; Naumkin 1993; Doe 1993; Beyhl 1998; Botting 2006; Cheung *et al.* 2006). As a result, previous studies of Socotra's historical narrative have mostly concentrated on specific periods and events in Socotra's history and have sought to identify and analyse the socio-political changes that occurred during these periods. This review will look at these earlier historical studies undertaken in conjunction with those primary sources that refer to Socotra. However, as the focus of my research is the fishermen of Socotra, the emphasis will be on those historical sources which either allude, or directly refer to the fishermen and their traditions.

The Classical Period (8th century BC to 6th century AD)

During the classical period little was apparently known about people of Southern Arabia and the island of Socotra other than that they were the principal exporters and producers of frankincense and myrrh (Groom 1981: 10). These highly coveted and expensive aromatics played a vital role in the ancient world and were used in huge quantities to pay tribute to a multiplicity of gods. Scholars studying the classical sources have been able to prove that there are a number of sources that do refer to Socotra, although the majority contain little more than brief descriptions referring to the existence of the island, or list products that can be obtained there, such as frankincense, Indian cinnabar (Dragon's blood), and Socotran aloes. Those accounts that did refer to the inhabitants called them either troglodytes or turtle eaters. The classical works within which Socotra has been referred to are: Herodotus, (*c.* 5th century BC), *The Histories* (2.3.107-112); Theophrastus, (*c.* 287 BC), *Historia Plantarum* (2.9.8-10); Agatharchides of Cnidus, (*c.* 2nd century BC), *On the Erythraean Sea* (5. 105a); Diodorus Siculus, (*c.* 1st century BC), *Bibliotheca Historica* (5.41.4; 5.42.5); the *Periplus Maris Erythraei*, (mid-1st century AD), (32. 10. 3-25); Pliny the Elder, (*c.* AD 79), *Natural History* (6.32.153; 6.34.170; 6.36.153), and Ptolemy, (*c.* AD 168), *Geography* (6.7.45; 8.22.17).

The earliest, most pertinent account for this study is that written by the historian and geographer Agatharchides of Cnidus (*fl.* 2nd century BC), who derived his information on Socotra or the 'Fortunate Islands', as it was known, from sailors that had visited the island. According to him, the inhabitants were known as turtle eaters, alluding to the fact that there was likely to have been a fishing community on Socotra, who were engaged in hunting and eating turtles (Agatharchides 1989: 169). By the mid-1st century AD Socotra, known as *Dioscuridês* at this time, was a major supplier of turtle shells (Casson 1989: 69). This would seem to indicate that the inhabitants on Socotra were hunting turtles to eat from at least the 2nd century BC, and by the mid-1st century AD were also keeping the shells to trade with visiting merchants.

The earliest detailed historical account of Socotra and its people was written by an anonymous Greek trader from Egypt in the mid-1st century AD in a book entitled the *Periplus Maris Erythraei* (Schoff 1912; Huntingford 1980; Casson 1989). This book was much like a modern day pilot guide which, in addition to describing the navigational directions to follow, also described the trading opportunities available at various ports throughout the Indian Ocean. The main points concerning Socotra were that it was possible to obtain frankincense, dragon's blood, turtle shells and Socotran aloe there; that the north coast was inhabited by Greek, Indian and Arabian traders, and that it was being ruled from the mainland of Yemen. This description is the best known classical account concerning Socotra and has been highly influential in many scholarly studies pertaining to the island's trading links, population and products (Bent 1900; Doe 1992; Botting 2006; Cheung *et al.* 2006). It also provided the main impetus for many archaeological expeditions to Socotra, whose aims were to unearth evidence for the presence of an earlier population residing on the north coast (Bent 1900, Shinnie 1960, Doe 1967; Naumkin and Sedov 1993). The *Periplus Maris Erythraei* is particularly important for this study in that it provides the earliest evidence of people engaged in hunting for turtles and possibly other marine species, and locates them geographically along the north coast, which was the main area of settlement on the island.

The Medieval Period (7th to 15th century AD)

Within the medieval period there are a prolific number of references to Socotra in the writings of Muslim, Chinese and European geographers, navigators and travellers. So abundant are these references that sifting through them can almost be overwhelming, and there is no certainty that all references relating to Socotra will be found. Furthermore, reading through the majority of these sources it is clear that few authors provide much new information and there is a great deal of repetition. The reason for this is likely to have been due to the fact that many of the Muslim, Chinese and European medieval authors copied earlier accounts and few actually visited the island, or were able to obtain first-hand information. Modern scholars using the medieval sources tend to have concentrated on specific events or topics relating to Socotra, notably the Christian inhabitants of Socotra, and that Socotra supplied highly prized aloes, dragon's blood and ambergris to various parts of the Indian Ocean, including China (Hirth and Rockhill 1911; Smith 1985; Ubaydli 1989; Doe 1992; Naumkin 1993; Müller 2001; Biedermann 2006; Cheung *et al.* 2006). This has resulted in several gaps in our understanding of the sources consulted, and has subsequently influenced what we know of the cultural makeup of the coastal population as well as the importance of Socotra in navigational traditions, and in the trade of marine species. Therefore, it is necessary to revisit the medieval accounts in order to ascertain what the Muslim, Chinese and European accounts can tell us about Socotra's inhabitants, in particular those who were involved in fishing.

The earliest medieval reference to Socotra is in the 6th century AD, when the Greek Nestorian Christian monk and merchant from Egypt, Cosmas Indicopleustes (*fl.* 6th century AD), refers to having met Greek Christians from Socotra in Ethiopia. According to Indicopleustes, the island of Socotra was inhabited by Greeks sent there by Ptolemy I Soter (d. 283 BC), and they were all Christians (Indicopleustes 1896: 119). The research of Müller (2001) and Biedermann (2006), would suggest, however, that the inhabitants of Socotra were converted by St Thomas the Apostle (d. AD 72), in 52 AD, when he was shipwrecked on the island en-route to India. The importance of this event is that it shows that the Christians on Socotra were likely Nestorians and that shipping to India must have passed if not stopped at Socotra. The presence of Christians on Socotra attracts a lot of attention in Muslim and European accounts throughout the medieval and post-medieval period. This can be attributed to the fact that Socotra was a Christian enclave in a predominantly Muslim area, a fact that led to the inhabitants being regarded with derision by the Muslim authors, who saw them as being involved in sorcery and piracy.

The Muslim Authors

The earliest Muslim author to mention Socotra was the Persian geographer and bureaucrat, Ibn Khurradādhbih (d. AD 911). Serving as a postmaster general and spy for the ᶜAbbāsid Caliph al-Muᶜtamid (r. AD 869-892) he gathered together one of the earliest administrative geographies entitled, *Kitāb al-masālik wa l-mamālik* (The Book of Routes and Provinces), (Khurradādhbih 1889: 73). This work, translated by De Goeje, outlines the major land and sea routes of this period and the trade in which various areas are engaged in. Socotra was noted as an important navigational landmark at the entrance to the Red Sea and was said to be famous for its trade in bitter aloes. No mention is made of the inhabitants. What is particularly significant here is Socotra's importance as a landmark into the Red Sea, which is repeatedly mentioned throughout the medieval and post-medieval period, and forms an important part of the 15th century Muslim navigational treatise.

The first Muslim medieval account to provide any indication of Socotra's population is al-Hamdānī (d. 945), a Yemeni geographer, historian and astronomer. In his *Ṣifat Jazīrat al-ᶜarab*, (Description of the Arabian Peninsula), Al-Hamdānī reiterates Indicopleustes's description of Socotra being inhabited by Christian Greeks, but identifies a tribe from al-Mahra in Hadhramaut that had also settled on Socotra and became Christian (Hamdānī and Müller 1968: 93-94). This provides the first indication of the origins of the Arabian settlers who, in 15th century accounts, are recorded as ruling over Socotra. Moreover, it also demonstrates the complexities involved in attributing an ethnicity to the Christian inhabitants. Al-Hamdānī also mentioned that the island was famous for the great quantities of aloes, dragon's blood and ambergris. These products are repeatedly referred to by the medieval and post-medieval authors and were amongst Socotra's main trading commodities. What is of particular interest here is the ambergris that was believed to have been extracted from captured whales (Yule and Cordier 1993: 2.406-407). This would appear to demonstrate that the inhabitants, whether native to the island or migrants from Greece and the Hadhramaut, had the knowledge and skill to capture whales and presumably other marine species.

The Baghdadi geographer and historian al-Masᶜūdī (d. AD 956), provides, in his *Murūg al-dhahab wa-Maᶜādin al-Jawhar* (Meadows of Gold), a very similar narrative to that of al-Hamdānī. Within it he too refers to the Greek and Christian inhabitants, and notes that Socotra was famous for its aloes, dragon's blood and ambergris (Doe 1992: 136-137). In addition, he provides the first account concerning pirates on Socotra. Within al-Masᶜūdī's description, the island was ruled over by Indian pirates, before the Greeks came to Socotra, who plundered passing merchant ships. This reference to Indian pirates is interesting in that if they were Christians, like the inhabitants, it is likely that they would have found a ready market for their spoils on the island. This would tie in with later accounts by Marco Polo of pirates trading with the Christian inhabitants (Yule and Cordier 1993: 2.407).

The next reference to Socotra's population is a compilation of travellers' accounts that was collected by Sulaymān al-Tājir (Sulaymān the Merchant) and others, and completed *c.* 851 AD. This compilation was re-edited and added to by Abū Zayd Ḥasan b. Yazīd of Siraf (*fl.* 10th century) and became known as, *Akhbār al-Ṣīn wa-l-Hind*, translated and edited by Sauvaget (1948: 228). This compilation repeats the earlier accounts concerning the presence of Christians, that Greeks once resided on the island and that Socotra was famous for its aloes.

This is similar to the description of Socotra by the Persian ship captain, Buzurg ibn Shahriyār, al-Rāmhurmuzī (*fl.* 10th century), who is famous for his book entitled, *Kitāb ᶜadjā'ib al-Hind* (The Book of the Marvels of India: Mainland, Sea and Islands), (Buzurg 1966: 82). This book is a compilation of stories and anecdotes from ships captains, pilots, traders and other seafaring men who sailed the Indian Ocean. Within Buzurg's narrative he also repeats earlier accounts concerning the Greeks and Christians that resided on the island, and how Socotra was famous for its aloes. In both of these accounts the importance of Socotra as a navigational landmark into the Red Sea is mentioned, yet neither provides any detailed information, reinforcing the fact that even though people are aware of Socotra little is actually known about the island.

The Indian pirates mentioned by Al-Masᶜūdī are again referred to by the geographical historian al-Muqaddasī (*fl.* 10th century), in his book *Aḥsan al-taqāsīm fī na'rifat al-aqālīm* (The Best Divisions for Knowledge of the Regions). According to him, Socotra was the haunt of Indian pirates, who patrolled the waters and caused sailors to fear for their lives until they had safely passed the island (Muqaddasī 2001: 13). He does not specify whether or not they were residing on Socotra although, in light of al-Masᶜūdī's account, and that the Christian inhabitants are likely to have traded with them, it is possible that they may have been.

The next account in the 11th century is that by the Iranian scholar al-Bīrūnī (d. AD 1048), who was noted for his work in the fields of mathematics, physics, geography and history. According to the translations of his works, Socotra was ruled by Christians and supplied the best myrrh and aloes for the drug trade (Bīrūnī 1983: 142). These two themes provide the basis for most earlier accounts and it is likely that al-Bīrūnī had copied his information from previous authors, emphasising the importance of Socotra as a supplier of aloes and once again the lack of first-hand knowledge about the island or its people.

Al-Idrīsī (d. AD 1165), a geographer, presents an illustrative account of Socotra in his maps and descriptions of the world. Al-Idrīsī's work is known either as, *Kitāb nuzhat al-mushtāq fī ikhtirāq al-āfāq* (The Delight of One Who Wishes to Traverse the Regions of the World) or *al-Kitāb Rujār* (The Book of Roger), after the Norman king Roger II who commissioned the work. Incorporating knowledge obtained from Muslim and Norman merchants and explorers, al-Idrīsī produced one of the most accurate maps of the world for the medieval period. Within his description of Socotra he referred to the island as being ruled by Christians and producing the world's finest aloes (Idrīsī 1836: 1.371). Al-Idrīsī's stylised maps place Socotra relatively accurately at the entrance to the Red Sea, similarly to the work of Ibn Khurradādhbih. That Socotra would feature in al-Idrīsī's world map demonstrates several important points already alluded to in earlier texts. First, Socotra was, during the medieval period, considered an important navigational landmark for entering the Red Sea, especially as it is depicted lying almost at the entrance of the Red Sea. Secondly, the Socotran aloe was an important export and finally that the island was a Christian enclave.

The work of Yāqūt (d. AD 1229) a celebrated traveller and scholar, entitled, *Kitāb mu'jam al-buldān* (A Lexicon of Countries), offers an insight into the general state of knowledge concerning Socotra and neatly sums up the overall themes in the Muslim medieval sources up to this period. According to his description of Socotra, the island was originally inhabited by Greeks and was ruled over by Christians (Yāqūt 1873: 6.237). He also refers to the Indian pirates that al-Ma^{c}ūdī and al-Muqaddasī warned sailors about and that the island supplied aloes, dragon's blood and ambergris.

The most descriptive examination of Socotra and its inhabitants from the Muslim sources is found in the traveller Ibn al-Mujāwir's (d. AD 1291) book entitled *Tārīkh al-mustab~ir* (A Chronicle for Someone who Seeks to Understand). This book presents a wealth of miscellaneous information concerning many aspects of the island, which include the physical geography of the island, its history, the position of its villages, people and their practises, and the methods sailors used to navigate to Socotra. It is also accompanied by a highly stylized map of the island, which depicts various navigational landmarks (Ibn al-Mujāwir 1954; Ibn al-Mujāwir 2008). In addition to the Christians, aloes, dragon's blood and ambergris found in earlier Muslim accounts, Ibn al-Mujāwir also refers to the two groups of people, those that live in the mountains and those that live along the coast (Ibn al-Mujāwir 1954: 2.264). According to him, the coastal people had an intimate relationship with visiting pirates and were sorcerers, who could cause the weather to change at will. The importance of this description is that it is a first-hand observation of Socotra and its people by someone who actually visited the island, and it clearly identifies a coastal population. In addition, he also discusses the coastal population's close relationship with pirates, which would allow for one to surmise that the pirates of earlier accounts were as intimate with the coastal population as had been reported by Ibn al-Mujāwir (1954: 2.265). Finally, he referred to the seas surrounding Socotra having been full of fish, even though he does not mention who or what was catching them. The significant of this reference to fish is noteworthy insofar as it alludes to a rich available resource that was undoubtedly being exploited by the coastal inhabitants, who are likely to have also been those trading in ambergris.

A further source of information on Socotra comes from a recently discovered manuscript entitled, *Kitāb gharā'ib al-funūn wa-mulaḥ al-'uyūn* (The Book of Curiosities). The manuscript, believed to have been copied from an anonymous work compiled in the first half of the 11th century in Egypt, was recently (2002), digitised and translated at the Bodlein Library, Oxford (The Book of Curiosities 2007). This manuscript contains a rich source of hitherto unpublished historical and cartographical information, and in its description of Socotra mentions the Socotran aloes and that Nestorian Christians inhabited the island. However, the most interesting part of this description is a passage that refers to Socotra as having been under the rule of black pirates, something which had not been recorded before. This account demonstrates a continuation with the earlier accounts of pirates and, when viewed in conjunction with Ibn al-Mujāwir's account, would appear to demonstrate that amongst Socotra's coastal population there may have been East Africans.

The island of Socotra also features in the works of the Persian historian and geographer, Ḥamd Allāh Mustawfī Qazvīnī, (d.*c.* 1340 AD), who wrote a book entitled, *Ḥudūd al-'ālam* (The Regions of the World). The translations of this book, unlike other accounts, makes no mention of Socotra's produce or history, instead it refers to Socotra as an island of little amenity, with many inhabitants (Qazvīnī 1970: 29). Due to the lack of detail it can only be surmised that he had little information available to him, especially as Socotra has never been considered by earlier authors to be particularly populous.

Ibn Baṭṭūṭa (d. AD 1368-9), the Moorish traveller born in Tangiers who travelled extensively around the Indian Ocean, does not describe Socotra in his *Riḥlah* (Book of Travels), but does refers to an encounter with Indian pirates off Socotra (Baṭṭūṭa 1956: 1.224). According to him, the pirates off Socotra were a continuing menace for shipping. What is of particular interest here is that there would appear to be two different pirate groups operating on or in the vicinity of Socotra, East Africans and people from western Indian which, when viewed in conjunction with Ibn al-Mujāwir's description, would appear to demonstrate that the coastal population of Socotra was possibly made up of both Indian and African inhabitants.

The final Muslim medieval author to be mentioned is Ibn Mājid (d.*c.* 1500 AD), a navigator and author of the navigational treatise, *Kitāb al-fawā'id fī uṣūl al-baḥr wa l-qawā'id* (The Book of Benefits in the Principles of Navigation). Ibn Mājid's navigational treatise was compiled from his own experiences, and the earlier works of his father and grandfather, both *mu'allims* (Masters of Navigation). His narrative of Socotra, translated by Tibbetts (1981), described in detail the sailing routes, seasons and dangers of the seas around Socotra, and how the island was utilised by navigators as a landmark to and from India and East Africa. Ibn Mājid also refers to the Christians on Socotra, although he remarks that they were no longer ruling over the island, but that it was being ruled by tribes from the mainland of Yemen.

The importance of this description is that it gives further evidence for the cultural makeup of the population and the environmental difficulties the coastal population would have had to face at differing times of the year.

The Chinese Authors

Chinese contact with the western Indian Ocean mainly began in the form of an indirect trading network, from around the 1st century AD. Evidence for this early trade came from the Chinese sources of the Han dynasty (r. AD 206-220), which mentioned how they had obtained pearls, tortoise shells, incense and spices in exchange for silk (Hirth and Rockhill 1911: 3). This trade in Chinese silk is also referred to in the *Periplus Maris Erythraei*, where silk from China was one of the products obtainable in *Barygaza*, on the northwest coast of India (Casson 1989: 22).

Several Chinese accounts mention the maritime trade China was involved in, yet few offer any detail about the people or places that they traded with. One of the most detailed descriptions of this trade and the people encountered comes from Chau Ju-kua (d. AD 1231), an Inspector of Maritime Trade at the great port of *Ts'üan-chóu* in *Fu-kién* (Hirth 1896). According to Chau Ju-kua's report, entitled *Chu-fan-chï* (A Description of Barbarous Peoples), Socotra was a supplier of *lu-weï* (aloes), *hüé-kié* (dragon's blood), *tei-meï* (tortoise shell) and *lung-hién* (ambergris), and the inhabitants were sorcerers, who could affect the weather and change shape at will (Hirth and Rockhill 1911: 130-132). This report of Socotra is likely to have been taken from Arabian traders, as the items of trade and descriptions of the people are the same, and there is no definitive evidence for the Chinese having visited Socotra.

The European Authors

During the medieval period there are several European adventurers who made various trips into Asia, although the only European travellers to have written about, or visited Socotra were Marco Polo (d. AD 1324) and Nicolò dè Conti (d. AD 1469).

Marco Polo, a Venetian merchant, who travelled extensively in Asia, was the first European to write about Socotra (Yule and Cordier 1993: 2.406-410). Within Marco Polo's description of Socotra there is a great deal of repetition of the earlier Muslim and Chinese accounts concerning the presence of Christians, that the inhabitants practice sorcery, how pirates frequented the island, and that ambergris and aloes were traded. However, he also refers to Socotra as having been an important trading port for all vessels bound to Aden and that salted fish was amongst the articles traded. In addition, he describes how the inhabitants were hunting whales to obtain ambergris and that they purchase the plunder of the pirates, who frequent the island (Yule and Cordier 1993: 2.406-407). Scholars studying Socotra's historical narrative often mention this account, yet have ignored this trade in salted fish and that the inhabitants were hunting whales, concentrating instead on the presence of Christians. This detail is of particular importance for my study as it provides the first direct evidence for a fishing community on the island. Moreover, it also gives an indication of the trade in fish, which was not being reported by the Muslim authors, although it is possible that Ibn al-Mujāwir had indirectly referred to this when he said that the sea surrounding Socotra were full of fish.

Nicolò dè Conti was, much like Marco Polo, a Venetian merchant who travelled extensively around Asia. However, he learnt to speak Arabic, which allowed him to travel to many places frequented only by Muslim merchants. During the twenty five years Nicolò dè Conti spent travelling in Asia, he is believed to have spent two months on Socotra. Unfortunately, his only record of this prolonged stay was that aloes could be obtained on the island and that it was inhabited by Christians (The travels of Nicolò dè Conti 1857: 20). This would seem to indicate that he had not actually visited the island, but had obtained all his information from the oral accounts of Muslim traders who had.

Throughout the medieval Muslim, Chinese and European accounts the main themes that dominate the historical narrative are the same as those that have monopolised the scholarly studies of Socotra. That Socotra was inhabited by Christians and was famous for its aloes is undoubtedly important, yet it has overshadowed scholarly discourse to such an extent that many other details concerning Socotra's inhabitants and their practices have been ignored. This is especially apparent when looking at the primary sources outlined above, a number of which refer to a coastal population that is engaged in fishing, hunting whales and probably piracy. These accounts also highlight the importance of Socotra for navigators travelling within the Arabian Sea and, as the post-medieval period will further demonstrate, its strategic importance for shipping travelling to and from the Red Sea.

The Post-Medieval Period (16th to 18th century)

Socotra's post-medieval narrative has attracted a great deal of attention from scholars, although the main focus has been the Portuguese accounts. This is especially apparent in the studies undertaken by Serjeant (1963), Beckingham (1983) and Doe (1992), whose writings on the history of Socotra were primarily concerned with the Portuguese subjugation and short-term settlement of Socotra, and the events that transpired during this period. Regardless of this bias, there are several accounts taken from other European visitors to the island, although these are brief. The main themes found within the post-medieval accounts of Socotra are surprisingly similar to those of the medieval period, and once again the main focus is on the Christian inhabitants and the availability of good quality aloes, dragon's blood and ambergris. However, as I shall demonstrate below, within these accounts there are several references that relate to the fishing communities on Socotra.

The Portuguese

The Portuguese discovery and involvement with Socotra is clearly documented in many accounts notably those by Brásio (1943) and Da Costa (1973). The (re)discovery of Socotra in 1503 was made by Captain, Diogo Fernandes Pereira (*fl.* 16th century), who was particularly surprised to encounter a Christian community on the island. The locating of Socotra generated a significant amount of interest on Diogo Fernandes's return to Portugal in 1505, both because of its Christian population and its strategic placement at the mouth of the Red Sea. Consequently, in 1506 the King of Portugal sent a fleet of fifteen ships, under the command of Tristão da Cunha (d. 1540), to conquer Socotra. The Portuguese hoped that by conquering Socotra and building a fort there it would be possible to disrupt the flow of Muslim trade into the Red Sea.

The subjugation of Socotra by the Portuguese in 1507 was undertaken by Tristão da Cunha and his cousin, Afonso Dalboquerque (d. 1515), who later became the Viceroy of India. A detailed account of how this expedition brought Socotra under Portuguese control, the difficulties faced by the Portuguese garrison stationed there and their eventual abandonment of Socotra in 1511 was written several years later by Afonso Dalboquerque's son (Commentaries 1884: 1.44-56). In addition to these details, this account also refers to the Christian inhabitants and the danger Socotra posed for shipping sheltering off the shores of Socotra. According to the commentaries, Dalboquerque also obtained a chart from a captured Muslim pilot, who was forced to help the Portuguese sail along the coasts of Arabia. Whether or not this pilot was a fisherman is not mentioned. However, it is not the first time that Portuguese and other European captains have been known to forcibly take fishermen to help them navigate in unfamiliar areas (Barendse 2009: 89), and it is likely that this may have been the case here.

The next Portuguese account of Socotra is taken from Duarte Barbosa (d. 1521) a travel writer, linguist and officer in the Portuguese navy. Duarte Barbosa's book contains a first-hand account of Tristão da Cunha's military campaign, the Christian inhabitants and that ambergris, dragon's blood and aloes could be obtained on the island (*The Book of Duarte Barbosa* 1967: 1.59-63). However, of particular interest are his references to the ethnic background of the coastal population, which are said to be African and Indian. This is strikingly similar to the medieval descriptions and reinforces the ethnic diversity of Socotra's coastal population.

Several years later a Portuguese apothecary Tomés Pires (d.1540), while stationed in Malacca, India wrote a monumental work on the historical, geographical, ethnographic, botanical and economic situation of the East Indies, entitled *Suma Orientale*. However, the only reference to Socotra refers to the Christians living on the island and the trade and medicinal benefit of Socotran aloes (*The Suma Orientale* 1967: 2.514-520). This account is much like that of the Muslim scholar al-Bīrūnī, and again demonstrates the importance of aloes in the drug trade and explains why they are constantly referred to in the historical sources.

Despite the fact that the Portuguese abandoned Socotra in 1511, it was still regularly used by them throughout the 16th century. This was due to Socotra having been a convenient stop for water and supplies for shipping going to and from the Red Sea, India and Africa. The importance of Socotra as a victualling station is noted by the Portuguese naval officer and fourth viceroy of Portuguese India, Dom João de Castro (d. 1548), who visited the island during a voyage from Goa to the straits of Bab al-Mandeb. João de Castro's descriptions of Socotra are similar to earlier accounts and focus on the island's Christian population, and aloes (Kammerer 1936: 25-48; Fontoura da Costa 1940). However, he also refers to the availability of water and supplies, and conducts a survey of the island, sketching the main ports and elements of the landscape which could be used as navigational aids. Interestingly, he records that the population is not engaged in fishing even though the sea is full of fish (Kammerer 1936: 39). The reason for this remark is likely to be due to the fact that he was referring to the interior population, who he considered to be the original inhabitants, and not the ethnically diverse coastal population Barbosa mentioned.

The final Portuguese report on Socotra was by João de Barros (d. 1570), who was considered to be one of the first great Portuguese historians and is most well known for his famous work *Décadas da Ásia* (Decades of Asia), a history of the Portuguese in India and Asia (Barros 1945: 3.35-51). This work collates a great deal of information from previous accounts and is mostly concerned with Tristão da Cunha's conquering of Socotra and the availability of aloes. The only mention of the population is that they are Christians, who dress in rags and are '*gente mui bestial*', uncivilised.

By the 17th century when the British, Danish, Dutch, French and other European nations began their voyages to the East, they too found Socotra a useful stopping point for water and supplies. However, unlike the Portuguese, they made no attempt to occupy Socotra, their primary interest being to obtain aloes, which were much in demand as a purgative (Beckingham 1983: 177).

The British

The British were mainly interested in the spice trade with India and establishing themselves as traders in the Indian Ocean. Consequently, the journals of most traders and captains that visited Socotra were concerned with weather, anchorages, the availability of water, and the price of aloes. However, some reports did refer to the presence of Arabian soldiers, who are said to have served ᶜAmr bin Saᶜīd, son of Sultan of Qishn of the Banū ᶜAfrār family, and that there were numerous slaves of 'African' descent on the island (Kerr 1811-1894; Purchas 1905-1907; Foster 1906-1927).

The earliest and most detailed of all these accounts comes from the diary of William Finch (d. 1613), an English merchant who spent three months on Socotra in 1608 (Geddes 1964: 70-77). During his stay William Finch reported on the inhabitants of Socotra, their customs and practices and the animals and plants he encountered. Although his original diary is lost, a summary of his description of Socotra can be found in Purchas's *Hakluytus Posthumus* (Purchas 1905: 4.13-19). Within Finch's narrative he reports on how the Arabians from the mainland were forcing the inhabitants to fish and dive for pearls, which demonstrates that the trade in fish described by Marco Polo was ongoing. While Finch does not say who the people fishing were, it may be surmised that they were part of the coastal population and were likely to have included Indians and Africans.

The next description of Socotra occurs in 1615, when Sir Thomas Roe (d. 1644) called at Socotra, on route to visit the Mogul Emperor Janhangir of India (r. 1605-1627). Sir Thomas Roe provided a rich descriptive narrative concerning the topography and weather, the aloes, dragon's blood and the customs and manners of the inhabitants (Roe 1899: 1.29-37). His description refers to the inhabitants as being a mixture of Arabians, their African slaves, Christians and the 'original' inhabitants whom he called the 'true ancient naturals' of Socotra (Roe 1899: 1.34). He also said that the 'African' slaves were being used as pearl divers, providing evidence for the ethnicity of Finch's divers, who we can presume were also of African descent.

The Dutch

Within Socotra's historical narrative several authors refer to Dutch shipping visiting the island, yet none provide specific accounts (Serjeant 1963; Beckingham 1983; Doe 1992; Naumkin 1993; Botting 2006; Cheung *et al.* 2006). During my research I was able to obtain and translate one specific account by Hendrick Hagenaer (*fl.* 17th century), a captain of the Dutch East India Company who visited Socotra sometime between 1631 and 1638. Hendrick Hagenaer's description of Socotra is not dissimilar to those accounts provided by the English and he also referred to aloes and how the island was ruled by Arabians from the mainland of Yemen. Interestingly, Hagenaer specifically referred to fishermen and how they were using nets and lines, and would fish from vessels (Hagenaer 1650: 56-57).

These post-medieval accounts are very similar to the earlier medieval accounts even though the majority of the accounts are European. The reason for these similarities would appear to be due to what was considered to have importance to the Portuguese, British and Dutch authors. However, I would argue that it is actually due to current scholarly bias that has concentrated on the articles that were being traded and the short-term events of occupation, which actually had very little effect on Socotra. Nevertheless, as I have demonstrated above, when reanalysing these accounts it is possible to obtain some detailed information concerning the fishing communities and the practices they were involved in which, together, help in the understanding of modern practices.

The 19th Century

By the end of the 17th century, as European shipping to the Red Sea and Gulf of Aden dwindled, accounts of Socotra become scarcer, and by the 18th century literature pertaining to Socotra is particularly sparse. As a result, very little is known about Socotra in the 18th century and it therefore necessary to resume from the 19th century.

The 19th century heralds a new phase in Socotra's narrative, one that is intimately linked with the aspirations of the British in the Middle East and the opening of a steamship route from Bombay to Suez. Socotra, by virtue of its strategic position and supplies of water, was an important geostrategic base for the British in the Red Sea and was proposed as a coaling stop for steamships on the India to Suez route (Gavin 1975: 197). As a result of this proposal, an expedition was sent to Socotra to survey the island and at the same time gather information on the island's fauna, flora, and people. This survey was undertaken by Captain Haines and several officers, namely Wellsted, Hulton, Cruttenden and Ormsby.

The findings of this expedition were almost exclusively published by Lieutenant Wellsted (d. 1842), a prolific writer who detailed many aspects of Socotra's fauna, flora, its inhabitants and their customs, manners and language (Wellsted 1835a, 1835b, 1838 and 1840). According to Haines (d. 1860), (1845:107), the reason that Wellsted's accounts were so comprehensive was that he copied and used information gathered by the other members of the expedition throughout his publications. Regardless of this apparent plagiarism, Wellsted's writings are an important resource for scholars studying Socotra and its interior population, particularly as his publications were the first scientific record of the little known interior mountain dwelling population and their hitherto unknown language. Despite his bias toward the interior population there are several references to the coastal population, their cultural makeup, fishing vessels and practices, although these lack the same detail afforded to the interior population. In addition to Wellsted's publications I also managed to locate Lieutenant Ormsby's (d. 1857) unpublished journal, found as an appendix in Haines's journal *Southern Arabia* (Ormsby 1844). Ormsby's journal provides a detailed description of his part of the expedition, which includes an account of the fishing communities, the vessels they were using and the trade they were engaged in.

Once the results of this expedition had been published it generated a significant amount of interest in the scientific community, and over the next two centuries several scientific expeditions visited the island. However, the focus for these expeditions were to investigate either the interior population and their language, or the endemic fauna and flora and few provide anything more than a casual observation of the fishermen (Hunter 1878; Schweinfurth 1993; Balfour 1888; Peucke 1899; Forbes 1903; Boxhall 1966). For example, within Schweinfurth's (d. 1925), study of the Socotri plants we learn that Africans make up the majority of the fishermen, while during Boxhall's (d. 2003) survey expedition we learn that the fishermen were using log rafts to fish from. These offhand remarks in the reports of these expeditions not only demonstrate the lack of studies concerning the fishing communities at this time, but also the necessity of having to trawl through seemingly unrelated studies to find any information about them.

The periods outlined above demonstrate the wide range of historical sources from which it is possible to find some information on Socotra. At the same time it is also possible to see how specific themes such as the presence of Christians and the availability of aloes have dominated both the primary and secondary historical discourse. In spite of this, I have shown that the historical sources do contain a rich source of information about the coastal population, which has previously been ignored by researchers and historians. Whatever the reasoning for this, the archaeological reports are little different.

Archaeological Accounts

> '...other ruins of a ruder and more irregular character lay scattered in the vicinity, and at some remote period, when Sokotra was in its brighter days, this must have been an important centre of civilisation' (Bent 1900: 375).

The ruins that lie scattered across the Socotra's northern coast can provide an important picture of who the island's coastal inhabitants were and what activities they were engaged in. Indeed it is only through the study of archaeological remains that we are able to understand many aspects of Socotra's prehistoric past and gain further insights into the historical narrative. In this study I seek to utilise archaeology to provide information on the historical and prehistoric inhabitants and attempt to determine to what extent they may have been engaged in exploiting resources from the sea. As such, this study examines the archaeological record from an aquatic perspective by looking at the maritime activities people were engaged in and how the settlements and other structures found along the coast reflect these activities. This differs in many ways from previous archaeological work that has been undertaken on Socotra, which has been primarily interested in finding evidence to support the historical accounts; trace the origins of the inhabitants and determine the earliest settlement of Socotra (Bent 1900; Shinnie 1960; Doe 1967; Naumkin and Sedov 1993).

The first archaeological expedition to Socotra was undertaken by the traveller and archaeologist Theodore Bent (d. 1897) and his wife Mabel Bent (d. 1929), who visited the island in 1897, with the aim of finding evidence for a Himyaritic and Christian civilisation on the island (Bent and Brisch 2010: 279). During this expedition the Bents travelled along Socotra's north coast, recording several inscriptions, graves and ruins, most notably a fort, which he attributed to an early Muslim presence.

Despite these findings, it was 60 years before another archaeological survey could be undertaken, as the British military control in Arabia throughout the First and Second World Wars prevented visitors from visiting the island (Peterson 1985: 23-35). Thus the second archaeological survey of Socotra was only undertaken in 1957, by the archaeologist Shinnie (d. 2007), who formed part of an Oxford expedition to Socotra. Limited by time and the difficulties of excavating on the island, Shinnie concentrated on surveying and excavating in several areas along the north coast, where he hoped to find evidence for a classical settlement. While structures including a mosque, fort and several graves were surveyed and excavated, no traces of any occupation dated to earlier than the 16th century was found (Shinnie 1960: 108). Of particular interest to this study are the findings of settlements that were linked to lagoons and landing places, which would indicate that access to the sea was important for the inhabitants.

The next expedition to investigate the archaeological remains on Socotra was undertaken between 17 March and 1 June 1967, in a joint British military and civilian scientific expedition lead by the military officer and archaeologist Brian Doe (d. 2006). The aims were to gather information on a wide variety of subjects that included archaeology, botany, entomology, geology, linguistics and meteorology (Doe 1992: 7). The archaeological survey of Socotra recorded over 18 sites along the north-western side of the island, which included forts, abandoned villages, graveyards, linear wall alignments and inscriptions, many of which had originally been recorded earlier by Bent and Shinnie. According to Doe (1992: 41), the archaeological evidence demonstrated that Socotra was once of agricultural importance and its inhabitants were farmers, who were forced by the decline of the incense trade to become herders and fishermen (Doe 1970: 151). Doe also records finding numerous sherds of pottery dated between the 10th to 17th century AD in and around the village of Suq, on the north coast. He suggests that this pottery is indicative of the long-term settlement of Suq (Doe 1992: 61). This reinforces the accounts of Ibn al-Mujāwir (d. AD 1292), Ibn Mājid (d.*c.* 1500 AD), and Afonso Dalboquerque (d. 1515), which all refer to Suq having been inhabited by Arabians and Christians, and the importance of this settlement for mariners and merchants visiting the island.

On 29 November 1967, several months after Doe's expedition, the British occupation ended and Socotra eventually became part of the Peoples Democratic Republic of Yemen (PDRY). This lead to a greater Soviet involvement with Socotra and in the 1980s several joint Soviet-Yemeni archaeological surveys were undertaken (Naumkin 1993; Naumkin and Sedov 1993). The most important discoveries made during these expeditions were the identification of flint tools, believed to be Neolithic, and the location of a settlement on the north coast, with pottery dated to the 1st millennium AD. These finds provide evidence to indicate that the earliest occupation on Socotra was along the north coast and was of an even earlier date than that proposed by Shinnie or Doe (Naumkin and Sedov 1993: 605). The importance of this evidence for this study is that it demonstrates a long-term coastal settlement that is likely to have been engaged in overseas trade and the exploitation of marine species.

The next archaeological expedition to survey Socotra was conducted by the University of Sydney, with the specific aim of investigating the southern part of the island (Weeks *et al.* 2001). During this survey numerous hitherto unknown structures and graves were recorded. This study was particularly important in that it demonstrated that the southern half of Socotra, originally believed to have been uninhabited, had several settlements, although the exact length of time these were settled is uncertain (Weeks *et al.* 2001: 120). The most significant finding of this archaeological survey with regards to my research was the discovery of numerous cave shelters along the coast. According to Weeks *et al.* (2001: 108), these cave shelters had been occupied for a significant length of time and contained large quantities of turtle shells, fish bones and shell. The presence of these marine species not only indicates that fishermen were inhabiting these caves, but that they were fishing from the southern side of the island for a much longer period than had originally been thought (Morris 2002: 222).

The importance of caves for the people on Socotra was again realised when the Belgian Speleological Mission (Socotra Karst Project 2000-2008), made one of the richest archaeological discoveries on Socotra, in a cave overlooking the north-eastern side of the island. Within this cave a wooden tablet with Palmyrene script, incense burners, pots and numerous Indian and Greek inscriptions were found (Dridi 2002, Robin and Gorea 2002, Dridi and Gorea 2003 and Strauch and Bukharin 2004). The importance of this cave is that it provides evidence for Socotra's maritime links from at least the 2nd century AD. Moreover, due to a ships motifs and several incense burners found within the cave it is also considered to have been a mariner's religious sanctuary (Dridi 2002: 589).

In 2004, further archaeological evidence in the form of five inscribed stone tablets were found in the fishing village of ᶜAririhun Di-Lisheh on the northeast coast of Socotra. These stones, dated to the 17th and 18th centuries, were written in Gujārāti and refer to sailor and merchants visiting Socotra to trade (Shelat 2012; Jansen van Rensburg 2012). These stones provide definite evidence for the numerous historical accounts referring to the presence of Indians on Socotra and, together with the Indian inscriptions found in the cave, demonstrate a long-term Indian influence on Socotra. This is of specific importance in that Indians were referred to by al-Masᶜūdī' and al-Muqaddasī, and this would seem to indicate that they were resident on the island. Furthermore, it is possible that the maritime sanctuary would indicate a strong link with the sea, whether as pirates, fishermen or traders.

From the archaeological accounts outlined above it is apparent that there is a significant amount of work that still needs to be done on Socotra. Within the various archaeological expeditions undertaken there have been many links to Socotra's maritime past, yet few attempts to determine what influence this had on the inhabitants living along the coast. Within Weeks *et al.* (2001), we obtain the first glimpse into the fishing communities living along the south coast and it is likely that similar finds can be made on the north coast where there was a long-term settlement of people engaged with the sea. The focus of these archaeological expeditions has been on the external cultural influences affecting Socotra and its interior inhabitants. Consequently, what the coastal inhabitants were engaged in and how they interacted with the interior population and overseas merchants remains virtually unexplored.

The Ethnographic Accounts

> 'They [coastal population] are a mongrel race, the descendents of Arabs, African slaves, Portuguese, and several other nations' (Wellsted 1840: 301).

The coastal population of Socotra is made up of an eclectic mixture of immigrants who are engaged in trade and fishing and come from a wide range of different social, economic and cultural backgrounds. The primary language of this population is Arabic, although many are bilingual and also speak Socotri. These people are strikingly different to the interior inhabitants, who are semi-nomadic pastoralists that have been living on the island for several generations and have their own native language, Socotri, although many do speak Arabic as a second language. The interior population and their language, which forms one of the six Modern South Arabian Languages (MSAL), has attracted the interest of ethnographers, linguists and anthropologists for several centuries (Hunter 1878; Leslau 1938; Lonnet 1998; Simeone-Senelle 1998; Naumkin 1993; Wranik 1999; Morris 2002; Elie 2007). Conversely, there are few ethnographic studies that have looked at the coastal population, and even fewer that have focused on the fishermen. This has made it necessary to consult various government publications that have reported on the fisheries sector (Brown 1966; Nichols 2001; Morris 2002), in an attempt to gather any information that may allude to the traditions and practices of the fishermen on Socotra.

The earliest account pertaining to the fishermen on Socotra is a 1966 British governmental report on the economic development potential of Socotra, undertaken by the Assistant Advisor in Aden, G. H. H. Brown. The aims of this report were to gather information on the social and economic conditions on Socotra, and determine how and in which sectors economic development would be possible. As a result, it provides a detailed analysis of the social and economic conditions on Socotra, including the fisheries sector. Importantly, it also presents a synopsis of fishing practices, the market for fish being caught, processing of fish, amounts being sold and the villages and inhabitants that are involved in fishing (Brown 1966). The breadth of information included in this report makes it particularly useful in understanding the fishing practices undertaken, the market for this fish and the socio-economic position of the fishermen. Indeed, it is the broad range of topics concerning fishing that it covers which makes it such a key resource for this study.

The first ethnographic account to focus specifically on the coastal inhabitants of Socotra was undertaken during the 1967 joint British military and civilian scientific expedition by the linguist R. B. Serjeant, who had already undertaken similar studies in Yemen (Serjeant 1991; 1995a). According to Serjeant (1992: 113-114), the aims of his visit to Socotra were to provide a report on the social organisation, maritime activities, fishing and navigational practices of the coastal population. Unfortunately, his work was limited, geographically, linguistically and due to the time constraints of the expedition (Serjeant 1992: 133). Geographically, his study concentrated on a few villages on the north coast, whilst linguistically he found the Arabic spoken by the Socotri fishermen to be difficult to understand, forcing him to rely on visiting Arabian sailors for a great deal of his information. Nevertheless, Serjeant was the first person to record a star calendar in use on the island and to describe the winds and seasons of the year as understood by the coastal population, the favoured seasons for visiting Socotra, and what equipment was used by the fishermen. The importance of his work for my study into the fishermen of Socotra is that it provides the earliest ethnographic analysis of the social organisation and maritime traditions of the fishermen of Socotra.

The next ethnographic study of the fishing communities on Socotra was undertaken between 1970 and 1988, when several joint Soviet-Yemeni studies of the island and its people were undertaken. These studies were brought together in an updated and translated book, *Island of the Phoenix* 1993, which represented the culmination of a multi-disciplinary range of Soviet ethnographic, archaeological, anthropological, historical, cultural and linguistic studies (Naumkin 1993). However, the conclusions drawn and methodologies employed were criticised by Weir (1994), Varisco (1994) and Elie (2006), as being too descriptive in nature, having little analytical content and making use of discredited methods of 19th century physical anthropology. Nevertheless, the descriptions of the social and economic lives of the fishermen, their fishing practices and equipment does provide additional information that is not included in Serjeant's work and, with certain caveats, is a useful source for this study.

Several years after the unification of Yemen in 1990, a series of scientific expeditions aimed at achieving a sustainable development programme on the island were undertaken on behalf of the Republic of Yemen by the Global Environmental Facility (GEF) and the United Nations Development Programme (UNDP). This lead to the publication of several scientific reports on Socotra within four volumes entitled, *The Proceedings of the First International Symposium on Socotra* 1996. Within these four volumes fisheries are dealt with, although other than describing the status of the fisheries resources and providing an outline of the management and potential for the fisheries sector, there is little information concerning the cultural practices of the fishermen (Dumont 1998; 1999). In addition to these publications there were also two unpublished reports on the fisheries (Nichols 2001) and traditional land use of the inhabitants (Morris 2002). Within these two reports there are several references to the fishermen and their settlements, practices, quantity and types of fish caught, and the traditional fisheries management practiced by them. The main focus of the first report (Nichols 2001) is on the traditional fisheries management and analysing the catches made by fishermen. Notwithstanding the lack of qualitative analysis concerning the fishermen and their practices, this report is useful insofar as it outlines where catches of specific marine species are more prolific and why fishermen favour certain fishing areas or types of fish. The focus of the next report (Morris 2002) is on the traditional land use of the inhabitants, and is primarily concerned with the interior population, although several references to the fishing community are made. Its importance is that it builds upon the studies of Serjeant and Naumkin and provides one of the most complete works on the traditional Socotri fishing practices to date. Nevertheless, as the focus of this report is primarily on the interior inhabitants, the descriptive accounts are relatively brief and lack analysis.

Conclusion

Throughout this review it is apparent that few studies pertaining to Socotra have focussed on the coastal population, and even fewer have sought to understand the fishing communities or their traditional practices. It is also clear that throughout the historical, archaeological and ethnographic accounts there are notable gaps in our knowledge of these communities. However, by collating what we know about them from the various disciplines outlined above it is possible to put together a holistic narrative that can shed light on the social, cultural and ethnic background of the contemporary fishing communities and their maritime traditions.

What I have demonstrated within the historical accounts is that there is a rich supply of information pertaining to the fishing communities, although it is widely dispersed throughout the classical, medieval and post-medieval periods. The classical period provides the first glimpse of Socotra's fishing community. The most important descriptions are those by Agatharchides and the *Periplus Maris Erythraei*, as they provide some of the earliest evidence for an active fishing community that is likely to have been part of an eclectic mix of people from India, Arabia and Europe. Comparing the classical period with the contemporary communities on Socotra would be foolhardy, yet one cannot help to see how there are similarities in the diversity of the coastal population and the ongoing practices of turtle hunting.

In the medieval period the sources outlined highlight the juxtaposition between how little was actually known about Socotra and how often it was referred to. The primary reason for this would seem to be due the island's remoteness; the presence of pirates; that it was inhabited by Christians, who were believed to be sorcerers, and the famous Socotran aloe. Within these descriptions there are numerous references which provide an insight into social and cultural lives of the coastal community. Within the Muslim accounts we learn that the population was made up of Greeks, tribes from the Hadhramaut, and possibly people from western India and East African pirates, who are most likely to have been involved with or formed part of the coastal community. In addition, Ibn al-Mujāwir also provides the first glimpse into the division between the coastal and interior population, which is mentioned in the 19th century and in various ethnographic reports. However, it is not until Marco Polo's description of Socotra that we obtain evidence for a fishing community engaged in hunting whales and trading in dried fish. What these medieval accounts demonstrate is that Socotra's coastal inhabitants are an ethnically diverse community, who are engaged in fishing and probably piracy, and that they are seen as being different to the interior population. These descriptions form the beginnings of a narrative for the fishermen and within this study are used to define their social and cultural makeup.

The records of the post-medieval period encompass a wide range of topics and observations, many of which pertain specifically to the fishing communities on Socotra. The various Portuguese observations refer to them as being made up of African, Arabians and possibly Indians, who were involved in fishing and pearl diving. This is elaborated upon by the British authors, Finch and Roe, who also examine the social status of those fishing and describe the various marine species being exploited. However, it is the Dutch captain Hagenaer, who documents the vessels and equipment they were using. The post-medieval accounts, much like the medieval accounts, provide this study with an understanding of the cultural makeup of the fishing community and importantly, details concerning their equipment and practices.

By the 19th century the focus of the various expeditions visiting the island was on the interior population and the endemic plants and animals of the island, yet several accounts do refer to the fishing community. The main two authors of relevance here are Wellsted and Ormsby, both of whom refer to the cultural makeup of the fishermen and provide further information on their vessels and fishing practices. The historical records play an integral part in this study insofar as they give an insight into social and cultural background of the contemporary fishing community. Furthermore, it also makes it possible to compare and analyse the similarities and differences of the traditions and equipment in the present with those in the past and identify the maturity of those traditions.

Archaeological investigations of Socotra have tended to focus on evidence to support the historical narrative, particularly the classical period and the short-lived Portuguese occupation. More recently, archaeologists Doe (1992) and Naumkin (1993) have sought to find evidence for the earliest inhabitants of Socotra, although these studies have focused primarily on the interior population. Nonetheless, the archaeological record has also provided an insight into the lives of the coastal population and their involvement in fishing. As the expedition by Weeks *et al.* (2001) has demonstrated, the archaeological record also highlights discrepancies within in the historical record. This is most evident in the caves filled with the remains of marine species that were being used by the fishermen on the south coast. The archaeological record highlights many aspects of the fishing community's lives, and may be used to question the historical record and give insight into the traditions of the fishing communities.

The ethnographic accounts outlined above provide a range of information on the fishermen of Socotra and their traditional practices. However, other than Serjeant, the focus of their interest has either been on the interior population (Naumkin 1993; Morris 2002) or the management of the fisheries resource (Brown 1966; Dumont 1998; Dumont 1999; Nichols 2001). These ethnographic reports form an integral part of this research, allowing for direct comparisons to be made with the ethnographic data gathered by myself. The ethnographic data gathered is used as a foundation from which to link to historical and archaeological accounts and address the numerous spatial and temporal gaps in our knowledge. The methodological and conceptual framework of how I propose to achieve this is outlined in the next chapter.

Chapter 3

The Conceptual Framework and Methodology

The research I will be using involves a transdisciplinary approach, which looks at past and present ethnographical studies in conjunction with historical and archaeological data. This approach is not new to the study of fishing communities and similar studies have been undertaken in the Gulf, Oman and East Africa (Donaldson 1979; Vosmer 1999; Beech 2004, Wynne-Jones 2007). The difference in my approach lies in the temporal and spatial structures I am using in the conceptual framework of this study and that the emphasis of my methodology is on maritime ethnography.

The Conceptual Framework

The temporal structure within which this study operates is based upon the Braudelian concept of historical time, in which time is seen as operating on a number of different levels (Braudel 1972, 1: 20-21). The first level of time is the *longue durée* (long-term realities), which is represented here by the monsoon winds whose ceaseless rhythmic cycle has played a defining role in the environmental, cultural, social and economic fortunes of the western Indian Ocean (Warren 1987: 137-158). The importance of this long-term event is that it has been a continuing influence over the lives of the fishermen on Socotra for millennia, influencing when and where it is possible for them to access the sea. In addition, the monsoon winds have played a central role in the island's environment and consequently its settlement. This is seen in the effect of the monsoon precipitation, which is highest along the northern more populous side of the island (Othman 1996: 213). The second temporal level, the *conjuncture* (medium-term realities), are occasional in nature and represent socio-economic and cultural changes, such as population growth and movement, warfare, production output, price change, taxation and social trends (Lai 2000: 69). The significance of these events is the social and economic changes that they bring and the effect this has on the fishermen's traditions. An important medium-term event was that of Socotra's political incorporation into the Peoples Democratic Republic of Yemen (PDRY), (1967-1990), which resulted in significant social and economic changes that are still being felt on the island today. The third level of historical time, the *événements* (short-term realities), are short-term events that are like 'fireflies', which for a brief period light up parts of the overall historical landscape (Braudel 1972, 2: 901). These events are typically isolated episodes in history which, for a brief period, result in a major environmental, social, economic or political change. The repercussions of these events can result in the introduction or cessation of certain cultural traditions. An example of this occurred in 2004 when Socotra was struck by a tsunami that destroyed the few remaining sewn vessels on the south coast and resulted in their complete abandonment.

This Braudelian division of time makes it possible to analyse the data gathered within three separate yet overlapping historical time frames. The strength of this temporal framework lies in both the vague and specific nature of the periods used, and that it allows for wider social and environmental influences to be analysed in conjunction with the more specific short-term events. Therefore, by analysing the ethnographic and archaeological data at different levels of historical time, it is possible to analyse and interpret the short and long-term effect these temporal episodes have on the maritime traditions of the fishing community.

Spatially this study seeks a holistic understanding of the fishermen's adaption to and use of the terrestrial and maritime landscape. As such, I have chosen to use a concept known as the maritime cultural landscape, a term which refers to both physical and cognitive aspects of the human interaction with the maritime and terrestrial landscape (Westerdahl 1992; Hunter 1994; Jasinski 1994; Parker 2001; Cooney 2003; Westerdahl 2008). However, my main focus is on the fishermen's physical and cognitive interaction with the landscape as it pertains to settlement, navigation and the exploitation of marine species, and how these interactions differ in a spatial and temporal context. Furthermore, I analyse how the fishing community reacts to social, economic and political changes and what influence these changes have had on the structure and organisation of their interaction with their physical environment (Vayda and McCay 1975; Feld and Basso 1996; Muir 1999: 115; Anschuetz *et al.* 2001: 164; Bender 2002: 104).

Separating the temporal and spatial frameworks used helps outline the conceptual approach adopted, yet the aim here is to combine them. This combined approach is used to engage with the complexities and influences of the social, cultural, economic and environmental factors influencing the fishing community and their maritime traditions. It also provides an insight into the differences and similarities of these influences on the fishermen and their traditions in a range of different areas and times.

The Methodological Framework

The challenges of devising a specific methodological framework for studying maritime traditions are numerous. The main reason for this is that these traditions are a mixture between the tangible and intangible and are shaped and influenced by social, economic, political and environmental factors. These factors each play a specific role in influencing the fishermen's relationship with the sea and all need to be taken into account when analysing tradition. To approach this diversity of human experience that is manifest in the creation of maritime traditions and the influences that affect this experience I have used a combination of quantitative and qualitative approaches in my data collection and analysis. The qualitative approaches allow me to generate a range of observational data that gives what Geertz (2000) described as 'thick description', or the reasoning behind human action. Whereas the quantitative approaches used, provides a range of thematic data, which allows for the qualitative data to be contextualised within broader social, cultural, economic, historic and environmental frameworks (Bray 2008: 298). Combining quantitative and qualitative methods of data collection and analysis adds value to this research in three ways: First, this mixed method approach contributes to an awareness of context when interpreting the data. Secondly, by using both a quantitative and qualitative approach it is possible to combine different spatial scales of analysis when viewing the data. Thirdly, bringing these two methods together allows for the data to be analysed and understood over a broader temporal range.

The defining methodological approach here is ethnography or more explicitly maritime ethnography. The reason for this is that the focus of my enquiries is fishermen, whose social, cultural and economic lives are intimately linked to the maritime environment. At this point it is worth mentioning that the term fishermen is used specifically to infer gender as it is rare for women on Socotra to be engaged in any form of fishing, although there are isolated accounts of this occurring. This qualitative approach gives a holistic view of the activities and experiences that influence the fishermen's creation and transmission of their maritime traditions. It also lays down a foundation of empirical data from which I am able to investigate the spatial and temporal factors influencing the fishing community's relationship with the sea and how this relationship affects their maritime traditions. This data is supplemented by archaeological, historical and meteorological considerations, which are used to contextualise the ethnographic data and provide a temporal and spatial structure within which maritime traditions can be further explored.

Maritime Ethnographic Methodology

The basis of this research is the maritime ethnographic fieldwork undertaken by myself over the course of two fieldwork seasons. The first season took place in February 2009 (4 weeks), and the second season between December 2009 and January 2010 (4 weeks). I chose to conduct my research during these two periods because of the influence of the weather on fishing activities. During earlier visits to Socotra, between 2003 and 2007, I realised that if I wanted to interview fishermen and observe their fishing practices the best period would be December to February, when the weather was calm and almost all fishermen were actively fishing. In addition, I also faced the challenges of language and being able to find people that would consent to being interviewed.

During my earlier visits (2003-2007) I was mostly engaged in recording and tracing evidence for the traditional vessels used by the fishermen, and while I did undertake several interviews with the fishermen, my primary aims were the documentation of their traditional vessels. Fortunately, during this fieldwork I had established several contacts within the fishing villages I visited and gained a good rapport with many of the fishermen. This helped me with regards to my current research as it expedited my access to fishermen and helped establish a sense of trust when conducting interviews. This was further aided by my use of guides from the English school in Ḥadiboh, who were able to translate for me and whose family and friends were active fishermen. Having guides who could also act as gatekeepers facilitated my research, helped provide me with access to the fishermen and gave me opportunities to observe and participate in various fishing activities. The importance of establishing trust is especially significant on Socotra as independent, financially deficient researchers have little to offer their subjects, and amongst the Socotri there is an inherent mistrust of researchers (Elie 2007: 34-35). This mistrust, with regards to the fishermen, is due to the actions of various conservation projects on Socotra whose efforts have successfully made the widespread hunting of turtles illegal and who, according to the fishermen, are trying to control their catches and hence influence their income.

During the course of my research I visited a number of fishing villages along both the north and south coast of the island. The aim of this geographical spread was to include as many villages as possible and gather information from as many fishermen as possible. The reason for this was that it would allow me to spatially compare and contrast the information gathered and look for regional similarities and differences. This is in stark contrast to my predecessors' work (Serjeant 1993; Naumkin 1993; Morris 2002), which was mostly limited to generalisations based on a few fishing villages along the north coast. Notwithstanding the fact that many fishing villages are situated in remote locations and require an off-road vehicle or boat to reach I was able to visit sixteen villages spread across both the north and south coast of Socotra and the only village in the

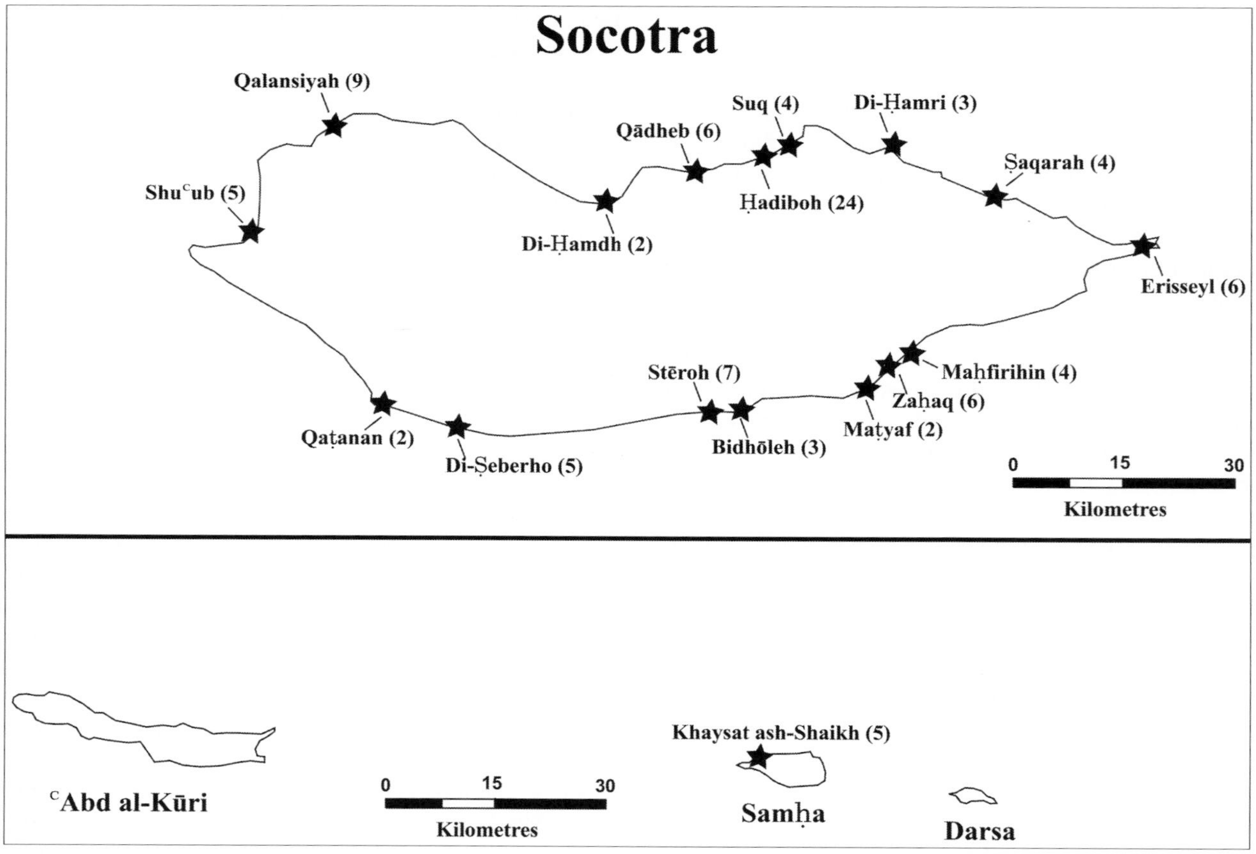

FIGURE 3. THE FISHING VILLAGES VISITED AND NUMBER OF PEOPLE WHO WERE INTERVIEWED, IN BRACKETS.

outlying island of Samḥa. The villages I visited and conducted interviews at were, for the north coast, west to east: Qalansiyah, Di-Ḥamdh, Qādheb, Ḥadiboh, Suq, Di-Ḥamri, Ṣaqarah and Erisseyl. The villages of the south coast I conducted interviews in were, from east to west: Maḥfirihin, Zaḥaq, Maṭyaf, Bidhōleh, Stēroh, Di-Ṣ eberho, Qaṭanan, Shuᶜub. I also visited Khaysat ash-Shaikh, on the island of Samḥa. The island of Darsa was briefly visited, but as it is uninhabited no interviews were conducted. The island of ᶜAbd al-Kūri was not visited due to the high cost of getting there and the danger of Somali pirates. The geographical distribution of the villages I was able to visit is given in Figure 3. The number in brackets next to the village name is representative of the number of fishermen who were willing to give me their names and does not include all those questioned during group interviews.

The 97 people who did provide me with their names are, according to a fisheries management report (Nichols 2001), representative of approximately 4% of the total fishermen on the island of Socotra and Samḥa respectively. The majority of those interviewed were full-time fishermen, from the populous north coast, notably in the capital Ḥadiboh, which has the largest single population of fishermen on the island. Four of those I interviewed were seasonal fishermen, or those for whom fishing is a supplement to their pastoral livelihood. Attempting to determine their age was particularly difficult, as many of those I interviewed were illiterate and had little knowledge of their exact date of birth. Furthermore, they would often round their perceived age up to a multiple of ten. In many cases the middle-aged fishermen would say that they were 30 years old, whereas the older fishermen would say that they were either 50 or 60. It is not certain why these numbers were chosen, although it is representative of the general age range of those interviewed. See Appendix 1 for a list of the fishermen interviewed.

As discussed above, maritime traditions encompass a broad range of tangible and intangible elements which are passed between individuals, groups and institutions over time. According to Hasslöf (1972: 20), this range of traditions is matched by the variety of traditional media by which these are passed. This diversity in traditions and transmissions makes it necessary for the researcher to devise a range of different methodological approaches to gather information about them. Within this study I have made use of a range of ethnographic methodologies that, in several cases, I have combined with historical and archaeological approaches.

Oral Traditions

The spoken word is the primary means of passing on traditions on Socotra, as approximately 50-60% of fishermen are illiterate. The problem for the researcher is that the spoken word is ephemeral, making it necessary for the researcher to reproduce the oral record in a written or recorded format. This process objectifies the researcher's experiences in the field, and at this stage it is important to continue to bear in mind how one's own sense of identity and capacity for interpreting what is communicated affects the information gathered (Blommaert and Jie 2010: 29). During the course of gathering oral data for my research I found that, as a sailor, my own knowledge and experience of the sea helped me to understand some of the more technical aspects the fishermen were telling me with regards navigation and seamanship. However, this was at times a hindrance and in several instances I had to curb my tendency to record the navigational terminology rather than the explanations used by the fishermen when writing up my field notes.

Ethnographic interviews are one of the main data gathering tools used in this study. It involves two stages, namely: developing rapport and eliciting information. Rapport provides the encouragement for the informants to talk, whilst eliciting information fosters the development of rapport (Spradley 1979: 44). Rapport also influences how it is possible to approach topics and the way in which these are negotiated and responded to (Sherman Heyl 2001: 379). Building upon previous relationships made, together with the use of a gatekeeper and interpreter, allowed me to gain the trust of the fishermen I interviewed. This helped me to explore a range of more sensitive topics related to fishing practices, social relationships, environmental concerns and socio-economic issues. During previous fieldwork I met with Abdullha Rahman Abod Ali Saeed, a past employee of the Socotra Conservation Development Programme, who was also a well known full-time fisherman in the village of Qalansiyah on the west coast. As a result of this meeting I was personally introduced to fishermen in Qalansiyah and other fishing villages. This was extremely useful when questioning the fishermen on more difficult questions concerning socio-economic conditions and illegal practices, as answering these questions required a significant amount of trust in that I would not report them to the authorities. Notwithstanding the importance of having gained the trust of the fishermen, I was faced with another dilemma. How is it possible to achieve a subjective and objective view of the fishermen I was interviewing? According to Bourdieu (1977: 1-3), it is the balance between the objective view that comes with the close association with one's subjects and the subjective view of a researcher that needs to be sought. The means by which I attempted to achieve this balance was by acknowledging my close association with the fishermen and the subjectivity this brought, and ensuring that this did not overly impose itself in my field notes and writing up.

The ethnographic interview techniques used during my fieldwork were adapted according to the circumstances in which I was able to conduct the interview and the information I wished to gather.

Open-ended Interviews

One technique I used was the open-ended interview, which can be defined as interviews in which there are no pre-defined options or categories. This allowed for the interviewee to speak about things that were important to them and reflect on topics that may not relate to the research undertaken (Schensul *et al.* 1999: 145-146). These interviews were particularly useful during the beginning of my research as they provided me with a general background to the issues and concerns of the fishermen, what was important to them and how they felt about the various socio-economic changes on Socotra. Notwithstanding the importance of the information that was gathered during these interviews I found that it was necessary to follow these up with a more structured interview technique that would allow me to explore the fishermen's traditions in more detail. This would have required me to revisit the people interviewed. Unfortunately, due to time and money restrictions and the difficulties of access this was not going to be feasible for all the fishing villages visited. As a result, I only used this technique in those villages where it was possible to revisit the fishermen interviewed, namely Ḥadiboh, Qalansiyah, Suq, Erisseyl and Maḥfirihin.

Semi-structured Interviews

The second technique used was the semi-structured interview. This interview technique can be defined as interviews in which the interviewee is asked open-ended questions about certain topics and the resultant conversation 'directed' towards the issues that the researcher wishes to explore in more depth (King and Horrocks 2010: 314-323). The questions I asked were directed toward five themes, namely: weather, settlement, traditional and modern fishing practices, navigation, and origins (Appendix 2). This was one of the main interview techniques used as it allowed me to explore a range of subjects within one interview and, where the interviewee was particularly knowledgeable about a particular topic, focus the interview questions on this. This proved extremely useful in gathering a wide range of data based loosely on specific themes. Moreover, during these interviews I found that it was also possible to gather information on topics that had not been previously considered. This was especially true during an interview in the fishing village of Di-Ḥamri when a fisherman interviewed said that he considered currents to be an important factor affecting when and where they will fish.

Guiding the questions toward his new information not only enabled me to gather new information, but also to adjust the questionnaire for later interviews. The nature of the semi-structured technique also helped in planning for subsequent interviews allowing me, where possible, to return to the people interviewed with specific questions based on the outcome of these interviews.

Focus Groups

A third technique employed was the focus group interview. The focus group interview is a technique whereby data is collected through group interaction on a topic determined by the researcher and, as such, it is the researcher's questions which provide the focus for group discussion, with the data generated coming from the group (Morgan 1997: 6). This technique is a rapid means of collecting data from a large number of participants (Wilkinson 2006: 180). During this study it was found to be helpful in situations where time constraints precluded undertaking a number of more in-depth interviews. This technique was particularly useful when on Samḥa, as the length of my visit was limited to a couple of days (Figure 4). While I was able to conduct several semi-structured interviews with some of the older fishermen, to ensure that I did not focus primarily on them I set up a focus group to include as many of the other fishermen as possible. This allowed me to supplement the data derived from individual semi-structured interviews with that gathered from almost the entire fishing community. The success of this technique was partly based on having a senior member of the community present, who helped facilitate the meeting. This technique was similarly employed in Ḥadiboh, where several fishing families were interviewed.

The interview techniques outlined above are ideally suited to understanding oral traditions and gaining an insight into the social, cultural and economic aspects that have influenced them. However, manual traditions, or those traditions that are passed on by observing and imitating the hand movements, gestures and behaviours of others, require a different approach. The reason for this is that it is not always possible for people to verbalise, or for researchers to visualise, the manual practices undertaken. Consequently, I also used another ethnographic technique known as participant observation.

Participant Observation

Participant observation, as used in this study, was overt and the fishermen, knowing that I wished to learn about their traditional techniques and methods, permitted me to accompany, observe and participate in their daily fishing activities. This technique is one of the core techniques in ethnographic research and enables a close and intimate familiarity with the communities under study (DeWalt and DeWalt 2002). According to Spradley (1979: 9), it also provides the underlying basis for ethnographic interviews as it allows for the researcher to verify whether that which was told to the researcher is actually practiced by the community under study. During my research I used participant observation in two ways. First, where a specific manual tradition had been mentioned during an interview I would ask the fisherman whether he could

FIGURE 4. A FOCUS GROUP INTERVIEW BEING UNDERTAKEN IN KHAYSAT ASH-SHAIKH, THE ONLY FISHING VILLAGE ON THE ISLAND OF SAMḤA (PHOTO: AUTHOR).

demonstrate this technique, which I would document using photographs, video recordings and field notes. I found this technique useful when documenting the process used to construct fish traps, a tradition which had been passed down from father to son through several generations, but was being rapidly supplanted by the introduction of industrial manufactured galvanised-wire fish traps. Secondly, where a specific technique was used, either to catch fish or navigate, I accompanied the fishermen out to sea where I could observe and engage in the techniques being used. The importance of this was that the fishermen would often refer to a technique as something one just knew, yet once out at sea they were able to demonstrate how and what techniques they used. In addition to the manual traditions I observed, I also used this technique to gather data on how the social relationships at sea operate and gain a deeper insight into many of the socio-economic and cultural influences affecting crew choice. It also allowed me to observe and acquire a deeper understanding of the traditions and ideational technologies employed. Much of the information gathered during the observation, participation and experience of the social and practical aspects of the fishing communities helped to reinforce and clarify the information gathered during interviews undertaken.

Object Traditions

The methodological approaches up to now are almost exclusively part of an ethnographic approach that has relied on what information can be observed or elicited from the fishermen being studied. However, examining objects, or more specifically the maritime material culture of these fishermen, requires a combination of archaeological and ethnologic methods. This is because ethnography and to a greater degree archaeology deal with material objects and their relationship to both the natural and social environment. As such, both disciplines inform and allow interpretation of the social, political, economic and environmental factors that influence when, how and what objects are adopted or rejected by a society. The methodology devised for this study uses ethnographic interviews and archaeological recording to shed light on various objects, notably the fishing equipment and traditional vessels. The aims of this are to look at the adoption, construction and use of the equipment and vessels; whether they are still in use or not. Tracing these 'survivals' or remnants from the past helps to open up perspectives into the past and aid in the interpretation and understanding of those periods for which there are few records (Hasslöf 1966: 130). Consequently, by combining ethnographic and archaeological methods it is possible to understand the technical aspects of the traditional maritime objects and determine how they have been adapted to the environment and social-economic structures the fishermen are working within. This approach also allows one to understand the social and cultural aspects that have influenced their acceptance and use, both today and in the past. Additionally, by recording the technical attributes of the traditional objects on Socotra one is able to make comparative analysis with similar objects recorded elsewhere and gain an insight into possible cultural links with other areas.

Social Traditions

The traditions outlined above all fall within a wider tradition known as a social tradition, which is articulated and spread by means of social groups, who have their own customs and rules (Hasslöf 1972: 25). Tracing these social traditions is complicated and requires a combined ethnographical and historical approach, as they are rarely apparent and often based upon half remembered standards and restrictions of the past. During my study it was apparent that the fishermen were operating within a set of customs and rules that affected not only the types of fishing equipment they were using but also when and where they would fish. According to the ethnographical evidence gathered, I realised that the customs and rules affecting the fishermen operated on a local and island wide level, and that to be part of a fishing community there were a number of social traditions one abided by. These traditions are strictly enforced amongst the fishermen and form an important part of what constitutes their social and cultural makeup.

The ethnographic methodologies used in this research has produced a significant amount of information concerning the interplay between individuals, their communities and the various United Nations organisations that are acting on behalf of the Yemen government. Consequently, a great deal of the information gathered has the potential to be damaging to the individuals and communities interviewed. In order to address these concerns I have placed them within an ethical framework (Murphy and Dingwall 2001: 347), outlined below.

Ethics

This research underwent a preliminary ethical review as part of the requirements set out by Exeter University. The participants interviewed were all recruited voluntarily. A written consent form was not considered to be necessary as the participants are mostly illiterate. Furthermore, the introduction of paper bureaucracy into the interview context was considered to be detrimental, in that forms would intimidate the interviewees, given the political culture of Yemen. The participants were all informed before the interview of the nature of my research by oral means. An assessment into the possible harm that could arise from the information that was obtained was done, and this was noted and acted upon. The main areas of concern were with regards the illegal fishing practices undertaken and the secrecy afforded to specific areas. To protect the participants from harm I have, where necessary, omitted their names and excluded the location of their villages. In addition, the names of all participants were kept anonymous, unless their express consent was obtained. The material gathered is kept by me in a secure archive and will not be used for commercial or governmental purposes.

Conclusion

The challenge of this study has been to find a way in which to it is possible to gather, analyse and interpret a wide range of traditions and to understand the social, economic, cultural and environmental factors that influence them. I have chosen a transdisciplinary approach that focuses on ethnography, but also looks at some historical and archaeological factors. This allows me to tackle a broad range of data and provide a narrative that is as holistic as possible. The starting point of this approach is ethnography, which provides a foundation of empirical data gathered from the contemporary fishing communities. With this foundation in place I am able to use archaeological, historical and meteorological studies to study the social, spatial and temporal factors that influence the fishing community's interaction with the sea and understand how these factors affect their maritime traditions.

Using a spatial and temporal framework allows this study to address the various factors influencing the fishermen's traditions from two separate yet interrelated perspectives. Furthermore, with the foundation of the information gathered coming from ethnographic accounts gathered from the contemporary fishing communities it is possible to work from the known present to the unknown past. As a result, this methodological approach is ideally suited to helping understand the complexities of the social, cultural, economic and political factors influencing their traditions. In addition, by encompassing several disciplines within a temporal and spatial framework this research presents a narrative of the fishermen and their maritime traditions that can be seen as being truly holistic.

Part Two:
The Fishermen

Chapter 4

The Historical Ethnic Groups

The coastal population of Socotra is made up of a culturally diverse mixture of people that is the result of several generations of historical migration and settlement. The aim of this chapter is to identify the main ethnic groups on Socotra in the past and find out which elements formed part of the coastal population. This is done by historically contextualising the various ethnic groups from the earliest known record of their existence up until the 20th century by looking at two groups of people on the island, the islanders and the foreigners. This division will help shed light on the social and cultural links of the island and assist in determining the role of each ethnic group and what influence they have had on the social and cultural traditions of the fishing community.

The Islanders

Archaeological evidence, in the form of stone tools found along the north coast of Socotra has demonstrated that the earliest known occupation of the island occurred approximately 1.4 million years ago (Sedov *et al.* 2009). An analysis of the mitochondrial DNA and Y-chromosomal genetic variation of the interior inhabitants revealed that this colonisation was followed by a second occupation phase from Arabia that took place approximately 11,000 years ago, in the early Holocene period. This was later followed by a third wave of colonisation from Arabia, which occurred during the Neolithic period, approximately 3000 years ago (Černý *et al.* 2009: 445). According to Černý *et al.* (2009: 138), the Socotri population living in the interior exhibit genetic evidence which shows that those who came to the island remained isolated for a long period of time and display signs of autochthonous evolution. The importance of this archaeological and genetic evidence is that it proves the settlement of Socotra took place over a period of several thousand years and that these settlers formed an indigenous population.

The next period within which it is possible to establish something about Socotra's inhabitants and ascertain what activities they were involved in is in the 7th century BC, when the island became a plantation colony for the provision of incense to the ancient Kingdom of Hadhramaut (Doe 1970: 151; Casson 1989: 46). Doe (1992: 41) and Naumkin (1993: 364), argue that the archaeological evidence demonstrates that this colony was made up of resident farmers and a number of migrant labourers from Arabia. The incense trade suffered a major decline during the 4th century AD, brought upon by increased aridification and a fall in the demand for incense (Groom 1981: 235). Doe (1970: 155), argues that this decline led to many migrant labourers and islanders abandoning Socotra. He also says that those who chose to remain would have been forced to rely on fishing, herding and farming. Genetically, it would appear that it was the remaining islanders, who must have settled in the interior as pastoralists, whereas the migrant labourers moved to the coast to fish.

Historically, the first evidence for this division in Socotra's population is found in an account by the traveller Ibn al-Mujāwir (AD 1292), who identifies two groups of people on the island, those who dwell on the plains and those who dwell in the mountains (Ibn al-Mujāwir 2008: 264). Thereafter, this geographical division is mentioned throughout Socotra's historical narrative and has come to represent two classes of people, namely: the indigenous mountain dwellers and the foreign coastal dwellers. Today the Socotri still differentiate between people according to where they live, namely: those who live above, *il-ṣaᶜanhen* (Soc), and those who live below, *di-gyēme* (Soc). This division also refers to those people who belong to a kin based tribal group, own land, and have access to specific land and water resources, and those who have no tribal affiliation and are not land owning (Morris 2002: 223). The latter are mostly settlers who live along the coast. Those with tribal affiliation mostly live in the mountainous interior and call themselves Bedouin. Today the term Bedouin is also used by those people who have family in the mountains and during my interviews with fishermen who live on the coast there are those who have been called or call themselves Bedouin by virtue of having this connection.

In spite of the decline in the incense trade in the 4th century AD, Socotra remained an important trading port for several centuries, with traders from ancient Greece, India and Arabia settling on the island to trade (Schoff 1912: 30-32). According to the *Periplus Maris Erythraei* (32.10. 3-25), an anonymous pilot guide written by a Greco-Egyptian in the mid-1st century AD, Socotra was a major supplier of dragon's blood, aloes and turtle shells (Casson 1989: 69). The *Periplus* also states that Socotra was under the rule of the 'king of the frankincense-bearing land', Hadhramaut, and was being leased by Arabian merchants from this area, who lived with the other foreign traders on the northern coast of the island (Casson 1989: 169-170). This has been archaeologically corroborated by the discovery of a settlement on the north coast, which has been securely dated to the 1st century AD (Naumkin and Sedov 1993: 605). Taken together, this evidence indicates Socotra's north coast has been inhabited for the longest period, and remains the most populated coastal stretch of the island. That the *Periplus* refers to the coastal population on Socotra as being made up of foreign traders from ancient Greece, India and Arabia would imply that there was likely to have been a native population on the island. However, attempting to trace the original islanders in the historical record is fraught with difficulties as there are few historical records that directly refer to them and when they do it is normally as 'natives', a term that is used by many authors to describe all the islanders they encountered. A noteworthy exception to this is given in an account by Sir Thomas Roe, an English diplomat, who visited Socotra in 1615 and described the ethnicity of the people he encountered. Within his portrayal of the inhabitants he refers to the 'Bedouin', as Christians living in the mountains and the 'true ancient naturals', as the original inhabitants (Roe 1967: 1.33-34). Interestingly, he groups the original inhabitants within his description of the coastal people he encountered, which would seem to imply that they may have formed part of the coastal population at this time. In the 19th and 20th century this situation changes and the 'native' inhabitants are all classed as pastoralists living in the interior, who only come to the coast for short periods to fish or trade (Wellsted 1840: 2.257; Ormsby 1844: 374; Balfour 1888: xxvii).

The Foreigners

The first constituent of the foreign coastal population that requires examination are the Greeks, who are referred to by both European and Muslim authors. After the *Periplus*, the next account to mention the presence of Greeks on Socotra is a 6th century AD description by Cosmas Indicopleustes (*fl.* 6th century AD), a Greek Nestorian Christian monk and merchant from Egypt (Indicopleustes 1896: 119). According to him, the island's inhabitants spoke Greek, having been originally sent to Socotra by the Ptolemy I Soter (r. 323-283 BC), who succeeded Alexander the Great (r. 332-323 BC). However, the Muslim sources from the 10th to 13th century AD claim the Greeks were sent by Alexander the Great to take control of the myrrh production on the island (Ubaydli 1989: 141). Regardless of who sent the Greeks to Socotra the only archaeological evidence to support their presence are two Greek inscriptions found in Hoq cave, dated to the first quarter of the 3rd century AD (Bukharin 2012: 497).

What is particularly significant about the presence of the Greeks is that they were, according to Cosmas Indicopleustes, Christians (Indicopleustes 1896:119). This is later corroborated by al-Hamdānī (d. AD 945), a Yemeni geographer, historian and astronomer, who not only referred to the Greeks as being Christians, but said that they were joined by people from Al-Mahrah, Hadhramaut, who like them became Christians (al-Hamdānī 1986: 93). The last reference to the presence of a Greek population is in the 16th century AD, when the navigator Aḥmed Ibn Mājid (d.*c.* 1500) said that the Christians on Socotra are the last remaining remnants of the Greek population that settled there (Tibbets 1981: 223). This would seem to contradict al-Hamdānī's account that the Christians were a mixture between Mahra tribesmen and Greek settlers, or it could be possible that these Mahra Christians were no longer considered to be affiliated with the tribesmen from Al-Mahrah. According to Serjeant (1992: 137-138), the reason for this difference is that the Mahra tribesmen who converted to Christianity were from a different tribal group than those who later came to rule over Socotra. The importance of this is that in many of the later 12th to 16th century descriptions the Christians are considered to be different to the Mahra who ruled over Socotra. This is clearly demonstrated in the Portuguese sources, which say that the island's Christian inhabitants were tormented by the 'Fartaquins', who were taking their children and wives and converting them to Islam (Commentaries 1884: 1.53; Brásio 1943: 12; *The Book of Duarte Barbosa* 1967: 1.62). Several authors state that the 'Fartaquins' and people from 'Fartaque' is a term used by the Portuguese to refer to the people living near Rās Fartaq, and was mostly used in reference to the Mahra tribes living along the Hadhramaut (Beckingham 1949: 165; *The Book of Duarte Barbosa* 1967: 1, n10; Serjeant 1992: 163). Later, in 1615, when Sir Thomas Roe (d. 1644) visited the island he too mentions a separate group of inhabitants, who are Christian, and live in the mountains (Roe 1899: 1.34). While there are a few descriptions in the 17th century that do refer to the presence of Christian symbols and architecture, there is little information on the Christian inhabitants. The final vestiges of Christianity on Socotra were eventually destroyed during a Wahhabi incursion in 1801 (Bent 1900: 361), although it is likely that Christianity had ceased to be practised on the island several centuries earlier. What this narrative demonstrates is that the Christian inhabitants constitute a wide range of different ethnicities that included Greeks, a tribe from Al-Mahrah that settled on the island, and an element of the original population. It would seem that initially they formed part of the coastal population, although later they moved inland, probably to avoid persecution. The importance of a Christian presence on Socotra is that it sheds light on one of the reasons for population movement and the dangers of attributing ethnicity to the geographical location of the islands inhabitants. Furthermore, it helps us to understand why, in the Muslim medieval accounts, the Christian islanders were attributed with supernatural powers and said to be involved with pirates, who were preying on Muslim shipping.

The second group of foreign settlers on Socotra to be examined are the Arabians, or more explicitly the Arabians from Al-Mahrah, who have been involved with Socotra for millennia. The question here is, who are the Mahra and what was their interest in Socotra? The Mahra are a tribe, or more correctly a people, that form part of the Mahra sultanate, which stretched along the south-eastern part of the Arabian Peninsula, between the Hadhramaut and Dhofar, Oman and included the island of Socotra (Carter 1976: 37). The capitals of this sultanate were a combination between Qishn on the south western coast of Yemen and Ḥadiboh on Socotra's north coast. The Mahra speak their own language, Mehri, of which there are three main dialects. Mehri, much like Socotri, is one of the six Modern South Arabian languages, although there are no similarities between Mehri and Socotri (Simeone-Senelle 1997: 378-379). Traditionally the Mahra people of the interior were semi-nomadic pastoralists, while those along the coast were also fisher-men and sailors. The most famous of these sailors was the 16th century navigator, Sulaymān al-Mahrī (d. 1550), who wrote several navigational treatises (Tibbetts 1981: 42). Epigraphic evidence indicates that Mahra were the descendants of the Himyarites (r. 110 BC-520 AD) and were involved in controlling the trade in incense (Müller 2012). This may explain their original connection with Socotra, which was an important source of frankincense. As mentioned above, Mahra involvement with Socotra began from at least as early as the 1st century AD, when the *Periplus* refers to them as being rulers of the island (Casson 1989: 169). During the medieval period they retained their hold on Socotra, but their main interests are in securing the island against invasion, to provide themselves with a temporary refuge from their political enemies, and to establish a tax farm (Tibbetts 1981: 223; Serjeant 1992: 162-163). According to Ibn Mājid, in the 15th century the island was ruled by two Mahri sheiks from the Beni ᶜAfār and Beni Sulaimān tribes, who were the descendants of the Beni Ziyād (Tibbetts 1981: 223; Serjeant 1996: 144). This would imply that at this period there were at least two different Mahri tribal groups on Socotra, although it is unlikely that these rulers were part of the initial Mahra settlement that converted to Chri-stianity. Consequently, it is possible that there was an earlier Mahri tribe that settled on Socotra and converted to Christianity and that they, together with the original population, were ruled over by other Mahri tribes. Attempting to trace the genealogy of the Mahri tribes and establish which tribe may have been part of this initial settlement is very nearly impossible as so many of the Mahri Sultans in the Muslim chronicles have similar names (Serjeant 1996: 162). Portuguese sources corroborate much of what was written by the Muslim authors, insofar as they encountered a well-fortified Muslim fort built by the Mahra from Qishn, which was used to control and impose tribute on the inhabitants (Commentaries 1884: 1.44-56; Serjeant 1963: 158). The short-lived occupation of Socotra by the Portuguese (1507-1511), appears to have little impact on Mahra claims to the island and soon after it was abandoned they returned to re-establish their dominance over the inhabitants (Serjeant 1992: 161-162). This dominance continued throughout the 17th and 18th centuries when, according to various European accounts, the island was ruled by a relation of the Sultan of Qishn, who imposed a tax on the inhabitants (Kerr 1811-1894; Foster 1906-1927). Mahra involvement in Socotra underwent a significant change in the 19th century as the British colonial interests in the island increased. This interest began in 1834 with the introduction of the steamship and the first direct sea passage from Bombay to Suez. Socotra, by virtue of its strategic position and supplies of water was considered an important coaling station for steamships travelling from India to Suez, leading to an agreement between the British government and the Sultan Omar ibn Tuārī of the ᶜAfār tribe, who had been ruling over the island for 30 years but resided in Qishn (Haines 1845: 109). The agreement allowed Socotra to function as a coal storage depot serving the steamships. However, with the British capture of Aden in 1838, the British no longer required Socotra, and for several years they were no longer interested in keeping the island under their control. This situation changed in 1874 when news of Turkish and Italian interest in the island was received, which would have had a detrimental effect on British military strategy in the area (Hunter and Sealy 1986: 112). Consequently, in 1876, the British concluded an additional treaty with the Sultan by which, in payment of an annual stipend, he agreed, 'never to cede, sell, or mortgage, or otherwise give for occupation, save to the British Government, Socotra or her outlying islands' (Hunter and Sealy 1986: 113). The significance of this treaty was that it initiated the gradual transfer of the official seat of the sultanate from Qishn in Al-Mahrah to Ḥadiboh in Socotra, where the sultanate eventually became established (Elie 2004: 54-56). The reason for this was that by residing on Socotra, the sultan could easily enforce taxation on the inhabitants and be assured of a guaranteed income from the annual payment of protectorate fees by the British. During this period of British interest, the island attracted successive waves of immigrants from the Arabian mainland. As a result, the Arabian coastal population on the island was, in 1967, recorded as being made up of a mixture of Mahra tribesmen, Hadramis, and various merchants and sailors from Saudi Arabia, Dubai, Oman and other areas in the Gulf (Serjeant 1992: 170-172). Despite this influx of immigrants in the late 19th and 20th century the Mahra still made up a significant part of the coastal population. While it is possible that some of the Mahra may have become pastoralists and intermingled with the interior inhabitants, those on Socotra were predominantly coastal people, who were more likely to have been engaged in trade and fishing.

The third ethnic group are the Indians, who according to Ubaydli (1989), Behyl (1998), Müller (2001) and

Dridi (2002), have had a presence on Socotra from at least the 1st century AD. Archaeologically, the discovery of several Indian inscriptions found in Hoq cave, on the north side of the island and dated from the 2nd to 4th centuries AD, provides further evidence to indicate their presence and origins (Dridi 2002; Robin and Gorea 2002; Dridi and Gorea 2003). Within the *Periplus Maris Erythraei*, the Indian traders are said to have come from Barygaza (modern Broach) in Gujārāt on the northwest coast of India (Casson 1989: 18). This is confirmed by the epigraphic evidence, yet there is also some limited evidence which indicates that they also came from Malabar on the southwest coast of India (Strauch and Bukharin 2004: 135). The presence of Indians on Socotra continues to be mentioned from the 10th to the 13th centuries, although by the 13th century they are increasingly portrayed as pirates rather than traders (Ubaydli 1989: 144-146). According to the geographer al-Muqaddasī (*fl.* second half of the 10th century), all vessels passing in the vicinity of Socotra were fearful of attacks by Indian pirates (al-Muqaddasī 2001: 13). These fears were well founded, and the Moroccan traveller Ibn Baṭṭūṭa (d. 1368-9) provides a graphic account of how a ship was attacked by pirates from India, when passing the island (Ibn Baṭṭūṭa 1956: 1.224). The portrayal of pirates within the Islamic sources as having an Indian origin, is based on the association of Indians with the word *bawārij* (pl. of *bārija*), meaning pirate ship. This word was initially used to describe the coastal people from western India who were involved in piracy during the 9th century AD, but later was used in reference to all pirates and pirate ships of Indian origin (Ubaydli 1989: 145; Agius 2008: 329). This is later contradicted in, *The Book of Curiosities*, a manuscript dated to the first half of the 11th century AD, which refers to shipping passing Socotra being stopped by pirates, not from western India, but from East Africa (Savage-Smith and Rapoport 2007: 24).

Within the traveller and merchant Ibn al-Mujāwir's (d. AD 1291) description of Socotra the pirates, or *surrāq*, were directly involved with the coastal population, who allowed them to stay on the island for six months of the year (Ibn al-Mujāwir 1954: 268). During this time they shared food and drink with the pirates and the men allowed them to have sexual relations with their wives (Ibn al-Mujāwir 2008: 265). The relevance of this is that Ibn al-Mujāwir does not specify whether the pirates were people from western India or East Africans, but does state that there was a close relationship between the pirates and coastal inhabitants. This relationship is also mentioned by Marco Polo (d. AD 1324), who comments on how the inhabitants were Christians that went naked 'like the other Indians' and that they traded with the pirates that frequented the island (Yule and Cordier 1993: 2.406-410). This would seem to confirm that there was a western Indian rather than East African presence on the island. However, the possibility of an East African presence is later confirmed by Duarte Barbosa (d. 1521), an officer in the Portuguese navy who refers to Socotra as being subject to the Mahra, who ruled over 'black' and 'brown' men. The ethnic background of the 'black' men is most probably the East Africans mentioned several centuries earlier, although it is not possible to totally exclude dark-skinned Indians or Arabians. The ethnic background of the 'brown' men is more difficult to ascertain, as in one instance he refers to them as Christians and then refers to them as being similar to the 'Canarins' (*The Book of Duarte Barbosa* 1967: 1.60-62). According to Longworth Dames (*The Book of Duarte Barbosa* 1967: 1.n 62), the term 'Canarins' is used by Barbosa to compare the inhabitants to the Indians of southern India. This could either imply that they resembled Indians or that they were Indians, which would reinforce the earlier accounts mentioning an Indian presence on the island.

Recently, in 2004, further evidence for the presence of Indians on Socotra was discovered, when five stone inscriptions written in Gujārāti and dating to the 17th and 18th centuries were found near ᶜAririhun Di-Lisheh, a village on Socotra's north coast (Figure 5). The stones were inscribed by several Indian merchants and each lists the name of the ship and the people onboard. In several cases they also refer to the port from which they sailed from and that they stayed on Socotra for up to seven months to trade. What is intriguing is that the names of the various merchants inscribed are similar to those recorded as merchants who traded with ports in East Africa (Strauch 2012). The importance of these stones is that it would appear that the Indians visiting Socotra during this period were traders, not pirates. Secondly, that many of the merchants on the island were trading with East Africa would imply that Socotra had a strong social and cultural links with East Africa, which would account for an East African presence on the island. Finally, it also provides an insight into the activities of the Gujārāti sailors, who were visiting Socotra in the 17th and 18th century (Kerr 1811-1894; Purchas 1905-1907; Foster 1906-1927). This Indian presence continues throughout the 19th century, and when the archaeologist and traveller Theodore Bent (d. 1897) visits the island in 1896 he too refers to Indian traders (Bent 1900: 345). In 1967, when a joint British military and civilian scientific expedition was undertaken to the island the Indian traders they encountered were said to come from Muscat, rather than the oft quoted Gujārāt (Serjeant 1992: 133). This could imply that these people were perhaps not Indian but Balochi, an ethnic group native to the Balochistan region, who have a strong presence in Oman and are mostly traders and farmers. The length of Indian involvement with Socotra demonstrates a longstanding interest, which began with piracy but later was based around trade. While it is possible that Indians made up part of the coastal population it is doubtful that they remained on the island for any significant length of time, but rather that they formed part of the a seasonal

Figure 5. The stone tablets with Gujārāti inscriptions found near ᶜAririhun Di-Lisheh on the north coast of Socotra (Photo: author).

influx of traders that stayed on the island for several months to trade.

The last ethnic group to be examined are the Africans. As mentioned, the earliest reference to Africans on Socotra is in *The Book of Curiosities*, which also referred to Socotra as being under the rule of East African pirates (Savage-Smith and Rapoport 2007: 24). In light of this it is also possible to argue that the pirates referred to by al-Masᶜūdī in the 10th century AD may have also been East African. The significance of this is that it would imply that the East Africans constituted part of Socotra's early coastal population, even though they are rarely referred to the Muslim and European accounts. Thus it would seem that the Africans may have been a mixture of slaves, pirates and possibly traders. While it is possible to argue that the ethnicity of Barbosa's 'black men' could have been dark-skinned Indians or Arabians, it is more likely that they were African. This is supported by Roe's description of the inhabitants several years earlier, in which he describes the slaves as being Ethiopians (Roe 1967: 1.34). During the 11th century there are several references to the presence of African slaves on Socotra, which are said to be especially numerous and forced by their Arabian masters to tend the date plantations and fish. They are also said to have been mainly brought from Zanzibar by the Omanis, who were running a lucrative trade in slaves at the time (Kerr 1811-1894; Purchas 1905-1907; Foster 1906-1927). The exception to this is found in the journals of an English captain William Keeling (d. 1620), who describes how the Mahra residing in Socotra would travel to the Comoros each year to purchase slaves (Purchas 1905: 2.515). While this provides an interesting insight into the procurement of slaves it is not an indication of their origins, as it was not uncommon for East African slaves that had been taken to Arabia to be sold on several times and find themselves moved from one area of the Indian Ocean to another (Grandidier *et al.* 1903: 68). The ethnicity of Socotra's slave population is elaborated on in the 19th century when Wellsted (1835a: 214) describes them as having been brought to the island by passing shipping from Somalia, Zanzibar and 'other areas'. The trade in slaves on Socotra appears to have ended by 1881, when the German botanist, Georg August Schweinfurth (d. 1925) wrote a report concerning the end of the slave trade on Socotra. In his report he remarks that slave ships which travelled from Zanzibar to Muscat no longer carried slaves to Socotra, implying that the Omanis had been supplying Socotra with slaves from Zanzibar (Schweinfurth 1993: 4.190). He also mentions that there were numerous second and third generation African families living in the coastal villages on Socotra, who had been freed by their masters (Schweinfurth 1881: 128). This is similar to that told to me by several African fishermen from Suq and Ḥadiboh. They recounted how their grandfathers had been brought to Socotra from East Africa, although several in Ḥadiboh said that their grandfathers had specifically come from Zanzibar. According to an African fisherman in Ḥadiboh, Jamen Mahafawl Saif,[1] 70 years old, his grandfather had come from Zanzibar, and when he had been freed had decided to stay on Socotra to fish, which was what he had

[1] Interviewed on 22 December 2009.

been doing before he had been freed. The final person to refer to the presence of slaves on Socotra is that of the archaeologist and traveller Theodore Bent (d. 1897), who visited the island in 1896. According to his description, the Africans on Socotra were slaves and soldiers (Bent 1897: 975-992). That Bent talks about African slaves seems at odds to the report submitted by Schweinfurth, and it would seem that either the Bents were mistaken or that slavery had returned to the island. The former would seem the most plausible explanation, as there are no further references to slavery after this account. During the 20th century we learn that, other than Ethiopia, Somalia and Zanzibar, some of the Africans on Socotra also came from Sudan (Serjeant 1992: 172). This was corroborated by a full-time fisherman in his 60s, Saad Dabowed Mousa,[2] who said that his grandfather had been brought from Sudan as a slave and was the Sultan's chief executioner. Throughout Socotra's historical narrative Africans have mostly been portrayed as slaves serving their Arabian masters and it is certain that they must have constituted a significant part of the coastal population. That most had been brought from East Africa is unsurprising when taking into consideration Socotra's strong trading links with East Africa and that Zanzibar was one of the Omanis main sources of slaves.

Conclusion

This historical overview of the various ethnicities on Socotra has outlined several important points with respect to Socotra's population. The first point concerns the geographic division between those who live in the interior and those who live along the coast. According to the archaeological and genetic studies undertaken, the interior population are the original inhabitants and the coastal population are migrant foreigners from a variety of ethnic backgrounds. However, the historical records present a rather more complex picture. This is firstly seen in the presence of Christians on the island, who are portrayed as Greeks, a tribe from al-Mahrah, and the original inhabitants. Initially the Christians seem to have lived both in the interior and coastal areas, although sometime in the 15th century most of them moved into the interior to avoid persecution. What is important here is that after they moved into the interior they became known as islanders, even though many of them had initially come to Socotra as settlers. Paradoxically the coastal population retained their ethnic identities in all but some of the vague 17th and 18th century European accounts that refer to almost all the people encountered as 'natives'. As a result, we learn that those living in the interior were considered islanders, even though they may have been foreign settlers. Conversely, those people living along the coast were always divided into their ethnic groups, which has also helped show that the islanders did live amongst the foreign settlers at various times.

The second point is in connection with the tribes from Al-Mahrah. Throughout the historical record we learn that the Mahra tribes were involved with Socotra, mainly as rulers but also as settlers, some of whom converted to Christianity. The importance of this is that it demonstrates two points. First, there were several different Mahra tribes settling or ruling over Socotra. This is clearly shown in the 16th century when we learn that two sultans from two different tribes ruled over the island. Secondly, notwithstanding the difficulties of determining the genealogies of the named sultans ruling over the island, it is apparent that these tribes were predominantly coastal people, engaged in trade. That several coastal tribes from Al-Mahrah were affiliated with those on Socotra reveals how intimate this long-standing relationship between the two areas must have been and more importantly that this association was between people with a strong link to the sea.

The third point is in relation to the nature of the coastal inhabitants' relationship with Socotra, in particular the Indian population. When looking at the presence of the Mahra on the island it is clear that, even though the sultans mainly ruled over the island from Qishn, there had always been a settled Mahra presence on the island. Consequently, it is probable that they would have had a significant part to play in the social and cultural traditions of the coastal population. Conversely, when looking at the presence of Indians on the island it would appear that they were not permanent residents. Indeed, it could be argued that the Indian pirates were only resident during those periods in which there was a high proportion of passing shipping to prey on and during the savage South West monsoon winds sought shelter elsewhere. Similarly, epigraphic evidence also refers to Indian merchants, who only stay on Socotra for several months of the year, presumably during those periods in which it was possible to trade. Therefore, even though Indians do make up an element of the coastal population, their numbers would have been small enough to suppose that they are likely to have had little influence over social and cultural practices.

The final point is in reference to Africans in the historical narrative of Socotra. The earliest description of Africans on Socotra is in the first half of the 11th century, which surprisingly refers to the island as being under the rule of East African pirates. While it is possible that, like the Indian pirates, they raided shipping passing the island it would seem unlikely that they had managed to oust the ruling Mahra. Nevertheless, what this description does show is that the East African people were not only slaves, but that it is possible that they were also engaged in various maritime activities. Certainly, it is not inconceivable that, with Socotra's strong trading links with East Africa, they too may have been engaged in the trade of slaves and other products. Throughout the rest of Socotra's historical narrative the only reference to

[2] Interviewed on 14 February 2009.

Africans are that they were brought to the island as slaves from East Africa, Somalia and Sudan and were forced to work in the date plantations or as fishermen. While the abolishment of slavery set the various African people on Socotra free, most remained on the island in the same occupation they had been doing under their Arabian masters. Consequently, they formed a significant ethnic group within the coastal population and are likely to have had an important influence on social and cultural traditions.

The ethnicities outlined in this historical overview have shown that Socotra's coastal population was made up of a wide range of different ethnicities that have almost all had a strong link with the sea. The next chapter explores this link by looking at which of these ethnic groups were involved in fishing and attempts to trace the length of their involvement.

Chapter 5

The Historical Fishing Community

Attempting to analyse the historical record and find evidence for fishing communities on Socotra is particularly difficult for a number of reasons. Firstly, the historical record is mostly concerned with the products from the sea rather than the people engaged in obtaining them. Secondly, those accounts which do refer to the people engaged in fishing refer to them by their occupation rather than cultural or ethnic background. This is exacerbated by the fact that many authors make little distinction between different elements of Socotra's population. As a result, the aim of this chapter will be to attempt to establish which of the historical ethnic groups identified in the previous chapter were involved in fishing and what the length of their involvement was.

The Fishermen

The earliest, most relevant account for my study is that written by the historian and geographer Agatharchides of Cnidus (*fl.* 2nd century BC), who derived his information on Socotra or the 'Fortunate Islands', as it was known, from sailors that had visited the island. Agatharchides (1989: 169) refers to the inhabitants as turtle eaters, which would indicate that they were fishermen, who actively hunted and ate turtles and probably other marine species. The importance of this is that by the mid-1st century AD Socotra or *Dioscuridês*, as it was known, was a major supplier of turtle shells (Casson 1989: 69). This would seem to indicate that the fishermen were exploiting turtles as food from at least the 2nd century BC, and by the mid-1st century AD had started selling the shells to the foreign traders referred to in the *Periplus Maris Erythraei*, as a means of supplementing their income. The ethnicity of these fishermen is most likely to have been the original inhabitants, although it is possible that they may have also been the migrant labourers that remained on Socotra after the collapse of the incense trade in the 4th century AD (Doe 1970: 155).

The trade in turtle shells is only recorded again in the 13th century AD by the Chinese inspector of maritime trade Chau Ju-kua (d. 1231), who lists it amongst the articles obtainable from Socotra (Hirth and Rockhill 1911: 130-132). Unfortunately, this record provides little insight into the ethnicity of the fishermen and it is only possible to surmise that during this period they may have been the original inhabitants living along the coast, although it is likely that they were joined by fishermen from various other ethnic groups, especially when there was a market for turtle shells. The decline of the trade in turtle shells seems to have had little impact on the exploitation of turtles as in the 20th century we learn that Socotri fishermen are still actively catching and eating turtles (Forbes 1903: xxvii; Frazier 1980: 331). This was corroborated by the Head of Fisheries, Fouad Naseb Saeed,[3] who said that the fishermen, townspeople and pastoralists today are all involved in hunting turtles that come to the beaches during the nesting season. He also said that turtles have been actively hunted for several generations, although it is the meat and eggs that are sought after rather than the shell.

The next reference to directly mention fishing activities on Socotra comes from Marco Polo (d. 1324), the Venetian traveller who may have visited the island sometime in the 14th century AD. Within his description he observes that Socotra was involved in a great trade with shipping coming from 'all quarters' and that all vessels bound for Aden would stop there. Among the main items of trade listed by Marco Polo are ambergris and salted fish 'of a large and excellent kind'. The ambergris was, according to Marco Polo, obtained by hunting whales with barbed iron darts attached to a buoy (Yule and Cordier 1993: 406-407). Having killed the whale it was dragged up onto the shore to extract the ambergris from its stomach and oil from its head (Yule and Cordier 1993: 407). This description provides a number of interesting and important facts concerning the trade in fish, the fishermen and their practices. The first of these is that salted fish is an important traded commodity. This is especially interesting in that salted fish remains an important export on Socotra to this day (Nicols 2001: 29). Secondly, not only does he inform us that ambergris was obtained on Socotra, but that it was actively being collected by people who hunted whales. The importance of this is that ambergris is a rare and much sought-after commodity, used in medicine, cookery and perfume (Dannenfelt 1982: 382-384). Consequently, it would have brought great wealth to those fishermen who had the equipment and knowledge that would allow them to hunt whales. Thirdly, Marco Polo describes the people on Socotra as being baptised Christians, who went naked 'like the other Indians' (Yule and Cordier 1993: 406). As discussed in the previous chapter, this reference to Indians indicates that there was an Indian presence on the island, although it is most likely that they were engaged in piracy or trade rather than fishing. This would make it appear that it was the Christian inhabitants

[3] Head of Fisheries, 30 years old, interviewed on 22 December 2009.

who were hunting whales and supplying the dried fish. The issue here is that, as mentioned earlier, Christians are not indicative of an ethnic group. However, it is possible to surmise that the Christian fishermen would have been a mixture between the original inhabitants and the Mahra tribesmen, especially those Mahra that had been fishermen and sailors in Al-Mahrah. Finally, Marco Polo also says that pirates frequented the island and sold their looted goods to the Christian inhabitants (Yule and Cordier 1993: 407), which in light of the comments made by al-Muqaddasī (*fl.* 10th century AD) and Ibn Baṭṭūṭa (d. 1368) on the presence of Indian pirates, would suggest that they were still operating and residing on the island in the 14th century AD. The Christian and pirate interaction outlined by Marco Polo is similar to an account by Ibn al-Mujāwir's (d. 1291), who states that not only did the pirates stay with the inhabitants but that they shared their food, drink and wives with them (Ibn al-Mujāwir 2008: 265). This ongoing relationship presents an interesting question. Could some of the coastal population have also been pirates, and which part of the coastal population would they have been? I argue that the fishing community was directly involved in piracy. First, fishermen on Socotra and elsewhere live a marginal existence and many seek alternative forms of employment to supplement their livelihood (Serjeant 1992: 171-172; Naumkin 1993: 165; Elie 2008: 101). Secondly, they would have an intimate knowledge of the weather and seas in and around Socotra, and could use this knowledge to aid in capturing ships by luring them into dangerous areas and causing them to wreck. Finally, there are many recorded cases of interaction between fishermen and pirates throughout the Indian Ocean, which are based upon similarities between fishing communities and pirates (Murray 1987: 6; Young 2007: 13; Barendse 2009: 391).

The arrival of the Portuguese in the 16th century AD provides the next source from which it is possible to determine the ethnic background of the people engaged in fishing on Socotra and the marine species they were exploiting, although there is little information concerning their fishing practices. Within the Portuguese sources Socotra's inhabitants are referred to as being Mahra tribesmen who ruled over Christians, who were likely to have been Arabians that resembled Indians in appearance, East Africans and Indians (Commentaries 1884: 1.53; *The Book of Duarte Barbosa* 1967: 1.60-62). Duarte Barbosa (d. 1521), an officer in the Portuguese navy, also states that it was possible to obtain great quantities of ambergris and 'conch' shells, that were known to be valuable in Mine, a Portuguese fort built on the coast of Guinea, which functioned as the centre of trade on the west coast of Africa (*The Book of Duarte Barbosa* 1967: 1.n 62). The 'conch' shells mentioned by Barbosa, actually refers to cowries, which were highly valued along the west coast of Africa as a monetary unit that was used to trade for slaves. The mention of ambergris further reinforces the descriptions by al-Hamdānī, Ibn al-Mujāwir, and Marco Polo, and it appears that, much the same as in Malindi, East Africa, whales were being actively hunted by the fishermen during this period (Agius 2008: 100). The trade in cowries is also of interest when we learn that their worth was still recognised several centuries later when West African troops stationed on Socotra during the Second World War gathered sack loads of these shells to take home with them (Botting 2006: n 90). The final Portuguese account by Dom João de Castro (d. 1548), a naval officer and the fourth viceroy of Portuguese India, who visited Socotra in 1541, only refers to the inhabitants as 'natives', which would imply that they were the Christians. According to de Castro, they did not practice any manner of navigation, or fishing, even though the seas were full of fish (Kammerer 1936: 39). This remark is difficult to understand when viewed in conjunction with Marco Polo's description of the fishing practices and trade in fish, as well as Barbosa's description of the ambergris and shells available. The most likely explanation is that he is referring to the inhabitants of the interior who have not been recorded as being involved in fishing at this time.

These descriptions bring to an end the 16th century and lead into the 17th century when other European nations began their voyages to the East. Unlike the Portuguese, there was no attempt by these nations to occupy Socotra, their primary interest being to obtain aloes and victual their ships before continuing on their voyages to the Red Sea, India or Africa. The 17th century contains numerous references to Socotra in the journals of sailors who visited the island, yet few of these provide information about the people engaged in fishing. The main themes are that the island is occupied by soldiers who serve a residing ruler from Al-Mahrah, that Gujārāti sailors and ships visit the island and that there are numerous slaves of African descent (Kerr 1811-1894; Purchas 1905-1907; Foster 1906-1927).

The first 17th century account to provide a description of the fishing population is that of William Finch (*fl.* 17th century), an English merchant who remained on the island for three months in 1608 (Geddes 1964: 70-77). Finch describes how the Mahra did not permit the 'natives' to kill animals, and forced them to live from fish and dive for pearl oyster shells. He also comments on how the 'natives' supplement their enforced diet with dates, milk and rice, which they obtained from prostituting their wives to the visiting Gujārāti sailors (Purchas 1905: 4.13). This is very similar to that recorded by Ibn al-Mujāwir, and it would seem that not only were the 'natives' being forced to become fishermen, but they were also obliged to foster a close relationship with visiting pirates and merchants to supplement their limited diet. In Finch's description he refers to visiting Gujārāti and English merchants stayed for a short time on the island to trade in aloes, dragon's blood, dates and black ambergris (Purchas 1905: 13-17). This corroborates the Gujārāti inscriptions found on stone tablets uncovered near ᶜAririhun Di-Lisheh on the north coast of Socotra and demonstrates a strong Indian presence on the island. Incidentally, the reference to black ambergris is interesting as the modern-day fishermen consider this colour ambergris to be of inferior quality, which implies that they were selling the inferior quality to the visiting Europeans. Finally, Finch also mentions that the 'natives' took fish and lobsters from a bay in the north coast called ᶜAririhun Di-Lisheh, and that many pearl oyster and other shells could be found on the beaches (Purchas 1905: 17-18). That the 'native' inhabitants are actively fishing and diving is in contrast to the account by da Castro, which says that they did not practice any form of fishing. However, as Finch does not clearly identify who the 'natives' are, it is difficult to determine the ethnicity of the fishermen being described, although it can be surmised that it was not the ruling Mahra tribesmen, who he claims were forcing the 'natives' to fish.

Sir Thomas Roe (d. 1644), an English diplomat who visited Socotra in 1615, provides a clearer account of the ethnic divisions within the population. According to Roe, the island is inhabited by four groups of people: the Mahra tribesmen; Christian 'Bedouin'; the 'true ancient naturals', or those who were the original inhabitants, and 'Abyssinian' slaves (Roe 1967: 1.33-34). The only ethnic group he refers to as having been involved in fishing are the slaves, who are referred to as divers. The identification of these divers as Africans poses an interesting possibility. Could the fishing population mentioned by Finch have been African slaves? This would certainly explain what the numerous slaves of African descent were doing on Socotra and why Finch said that they were being forced by the Mahra to fish and dive for pearls. This would also explain the large number of Africans involved in fishing today.

The last 17th century reference to Socotra's fishing population is found in archives of the Dutch East India Company. Established in 1602, the Dutch East India Company was formed for the express purpose of extending the commercial interests of the Dutch into Asia and establishing colonies that would secure their position in the spice trade (Beckingham 1951: 1/2.65-66; Ingrams and Ingrams 1993: xxxi). The first Dutch mention of Socotra was written by Jan Huyghen van Linschoten (d. 1611), a merchant and traveller who published several books concerning the early East India trade. Within his writings he observes that Socotra supplied 'highly esteemed' aloes, which were famous for their medicinal effects (*The Voyage of John Huyghen van Linschoten to the East Indies* 1885: 2.126-127). As a result of the high value aloes that could be obtained on Socotra it was visited by numerous Dutch captains, but few provide any descriptions of its inhabitants. The most detailed report is found in the journal of Hendrik Hagenaer, a captain of the Dutch East India Company who visited the island sometime between 1631 and 1638. Hagenaer says that the inhabitants were all under the rule of a Sultan from Arabia and that the 'natives' bear arms and are all Muslims (Hagenaer 1650: 24-26). While he does not elaborate on this, it is likely that the 'natives' bearing arms were the Mahra tribesmen who served the Sultan of Al-Mahrah, as they were the only ones in the 17th century who were said to be carrying arms. He also mentions how the inhabitants would fish using rafts, fishing rods and seine nets (Hagenaer 1650: 25). That he refers to the inhabitants as 'natives', who were fishing makes it difficult to determine whether they were the Mahra tribesmen, which in light of earlier accounts would seem unlikely, or another part of the 'native' population. As he does not refer to the Christians, East Africans, or people from western India mentioned in earlier narratives, it is difficult to do little more than speculate who they may have been.

During the 18th century there are few European trading vessels passing Socotra to visit the Red Sea, which is seen in the very limited number of 18th century records available, most of which supply little or no evidence for Socotra's inhabitants (Beckingham 1983: 179). The 19th century begins with British colonial interests in Socotra, which started in 1834 with the signing of a treaty between the British government and Sultan Omar ibn Tuārī of the ᶜAfār tribe. Following the signing of this treaty a general survey of the island was undertaken by Commander Haines (d. 1860), Lieutenant Wellsted (d. 1842), Lieutenant Ormsby (d. 1857), Midshipsman Cruttenden and Dr Jessop Hulton (d. 1836). During this survey they provided several descriptive accounts of the population and their activities. Lieutenant Wellsted, the officer in charge of surveying the interior and the most prolific writer of the expedition, described the coastal population as being the descendants of a 'mongrel race' of Arabians, African slaves, Portuguese and people from other 'nations' (Wellsted 1840: 301). Elaborating on this, he says that the coastal inhabitants were all classed as foreigners, principally made up of Arabians who were left on Socotra by passing shipping and Africans brought from Somalia, Zanzibar and other areas (Wellsted 1835a: 214). Wellsted reports that the coastal 'Arabs' were primarily engaged in tending their date plantations and flocks of sheep, making ghee and trading with passing ships. He also observes how the Arabians often embarked on these ships, leaving many homes empty for several months (Wellsted 1835b: 323). The original inhabitants he describes as being as either 'natives' or Bedouin pastoralists, who were primarily involved in caring for their livestock in the hills and only came down to the coast to trade with passing ships. However, he does mention that some engaged in fishing, while retaining their livestock in the hills for those periods when it is not possible to fish (Wellsted 1840: 257). This is very similar to the situation today, and during the calm weather of the North East monsoon there is an influx of Bedouin who come down to the coast to fish. In his most direct reference to the fishing villages on the island, he identifies several fishing hamlets that can be found throughout the island and that in Qalansiyah, on the west coast, there were fifty fishing families who supplement their income by supplying water to passing vessels. These descriptions by Wellsted are based upon much of the work undertaken by the other members of the expedition, although these people are not referenced in Wellsted's work (see Haines 1845: 110). In a separate journal, the ship's surgeon, Jessop Hulton, also talks about the coastal population, although he only refers to them as being Arabians with distinctive African characteristics (Hulton 2003: 79). The next written description of the fishermen is that of Lieutenant Ormsby, who surveyed the interior and coastal areas of Socotra. Within Ormsby's journal the African slaves are said to have been bought from passing ships voyaging between Zanzibar and Muscat and were used by the Socotri 'Arabs' as fishermen and labourers in the date plantations (Ormsby 1844: 374). He also says that the 'native' inhabitants living on the south coast of the island would fish seasonally, using log rafts when the sea is calm (Ormsby 1844: 361-362). The importance of these expedition reports are that they provide one of the most comprehensive studies of Socotra's inhabitants and give an insight into diversity of the ethnic and cultural makeup of the coastal population at this time. What is clear is that the Africans divers and fishermen referred to in the 17th century are still actively fishing and constitute a significant part of the north coast's coastal population. The occupation of the Arabians referred to appear to be slightly more complex and it would seem that they were involved in various different activities, such as cultivation, pastoralism and trade, although fishing cannot be ruled out. These reports also provide a significant insight into the interior population in that it would appear that the interior inhabitants would not only come down to the coast to trade but, especially along the south coast, also to fish. This would imply that the interior population may have been fishing from a much earlier period, although it was only along the north coast where this was initially reported.

A botanical expedition led by the British botanist Issac Bayley Balfour (d. 1922) visited the island in 1880 to undertake a scientific survey of Socotra's plants and animals. Balfour, much like earlier accounts by Ibn al-Mujāwir and Sir Thomas Roe, also distinguishes between two communities, those living on the coast, and those living in the highlands. He describes the two communities as the native Socotri Bedouin, who lived in the hills, and a mixed population of Arabians, Indians, and Africans of 'various tribes', who lived along the coast. According to him the coastal inhabitants resided in several small villages on the north coast, the chief being Ḥadiboh, Qādheb and Qalansiyah, and that they were all engaged in fishing (Balfour 1888: xxvii). Balfour's description that all of the coastal inhabitants were fishing seems unlikely, in view of earlier narratives. However, what is particularly interesting is that the three villages he refers to are today amongst Socotra's main fishing villages.

Balfour's expedition was followed a year later by that of the German botanist, Georg August Schweinfurth (d. 1925), who spent several months on the island collecting specimens. Schweinfurth describes the villages of the coast as being inhabited by 'Arabs', who were primarily facilitating trade between the Bedouin and passing ships and would often embark on these vessels, leaving many houses in the main town of Ḥadiboh empty (Schweinfurth 1993: 4.190). He also refers to Socotra as being a refuge for slaves from Zanzibar and Muscat, many of whom were then second and third generation families (Schweinfurth 1881: 128). Notwithstanding the fact that Schweinfurth does not say what these African families were doing on Socotra it is possible to surmise that, much like in the past, they were fishing.

The last major expedition of the 19th century was undertaken by the archaeologist and traveller Theodore Bent, his wife, Mabel Bent and a Mr Bennett, who visited Socotra in 1896. They say that the inhabitants of the coastal villages were made up of Mahra and Indian traders and Africans from Zanzibar, and that they were ruled over by Sultan Salem, the nephew of Sultan Ali of Qishn (Bennett 1897: 410; Bent 1897: 975-992; Bent 1900: 343-396). Theodore Bent reiterates a great deal of what is said in earlier reports and even though he refers to the fishing population and their practices there is no mention of their ethnicity. Consequently, it is only possible to surmise that, in light of his descriptions of the population, the fishermen were predominately East Africans and Arabians.

Lastly, it is worth noting that both Wellsted (1840: 323) and Schweinfurth (1993: 4.190) point out that the Arabians on Socotra embarked on passing vessels, leaving many homes empty. It could be surmised that they were travelling to Al-Mahrah or Muscat. However, when the Italian traveller Luigi Robecchi-Bricchetti (d. 1926) was travelling in Somalia he reports coming across Mahra tribesmen from Socotra in Rās el Khail and Obbia. He also mentions that these Socotri Mahra were engaged in the trade of sheep and dried shark (Robecchi 1893: 360-361). Their presence in Somalia could imply that there was some relationship between these two areas, or that before the winds of the South West monsoon cut off all shipping to and from Socotra, that the Mahra living on Socotra travelled to Somalia to continue fishing and trading. That they are reported as being involved in the trade of dried shark could imply that they may have been catching them, which would indicate that they may have also been fishing for shark on Socotra.

The first expedition of the 20th century was a zoological expedition led by Henry Forbes, which visited Socotra and the outlying island of ᶜAbd al-Kūri. According to Forbes (1903: xxx), the islanders of ᶜAbd al-Kūri lived almost exclusively on fish, molluscs and turtle. The large quantity of turtle shells he finds on the island leads him to refer to the inhabitants as '*chelonophagi*', turtle eaters. The last product he talks about is ambergris, which is in direct correlation to the 10th and 17th century accounts, although he does not specify who is trading it. On Socotra, he says that the main employment of the coastal population was fishing and that when the pearling vessels come to the island they all dived for pearls. During his expedition Forbes encountered difficulties with the Sultan of Qishn and governor of Socotra because of an ongoing dispute between him and the British Government, in which the Sultan had been permitting numerous acts of piracy to take place (Forbes 1903: xx). This is particularly interesting in that it would seem that piracy must have continued to have been taking place for a lot longer than has been recorded, and that it was used by both the coastal inhabitants and the Sultan as an additional source of income. Today this situation is very different, and pirates attempting to buy supplies on the island are quickly reported and arrested.[4] The difficulty in identifying the ethnicity of the inhabitants within Forbes's descriptions is that he only ever refers to them as Socotri, and makes no differentiation between the ethnic groups mentioned previously.

The United States Consul-General to Aden, Charles Moser visited the island in 1918 to procure frankincense trees for the Bureau of Plant Industry in Washington. During his short stay he states that the coastal Socotri were predominantly Africans and that the 'original inhabitants' were mostly pastoral, although those who lived by the sea would catch fish or dive for mother of pearl (Moser 1918: 267-278). Moser's observations reinforce many of the earlier accounts concerning the presence of a large African community involved in fishing. Furthermore, it also shows that the Bedouin living near the coast were more involved in fishing than had been previously thought. An interesting aside here is a report by Samuel Barrett Miles (d. 1914), a political agent and consul in Muscat, who explains that during the fishing season the Socotri would visit the port of Muscat on their log rafts (Miles 1919: 2,414). This is reinforced by a 1925 report of Oman by Percy Cox (d. 1937), a political agent for the Government of India. In his description of the main harbour at Muscat, he too refers small parties of fishermen from Socotra, who camped in the neighbouring coves and made a living by diving and fishing from their 'catamarans' (Cox 1925: 195). These catamarans and log rafts are the same type of vessels in use on Socotra at the time and both Ormsby and Bent refer to them. Today, many fishermen will still leave Socotra during the monsoon season, although they mostly travel to villages along the south east Hadhramaut coast to fish. That the fishermen of Socotra were travelling to Oman to fish provides additional evidence for destination of and relationships between the fishermen on Socotra and those recorded as embarking on vessels bound for Zanzibar, Somalia and other areas (Wellsted 1840: 323; Schweinfurth 1993: 4.190). The relationship between some of the Socotri and Omani fishermen is especially noticeable in Qalansiyah, where four informants told me they had family relations in Oman.[5] According to one of these fishermen, Abdulla Rahman Abod Ali Saeed, his grandfather had heard that fishing on Socotra was better than in his village near Salalah, Dhofar. Consequently, he said that his grandfather had come to Socotra to fish and, having found it particularly favourable, decided to stay. He said that this was also due to his grandfather having married a Socotri woman. This is similar to stories told to me by the other fishermen. In addition, I was also told that many fishermen from Arabia that had travelled with the Socotri fishermen back to Socotra ended up staying on the island because of their involvement with Socotri women.

In 1956, Douglas Botting's Oxford University expedition aimed to conduct a zoological, botanical, archaeological and anthropological study of the island and its inhabitants, although this was mainly limited to the interior population. Within his report he refers to the island's people as being divided between those who live on the coast and those living in the interior. This division is similar to many earlier accounts concerning the division of the population. According to Botting (1958: 200), the people of the north coast lived in several hamlets, and all were engaged in fishing and trade. He also explains that they were mostly manumitted slaves from East Africa and Arabians from Al-Mahrah and Dhofar, Oman. That he talks about the people from Dhofar sheds further light on the earlier descriptions of this relationship between the fishermen from Al-Mahrah and Socotra, and what Abdulla Rahman Abod Ali Saeed told me about his grandfather coming from Dhofar. Describing the Africans, Botting says that they were pearl divers and dhow sailors (Botting 1958: 203). Interestingly, Botting also remarks that the *wazīr* (Ar), governor, of Socotra was of African descent and reached this position by becoming literate through Qurᵓānic education (Botting 2006: 72). That this could occur is worth bearing in mind as, even though certain ethnic backgrounds are more likely to be associated with certain occupations, such as fishing, it would be unwise to suggest that all Africans were fishermen.

[4] Two reports bear testament to this: http://www.socotraproject.org/index.php?page=content&id=113 accessed 23/06/2011 and http://www.socotraproject.org/index.php?page=content&id=119 accessed 23/06/2011.

[5] Abdulla Rahman Abod Ali Saeed, full-time fisherman, 38 years old; Anwar Khamis Abdul Adob Ali Saeed, full-time fisherman, 32 years old; Ali Salim Da-Salmoho, full-time fisherman, in his 60s; Abaid Salem bin Awailan, full-time fisherman, in his 50s, all interviewed on 16 December 2009.

Botting's expedition was followed by a joint services expedition lead by Captain Peter Boxhall (d. 2002), whose aim was to survey and attempt to accurately map the island. In addition to this report, Boxhall briefly refers to the coastal population, observing that the fishing villages he visited along the north coast were inhabited by Arabians and Africans, who were all engaged in fishing for fish and shark (Boxhall 1966: 213-222). This provides further evidence for the involvement of the Arabians, who were mainly thought of as traders.

In 1966, the British government commissioned a report on the economic development potential of Socotra, by the Assistant Political Advisor at Aden, G. H. H. Brown. The aims of this report were to gather information concerning the social and economic conditions on Socotra, and determine how and in which sectors economic development would be possible. In Brown's report he identifies fishing as one of the main economies of Socotra (Brown 1966: 28). He also states that people fished both for subsistence and trade, with the larger pelagic fish species being salted and dried for export to East Africa where they were exchanged for grain. The fishing population he describes as being mostly comprised of Arabians and Africans, and that the Socotri of the interior were also fishing seasonally, as an additional means of sustenance. Brown's description emphasizes the role of fishing on Socotra and reinforces earlier descriptions of the role of the Arabians, Africans and pastoral Bedouin of the interior in the fisheries economy. This also helps us to understand the extent of the trade in salted fish and Socotra's long-term trade with East Africa.

The final British expedition undertaken between 17 March and 1 June 1967 was a joint military and civilian scientific effort. As part of this expedition, R. B. Serjeant, a linguist and ethnographer, spent several months investigating the fishing population, providing the most detailed description to date. Serjeant's informants tell him that there are two types of people, namely: the people of the plains, *sahriyah*, and the people of the hills, *joboliyah* (Serjeant 1992: 164). As mentioned in chapter four this geographical division has been referred to from at least the 7th century and is still used on Socotra today. Serjeant divides the coastal population into two groups of people, the Arabians and Africans. The Arabians are said to be Mahra tribesmen, Hadramis, and various merchants and sailors from Saudi Arabia, Dubai and Oman (Serjeant 1992: 170-172). The Africans he divided between those coming from East Africa, Somalia and southern Sudan, most of whom were fishermen (Serjeant 1992: 170-172). Commenting on the class system on Socotra, Serjeant says that amongst the Arabians, there was a strict class system. Those at the top of the hierarchy were the Sultan of Socotra and his tribesmen from Al-Mahrah, followed by the other Arabian tribes. The Mahra controlled the affairs of the port and state council, and various monopolies including pearls, the import and export of supplies and camel transport. These monopolies were either sold or rented to other Arabian merchants and those who were not able to afford to become involved would form part of the working class, whose main occupation was fishing. Indeed, Serjeant even refers to some Mahra tribesmen who had become fishermen (Serjeant 1992: 165). He also mentions that the provision of goods to visiting vessels was strictly controlled by a Socotri African originally from Sudan, who was given the title *ᶜAmīr al-Baḥr*, Commander of the Sea, and he collected the custom duties for the Sultan (Serjeant 1992: 171). The importance of this is that it was possible for slaves to attain positions of power and reinforces the point made above that an African ethnicity does not immediately make one a fisherman. Instead, fishing as an occupation can be seen as having been undertaken by those who were in difficult economic circumstances and was not always based upon tribal or ethnic affiliation. Finally, Serjeant refers to marriage ties between people from the island and those along the Hadhramaut coast (Serjeant 1992: 164), which links directly to that told to me by fishermen in Qalansiyah and other villages on Socotra.

After the end of the British occupation of Socotra, the island came under the control of the Peoples Democratic Republic of Yemen (PDRY), whose Socialist administration and policies had a great effect on the island's inhabitants. The greatest change that this regime brought was replacing the sultanate with a hierarchical system of committees. This was done in an effort to remove all clan affiliations, social status distinctions, socio-ethnic boundaries and religious practices (Elie 2008: 339). During the PDRY occupation (1970-1990), several Russian ethnographic and archaeological expeditions visited the island. The most notable being the 1983 and 1988 joint Soviet-Yemeni study by Vitaly Naumkin, which explored several themes concerning ethnography, history, archaeology, linguistics, culture and medico-biological studies (Naumkin 1993: ix). Owing to Naumkin's Marxist ideologies, the population was divided into two main economic types: the herders, and the fishermen (Naumkin 1993: 364). Furthermore, the fishermen were divided between those for whom fishing was their only occupation, and those for whom fishing was only used to supplement their food supplies, especially during periods of drought (Naumkin 1993: 162-173). Naumkin also refers to the 'pure' fishermen, who were mainly Africans, the descendants of former slaves. Finally, he suggests that the Bedouin were involved in fishing only when drought or economic circumstances forced them to. This differs to the accounts by Wellsted and Brown, who refer to seasonal and full-time Bedouin fishermen and demonstrates the difficulties of untangling Bedouin involvement in fishing.

In the 21st century, the island has become the focus of several scientific expeditions aimed at achieving a sustainable development programme. The Global Environmental Facility (GEF) and the United Nations Development Programme (UNDP) were instrumental in commissioning several scientific expeditions to report on the conservation and sustainable use of the biodiversity of the island. Two of the reports covered the fisheries sector, the first was based upon managing the fisheries resource and the second on the traditional land use of the inhabitants. The fisheries management report contains a wealth of data concerning the fishing vessels and practices, although there is little information on the people involved (Nichols 2001). The second report on the traditional land use of the inhabitants is primarily based upon the pastoral inhabitants, and there is limited information on the fishing communities. However, within this report Morris (2002: 221-231), does say that the fishing villages were made up of local and overseas fishermen. The full-time fishermen she describes as having been manumitted slaves and immigrants, wrecked mariners and others, whilst the seasonal fishermen were said to be islanders, implying that they were the pastoral Bedouin (Morris 2002: 221). This information concerning those involved in fishing provides little new information and it can only be surmised that there has been little change in the cultural make up of the coastal population during this period.

Conclusion

Throughout Socotra's historical narrative the coastal inhabitants have been referred to as being an eclectic mixture of people that were made up of Arabians, Africans, Indians and elements of the interior population. Having attempted to trace the historical involvement of these ethnic groups in fishing has demonstrated two important points. The first is that most of the ethnic groups that make up the coastal population have, at some period, been involved in fishing, whether seasonally or full time. Secondly, many of them became fishermen as a result of a complex set of social, economic and cultural factors, which has also influenced the length of their involvement.

With regards Indian involvement in fishing, it is possible that sometime during the 13th century there may have been some Indian fishermen on the island and that they were interacting with the Indian pirates. However, the role of Indians in the fishing community remains doubtful. Instead I would argue that, even though early accounts refer to them as being involved with the inhabitants, they were most likely traders whose only involvement in fishing was to facilitate the sale of fish, especially with East Africa. This fits with the archaeological and historical evidence outlined in chapter four, which shows the Gujārāti merchants and sailors were involved in an established trade in salted fish between Socotra and East Africa.

The earliest mention of an East African presence on Socotra is that of the East African pirates observed during the 11th century. While not conclusive, it is possible to surmise that during this period there were East African fishermen on the island, who were assisting the pirates and probably engaging in piracy. However, the first direct indication of their involvement in fishing only occurs in the 16th and 17th century when, as slaves, they were being forced to fish and dive for pearls. References to African fishermen continue throughout the rest of Socotra's historical narrative and today they are the largest ethnic group to be involved in fishing. The length of their involvement is primarily due to their social status which, as slaves, gave them little opportunity to have been involved in any other occupation, although there were a few exceptions. Once the slaves had been manumitted there would have been little need for them to have remained fishermen, yet most did. I would argue that the main reason for this is that socially it would have been extremely difficult for them to have become involved in anything else and economically fishing provided them with a relatively good income.

Tracing the involvement of the Mahra and other Arabians in fishing is difficult as within the historical accounts there is a great deal of confusion between the settled Arabians and the 'native' interior pastoral inhabitants. Notwithstanding this confusion it is possible to argue that some of the Mahra tribesmen on Socotra were not only engaged in the trade in fish but were actually fishermen at various periods. Historically the Mahra have always been portrayed as rulers yet, as mentioned in chapter four, not only were there at least two Mahra tribes on Socotra, but these tribes were predominately made up of sailors and fishermen. Therefore, it is plausible that not all the tribesmen were involved in exacting taxes and trade, but that there were those in less favourable economic circumstances that would have become fishermen, much as they had been in Al-Mahrah.

Unfortunately, the historical sources provide too little information on the ethnicity of the Arabians and it is not possible to determine the exact length of their involvement in fishing. During the 19th century, with the influx of other Arabians coming to Socotra there is likely to have been little change and all those Arabians without the necessary social and economic means would have probably become fishermen.

Finally, when tracing the involvement of the original inhabitants in fishing in the historical record we are presented with a similar problem to that of the Arabians namely, the difficulties of disentangling the islanders from the so-called 'native' population. This is especially true up until the 17th century and, even though the 'natives' are said to be hunting turtles and whales, it is difficult to be certain that they are the original inhabitants. Unfortunately this situation is exacerbated by the classification used by many of the authors outlined above, who refer to all the original inhabitants as Bedouin pastoralists. That they were pastoralists is not disputed, yet what I would argue is that their level of involvement in fishing was either an essential part of their livelihood or a seasonal necessity. This would then demonstrate that there were two groups of original inhabitants involved in fishing, which goes some way to disentangle them from the other ethnic groups involved in fishing.

Historically contextualising the fishing communities has provided the necessary background to help develop an understanding of the cultural and ethnic background of these communities on Socotra. The next chapter builds upon this by looking at issues of ethnicity and ethnic identity in the contemporary fishing community, and how this affects social interaction.

Chapter 6

The Contemporary Fishing Community

The contemporary fishing communities of Socotra have undergone a radical change over the past 20 – 30 years. This change has mostly been due to an increasing market for fish, which has had a direct effect on the number of people who have become involved in fishing. It has also resulted in an island wide expansion in the number of fishing villages and put increasing pressure on the local fisheries resource. The aim of this chapter is to look at this change and investigate how these changes have affected the social interactions of Socotra's contemporary fishing communities. Firstly I look more closely at the ethnic identity of the contemporary fishermen in conjunction with the findings made in chapter five. This section analyses how the ethnicity of the fishermen has shaped their distribution and social interaction. Secondly, I will analyse the social relationships between fishermen, the interior population and the state, focussing on fishing activities and fisheries resource management. This provides the basis for understanding how social changes have affected the maritime traditions of the fishermen.

Ethnic Identity and Ethnicity

As discussed in chapter five, the fishing communities on Socotra have constituted a hybridised mixture of cultural fragments from a multitude of sources, and it is perhaps not surprising that the ethnicity of the contemporary fishing communities is little different. During interviews with the fishermen about their ethnic identity and origins I found that even though they recognised the ethnic differences within the fishing villages they rarely referred to people as having come from Africa or Arabia. Instead they would tell me that they were all Socotri. Elie (2007: 213-215), states that the adoption of this national Socotri identity is a relatively new concept which has replaced clan and tribal based affiliations and is centred upon a form of self-identification and cultural identity. This is important for the fishermen, who belong to a community who are said to be amongst the poorest on the island, having no tribal affiliations and no rights to land or water resources (Morris 2002: 223). By adopting a national Socotri identity the fishermen have been able to circumvent their lack of tribal affiliation and become part of a recognised national ethnic, which encompasses a range of different ethnicities and social groups. According to 11 fishermen, in their 60s, interviewed in Ḥadiboh, and four, in their 30s, interviewed in Qalansiyah, they are legitimately Socotri both by virtue of having been born on Socotra and having family that have been resident on the island for several generations. Nevertheless, I did find that, even though the fishermen regard themselves to be part of this seemingly egalitarian Socotri national identity, there remains an underlying social division which still separates them from the merchants and interior pastoral inhabitants, and an ethnic division which divides the fishing communities. These divisions are examined below.

The Socotri fishermen are divided into three major ethnic groups that are still present on the island today. First are the Africans, who make up the majority of fishermen in several villages along the north coast, notably Ḥadiboh, Suq and Qādheb. They have the lowest social standing on the island and are known as *muwalladīn* (Ar), a term used as a socio-cultural reminder that they are of slave descent and one that continues to separate them from the rest of the Socotri community. As mentioned by Serjeant (1992: 170) and Schweinfurth (1881: 128), the African slaves were originally from Zanzibar, an important slaving port in East Africa. This was corroborated by four Socotri Africans living in Ḥadiboh,[6] who said that their grandfathers had been brought to Socotra from Zanzibar, Tanzania and Mombasa, Kenya. In Suq, a full-time fisherman in his 60s, Saad Dabowed Mousa,[7] said that his grandfather had come from Sudan. The relevance of this is that it demonstrates the wide range of African countries which slaves on Socotra were coming from, and that it was unlikely that they would have had many tribal similarities.

The second group of fishermen are the Arabians, who represent one of the more complex ethnic groups. The reason for this is that the Arabians are said to be those who own date palms and engage in trade (Morris 2002: 143). In fact these fishermen own no date gardens and are rarely involved in anything other than supplying merchants with fish. Therefore, like the Africans, they are also considered to be amongst the poorest on the island, although they do hold a higher social position. During interviews with 12 Arabian fishermen in Qalansiyah, Qādheb and Ḥadiboh, seven said that their grandfathers had come from villages along the Hadhramaut coast and five said that they had come from Dhofar, Oman. These links reinforce the historical relationship between

[6] Khames Abdulah Salem, full-time fisherman, 75 years old; Jamen Mahafawl Saif, full-time fisherman, 70 years old, both interviewed on 22 December 2009; Esso Ibn Seyaka, full-time fisherman, in his 60s; Aneen Ibn Sankour, full-time fisherman, in his 60s, both interviewed on 7 February 2009.

[7] Interviewed on 14 February 2009.

Socotra and the sultanate of Al-Mahrah, which governed this stretch of coastline up until 1967, when it was abolished and became part of South Yemen. The reasons for coming to Socotra were similar for all the fishermen interviewed. First, their grandfathers came to the island to fish, as the fishing grounds off Socotra were regarded as being better than the fishing grounds of Oman and Yemen, although the influence of the monsoon winds on the island are worse. Secondly, they said that their grandfathers had also recognised that it is possible to catch more fish and make more money on Socotra than if they were fishing along the Hadhramaut coast, or Oman. Finally, they also said that their grandfathers had married Socotri women and had decided to remain on the island to support their families. These marriage ties between Socotra and Arabia are also referred to by Serjeant (1992: 164) in the 1970s, and give an important reason for the presence of Arabian fishermen on the island and the relationship between Socotra and Al-Mahrah. This has also contributed to the complexities surrounding the ethnicity of the Arabian fishermen, who consider themselves to be Socotri, yet are still regarded by the Bedouin to be foreigners from Arabia.

The final group are the interior pastoralists, also known as Bedouin, many of whom have only become fishermen in the last 20 years. Morris (2002: 221), reports that they are seasonal fishermen, who come down to the coast to fish during periods of drought or hardship. However, Naumkin (1993: 165-167) says that they are a mixture between seasonal and full-time fishermen, and that many are involved in a 'mixed economy' caring for livestock and fishing. Today Bedouin involvement in fishing is even more complex, especially with the substantial growth in the fishing industry, which has seen more Bedouin becoming involved in fishing and an increase in seasonal fishermen becoming full time. This is reflected in the interviews undertaken with the four seasonal pastoral fishermen,[8] who had only started fishing in the last five years. These fishermen said that they began to fish for economic reasons, but that they would only fish during calm weather and preferred to look after their livestock in the mountains. Nevertheless, they did know of some Bedouin that did not have livestock and were now full-time fishermen. Having outlined the three main ethnic groups of the contemporary fishing community and looked at their involvement in fishing, it is now possible to look at how their ethnicity and involvement in fishing has affected their geographical distribution.

Distribution

The population of Socotra has been divided between the settlers that live on the coast and the residents that live in the mountains from at least the 13th century AD (Ibn al-Mujāwir 2008: 264). This division was probably, as recorded by Morris (2002: 223), based upon kin-based tribal affiliation, in which only those belonging to a tribal group could own land and have access to specific resources. As most of the fishermen were settlers they had no tribal affiliation and could not own land or access resources without the permission of a land-owning tribe.

This division between the settlers of the coast and the tribal land-owning interior population first underwent a change during the Peoples Democratic Republic of Yemen (PDRY) occupation of Socotra (1970-1990), when tribally-owned land was forcibly redistributed amongst the landless people, especially those of mixed, but non-tribal origin, who were settled along the coast. The land redistribution policies implemented saw an increase in the number of houses and villages being built, both by those who had been granted land rights and those tribes wishing to retain their rights to tribal land which lay on the coast. This led to a substantial increase in the number of fishing villages being established, especially along the south coast (Morris 2002: 221-222). This development was further exacerbated by the burgeoning tourism and fishing industry, which saw a second substantial increase in the number of fishing villages and coastal eco-lodges being built along the coast. The results of this land redistribution and building of houses and eco-lodges in tribally-owned land is still being felt on Socotra today and there are numerous cases concerning the legitimacy of land ownership, with many land-use law cases, *dāʿwa* (Ar), filling the courts today.[9] As a result, when I asked fishermen about how long they had been living in a particular village and where they had originally come from the answers given were either evasive or vehement, and it remains a minefield for the unwary researcher.

Notwithstanding these difficulties, it is still possible to provide a generalised view of this distribution by looking at the presence of different ethnicities in villages along the coast. Today the majority of the African fishermen live in the present day capital of Ḥadiboh, the former capital Suq and Qādheb. This distribution is largely historically based, as these villages were the main areas in which the slaves were being housed by their Arabian land-owning masters and is where the manumitted slaves remained. This distribution is also based on having permission to live on the land, as land ownership and the right to access resources is strictly controlled (Morris 2002: 223), giving them little choice in where they were able to live. The PDRY land redistribution did little to change where they lived, although it did allow them to build permanent stone and coral-rag houses. Today the fishermen's houses in Ḥadiboh and Suq form a distinctly segregated African housing district that lies close to

[8] Mohammed Aldolah, in his 60s, interviewed on 8 February 2009; Said Saeed, in his 30s, interviewed on 11 February 2009; Saeed Salem Ali, 35 years old, interviewed on 17 December 2009; Ali Omar, 48 years old, interviewed on 23 December 2009.

[9] Miranda Morris personal comment July 2010.

FIGURE 6. PALM-FROND BOAT SHELTER EAST OF QĀDHEB (PHOTO: AUTHOR).

the coast in an area which they had initially only been granted rights to stay in temporary date palm-built structures.

During the land redistribution process of the PDRY the distribution of the Socotri Arabian fishermen, who also had no rights to land and were confined to temporary structures along the coast, underwent a substantial change. These fishermen, once confined to a few villages on the north coast, spread throughout the island's perimeter forming new villages and establishing themselves more permanently in others. This was further influenced by the rapidly developing fishing industry, which also saw more villages established along the south coast. Today the Socotri Arabian fishermen are widespread in fishing villages along the north and south coast of Socotra.

The Bedouin engaged in fishing have mostly lived seasonally along the coast, and it was not until they became more established as full-time fishermen that they began to live permanently near the coast. As a result of this, the seasonal Bedouin fishermen can be found fishing throughout the island, while the full-time fishermen tend to be congregated along the eastern coast in Di-Lisheh, Di-Ḥamari, Erisseyl, and Maṭyaf, where, according to Morris (2002: 222) and Naumkin (1993: 166), the Bedouin tribes were more involved in fishing. While the Bedouin full-time fishermen still remain concentrated along the eastern side of Socotra, today, it is possible to find them throughout the island. Seasonal fishermen have and continue to be found fishing throughout the island, although those I spoke to said that they normally only fish in the coastal areas near their villages in the mountains. This is due to these areas being part of their tribally owned land, as coastal areas are still considered to be belonging to a specific tribal group. These factors affecting the distribution of the fishermen on Socotra are also manifest in the distribution and construction of boat shelters found all along the coast, and is what will be looked at below.

Boat shelter, *ᶜarish* (Ar)

Two experienced fishermen in their 70s[10] interviewed in Ḥadiboh, stated that boat shelters were first built to house *hūrīs*, as they needed to be protected from the sun, which could cause them to dry and crack. The *hūrī* is a dugout canoe that has been in use on Socotra from at least the 18th century and was, up until the introduction of glass reinforced plastic (GRP) boats, widespread throughout the island. Further details concerning the *hūrī* and other vessels in use on Socotra can be found in chapter nine. In Qādheb, three fishermen[11] I spoke to said that boat shelters were also used when fishing around the island, either as a place to store dried fish or to sleep. Today the boat shelters are mainly used to store vessels, fishing gear and dried shark. On Socotra there are three main types of boat shelters. The first of these are the naturally occurring rock caverns which lie close to the coast and are used for the long-term storage of fishing vessels. The other two are built from stone or palm fronds, and are known as, *ᶜarish* (Ar). This word is used to describe any

[10] Jamen Mahafawl Saif, full-time fisherman, 70 years old; Khames Abdulah Salem, full-time fisherman, 75 years old, both interviewed on 22 December 2009.

[11] Salim Games Saaed, full-time fisherman, 45 years old; Salim Saaed Atman, full-time fisherman, 55 years old; Abdullah Ali Muhammed, full-time fisherman, in his 60s, ail interviewed on 2 January 2010.

FIGURE 7. STONE BOAT SHELTERS IN ḤĀLLAH (PHOTO: AUTHOR).

building of inferior construction, and can also be used to describe a building with a palm-frond roof.

The palm-frond boat shelter is found throughout the island, and is made using palm tree trunks and fronds, which are bound together with rope made from palm tree fibre. This structure has three walls and a roof, within which vessels and fishing gear are kept. The roof is normally made from palm tree fronds, although bits of plastic are also incorporated (Figure 6).

The stone built boat shelter is a robust building, constructed from coral or rock with palm trunks laid across the roof. The roof is covered with palm tree fronds, metal sheets or jetsam, held in place by rocks (Figure 7). The material used to construct these boat shelters is always taken from the immediate vicinity. This is similarly reflected in the housing, which is also based upon the availability of local material (Naumkin 1993: 227; Stein 1996: 271). Furthermore, much like the housing, boat shelters also require tribal permission, and even then only temporary structures were normally allowed. Abdullah Ali Muhammed[12] from Qādheb and Ali Ibn Aneen[13] from Ḥadiboh, said that it is still not possible today for anyone to build a stone boat shelter, and those that are built have been done so by the tribes fishing in that area or with their permission. They also said that it was possible to build the palm-frond boat shelters without permission, although it was rarely done.

[12] Full-time fisherman, in his 60s, interviewed on 2 January 2010.
[13] Full-time fisherman, in his 60s, interviewed on 7 February 2009.

Social Relationships

As mentioned earlier, the fishermen on Socotra are amongst the lowest on the social and economical scale, a situation which has recently begun to change with the rapidly expanding market for fish from abroad. While this expanding market has resulted in the fishermen today being economically much better off, it has done little to affect their social status. Instead it seems to have reinforced social divisions within the fishing communities and, with greater state intervention in the fisheries economy, has created additional tension in the way the fisheries resource is managed.

Relationships between the Fishermen

The social relationships between fishermen are enacted on land and at sea and encompass ethnicity, gender, family ties and experience. The first item to explore is the ethnic relationship between fishermen on land and sea. Within the fishing community there is a distinctive racially based division between the Africans and the Socotri Arabians. As mentioned above, the Africans in Ḥadiboh and Suq live in a segregated African housing district that lies close to the coast; within these areas it is rare to find any Arabians living. This segregation is most apparent in these two villages as there is a larger African population, but it can also be found in other villages where they form the minority. The division between African and Arabian fishermen also extends to fishing vessels, which are run either by an all African or all Arabian crew and owner. This division did not extend to the Bedouin, who would crew in either, although those I knew were young fishermen who could not afford their own boat or did not belong to a fishing family with a boat.

In addition to this ethnic division there is a very distinctive gender bias and the crew onboard is always made up of male family members or relations, women are never found onboard. This is much the same situation as found in many fishing communities throughout the Indian Ocean, and has been recorded in Suakin, Sudan; along the Hadhramaut and Al-Batinah coast, Oman (Donaldson 1979: 175; Kentley 1988: 176; Bonfiglioli and Hariri 2004: 25; Camelin 2006: 46; Wagenaar and D'Haese 2007: 267). Nevertheless, in Ḥadiboh, several fishermen[14] I interviewed said that on the outlying island of ᶜAbd al-Kūri women use *hūrīs*. The reason given for women to be engaged in fishing was that their men had left the island to fish on the mainland and, because the women were hungry and had no one to catch fish for them, they were forced to take their husband's *hūrīs* and go fishing. According to Morris (2002: 134), the women on ᶜAbd al-Kūri and Samḥa were only engaged in fishing and diving for shells from the shore. This change to using boats is likely to be a more recent phenomenon, which I believe can be explained by the introduction of GRP boats and the eventual abandonment of the *hūrīs*, which were still seaworthy. Therefore, it is likely that when the fishermen from ᶜAbd al-Kūri left to fish with their GRP vessels, the women were left with the abandoned *hūrīs*, which had not previously been available to them. Consequently, rather than having to fish from the shore, they could now use these vessels to access the richer offshore fishing grounds.

The third item is the number of people found onboard a vessel. In interviews conducted throughout Socotra and Samḥa almost all the fishermen interviewed told me that the number of people onboard a vessel is determined by the type of vessel, its size, whether they were fishing with handlines or nets and the size of the owners family. In Suq, Ḥadiboh and Qādheb six of the fishermen I interviewed,[15] who used *hūrīs*, said that the number of people on board a small *hūrī* is usually one or two, and they would normally only use handlines. They also said that the larger *hūrīs* have between three to four people as crew and that they would use a combination of handlines and nets. Whereas over 20 fishermen in their 30s to 60s, who use GRP vessels, in Ḥadiboh, Qalansiyah, Shuᶜub, Maḥfirihin, Ṣaqarah and Erisseyl said that that the crew sizes can range between two and five. This was partly due to the choice of nets or handlines. When using a net more people are required as it can be difficult to haul, especially during the more productive fishing seasons, when the quantity of fish caught in nets is significantly higher. The crew size is also influenced by the size of a fisherman's family, if a fisherman has a large family and only one boat he has a larger crew.

The number of crew onboard is also influenced by the economics involved in sharing the catch as, when fishing with nets it is easier to have four to five people hauling the nets, but if the catch is not good then each fisherman only receives a small return. This is an important concern for all the fishermen and they often said that it is better to have less people when using nets, even though it would be harder to retrieve them, as fewer people would mean bigger returns. This level of return only influences the number of people that would be used to fish with nets as, when handlining, the amount of fish caught is very much dependant on how many people are catching fish. Nevertheless, I rarely saw crew sizes larger than five. The reason for this is due to the seaworthiness of the vessels, which could capsize if too many people were onboard.

The proceeds of the catch, as stated by almost all the fishermen in their 60s interviewed, has always been divided between the boat and the number of people on board, with one share going to the owner of the boat and the rest being divided between the fishermen. They also said that if the boat owner was on board then he would receive two shares, one for the boat and one for himself. The only change occurred during extended fishing trips when, as I was told by fishermen in their 30s and 40s, interviewed in Qalansiyah, Ḥadiboh, Stēroh, Maḥfirihin and Samḥa, the expenses of food and equipment had to be taken out. This could result in very little possibility of an income if fishing had not been good and is one of the main reasons why crew sizes are kept to a minimum. The division of the catch as recorded on Socotra is identical to that recorded along the Hadhramaut coast and in Al-Batinah, Oman, and has remained the same even though the vessels in use have changed (Bonfiglioli and Hariri 2004: 25; Wagenaar and D'Haese 2007: 268; Al-Oufi 1999:143-144).

The sharing of the catch as outlined above, whilst the norm, was not the same for all the fishermen on Socotra and in Ḥadiboh some owners employ a different system. An experienced full-time fisherman who could not afford his own boat, Faisal Ahmed Khalif,[16] in his 30s, said that the catch on the boat he works on is divided into, two shares for the boat and one share for each of the fishermen. This is due in part to the fact that fishing

[14] Ashish Hazeem Hilaal, full-time fisherman, in his 30s, interviewed on 16 February 2009; Khanem Salem Mohammed, full-time fisherman, in his 40s, interviewed on 3 January 2010; Jamen Mahafawl Saif, full-time fisherman, 70 years old, interviewed on 22 December 2009.

[15] Rabain Mobarek al-Noby, full-time fisherman, in his 60s; Saeed Ahmed Nashran, full-time fisherman, in his 60s, both interviewed on 14 February 2009; Heni Mohammed Saeed Abdullah, full-time fisherman, in his 60s; Khamic Amer, full-time fisherman, in his 60s, both interviewed on 15 February 2009; Salem Saeed Tamook, full-time fisherman, in his 40s, interviewed on 1 January 2010; Omar Abdullah Saleh, full-time fisherman, in his 60s, interviewed on 8 February 2009.

[16] Interviewed on 1 January 2010.

equipment was supplied by the owner. Three younger fishermen I interviewed in Ḥadiboh[17] said that they had leased their boat from a merchant, who took a much larger share of the catch and left them with only half a share each. This disparity in the catch share is due to the increased involvement of people in fishing, and is reflective of how merchants and fishermen with additional resources are using those who do not have boats to increase their earnings by leasing their vessels at higher rates of return, thereby corrupting an earlier tradition. How this will affect both the aforementioned and other fishing traditions remains to be seen.

The fourth point to be analysed is to do with spatial division onboard. This came about during personal observations, which were followed up by interviews with five full-time fishermen in their 60s, in Ḥadiboh and four in their 30s, in Qalansiyah.[18] What I observed and was told is that spatial division on board a vessel is based upon the type of vessel, the number of people on board and the experience of the crew. Those fishermen interviewed said that the owner or most experienced fisherman sits at the rear of the *hūrī*. The reason given for this was that he would chose where they would fish, and would need to be able to see the landmarks to guide them there. This position is also said to be the best when travelling through the surf, as it kept the prow up and prevented the boat from being swamped by waves. Where two people were on board, one would sit at the prow and one in the stern, whereas if there was a third person they would be positioned in the centre. The spatial division on board a *hūrī* is set once the vessel has been launched, as the narrowness and instability of these vessels makes movement between different areas of the boat difficult.

The crew layout of the GRP vessels is very similar to that of the *hūrī*, and the owner or most experienced person normally always sits at the stern. During my time fishing with the fishermen in Ḥadiboh I noticed that the father would sit at the stern and his son at the prow, whilst the other crew members, including myself, were allowed to sit anywhere in between. The fishermen I was with stated that the most experienced person is at the stern because he needs to be able to see where they were going. I also noticed that in this position he is also able to see what everyone is doing and would quickly correct anyone who was not following his orders, especially when we were preparing to catch baitfish or nearing a fishing area. The only time in which this division on board is operational is when underway, and when a fishing area has been reached it is not uncommon for everyone to move around the boat to get into their favoured fishing position.

The fishermen also said that the reason for the son to be in the prow is for him to gain sufficient experience to be able to locate the different fishing areas. The exceptions to this occurred when the father wished to undertake some task on deck, and it was not unusual for his son to then take the helm. In Ḥadiboh and Qalansiyah, the fishermen I spoke to said that they would show their sons how to recognise the different fishing areas, and when they were able to correctly identify them they would then be allowed to take over from them at the stern. They also said that it was always the father or most experienced fishermen who chose where to fish. Two full-time fishermen in their 70s in Ḥadiboh[19] said that the son would only begin to make decisions on where to fish when his father became too old to fish, or when his eyesight began to deteriorate to such an extent that he was not able to make out the landmarks necessary to find the fishing areas. Partial blindness amongst elderly fishermen is prevalent due to the harsh sun reflecting off the sea and the lack of any eye protection.

Comparing the crew structure and method by which the son learns how to find a fishing area on Socotra with a similar study undertaken by Camelin (2006) in al-Shihr, Hadhramaut, demonstrates a distinctive difference between the two areas. According to her (2006: 41), the fishing vessels in al-Shihr are strictly divided into spatial areas, with the *rabbān* or captain at the stern and the other crew members sitting in a specific order of hierarchy up to the prow where the youngest member of the crew sits. Furthermore, the young fishermen do not get taught where to fish, but must learn to recognise the fishing areas for themselves (Camelin 2006: 44). The reason that even family members are not taught how or where to fish is due to the high competition between fishermen (Camelin 2006: 46-47). Interestingly though, the older fishermen on Socotra I spoke to were not worried about competition from family members, or other Socotri fishermen. They said that as long as people fishing used the same fishing equipment they did, they could fish wherever they wanted.

Finally, launching and landing of vessels on Socotra is a laborious task that requires a large number of people to successfully bring a vessel far enough up the shoreline to be safe, especially during bad weather. During the launching and landing of vessels, all people present on the beach help, even if it is just to move the log rollers to the front of the boat. This is carried out without any form of payment although, in some cases, the fishermen hand out less expensive fish to those that help. When the fishermen come back from fishing they either leave their

[17] Hamed Saeed Ahmed, full-time fisherman, 17 years old, interviewed on 26 December 2009; Ahmed Eisa Abdullah, full-time fisherman, 18 years old, interviewed on 26 December 2009; Eisa Atman Salem, full-time fisherman, 18 years old, interviewed on 25 December 2009.

[18] Abdullah Mohammed Hamadan, in his 60s; Heni Mohammed Saeed Abdullah, in his 60s; Nasieb Saeed Khamis, in his 60s; Khamis Amer, in his 60s; Mobarik Ali Abdulla, in his 60s, all interviewed on 15 February 2009; Jamen Saeed Abdullah, in his 30s; Anwar Khamis Abdul Abod Ali Saeed, 32 years old, both interviewed on 16 February 2009; Salam Saeed Martah, 39 years old; Omar Saeed Abod Ali Saeed, 31 years old, both interviewed on 18 February 2009.

[19] Jamen Mahafawl Saif, 70 years old; Khames Abdulah Salem, 75 years old, both interviewed on 22 December 2009.

FIGURE 8. 'THE GATE OF FORTUNE', AFTER A FRESH COATING OF SHARK LIVER OIL (PHOTO: AUTHOR).

vessel anchored in a safe area offshore or drag it up onto the shore. When returning to sea later during the day, either to retrieve nets, traps or go line fishing, they would leave their vessels anchored in the bay. However, if they had finished fishing for the day or the weather is rough they take their vessels out of the sea. Along the south coast several full-time fishermen in Stēroh, Bidhōleh and Maḥfirihin[20] said that if there were not enough people to help drag their vessels up the beach they would either attempt to drag the vessel up as far as possible themselves and secure it with an anchor in the sand, or anchor it in the bay. This was not considered ideal and they said that they would often wait by their vessels for more people to come, or get someone to ask for help so that it could be dragged further up the shoreline, where it would be safer. Launching of vessels never seemed to present a problem as most fishermen go fishing at the same time during the day.

The Relationship between the Fishermen and the Interior Population

This relationship was initially reported on by Morris (2002: 221), who says that the fishermen would seek to develop a relationship with the interior population, in an exchange system known as *maḥrif* (Soc). The word *maḥrif* can be loosely translated as friend or acquaintance, and is used to describe a relationship based upon a system of mutual assistance and dependency that operates on different levels and within different groups of society. This relationship is based upon an exchange of surplus products between different areas on Socotra, although it now also includes the provision of accommodation abroad (Elie 2007: 223-224). Consequently, when a Socotri travels abroad he can expect to receive free accommodation from other Socotris, by virtue of coming from the island. The focus here, however, is on the *maḥrif* relationship between the fishermen and the pastoral inhabitants of the interior. The way in which this relationship works is that the pastoralist has a family on the coast with whom he could go to stay and eat fish and other marine species during periods of drought. In exchange, male members of the fisherman's family would be able to go to stay with the pastoralist's family during or after the rains, when there was an abundance of milk and meat. Outside these periods the families may also exchange gifts, such as dried fish, salt, ghee and honey (Morris 2002: 150-151). Several fishermen in Qalansiyah, Qādheb, Ḥadiboh and Suq told me that they were involved in this mutual exchange relationship, and continued to exchange gifts with families in the interior. The gifts from the pastoralists are mostly goats, whilst the fishermen provide fish, rice or some other staple. Saad Dabowed Mousa, [21] a full-time fisherman in his 60s living in Suq, said that his family had been involved with a Bedouin family in the interior for at least three generations. He also said that he remembered that, when he was a child, members of the Bedouin's family had come down to the coast to eat fish, and later he had gone into the hills to drink milk. Interestingly, he told me that as a result of this relationship the Bedouin family had named his grandfather's vessel, *Bāb al-Khayr* (Ar), the Gate of Fortune (Figure 8).

[20] Mohammed Abdullah Ahmed, 35 years old; Ali Eisa Abdulla, in his 30s; Ali Abdullah Ahmed, in his 40s, all interviewed on 30 December 2009; Mohammed Saeed, Mohammed, 33 years old; Hadad Eisa Mohammed, 45 years old, both interviewed on 29 December 2009; Muslim Abdullah, in his 30s; Salim Saeed, in his 30s, both interviewed on 11 February 2009.

[21] Interviewed 14 February 2009.

The Relationship between Fishermen and the State

The historical evolution of Socotra's political incorporation underwent four conjunctural shifts, from sultanate fiefdom, Socialist administration, unity government, to post-unity regime (Elie 2008: 337-339). These all had an effect on Socotra's fishing population, although none more so than the Socialist administration, which was particularly interested in promoting fishing as an alternative means of livelihood. To support the development of the fishing sector this administration set up fishing cooperatives under the auspices of the Ministry of Fish Wealth (MFW), through which it purchased fish for sale abroad (Elie 2009: 376). With the unification of Yemen in 1990, fishing in Yemen remained under the auspices of the MFW, which is now responsible for all aspects of fisheries policy, research, development, fish quality control, monitoring, control and surveillance and management (Nichols 2001: 7). On Socotra, the MFW has an office in Ḥadiboh which, as is the case with other branches and departments of the MFW in Yemen, is hampered by severe lack of funds, equipment and training. Consequently, compliance with national regulations is poor, and fishing takes place virtually outside the national regulatory framework, due to a lack of understanding of the laws (Nichols 2001: 25). On Socotra this is exacerbated by the limited fishing season and that the fishermen are almost completely reliant on visiting vessels buying their catch. Despite this the fishermen are aware of the need to look after their fisheries resource, and have a long history of traditional fisheries management.

Fisheries resource management is practiced by fishing communities throughout the world who actively seek to regulate their fishing grounds (Acherson 1981: 281). On Socotra this was first recorded by Serjeant (1992: 176), who said that the village leader or *muqaddim* (pl. *muqaddamīn*) (Ar) enforces restrictions on fishing equipment, which even visiting fishing vessels are required to abide by. This is elaborated on several years later when we learn that the *muqaddamīn* also impose restrictions on where and when specific gear can be used, and what species can be taken (Wranick 1999: 170; Nicols 2001: 427-435; Hariri and Abdulaziz 2006: 356).

The Socotra Conservation Development Program (SCDP) marine officer, Fouad Naseb Saeed, [22] 30 years old, confirmed these findings and said that the *muqaddamīn* are elected by the fishermen in each village, and that they are normally older experienced fishermen. He also said that the elected village leaders normally meet in the first week of September, before the fishing season starts, to decide on what management measure need to be enforced where. This meeting is followed by several additional meetings that take place if and when a particular problem is reported. The management measures that were mentioned by the fishermen interviewed throughout the island are based upon three main themes, namely: ensuring that there is fair competition between the fishermen; protecting the sea against pollution (this was primarily to do with the belief that discarded fish remains polluted the sea), and ensuring that fish stocks were not being over exploited.

According to Wranick (1999), Nicols (2001), Hariri and Abdulaziz (2006) and Fouad Naseb Saeed, the agreed measures are strictly enforced by the fishermen and violation of them is rare. In spite of this, several fishermen[23] stated that they had and still are secretly fishing with nets and fish traps in areas where they were prohibited to do so. They also said that they would fish for any species they wished, even if their *muqqadīm* had agreed that it was not to be fished. The reasoning given was that some village leaders used their position to benefit the fishermen from their own villages, and that this created unfair competition. In addition, some fishermen said that their *muqqadīm* is weak and does not represent them properly. These problems have led to a lot of tensions between different villages, and together with uncontrolled buying of fish by vessels from the mainland, seems to be eroding the traditional resources management that has been practiced for generations. The fishermen I interviewed along the north and south coast of Socotra said that these fishermen are a small problem; the biggest problem is the large illegal foreign fishing vessels that are catching too many fish. Fishermen in several villages on the south coast said that these vessels came close inshore at night to fish and would even take those nets left out at sea overnight. These vessels are believed to be mainly vessels from India.

The fishermen also said that they were not happy with their reliance on the visiting vessels that buy their fish, as it is difficult to get a good price for their catch. This has led to many of them joining fishing cooperatives, which they said gave them more control over the sale of their fish. The establishment of fishing cooperatives has gradually gained impetus throughout the world as, like on Socotra, the fishermen attempt to regain some form of control over their fisheries resource (Acherson 1981: 284). On Socotra the cooperatives have been established by fishermen, in cooperation with the MFW, to enhance fish production, improve their economic and social conditions and develop new fishing methods. The fishermen use the cooperatives to set fixed prices on the sale of fish and use a percentage of their catch to establish and maintain maintenance and storage facilities (Hariri *et al.* 2002: 45-47). The cooperatives also provide assistance in obtaining access to credit for fishermen and allow them to buy new vessels and equipment.

[22] Interviewed 22 December 2009.

[23] I have omitted their names and the villages I interviewed them in because of state policing.

Hariri and Yusif (1999: 6) reported that the establishment of fishing cooperatives on Socotra began in 1970, and by 1993 the fishing cooperative in Ḥadiboh had 1,500 members. However, it is likely that the cooperatives may have been established even earlier as Serjeant (1992: 166) refers to the 'Blacks' as belonging to an organisation, headed by a village leader. Whilst he does not specify the purpose of this organisation, it is likely that, as the Africans were mostly engaged in fishing, the organisation was to do with fishing. Today there are approximately eight fishing cooperatives established throughout the island. Most of the fishermen I spoke to have joined fishing cooperatives, although this remains much more focussed in Ḥadiboh, where the cooperative has a functioning ice-making facility and maintenance shed for vessels. The fishermen in Stēroh[24] said that the cooperative there had allowed them to establish facilities for the maintenance of outboard engines. In Di-Ṣeberho a full-time experienced fisherman, Abdullah Eisa Ahmed, [25] in his 50s, said that through the fishing cooperative the fishermen had managed to get funding from the Italian Red Cross, which built an area for them to safely launch and land their vessels. The fishermen I interviewed also said that the cooperatives, in conjunction with the *muqaddamīn* agree on management measures. This mutual agreement allows fishermen from the cooperatives and those who do not belong to the cooperatives to be represented and, according to the fishermen, also helps to prevent unfair competition.

Conclusion

The ethnicity of Socotra's contemporary fishing community is representative of their historical background and the complexities involved in the relationships between the different ethnic groups. This complexity is clearly demonstrated by the Socotri Arabian fishermen who form part of an intricate interplay that is viewed and perceived differently by them, the Bedouin and those Arabians who are not fishermen. The distribution of the different ethnic groups provides further evidence for the historical and contemporary divisions between the population of Socotra, and demonstrates how the social and economic status of the fishermen has become manifest in where they have come to settle on the island. The contemporary African fishing community provides a clear indication of the social, geographical and economic prejudices that have influenced the geographical distribution of ethnic groups on Socotra. These prejudices also help understand why the fishermen consider themselves to be Socotri and possibly why it is that many of the historical accounts referred to the coastal people encountered as 'natives' or Socotri.

Looking at the relationships between the fishermen, the interior population and the state provides another insight into the lives of the fishing communities of Socotra. First, it would seem that by adopting a common Socotri identity the fishermen were attempting to integrate themselves into an egalitarian community that allowed them to move away from the social, economic and racial stigmas attached to fishermen. This stigma may have been slightly altered but fishermen are still regarded as being the lowest on the social hierarchy. What is particularly noteworthy is how the fishermen still use race to segregate themselves, as is seen in their housing and the crewing of their fishing vessels. While the crewing of vessels is racially divided, there are additional factors such as gender, family, economics and experience that also affect their makeup. These factors also influence the number of fishermen on board, where they fish, what they fish with, and how they divide their catch, providing an additional insight into the influences that affect their fishing activities. Secondly, whilst many of the Socotri Arabian fishermen have marriage ties to the Socotri Bedouin families, others also entered into relationships based upon a system of exchange. Initially, this provided the fishermen and the Bedouin of the interior with a mutually beneficent system that allowed them to survive periods of drought and bad weather. Today, this system of exchange still allows each family to lessen the hardships that occur during times of drought and bad weather, but also provides them with access to meat and staples that would otherwise not form a regular part of their diet.

Finally, state intervention has been instrumental in changing many aspects of the fishermen's lives, especially the Socialist's land redistribution policy and the promotion of the fisheries industry. These policies and the continuing promotion of the fisheries economy on Socotra have brought about significant changes to the quantity and geographical distribution of fishing villages, and have changed the economic fortunes of fishermen throughout the island. These changing fortunes have also led to a more structured approach to marketing fish to overseas buyers through the establishment of fishing cooperatives, which have been integrated into the traditional fisheries management systems practiced by the fishermen in the past. Unfortunately, substantial economic returns afforded to those who can sell their fish, together with the lack of state control and unscrupulous buyers has led to occurrences in which state and traditional management measures have broken down. These instances, in which the management measures have broken down, are hopefully limited to several rogue fishermen, yet may be an indication of a far wider ranging breakdown in the control exercised by the state and the *muqaddamīn*.

Notwithstanding the social and cultural differences between the fishermen and how they interact, they are all

[24] Mohammed Abdullah Ahmed, full-time fisherman, 35 years old; Ali Eisa Abdullah, full-time fisherman, in his 30s; Ali Abdullah Ahmed, full-time fisherman, in his 40s; Saeed Mohammed Abdullah, 27 years old, full-time fisherman, all interviewed on 30 December 2009.
[25] Interviewed on 30 December 2009.

engaged in the same occupation that is not only regulated by the state and *muqaddamīn*, but also the environment. Throughout this chapter I have alluded to the influences of the climate and maritime landscape within which the fishermen are living their lives. In part three the focus is specifically on these two elements, which are analysed in conjunction with the social, ethnic and economic factors, which are outlined here. In addition the distribution of the fishermen is also analysed in more detail, by combining the observations made here with the effect environmental influences have on this.

Part Three:
The Maritime Landscape And Climate

Chapter 7

The Maritime Landscape

The maritime landscape embodies both physical and cognitive aspects of human interaction with the maritime and terrestrial landscape (Westerdahl 1992; Hunter 1994; Jasinski 1994; Parker 2001; Cooney 2003; Westerdahl 2008). Consequently, when studying the maritime landscape of Socotra it is also necessary to understand how fishermen interact and perceive various physical features in the landscape. The aim of this chapter is to look at how the maritime landscape is used by the fishermen of Socotra to name and identify fishing areas and navigate. Firstly, this chapter outlines the physical topography of the land and sea of the Socotra archipelago. Secondly it looks at the physical topography of the land and sea at individual fishing villages. The aim of this is to demonstrate the similarities and differences between the villages of the north and south coast, and look at how the fishermen in these villages perceive and use the landscape. This section will focus on two themes, namely: how the fishermen use the landscape to name and identify their fishing areas and how they use their knowledge and experience of the maritime landscape to navigate.

The Physical Landscape

The island of Socotra is approximately 135 kilometres in length and 42 kilometres in width and has a surface area of 3650 square kilometres (Othman 1966: 204). This surface area is physiographically diverse in nature, with almost every area of the island having its own distinct characteristics. Notwithstanding this diversity it is possible to divide the island into three areas based on the predominant landforms. The first and most striking of these is the central mountains, whose spires of granite are a central feature of Socotra's landscape. These mountains are surrounded by the second landform, a series of rugged limestone plateaus. These are criss-crossed by a series of valleys and non-permanent streams that run down toward the coast. The final landform is the coastal plains and shores of Socotra. The topography of Socotra and the outlying islands, together with the fishing villages can be seen in Figure 9.

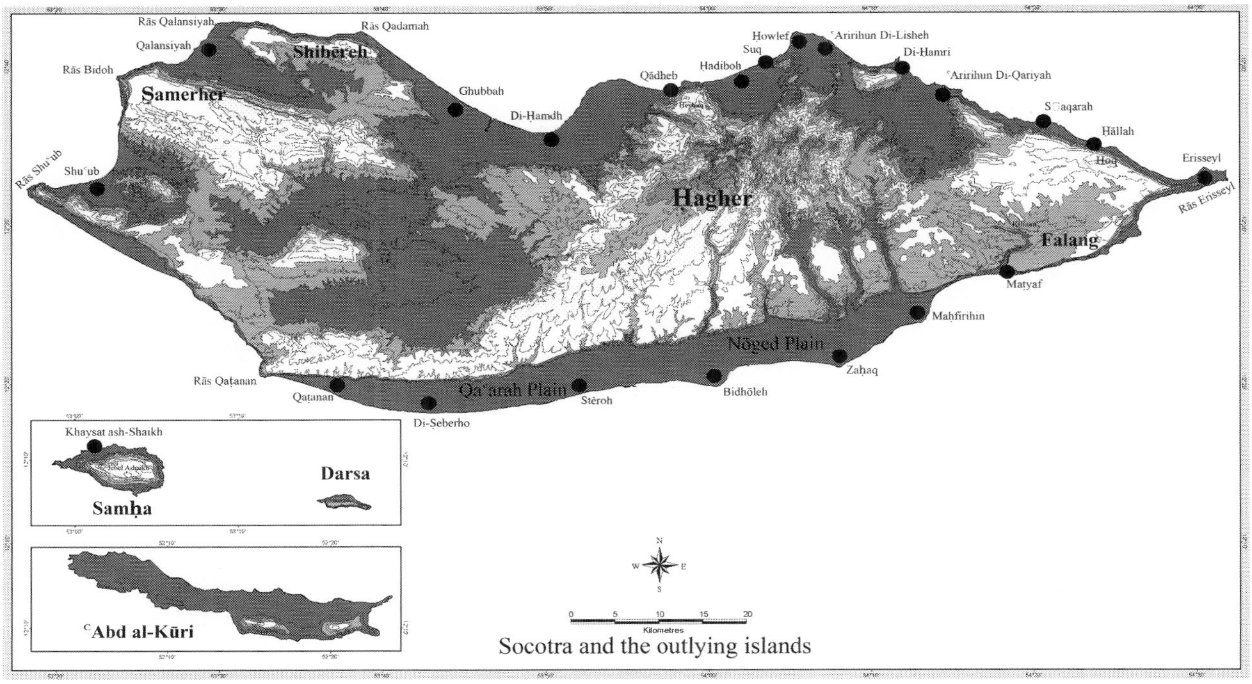

FIGURE 9. TOPOGRAPHICAL MAP OF SOCOTRA AND THE OUTLYING ISLANDS OF SAMḤA, DARSA AND ᶜABD AL-KŪRI, SHOWING THE FISHING VILLAGES MENTIONED IN THIS STUDY.

The Mountainous Interior

The dominant feature of Socotra is the Ḥagher, a mountain range made of granite rock that stretches across the central part of the island in a west south-westerly to east north-easterly ridge. This mountain range rises over 1000m above sea level throughout its extent reaching its highest point in the north east at Jebel Skand, which rises up to approximately 1550m (Miller and Morris 2004: 6). The slopes of this mountain range are well vegetated with perennial streams of water running down them, although the pinnacles and steeper slopes tend to be bare rock. The bare rock is generally red in colour, although on the higher rocky slopes where lichen grows upon them they often appear white. According to Forbes (1899: 635), the Ḥagher were known locally as the 'white rocks', a name that was derived from this white coloured lichen. This colour makes the Ḥagher visible for a significant distance out to sea and plays an important role in navigation. The Ḥagher also plays an important role in influencing the weather systems of Socotra by trapping the moisture-laden air of the NE and SW monsoon winds, allowing Socotra to enjoy two rainy seasons. However, due to the morphological nature of the Ḥagher, the water drainage of Socotra flows almost entirely in a north north-easterly direction across the northern plains. The two exceptions to this are the westerly flow of the wādīs in the valleys of Qalansiyah and Shuᶜub, and the southerly flow of a limited number of wādīs along the southern Nōged coastal plain (Beydoun and Bichan 1970: 415). As a result of this drainage the northern and eastern plains receive the greatest amount of water, and have an abundance of water sources, in comparison to the rest of the island. This also means that the northern side of the island is richer in vegetation. The availability of water and its predominance in the northern and eastern side of the island is illustrated in Figure 10.

The Limestone Plateau

Bordering the Ḥagher is a limestone plateau that covers almost half of the island's surface, averaging between 300-700m above sea level. In some areas of the western plateau of Diksam, this limestone plateau can reach heights of up to 1000m (Cheung *et al.* 2006: 31). Along the southern extent of Socotra, the plateau drops in near-vertical cliffs onto the coastal plains of the south, while further westward they drop steeply into the sea (Figure 11). Along the northern and part of the southern side of the island the plateau is dissected by numerous gullies and valleys. In the areas in which these plateaus reach the coastline they form projecting headlands that terminate in undercut cliffs, making it impossible to land or launch vessels.

The limestone plateau is also characterised by numerous karstic features, which include large natural rock cavities and several extremely large cave systems (De Geest 2006: 7-8). The natural rock cavities, or tafoni (sing. tafone), are formed through a process of weathering, which creates holes in the rock that can range in size from tiny pits to large openings. The larger holes have, for several centuries, been used by pastoral Bedouin as enclosures for their animals and general living quarters.

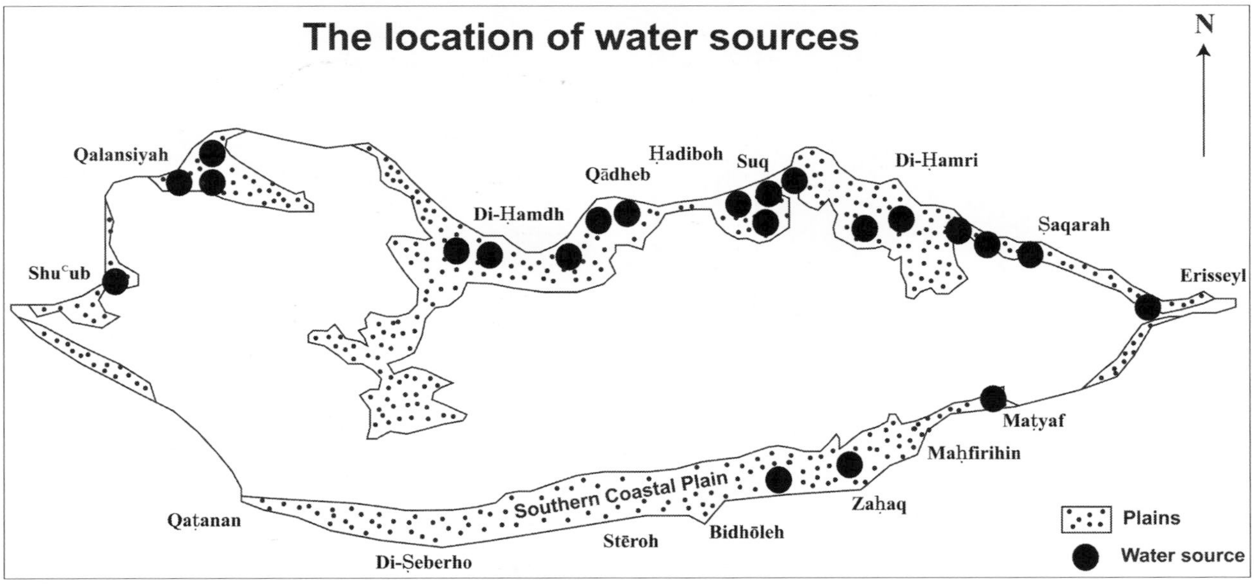

FIGURE 10. SOCOTRA'S WATER SOURCES, SHOWING THE LOCATION OF WELLS, LAGOONS AND SPRINGS, AND THE LOW LYING PLAINS IN WHICH THEY OCCUR.

FIGURE 11. THE SHEER LIMESTONE UNDERCUT CLIFFS OF THE NORTH WESTERN SIDE OF SOCOTRA. NOTE THE LACK OF ANY LANDING PLACES (PHOTO: AUTHOR).

FIGURE 12. A LARGE TAFONE OPENING NEAR THE COASTLINE THAT IS BEING USED TO STORE VESSELS (PHOTO: AUTHOR).

Along both the northern and southern areas of the coast these tafoni are also used by the fishermen, and in several instances I found logboats, *hawārī* (sing. *hūrī*), stored in them (Figure 12). Further evidence for the use of these by the fishermen was made in 2001, during an archaeological survey conducted along the south eastern coastline (Weeks *et al.* 2002). According to Weeks *et al.* (2002: 108), several openings near the coast contained the remains of fish bones, oyster shells, turtle shells and coral. These had been used by fishermen and appeared to have functioned as either a temporary shelter or storage area. Several elderly fishermen interviewed in Qalansiyah and Qādheb[26] told me that they still use these tafoni openings as temporary shelters when travelling around the island to fish. They said that they would

[26] Ali Salim Da-Salmoho, full-time fisherman, in his 60s, interviewed on 16 February 2009; Abaid Salem bin Awailan, full-time fisherman, in his 50s, interviewed on 17 December 2009; Omar Abdulla Saleh, full-time fisherman, in his 60s; Mohammed Aldolah, full-time fisherman, in his 60s, both interviewed on 8 February 2009.

FIGURE 13. A VIEW OF THE LARGEST NORTHERN COASTAL PLAIN LOOKING EAST OVER THE FISHING VILLAGE OF SUQ AND ḤADIBOH. NOTE THE LIMESTONE ESCARPMENT IN THE BACKGROUND WHICH SEPARATES THIS PLAIN FROM THE NEXT (PHOTO: AUTHOR).

mainly stay in these openings overnight when travelling from one area of the island to another, or when they were fishing far from their own villages and needed a place to stay. These were not owned by any of the fishermen, although they did say that they would return to the same ones used, if they were fishing in the vicinity.

As mentioned, the limestone plateau is also riddled with cave systems, some of which reach almost a third of the length of Socotra.[27] These caves, unlike the tafoni openings, extend for a significant distance underground. While it would be possible for several large families to use these caves and the water found therein, there is a strong aversion amongst the Socotri people against entering caves. This aversion is based on the belief that the caves are inhabited by spirits or *jinn* (Ar). Furthermore, there is also a legend amongst the interior Bedouin concerning a large man-eating snake said to live within the caves.[28] The majority of the largest cave systems have been explored by numerous expeditions undertaken by the Belgian Speleological Mission (Socotra Karst Project 2000-2008), led by Peter De Geest (De Geest 2006). During one of these caving expeditions in Hoq cave, a cave overlooking the north eastern side of the island, the project made one of the richest archaeological discoveries on Socotra. Hoq cave contained an array of archaeological remains, which included a wooden tablet with Palmyrene script, incense burners, pots and numerous Indian and Greek inscriptions (Dridi 2002, Robin and Gorea 2002, Dridi and Gorea 2003 and Strauch and Bukharin 2004). Preliminary studies of the inscriptions are providing glimpses into Socotra's historical contacts with traders throughout the Indian Ocean from at least the 2nd century AD (Strauch and Bukharin 2004: 135). According to Dridi (2002: 587-590), the presence of ships motifs and incense burners could mean that the cave was used by overseas mariners as a religious sanctuary, although the cave does not overlook any historical anchorages. I argue that, as a religious sanctuary, it would have been part of a pilgrimage for sailors visiting the island as it is not possible for ships to safely anchor in the vicinity of the cave, and that the closest historical anchorage is several kilometres away.

The Coastal Plain

As the plains of Socotra's northern and southern coasts are so dramatically different to each other, in terms of their physical geography, it is necessary to treat them as two separate areas.

The Northern Coastal Plain

The northern coastal plain is made up of a series of smaller coastal plains, which are bordered by the aforementioned limestone escarpments along their landward side and separated from each other by rocky headlands along their seaward extent (Figure 13). These plains vary between 100m to 8km in length and, although generally flat, they are often dissected by gullies and

[27] De Geest personal comment April 2009.
[28] De Geest personal comment May 2009.

FIGURE 14. A VIEW OF THE SOUTHERN PLAIN WITH THE LIMESTONE ESCARPMENT IN THE BACKGROUND (PHOTO: AUTHOR).

run-offs (Morris 2002: 55). There are no permanent streams that cross these plains, although during the two rainy seasons non-perennial streams, wādīs, can flow with great force, resulting in villages being cut off for several hours or days and causing the sea to be filled with brown sediments and detritus from the land. During this period the sea conditions are generally rough which, together with the sediments and other detritus entering the sea, makes it impossible for fishermen to fish close to the shore. Along these plains there are several wādīs which flow into small fresh or brackish lakes or *khāwr* (sing. *khāwr*) (Ar). These are mostly separated from the sea by cobble or sand bars and are normally lined with large plantations of date palms.

The Southern Coastal Plain

The southern coastal plain is the longest on Socotra, stretching approximately 80km in length and reaching approximately 6km inland (Cheung *et al.* 2006: 31). The plain is divided into two areas, namely: Qaᶜarah, the western half and Nōged, the eastern half (Morris 2002: 64). The landward side is bordered by the sheer cliffs of the limestone escarpment, which run in an almost unbroken line along the plain (Figure 14). The eastern and western edges of the plain end in steep cliffs that drop directly into the sea. During the rainy season there are several wādīs that traverse the central and eastern parts of the plain, flowing along single, well-defined beds of boulders and rock slabs (Popov 1957: 706). Outside of the rainy season the only available water is found within the central and eastern part of the plain, where several shallow wells tap into a subterranean water resource. The majority of these wells are brackish and are primarily used for date cultivation, washing and watering livestock (Morris 2002: 64).

The Coast

The coast of Socotra has one of the most physically diverse characteristics of all the landforms on the island, and varies between sand, cobble, or a mixture of sand and cobble beaches to relict reef platforms, rocky headlands, lagoons, mangroves and vertical and undercut cliffs. The majority of the north coast consists of sand, sand and cobble or outcroppings of fossil-reef platforms and rock. During the storms of the monsoon period, large quantities of dead corals and cobbles are driven up onto the north shore. The dead corals are collected and burnt in lime pits for the recent upsurge in building projects on the island. The north coast of Socotra, from the bay at Ḥowlef to the east of Ḥadiboh, forms a natural harbour that affords shelter to vessels for the majority of the monsoon seasons. The shore of this area is almost all sand, which stretches back into large sand dunes that almost cover the hills backing this area of coastline. Along the northwest coast is a large shallow lagoon that is sheltered behind a bank of sand. To the west of this lagoon lie two bays, Qalansiyah and Shuᶜub, which are separated by a sheer cliff headland. The littorals of Qalansiyah and Shuᶜub are the same as the rest of the north coast and consist of sand with some areas of elevated fossil or relict reef platforms. The southern littoral is primarily comprised of either cobble, sand or cobble, or sand bays. These bays are flanked by elevated rock, or undercut relict-reef platforms with a small spit of sand that stretches seaward (Klaus *et al.* 2002: 11-158).

The Physical Seascape

In this study I have divided the seascape of the Socotra archipelago into two parts, based upon the way in which it is perceived and used by mariners and fishermen. The first of these are the islands and rocky outcrops, which lie to the southwest of the main island of Socotra and form prominent land markers within the sea. The second is based upon the bathymetry surrounding the archipelago, which influences the currents and species of fish that can be caught.

The Outlying Islands

The islands of Samḥa, Darsa and ^{c}Abd al-Kūri lie almost directly southwest of Socotra, whilst the two rocky outcrops Sābūniyah and Ka^{c}al Fīr^{c}ūn lie further westerly. The island of ^{c}Abd al-Kūri lies approximately 52Nm from Somalia and consists of a mountain range that is cut in the middle by an area of low-lying land. It has two summits that rise to 573m in the west and 558m in the east respectively (Vora and Grattan-Cooper 2007: 380). The two islands of Samḥa and Darsa, also known as 'The Brothers', are approximately 35Nm east of ^{c}Abd al-Kūri and 20Nm southwest of Socotra. The island of Darsa is the most easterly of the two Brothers. Its coast is, for the most part, made up of vertical rock cliffs that rise to a height of approximately 392m. There are no settlements, and it is completely uninhabited. Samḥa is the most westerly of the two brothers and is made up of sheer rocky cliffs and headlands to the south, and rocky foothills that slope down to the sea along its northern extent. The island of Samḥa has several small bays along its northern and eastern side. The only permanent settlement, Khaysat ash-Shaikh, lies on the north western side of the island in an area where there is a naturally protected bay that is used by the fishermen. The highest point of the island lies at its centre and rises to approximately 779m. The rocky outcrop of Sābūniyah is situated approximately 11Nm northwest of the western-most headland on Socotra, Rās Shu^{c}ub, and consists of three white-granite peaks which reach a height of approximately 69m. According to several European accounts, the white rocks of Sābūniyah resemble two vessels under sail. This misconception has caused vessels to founder on the surrounding reefs (Vora and Grattan-Cooper 2007: 383, Horsburgh 1843: 293). Locally, these rocks are used by fishermen to navigate to the outer islands of Samḥa and Darsa. The second rocky outcrop, Ka^{c}al Fīr^{c}ūn, is approximately 12Nm north of ^{c}Abd al-Kūri and consists of two rocky islets separated by a shoal bank. The islets both reach a height of approximately 86m. According to Horsburgh (1843: 292-293), when these two islets are viewed by shipping approaching Socotra from the west they form five high perfectly white peaked rocks. According to Serjeant (1995: 118), Ka^{c}al Fīr^{c}ūn (Ar), (The Pharaoh's testicles), was a well-known landmark for Arabian navigators travelling to and from the Red Sea from at least the 15th century.

Bathymetry

The Socotra archipelago is situated on a small continental shelf known as the Socotra platform (Birse *et al.* 1997:

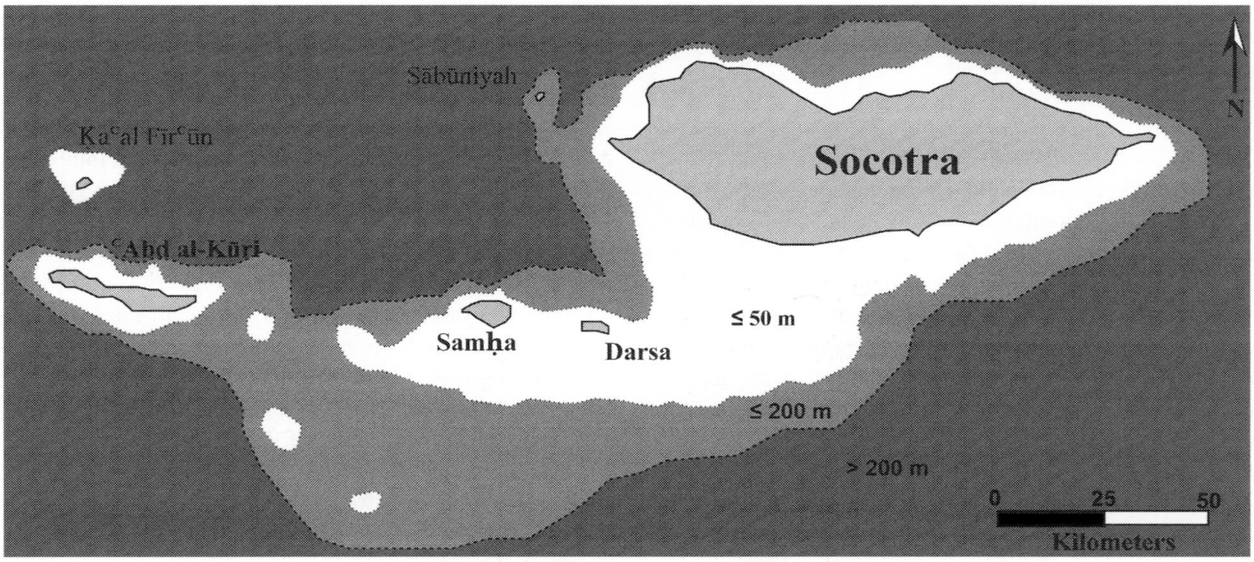

FIGURE 15. A SCHEMATIC REPRESENTATION OF THE BATHYMETRY OF THE SOCOTRA ARCHIPELAGO SHOWING THE OUTLYING ISLANDS AND ROCKS.

675). This was formed through several major tectonic events that have played a significant role in the formation of the islands topography and bathymetry. The marine topography surrounding the Socotra archipelago almost mirrors the topography of the islands, in particular Socotra (Leroy *et al.* 2002: 1-7). The sea-floor off the south coast appears as a submarine continuation of the flat plains on land, with a shallow platform extending approximately 15km offshore. This shallow plain stretches out in a westerly direction, linking the two islands of Samḥa and Darsa. The undersea terrain off the northern coastline is made up of a narrow shallow platform that extends out approximately five kilometres offshore. The submarine topography surrounding the Socotra archipelago is shown in Figure 15.

The bathymetry surrounding the archipelago has a significant influence on the deep sea currents and consequently the presence of fish. The steepness of the undersea topography surrounding the archipelago causes deep-water, cold nutrient-rich currents to be deflected up to the surface in an event known as upwelling (Banaimoon 1996: 20). This nutrient-rich water results in an abundance of fish occurring in these upwelling areas, which has a direct impact on the quantity of fish being caught. This is especially well demonstrated along the coastal waters of the northern and eastern side of the main island, where a narrow shallow-platform results in upwellings occurring closer to the coast. Consequently, fishermen along the north coast are able to catch greater quantities of demersal and pelagic species than those fishermen along the southern and western coast (Zajonz and Khalaf 2002: 246).

The Inshore Physical Land and Seascape

While a generalised view of the physical landscape and seascape of the island helps us to understand overall physical land and seascape, it is nevertheless important to view the land and seascape on a more local level. The importance of undertaking a micro-scale view is that it makes it possible to determine what influence specific land and seascape characteristics have on the location of fishing villages, and how the fishermen use and perceive these features in relation to their fishing areas and methods of navigation. Fishing villages outlined below are those which I have visited and chosen, during the course of my research, as being a representative sample of the types of villages that can be found along both the north and south coasts of Socotra. They are grouped together geographically according to topographical features that they share, whether on land or at sea. The aim here is to place these villages into the context of their surroundings and then look at how this affects the fishermen's perception and use of the surrounding landscape.

The Northwest Coast (Figure 16)

Shu^c^ub

The village of Shu^c^ub lies within the plain of Shu^c^ub in the bay of Bandar Shu^c^ub on the eastern edge of Socotra, Figure 16. According to Agius (2008: 174), the word Bandar means a port or port town and, although the village does not feature prominently in the historical accounts, it was visited from at least the 16th century.

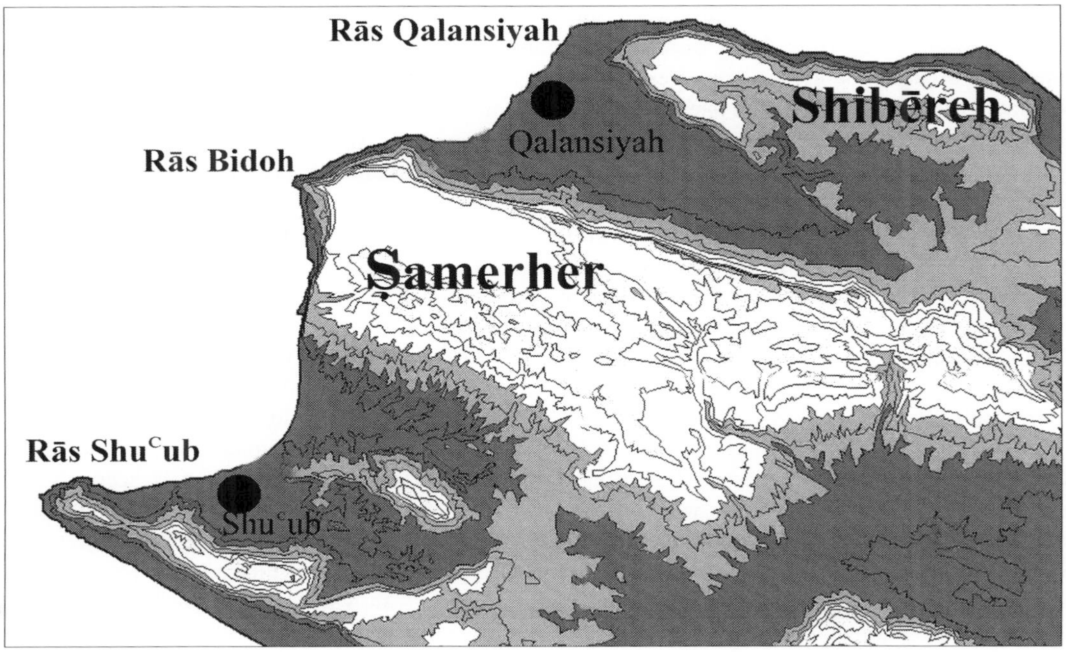

FIGURE 16. THE NORTHWEST COAST SHOWING THE LANDSCAPE IN THE VICINITY OF THE VILLAGES OF SHU^C^UB AND QALANSIYAH.

FIGURE 17. THE COAST OF SHU^c^UB AS SEEN FROM THE SEA. NOTE THE NARROW COASTAL STRIP AND THE LIMESTONE ESCARPMENT OF ṢAMERHER IN THE BACKGROUND (PHOTO: AUTHOR).

The eastern and western extent of the bay ends in a rocky cliff-lined shore, which provides the fishermen with a number of useful reference points for navigation. The shoreline is made up of sand and cobbles and extends the length of the bay ending at the rocky cliff headlands of Rās Bidoh in the east and Rās Shuᶜub in the west (Figure 17). This makes it possible for the fishermen to launch or land their vessels all along the bay, although they prefer to remain close to the village in the south western part of the bay. The main reason for this is the availability of fresh water in this area, which comes from the spring, Ḥalmi Di-Qaᶜarah. Toward the south western part of the bay is a wādī which runs down from the surrounding limestone escarpment into a large fresh water lagoon, separated from the sea by a sand bar. The lagoon is home to a large mangrove habitat, from which wood has been gathered from at least the 16th century (Kerr 1824: 217). The depth of the sea surrounding Shuᶜub is generally less than 50m for up to seven nautical miles from the shore before it drops steeply to depths in excess of 200m. As a result, fishermen targeting high-value pelagic species like shark and kingfish do not need to travel a significant distance offshore.

Qalansiyah

The village of Qalansiyah lies at the seaward end of a wide plain, Śeteh Qalansiyah, which is flanked by two limestone escarpments, Ṣamerher in the west and Shibēreh to the east (Figure 16). These two escarpments can be seen from a significant distance out to sea, and various features along them are used by the fishermen for navigation. The coast is mainly sand with a few cobbles, although at the eastern and western edges of the bay the sand gives way to a rocky outcrop that extends into the sea (Figure 18). The village is flanked to the west by a fresh water lagoon that is separated from the sea by a wide beach. This lagoon and several nearby wells have been used to supply both passing vessels and the village with fresh water for several centuries (Bent 1900: 347). The fishermen generally anchor their vessels offshore during most of the fishing season, although during bad weather or when they need to work on their boats or nets they bring their vessels up onto the beach in front of their village. The depth of the sea in the vicinity of Qalansiyah drops sharply to the north and reaches in excess of 200m approximately three nautical miles from the coast. Consequently, fishermen do not travel a great distance offshore when fishing for pelagic species.

The Central North Coast (Figure 19)

Qādheb

The village of Qādheb lies on the eastern edge of the central northern plain and is flanked to the east and south by the limestone escarpment Ḥeybaq. The coastline is predominantly made up of cobbles and sand, which backs onto a salt marsh that is accessible through a narrow channel to the west (Figure 20). The channel is used by the fishermen to access the seaward side of the salt marsh, where they are able to safely anchor their vessels. Fresh water is available from deep wells situated in the foothills to the south, although it is now also piped from

FIGURE 18. THE VILLAGE OF QALANSIYAH LOOKING WEST TOWARD THE LIMESTONE ESCARPMENT OF ṢAMERHER (PHOTO: AUTHOR).

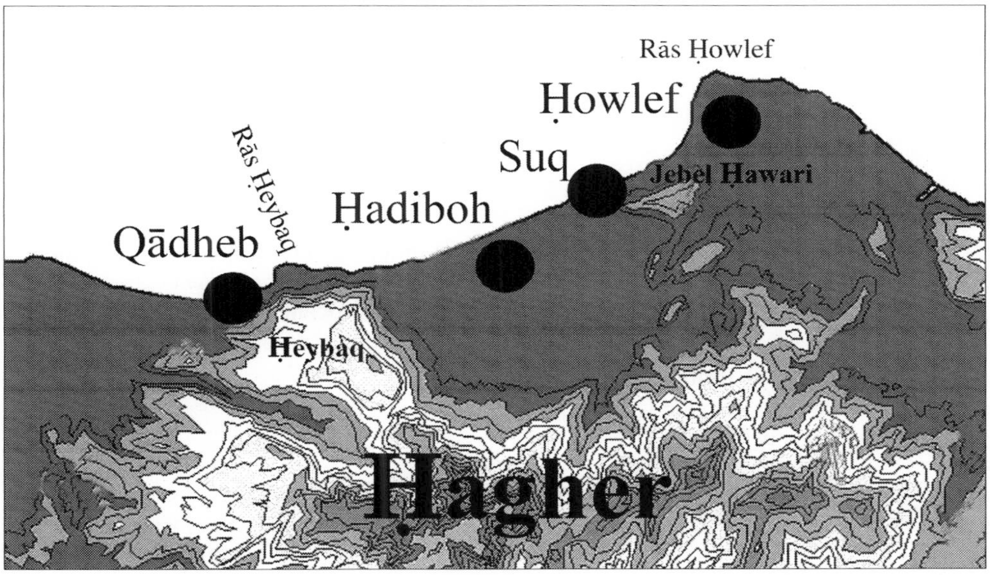

FIGURE 19. THE CENTRAL NORTH COAST SHOWING THE LANDSCAPE IN THE VICINITY OF THE VILLAGES OF QĀDHEB, ḤADIBOH AND SUQ.

FIGURE 20. THE LANDING AND LAUNCHING AREA IN FRONT OF QĀDHEB, LOOKING WEST OVER THE CHANNEL USED BY THE FISHERMEN (PHOTO: AUTHOR).

FIGURE 21. ḤADIBOH AS VIEWED FROM THE SEA. NOTE THE PEAKS OF THE ḤAGHER IN THE BACKGROUND (PHOTO: AUTHOR).

wādī ᶜAyḥeft. The depth of the sea remains at under 50m for approximately 13Nm offshore, and forms part of a basin of shallow water that extends from Rās Qadamah in the east to Rās Ḥowlef in the west. This shallow area makes it necessary for the fishermen to travel further when fishing for pelagic species, which may explain why fishermen here told me that they mostly fish for demersal species.

Ḥadiboh

The village of Ḥadiboh is today the capital of Socotra, and encompasses a large conglomeration of permanent settlements. The town and most of the outlying settlements lie within a plain that is encompassed by the limestone escarpment of Ḥeybaq to the west and the foothills of the Ḥagher in the south, providing fishermen with numerous landmarks (Figure 21). The coast is made up of sand and cobbles with some outcroppings of rock, which extend into the sea. The town encompasses a wādī that ends in a freshwater lagoon, separated from the sea by a sand and cobble beach. During the rainy season the flow of the wādī causes the lagoon to breach the sand and cobble spit, dumping large quantities of alluvium and other detritus into the sea and causing the sea to turn brown for several days. The residents obtain their freshwater from numerous wells to the west and water is also piped from Ferźaḥah, in the foothills of the Ḥagher (Morris 2002: 62). The sea off Ḥadiboh falls within the western half of the shallow basin which encompasses this section of coast and extends to approximately 12Nm out to sea before dropping into deeper water. Similarly to the fishermen in Qādheb, fishing for pelagic species requires travelling a significant distance from the shore, and many fishermen tend to concentrate on demersal species.

Suq

The village of Suq is the former capital of Socotra and today it is mostly inhabited by Africans, who were once slaves (Morris 2002: 56). The village lies at the eastern edge of the Ḥadiboh plain and is overlooked by Jebel Ḥawari to the east (Figure 19 and 22). The shoreline is mainly composed of sand and cobbles, although further to the east, sand predominates. Suq's fresh water is obtained from several nearby wells and the wādī Di-Suq. This wādī flows to the east of the village terminating in a large lagoon that is fringed with date palms. The sea off Suq sits within the eastern edge of the shallow basin which projects out along this section of coast. However, at this section of the basin the depth drops to in excess of 200m just seven nautical miles from the shore, making it easier for fishermen to reach pelagic species.

The Northeast Coast (Figure 23)

Ṣaqarah

The village of Ṣaqarah lies on a relatively long narrow coastal plain backed by a steep limestone escarpment to the south. The coast of this area is made up of relict

FIGURE 22. A VIEW OF THE COAST OF SUQ FACING EAST, SHOWING THE DATE-PALM PLANTATIONS AND JEBEL ḤAWARI IN THE BACKGROUND (PHOTO: AUTHOR).

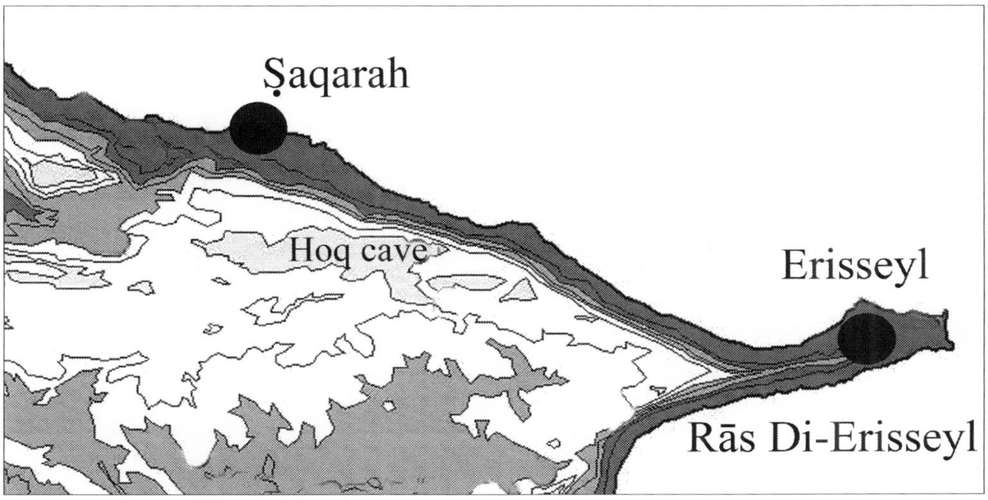

FIGURE 23. THE NORTHEAST COAST SHOWING THE LANDSCAPE IN THE VICINITY OF THE VILLAGES OF ṢAQARAH AND ERYISSEYL.

reef and rock outcrops which extend into the sea, broken periodically by sand and cobble bays (Figure 24). These bays are the only areas along this section of coast in which it is possible for the fishermen to land and launch their vessels. Fresh water is obtained from wells that lie along the foothills of the limestone escarpment. The depth of the sea drops steeply to in excess of 200m some three nautical miles from the coast and fishermen need travel only a short distance to fish for high-value pelagic species.

Erisseyl

The village of Erisseyl is situated at the eastern most point of Socotra at Rās Di-Erisseyl, a slightly raised limestone plateau that is almost surrounded by the sea. The coast is a mixture of sand and some rock outcropping to the northwest. The southwest coast is made up of outcroppings of rock interspersed with small bays of sand (Figure 25). The launching and landing of vessels normally takes place in the southwest, which provides a protected anchorage. Fresh water is piped from the base of a steep cliff to the southwest; today this is supplemented by a recent find of fresh water from the caves further west (De Geest 2006: 36). To the north, the depth of the sea off Rās Di-Erisseyl remains under 50m out to approximately three nautical miles before it begins to drop into deeper water. Whereas to the west and south the depth remains under 50m out to approximately nine nautical miles before it drops steeply to in excess

FIGURE 24. THE COAST LOOKING WESTWARDS TOWARD ṢAQARAH. NOTE THE COBBLE AND SAND LAUNCHING AND LANDING PLACES AND THE RELIC REEF AND ROCK OUTCROPPINGS. (PHOTO: AUTHOR).

FIGURE 25. THE MAIN LAUNCHING AND LANDING PLACE ON THE SOUTHWEST COAST OF RĀS DI-ERISSEYL, SHOWING THE NARROW SANDY BAY, SHARK CARCASSES AND EVIDENCE OF A RECENT SHIPWRECK (PHOTO: AUTHOR).

of 200m. The sea off Rās Di-Erisseyl forms part of the western-most section of a large shallow basin which extends along the entire southern part of the island. Several extant rocky reefs lie to the west of Rās Di-Erisseyl and numerous shipwrecks can be found among them. This area is rich in demersal and pelagic species, although fishermen mainly target shark.

The Southwest Coast (Figure 26)

Maṭyaf

The village of Maṭyaf is situated at the eastern edge of the Noged plain, just before the sheer-cliff headland of Rās Maḥfirihin and is flanked to the east and north by the limestone escarpment Falang, which is a significant navigational feature on this side of the island (Figure 26 and 27). The coast is generally sand with some cobbles and an extent rocky outcropping to the east, making it easy for fishermen to launch and land their vessels. Fresh water is obtained from a permanent stream running from Kilisan, which ends in a large fresh water lagoon close to the village. The depth of the sea remains at under 50m some 11Nm offshore before it begins to drop into deeper water. The sea forms the western part of a large shallow basin that extends the length of the south coast, making it necessary for fishermen to travel a significant

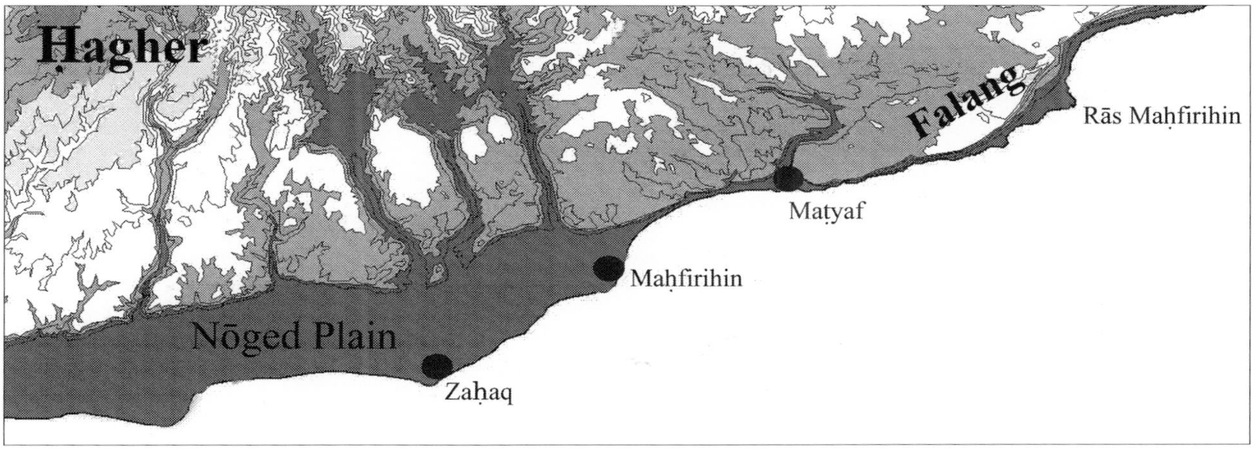

FIGURE 26. THE SOUTHWEST COAST SHOWING THE LANDSCAPE IN THE VICINITY OF THE VILLAGES OF MAṬYAF, MAḤFIRIHIN AND ZAḤAQ.

FIGURE 27. THE COAST OF MAṬYAF LOOKING EAST. NOTE THE LIMESTONE HEADLAND OF RĀS MAḤFIRIHIN IN THE BACKGROUND (PHOTO: AUTHOR).

distance from the shore to be able to fish for pelagic species.

Maḥfirihin

The village of Maḥfirihin lies at the western edge of the dry sandy Nōged plain and is backed by a limestone escarpment to the north. The village lies within a wide bay that opens to the east and has a shallow sloping shoreline that is made up of cobbles and some sand (Figure 28). The shallow water of the bay extends several hundred metres into the sea before it begins to get deeper. The westerly extent of the coast gradually gives way to a narrow sandy beach which is backed by rocky headlands and undercut fossil-reef platforms, restricting the launching and landing of vessels to very specific areas along the coast. Fresh water is taken from wādī Di-Faᶜar to the north. The sea remains under 50m in depth approximately 14Nm from the coast, after which it drops steeply to in excess of 200m, which, similarly to Maṭyaf, makes it necessary for fishermen to travel further to target pelagic species.

Zaḥaq

The village of Zaḥaq is almost entirely surrounded by sand dunes, interspersed with rock outcrops, which make it extremely difficult to reach from the land. The coast is made up of a steep sloping cobble beach, with cobbles and some rocky outcroppings extending several hundred meters out to sea (Figure 29). Due to the difficulties of hauling a vessel up the steep-sloping cobble beach,

FIGURE 28. THE SHALLOW-SLOPING COBBLE BAY OF MAḤFIRIHIN (PHOTO: AUTHOR).

FIGURE 29. THE COAST OF ZAḤAQ. NOTE THE STEEPNESS OF THE COBBLE BANK (PHOTO: AUTHOR).

fishing vessels are generally only brought up during bad weather or to effect repairs. Fresh water is obtained from deep wells to the south and wādī Di-Faᶜar to the east. The sea remains up to 50m in depth for approximately six nautical miles out before it begins to drop to depths in excess of 200m, forcing fishermen to target demersal species that, unlike the pelagic species, do not require a significant journey to reach.

The Central South Coast (Figure 30)

Bidhōleh

The fishing village of Bidhōleh lies in the middle of the Nōged plain and is overlooked by the cliffs of the limestone escarpment to the north. This section of coastline is made up of extant rocky outcrops interspersed by areas of low-lying cobbled beaches. Fresh water is obtained from wādī Iᵓirih, which runs from the limestone escarpment directly into a small sheltered bay. The wādī is joined to the sea by a narrow inlet which allows fishing vessels to access it, providing one of a few safe places within which it is possible to store vessels (Figure 31). This inlet allows the vessels to be brought into the safety of the wādī. Partly as a result of this, this area has a boat repair yard that services the entire south coast. The sea remains shallow for approximately nine nautical miles offshore before dropping steeply to in excess of 200m, and much like the southwest coast fishing is mostly for demersal species.

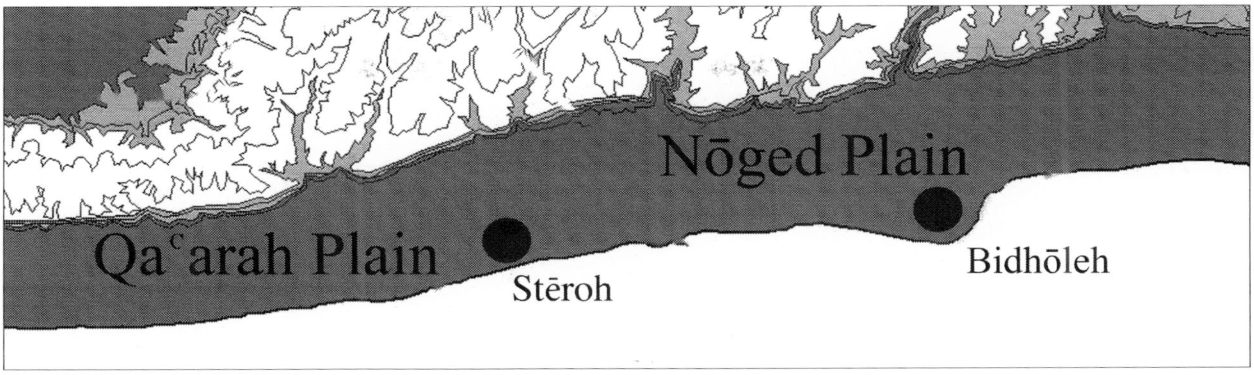

FIGURE 30. THE CENTRAL SOUTH COAST SHOWING THE LANDSCAPE IN THE VICINITY OF THE VILLAGES OF BIDHŌLEH AND STĒROH.

FIGURE 31. A VIEW OF WĀDĪ Iᵓ IRIH AS IT ENTERS THE SEA. NOTE THE FISHING VESSELS AT ANCHOR WITHIN THE SHELTER OF THE SAND SPIT (PHOTO: AUTHOR).

Stēroh

The village of Stēroh lies at the western end of the Nōged plain and marks the beginning of the Qaᶜarah area, which lies to the west. The coast is predominantly sand with some cobbles, although only a few hundred metres to either side of the bay relic fossil-reef outcrops dominate (Figure 32). The fishermen have recently obtained funding through their cooperative to have an artificial breakwater installed along one side of the bay. This breakwater provides them with more security for their fishing vessels. Stēroh obtains its fresh water from several wells that have been dug a short distance away. The sea off Stēroh forms part of the shallow water basin that dominates the undersea landscape of the south coast, and remains shallow for approximately 20Nm offshore before it drops into deeper water. This makes fishing for pelagic species difficult, due to the distance fishermen need to travel.

The Southwest Coast (Figure 33)

Di-Ṣeberho

The village of Di-Ṣeberho lies at the western edge of the Qaᶜarah plain. This plain is relatively flat and more verdant than the Nōged plain. The coast is made up of a series of narrow cobble bays that are surrounded by high cliffs of extant fossil-reef and rock. The Italian Red Cross recently paid for a landing place to be cut into the cliffs of fossil-reef near this area in order to provide fishermen with an additional launching and landing place (Figure 34). This is now being used by fishermen from Di-Ṣerberho and the nearby village of Ḥazaḥaz. Fresh water is obtained from the nearby wādī Di-Daᶜan. The sea in this area remains at depths of under 50m for approximately 22Nm from the coast before dropping steeply into deeper water. Fishermen told me that they concentrate on fishing for demersal species due to the

Figure 32. The bay used by the fishermen of Stēroh. Note the breakwater in the background (Photo: author).

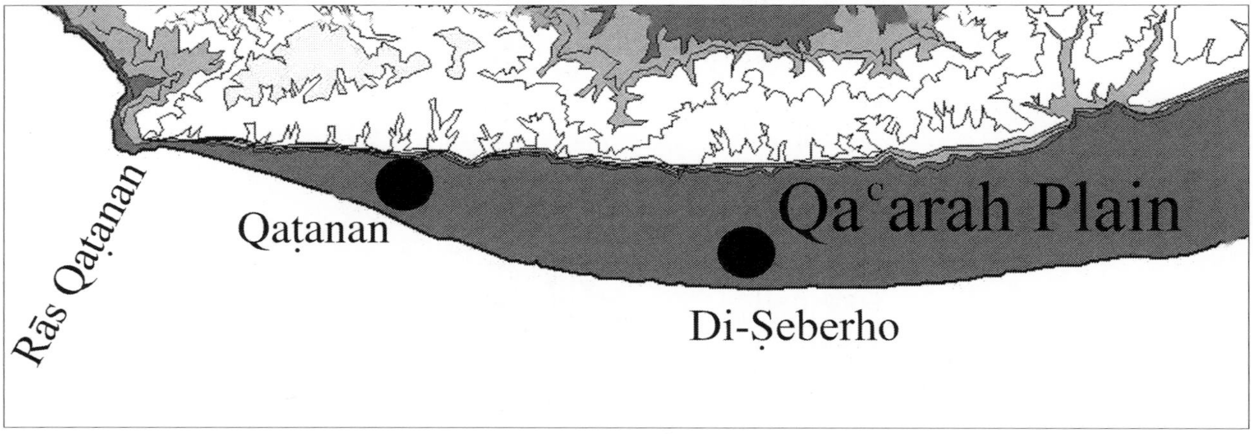

Figure 33. The southwest coast showing the landscape in the vicinity of the villages of Di-Ṣeberho and Qaṭanan.

Figure 34. A view of recent Italian Red Cross efforts to provide further launching and landing places (Photo: author).

FIGURE 35. THE LIMESTONE HEADLAND OF RĀS QAṬANAN FORMS THE BACKDROP TO THE VILLAGE OF QAṬANAN (PHOTO: AUTHOR).

expense of taking a boat out to sea to catch pelagic species.

Qaṭanan

The fishing village of Qaṭanan lies at the very western edge of the Qa^carah plain and marks the western end of the southern plain. It is bordered to the west by the cliffs of Rās Qaṭanan and to the north by the cliffs of the limestone escarpment, from which the village obtains its fresh water (Figure 35). The coast is made up of a long sandy stretch of beach that ends abruptly in the west at the limestone headland of Rās Qaṭanan, which drops straight into the sea. The depth of the sea in this area remains shallow out to approximately 28Nm offshore before dropping steeply to depths of in excess of 200m. Similarly to Di-Ṣerberho, fishermen mostly target demersal species.

Samḥa (Figure 36)

Khaysat ash-Shaikh

Khaysat ash-Shaikh is a small fishing village which lies on the north-western edge of Samḥa. The village lies within a narrow valley, surrounded on all sides by the foothills of Jebel Ash-Shaikh (Figure 37). The coast of the small bay used by fishermen is made up of a narrow sandy shore with outcroppings of rocky cliffs to either side. The northern coast consists of a series of narrow rocky plains and several small bays of sand and cobbles, while the southern littoral is almost all sheer cliffs. The inhabitants get fresh water from several small springs and a few wells situated at the foothills to the north of the village. The sea to the southeast and west of the island remains shallow for approximately 15Nm out to sea, whilst to the north the sea drops steeply into

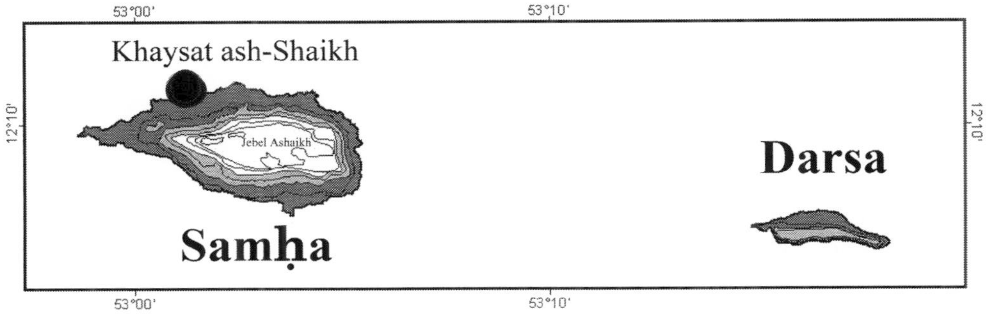

FIGURE 36. THE ISLAND OF SAMḤA AND DARSA SHOWING THE VILLAGE OF KHAYSAT ASH-SHAIKH.

Figure 37. The village of Khaysat ash-Shaikh as viewed from the sea (Photo: author).

deeper water little more than one nautical mile from the coastline, providing the fishermen with a range of fishing opportunities for pelagic and demersal species.

This brief synopsis outlines the major physical land and sea features found within the vicinity of the villages I am using in this study. Looking at the landscape surrounding the various fishing villages it is clear that there are distinctive differences between the north and south coast. Firstly, the north coast, is generally composed of headlands and mountains which make good visual points of reference for locating fishing areas at sea and navigation, whereas the landscape of the south coast has few if any landscape features and it is only the eastern and western most cliffs of the limestone escarpment that form useful points of reference. Secondly, along the north coast the water shelves rapidly into deep water relatively close to the shore, which not only means that upwellings occur closer to the shore, but that fishermen need only travel a short distance to fish for the high-value pelagic species, like shark and kingfish. This is especially apparent in the villages of Shu^{c}ub, Qalansiyah, Ṣaqarah and Erisseyl. Conversely, in areas where the depth of the water remains shallow for a significant distance offshore, especially along the south coast, it is difficult for fishermen to target pelagic species. Fishermen on the south coast I spoke to told me that this is due to the expense of the fuel required to travel out to deeper water and the dangers of the winds and currents when fishing this far from the shore. The near-shore bathymetry also has a significant effect on the type of fishing equipment used by fishermen.

Looking at the shoreline from which fishermen launch and land their vessels it is clear that favoured areas are composed of low-lying bays of sand and cobbles, where it is possible to drag ones vessel out of the sea. The villages of Ṣaqarah, Erriysel and Zaḥaq with their narrow bays and steep inclines are noticeable exceptions. However, when looking at the surrounding topography and sources of water the reasons for this become apparent, as not only are there few suitable launching and landing places in the vicinity, but there are even fewer that have a source of fresh water nearby. The importance of fresh water cannot be overemphasised; all the villages looked at here have access to some form of fresh water resource, although the quality and quantity can differ significantly. Access to a regular, good quantity of fresh water has a direct effect on the number and size of villages in any particular area. This is demonstrated by the profusion and density of settlements along Socotra's north coast, which has a more plentiful supply of water than the south. The factors outlined above provide a general idea on the effect the land and seascape has on the fishermen. With these factors in mind, it is now possible to look at how fishermen in specific villages use the land and seascape to identify fishing areas.

Fishing Areas

Attempting to gather a corpus of data for fishing areas was particularly difficult for a number of reasons. Firstly, in several instances the fishermen I interviewed did not want to give me the names or actual locations of their fishing areas because they wished to keep the names and

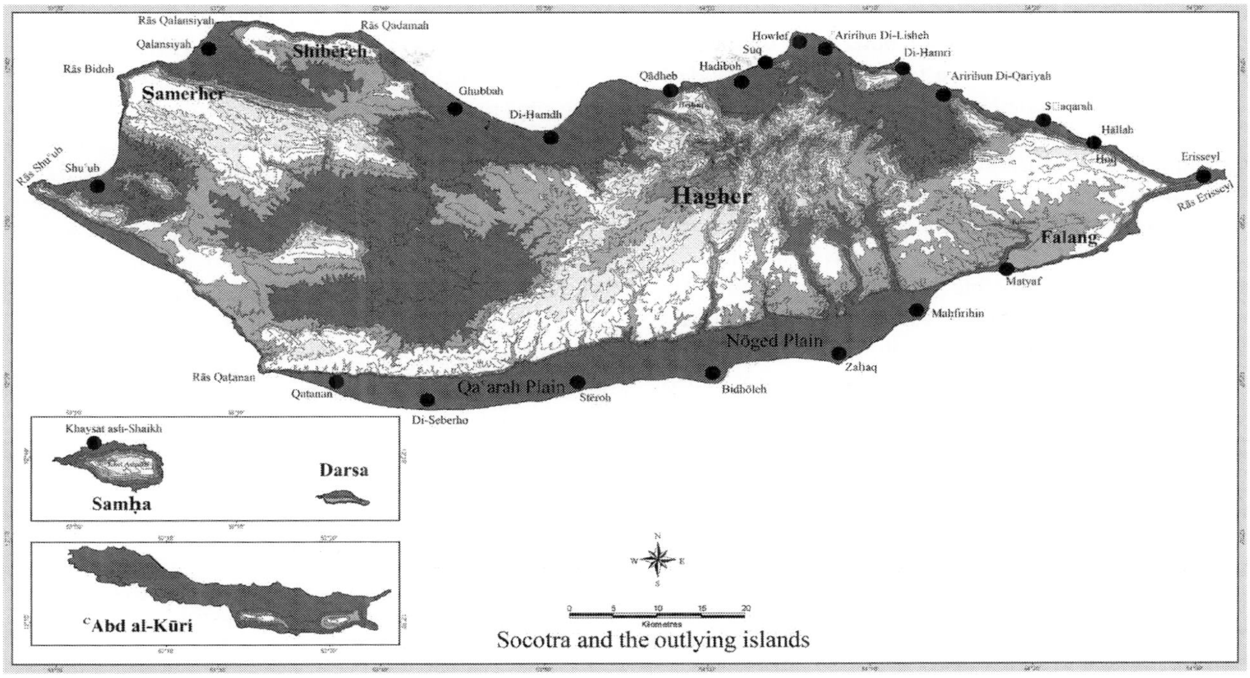

FIGURE 38. SOCOTRA AND THE OUTLYING ISLANDS OF SAMḤA, DARSA AND ᶜABD AL-KŪRI SHOWING THE FISHING VILLAGES WHERE INTERVIEWS WERE CONDUCTED.

locations secret from myself and the other fishermen. This has made it necessary for me to concentrate on those villages in which I was able to gather sufficient information namely, Shuᶜub, Qalansiyah, Qādheb, Ḥadiboh, Suq, Ṣaqarah, Erisseyl, Zaḥaq, Stēroh and Khaysat ash-Shaikh (Figure 38).

Secondly, I found that because the fishermen would use both Arabic and Socotri terminology to identify specific areas or landmarks, it was not always possible to clearly determine which landmarks they were referring to, as local names differed to those marked on maps and charts of Socotra. Furthermore, in several instances I found that fishermen also used generic names for specific landscape features. An example of this is the word *Shibereh* (Soc), which is used by people throughout the island to denote a ridge, plateau, or escarpment that overlooks the sea. Consequently, when interviewing fishermen in villages where more than one escarpment is in the vicinity, such as Shuᶜub and Qalansiyah, it was not always clear as to which escarpment they are referring to. Finally, when I attempted to translate and determine the meanings for the various fishing areas, I found that many of them do not have any meaning for the fishermen, other than being a name for a specific place, or that the word is no longer understood. As a result, it has not been possible to translate a number of the names for specific fishing areas.

The fishermen's identification of the species of fish found in various areas made it clear that the distribution of marine species is well known to the fishermen who, through several generations of experience, have learnt to recognise areas in which specific species are known to occur most frequently. The reason for this species distribution is based upon a number of factors which include the availability of food, changes to the water temperature, the dynamics of water movement and even the nature of the seabed (FAO 2005-2011). On Socotra, the distribution and richness of the fisheries resources is also influenced by the bathymetry and seasonally changing winds and currents around the Socotra archipelago. Studies of marine species richness on Socotra have demonstrated that there is a general decrease from west to east; that fish assemblages along the north coast are more diverse than those occurring along the south, and that the outer islands host a large proportion of the archipelago's fish biodiversity (Zajonz *et al.* 2000: 127). This species richness is likely to have played a role in the settlement of fishing villages, as it cannot be pure coincidence that the three main fishing villages of Qalansiyah, Qādheb and Ḥadiboh are all situated along the richer fishing grounds of the north coast. These three villages have the longest period of occupation and fishing, which can be traced back several centuries. This long-term period of fishing and the accumulation of knowledge by fishermen along the north coast have played a significant role in the location and identification of fishing areas. Conversely, the south coast fisheries are a relatively recent phenomenon, having only properly developed at the beginning of the 21st century (Morris

2002: 222). Many of the fishermen along the south coast are migrants who have come from other areas of Socotra, or have only fished there for a relatively short period of time; few have a detailed knowledge of the area.

In addition to this local knowledge, the diverse topography of the landscape is also instrumental in the location and identification of fishing areas. Geographically, the north coast of Socotra presents the fisherman with a number of distinctive and clearly visible headlands, mountain peaks and sand dunes, all of which can be seen a significant distance out to sea. In comparison, the south coast of Socotra presents the fishermen with a flat, featureless plain backed by a relatively uniform limestone escarpment that stretches along the entire length of the south coast, with the only exception being the distinctive projecting headlands of the east and west side of the island. This broad view of the north and south coasts of the island reinforces the commonalities and differences of the maritime landscape between the various villages. However, in order to develop this it is necessary to look at the individual villages and determine what factors have directly influenced the identification of their fishing areas. Detailed information concerning the land and seascapes of the various fishing villages has been outlined above, and in the next section I will concentrate only on those features which are relevant to the fishing areas mentioned by the fishermen. I have combined those villages in close proximity, as fishermen in these areas fish in the same areas and use the same landmarks to name their fishing grounds.

The Northwest Coast

Shuʿub and Qalansiyah

The names of the fishing areas used by the fishermen from these two villages are based upon the surrounding landscape and in both villages the names of the surrounding headlands are used by the fishermen to name and navigate to fishing areas. The names of the fishing areas that were named after features on land are: *Rās Qalansiyah* (Ar), meaning the headland Qalansiyah; *Rhˈiy bə̄do* (Soc), meaning the headland with strips of vegetation; *Rhˈiy d-ˈiṣfer* (Soc), translated as the headland of the birds, after the many cormorants that can be found in this area; and *Rhˈiy di-śyˈuʿub* (Soc), a headland named after Shuʿub, which in Socotri is known as Śyˈuʿub. While it was not possible to accurately identify or translate all of the named sea areas, in several instances they were prefixed by the word *mgˈibbə* (Soc), meaning an area where the sea is deep. The deep water sites named by the fishermen are, *mgˈibbə dˈeʿef*, *mgˈibbə sūkāk* and *mgˈibbə samara*. The only one I was able to translate is, *mgˈibbə dˈeʿef*, the deep area of the lengthening shadows of the early afternoon. The fishermen in Qalansiyah[29] and Shuʿub[30] told me that all these fishing areas named above are deep water sites where it was possible to catch pelagic species such as kingfish, tuna and shark. In addition to these sites the fishermen also identified several shallow water sites. The names of these sites were given in Socotri and are known as, *ḳʌ̄ṭi*, meaning two rock water pools; *gīd*, which literally means, a good spot; *ġˈubba śyˈuʿub*, which translates as the bay of Shuʿub; *sāle*; *dɔ̄l*; *ligda*, and *sɔ̄rīn*. The names of the latter four fishing areas had no apparent meaning for the fishermen. Those interviewed said that these shallow sites are best for rock fish, and are mostly fished when the weather makes it too dangerous or difficult to head further out to sea to catch shark, tuna or kingfish.

The Central North Coast

Qādheb, Ḥadiboh and Suq

Several names fishermen used for fishing areas off these villages matched nearby topographical features on land, which were also used in navigating to the areas. These are, *Rhˈiy ḥɔ̄lef* (Soc)/*Rās Ḥowlef* (Ar), meaning the headland of Ḥowlef; *šīmi di-ḥɔ̄lef* (Soc), which translates as the sand dunes of Ḥowlef, and *Jebel Ḥawari* (Ar), the mountain Ḥawari. The fishermen also identified a fishing area off the headland Rās Ḥebaq, which was known as *Rās b-rʾs* (Ar), and translates as a headland inside/beside a headland. Fishermen interviewed in Qādheb,[31] Ḥadiboh[32] and Suq[33] said that these fishing areas fall within a larger sea area known as *ḳeneʿˈiti* (Soc), which means the end, tip, or extremity. The reason these features on land were used to identify fishing areas within *ḳeneʿˈiti* was, according to the fishermen, that they were still visible at this distance and made good navigational landmarks. They also said that this area is the best place to catch shark, kingfish and tuna. The fishing areas closer to land are considered to be best for catching rock fish, and are known as: *ɔ̄ʾbeni* (Soc), meaning the two rocks; *kˈənəhor* (Soc), a type of tree known as the Lannea tree; *rēmo*

[29] Jaman Saeed Abdullah, full-time fisherman, in his 30s; Ali Salim Da-Salmoho, full-time fisherman, in his 60s; Abdullha Rahman Abod Ali Saeed, full-time fisherman, 38 years old; Anwar Khamis Abdul Abod Ali Saeed, full-time fisherman, 32 years old, all interviewed on 16 February 2009.

[30] Abdullah Salem Saaed Abokakibak, full-time fisherman, 45 years old; Mohammed Malak Masham, full-time fisherman, 35 years old; Kamis Jaman Hamond, full-time fisherman, in his 30s, all interviewed on 20 December 2009.

[31] Mohammed Aldolah, full-time fisherman, in his 60s; Omar Abdulla Saleh, full-time fisherman, in his 60; Abdullah Mohammed Sallim, full-time fisherman, in his 60s, all interviewed on 8 February 2009; Salim Games Saaed, full-time fisherman, 45 years old; Salim Saaed Atman, full-time fisherman, 55 years old, both interviewed on 2 January 2009.

[32] Abdullah Mohammed Hamadan, full-time fisherman, in his 60s; Heni Mohammed Saeed Abdullah, full-time fisherman, in his 60s, both interviewed on 15 February 2009; Khames Abdulah Salem, full-time fisherman, 75 years old; Jamen Mahafawl Saif, full-time fisherman, 70 years old, both interviewed on 22 December 2009; Minathal Eisa Mobarak, full-time fisherman, 34 years old; Selemann Safi Abeed, full-time fisherman, 45 years old, both interviewed on 3 January 2010.

[33] Rabain Mobarek al-Noby, full-time fisherman, in his 60s; Saaed Ahmed Nashran, full-time fisherman, in his 60s; Saad Dabowed Mousa, full-time fisherman, in his 60s, all interviewed on 14 February 2009.

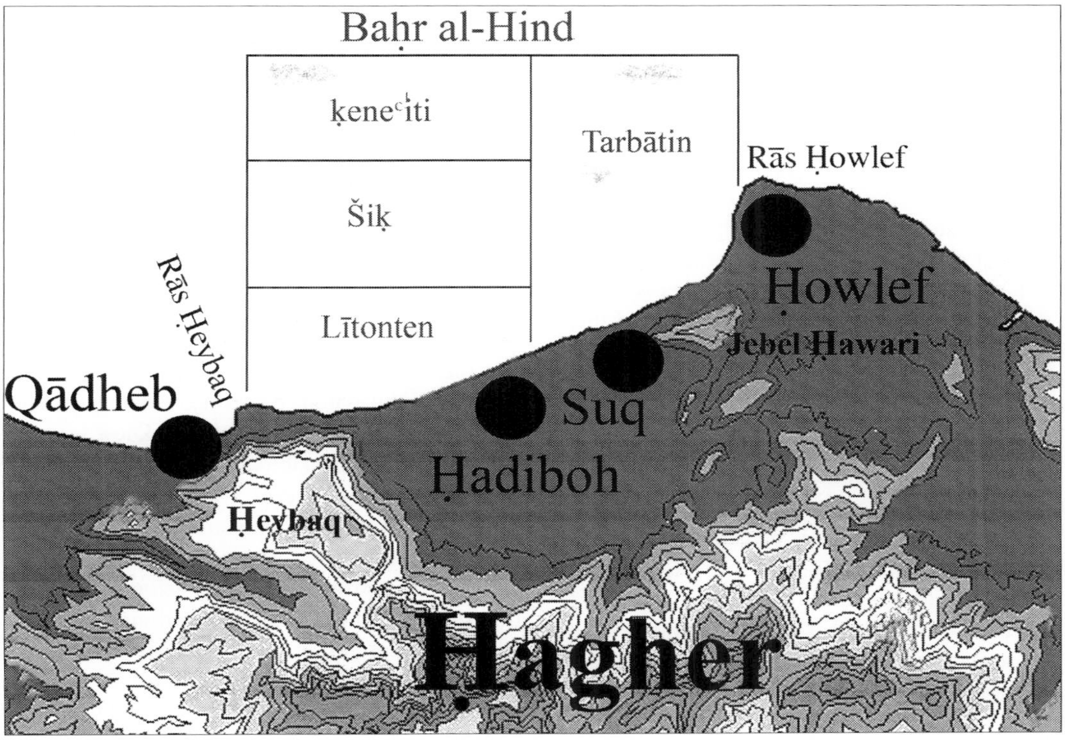

FIGURE 39. THE FISHING AREAS *ḲENEᶜITI, ŠIḲ, LĪTONTEN* AND *TARBĀTIN*.

(Soc), meaning long; *nimihər* (Soc), meaning a moray eel, and *ḳáśᶜer śēbəhon* (Soc), meaning a rock emerging from the sea, 'of the old people'. According to Morris,[34] 'of the old people' refers to an early period, possibly four to five generations ago. The other fishing areas named were known as: *ḥajrān* (Soc/ Ar); *nēkab* (Soc/ Ar); *taᶜbēna* (Soc/ Ar); *ᶜabud* (Soc/ Ar); *dīmāza* (Soc/ Ar), and *dībeni* (Soc/ Ar). These names had no apparent meaning for the fishermen, and appear to be creolised Arabic words. The reason for this is that in these villages there has been an influx of Arabians, whose language has become the most commonly spoken. Consequently, it seems to have penetrated into the language used by the fishermen to identify their fishing areas. This would indicate that these are relatively new fishing areas.

In addition to these names, the fishermen in these villages also recognise four fishing areas, which they say are the oldest and most widely recognised areas. These are known as, *ḳeneᶜiti* (Soc), *šiḳ* (Soc), *lītonten* (Soc), and *tarbātin* (Soc). According to the fishermen in Ḥadiboh and Suq,[35] they are used to identify an area of sea that lies between the two headlands at either end of the Ḥadiboh plain (Figure 39). They said that the area of *tarbātin* lies between, Rās Ḥowlef in the east and an area of beach midway between Ḥadiboh and Suq. The other fishing areas, *ḳeneᶜiti*, *šiḳ*, and *lītonten*, lie to the west of *tarbātin*, and are bounded between a midway point that lies between Ḥadiboh and Suq, and Rās Ḥebaq in the west.

Several experienced fishermen interviewed in Ḥadiboh[36] said that the distance between the start and finish of the fishing areas *ḳeneᶜiti*, *šiḳ*, and *lītonten* is determined by the time it takes to paddle out to sea, the depth of the water, and how much of the land is visible. The first area, *lītonten*, begins from the shore and ends after approximately 20 minutes, when paddling out to sea, at a depth of about 10m. At this distance it is possible to see the houses, foothills and peaks of the Ḥagher. They said that this area is good to catch bait fish and is the furthest distance that is safe to fish during the beginning or end of *ḥorf* (Soc), the SW monsoon season, as beyond this

[34] Miranda Morris personal communication December 2011.

[35] Abdullah Mohammed Hamadan, full-time fisherman, in his 60s; Heni Mohammed Saeed Abdullah, full-time fisherman, in his 60s, both interviewed on 15 February 2009; Khames Abdulah Salem, full-time fisherman, 75 years old; Jamen Mahafawl Saif, full-time fisherman, 70 years old, both interviewed on 22 December 2009; Minathal Eisa Mobarak, full-time fisherman, 34 years old; Selemann Safi Abeed, full-time fisherman, 45 years old, both interviewed on 3 January 2010; Rabain Mobarek al-Noby, full-time fisherman, in his 60s; Saaed Ahmed Nashran, full-time fisherman, in his 60s; Saad Dabowed Mousa, full-time fisherman, in his 60s, all interviewed on 14 February 2009.

[36] Khames Abdulah Salem, full-time fisherman, 75 years old; Jamen Mahafawl Saif, full-time fisherman, 70 years old, both interviewed on 22 December 2009; Nasieb Saad Khamis, full-time fisherman, in his 60s; Khamis Amer, full-time fisherman, in his 60s, both interviewed on 15 February 2010.

area strong winds and currents can drag one out to sea. The second area, *šiḳ*, ends approximately 40 minutes to an hour from the shore; at this distance the houses and foothills of the Ḥagher are no longer visible. Fishermen said that, on a calm day it is sometimes possible to see the seafloor here. They also said that this area is best for catching rock fish, especially groupers, although it is also possible to catch some pelagic fish species, such as snapper. The third area, *ḳeneᶜiti*, is the outermost area for fishing. They said that the limit of this area is when the peaks of the Ḥagher disappear into the sea, and this is the best place to catch shark, kingfish and tuna. The area beyond *ḳeneᶜiti*, is known as *al-baḥr* (Ar), 'the sea', or *baḥr al-Hind* (Ar), 'the Indian Sea', and is considered as the outer limits beyond which no fishing takes place. However, according to several fishermen, the few people who used GPS handheld units extend the traditional limits of *ḳeneᶜiti* further out to sea, as it is possible for them to use the GPS unit to find their way back to land. Whereas most fishermen consider the limit of *ḳeneᶜiti* as the point at which the peaks of the Ḥagher disappear, those with a GPS unit base its limits upon how far out to sea they think it is safe to travel. The use of GPS handheld units amongst the fishermen on Socotra is rare, although many are aware of them and in some cases have used one. The fishing area of *tarbātin* is completely different to these areas. According to fishermen in Suq, it is not subdivided into different areas, but represents a single fishing area that extends out to *baḥr al-Hind*. There was no apparent reason for this difference and it can only be surmised that it formed part of an earlier traditional fishing ground that may have had some significance in the past.

The Northeast Coast

Ṣaqarah and Erisseyl

Fishermen in Ṣaqarah[37] and Erisseyl[38] said that their fishing areas are named according to the mountains and rocks at sea. In Erisseyl, they also use a submerged shipwreck as a fishing area; they say that this is a very good area for rock fish. The names of the fishing areas are mostly a mix of Arabic and Socotri. The deep sea fishing areas off these villages are named, *ēdho*; *rūsh*; *sharāfi*; *dīdom*, and *mātaḳal*. Unfortunately, other than being able to tell me that these specific landmarks are used to identify deep water areas where shark, tuna and kingfish can be caught, I was unable to determine which features on land they represented and what the words meant. The main reason for this is that the fishermen wished to keep these areas secret, as they did not want others fishing there. The names of shallow sites proved to be less problematic. These are, *gālus*, an area named after a shipwreck found there; *ḳaśᶜer* (Soc), meaning rock, and *ḳaśᶜer men djēme* (Soc), meaning a rock from below. According to two elderly fishermen,[39] *ḳaśᶜer* and *ḳaśᶜer men djēme* refers to the rocky nature of the seafloor, which is a good area to catch rock fish.

The South Coast

Zaḥaq and Stēroh

Fishermen I interviewed on the south coast told me that there are no specific fishing areas, and they would fish along the whole coastline. However, fishermen in Zaḥaq[40] and Stēroh[41] said that they knew several shallow sites where it is possible to catch a lot of rock fish. The first area is *ġubba stēroh* (Soc/Ar), meaning a shallow area near Stēroh. The other sites are: *ḳaśᶜer ḥadēr*; *ḳaśᶜer gafān*; *maṣhor*; *ᶜaṣed* and *nāḳor*. Unfortunately, due to the secrecy surrounding these fishing areas I could not find out what these names meant, and was only able to determine that *ḳaśᶜer ḥadēr* and *ḳaśᶜer gafān* refers to a named rock, where fishing is good.

Samḥa

Fishermen interviewed[42] in Khaysat ash-Shaikh told me that they fish all around the island, targeting shark, kingfish, tuna and other pelagic species. The names of several fishing areas given were prefixed by the word, *qaṭaᶜat* (Ar), meaning an area. These were identified by the fishermen as, *qaṭaᶜat zujash*, *qaṭaᶜat ṣhayna*, *qaṭaᶜat sāmḥa*, and *qaṭaᶜat b-il-ḥeymer* (Figure 40). According to fishermen interviewed, the fishing area of *qaṭaᶜat sāmḥa* refers to the Samḥa fishing area; *qaṭaᶜat hindi*, refers to the fishing area of the eastern wind *hindī*, and *qaṭaᶜat b-il-ḥeymer*, refers to a star *al-ḥeymar*. They said that *qaṭaᶜat sāmḥa* and *qaṭaᶜat hindi* lie to the east of Samḥa and are protected from the winds that come from the east. They also said that *qaṭaᶜat zujash* and *qaṭaᶜat shayna* lie between Samḥa and Darsa, and can only be fished when the wind is calm. Unfortunately, I was not able to determine what star *al-ḥeymar* represented. Therefore, it is only possible for me to say that *qaṭaᶜat*

[37] Salem Abdullah Saeed, full-time fisherman, 45 years old; Thaili Hamoadi, full-time fisherman, in his 60s; Mobark Wilaal Saad, full-time fisherman, 25 years old; Salam Rashid Hamoadi, full-time fisherman, 25 years old, all interviewed on 23 December 2009.

[38] Mohammed Selem Abo, full-time fisherman, 56 years old; Sindowa Ali Ahmed, full-time fisherman, in his 40s; Frzir Ahmed Hamed, full-time fisherman, 28 years old, all interviewed on 23 December 2009.

[39] Saleman Hamodi Ahmed, full-time fisherman, in his 50s; Ahmed Mohammed Saaed, full-time fisherman, in his 50s, both interviewed on 9 February 2009.

[40] Jamen Khamis Saeed Marjan Saeed, full-time fisherman, in his 60s, interviewed on 12 February 2009; Abdullah Saeed, full-time fisherman, 25 years old, interviewed on 28 December 2009; Jamen Ahmed Salem, full-time fisherman, in his 40s, interviewed on 28 December 2009; Ali Saeed, full-time fisherman, in his 60s, interviewed on 29 December 2009.

[41] Mohammed Abdullah Ahmed, full-time fisherman, 35 years old; Ali Eisa Abdullah, full-time fisherman, in his 30s; Saeed Mohammed Abdullah, full-time fisherman, 27 years old; Ali Abdullah Ahmed, full-time fisherman, in his 40s, all interviewed on 30 December 2009.

[42] Saeed Masour Ahmed, full-time fisherman, in his 60s; Mohammed Ali Saliman, full-time fisherman, 35 years old; Mohammed Sabhan Mohammed, full-time fisherman, 45 years old; Abdullah Ali Saeed, full-time fisherman, 35 years old, all interviewed on 19 December 2009.

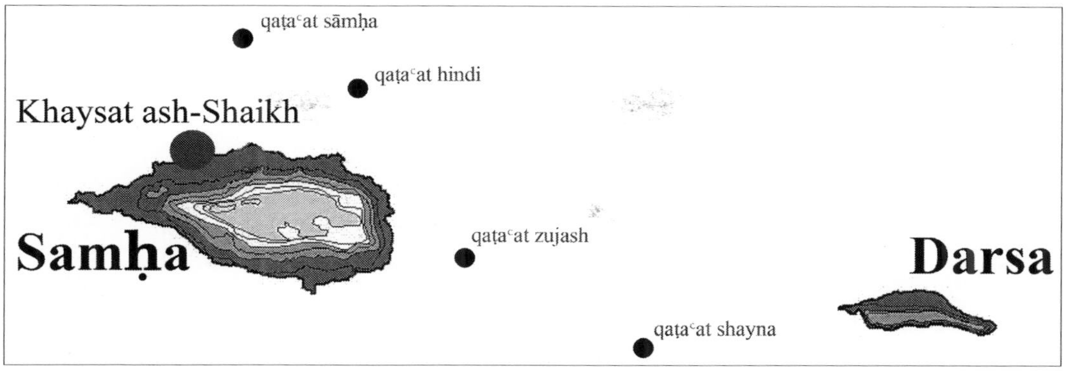

FIGURE 40. THE ISLAND OF SAMḤA, SHOWING THE LOCATION OF SOME FISHING AREAS.

b-il-ḥe̍ymer is fished during a specific period in which this star is visible. The other fishing areas identified by the fishermen are *ḳa̍śᶜer mjērī*, which refers to a rocky area below *mjērī*, a headland I was unable to identify; *mgi̍bbə zujash*, which refers to an area of deep water called *zujash*, and ᶜ*aqd* (Ar), which means contract or joining in Arabic and may refer to an area between the two islands.

The fishing areas outlined above demonstrate several similarities and differences in the naming and identification of fishing areas between villages on the north and south coast, and the outlying island of Samḥa. A complete list of the fishing areas off each village is given in Figures 41-45.

Figures 41-45 demonstrate the relationship between the naming and identification of fishing areas, the depth of the sea and the surrounding landscape. When comparing the number of deep and shallow water sites in relation to the land and seascape it is apparent that the fishermen recognise the extent of the shallow and deep-water areas off their villages and adapt their fishing accordingly. Furthermore, when looking at the naming of fishing areas it is clear that the fishermen rely on the presence of land and seamarks, which partially explains the lack of fishing areas along the south coast. The reason for this is that the south coast is composed of a wide, flat and virtually featureless plain that extends several kilometres inland and the only features that can be clearly seen when at sea are the headlands, which drop steeply into the sea at either end of the plain. In contrast the north coast is composed of a multitude of headlands and peaks that can be seen a significant distance out to sea. Therefore, one reason for the lack of defined fishing areas along the south coast is the lack of suitable landmarks. The

Villages	Fishing area	Language	Tentative interpretation of the topography	Area
Shuᶜub and Qalansiyah	*Rās Qalansiyah*	Ar	Headland of Qalansiyah.	Deep
	Rhi̍y bədo	Soc	Headland with strips of vegetation.	Deep
	Rhi̍y d-i̍ṣfer	Soc	Headland of the birds.	Deep
	Rhi̍y di-śyu̍ᶜub	Soc	Headland of Shuᶜub	Deep
	mgi̍bbə de̍ᶜef	Soc	Deep area of the lengthening shadows of the early afternoon.	Deep
	mgi̍bbə sūkāk	Soc	None	Deep
	mgi̍bbə samara	Soc	None	Deep
	ḳʌ̄ṭi	Soc	Two rock water pools	Shallow
	gīd	Soc	A good spot	Shallow
	ġu̍bba śyu̍ᶜub	Soc	Bay of Shuᶜub	Shallow
	sāle	Soc	None	Shallow
	dɔ̄l	Soc	None	Shallow
	ligda	Soc	None	Shallow
	sɔ̄rīn	Soc	None	Shallow

FIGURE 41. FISHING AREAS ALONG THE NORTHWEST COAST.

Villages	Fishing area	Language	Tentative interpretation of the topography	Area
Qādheb, Ḥadiboh and Suq	*rhi̍y ḥōlef* / Rās Ḥowlef	Soc / Ar	Headland of Ḥowlef	Deep
	šīmi di-ḥōlef	Soc	Sand dunes of Ḥowlef	Deep
	Jebel Hawārī	Ar	The mountain *Hawārī*	Deep
	raʾs b-rʾs	Ar	The headland besides a headland	Deep
	ōᵊbeni	Soc	The two rocks	Shallow
	ḥajrān	Soc / Ar	None	Shallow
	kə̍nəhor	Soc	The *Lannea* tree	Shallow
	rēmo	Soc	Long	Shallow
	tarbātin	Soc / Ar	None	A large sea area, both shallow and deep
	nēkab	Soc / Ar	None	Shallow
	taʿbēna	Soc / Ar	None	Shallow
	ni̍mihər	Soc	Moray eel	Shallow
	ʿabud	Soc / Ar	None	Shallow
	dīmāza	Soc / Ar	None	Shallow
	ḳa̍śʿer śēbəhon	Soc	A rock emerging from the sea, of the old people.	Shallow
	dībeni	Soc / Ar	None	Shallow
	ḳeneʿi̍ti	Soc	The end, tip or extremity	Deep
	šiḳ	Soc	The town of Suq	Deep
	lītonten	Soc / Ar	None	Shallow

FIGURE 42. FISHING AREAS ALONG THE CENTRAL NORTH COAST.

Villages	Fishing area	Language	Tentative interpretation of the topography	Area
Ṣaqarah and Erisseyl	*ēdho*	Soc / Ar	None	Deep
	Rūsh	Soc / Ar	None	Deep
	sharāfi	Soc / Ar	None	Deep
	dīdom	Soc / Ar	None	Deep
	mātaḳal	Soc / Ar	None	Deep
	gālus	Soc / Ar	None	Shallow
	ḳa̍śʿer	Soc	Rock	Shallow
	ḳa̍śʿer men djēme	Soc	Rock from below	Shallow

FIGURE 43. FISHING AREAS ALONG THE NORTHEAST COAST.

Villages	Fishing area	Language	Tentative interpretation of the topography	Area
Zaḥaq and Stēroh	*ġu̍bba stēroh*	Soc	Inlet of Stēroh	Shallow
	ḳa̍śʿer ḥadēr	Soc	Rock emerging from the sea	Shallow
	ḳa̍śʿer gafān	Soc	Rock emerging from the sea	Shallow
	maṣhor	Soc	None	Shallow
	ʿaṣed	Soc	None	Shallow
	nāḳor	Soc	None	Shallow

FIGURE 44. FISHING AREAS ALONG THE SOUTH COAST.

Villages	Fishing area	Language	Tentative interpretation of the topography	Area
Khaysat ash-Shaikh	*qaṭaᶜat zujash*	Soc	The *zujash* section	Between Samḥa and Darsa/Deep
	qaṭaᶜat shayna	Soc	The *shayna* section	Between Samḥa and Darsa/Deep
	qaṭaᶜat sāmḥa	Soc	The *sāmḥa* section	East of Samḥa/Deep
	qaṭaᶜat hindi	Soc	The *hindi* section	East of Samḥa/Deep
	qaṭaᶜat b-il-ḥeymer	Soc	The *b-il-ḥeymer* section	Deep
	ᶜaqd	Ar	Contract or Joining	Shallow
	ḳaśᶜer mjērī	Soc	A rocky area below *mjērī*	Shallow
	mgibbə zujash	Soc	A deep area in *zujash*	Deep

FIGURE 45. FISHING AREAS OFF SAMḤA.

second reason is based upon experience. Fishermen along the north coast have been fishing there for several generations and know the land and seascape intimately, whereas along the south coast they are less experienced, either because they have only been fishing for two to three generations, or because they have less experience in fishing along the south coast and are less accustomed to the land and seascape. The large number of shallow-water fishing sites along the north coast is also related to the market for fish and the fishing methods and equipment used by the fishermen. The influences of these factors will be discussed later, but for now it is worth mentioning that deep-water sites are areas in which the highly-marketable pelagic species are caught, whereas shallow water sites are areas in which demersal rock fish are more prevalent.

Finally, when looking at the location and naming of fishing areas off Socotra and the island of Samḥa it is apparent that the fishermen use distinctive, highly-visible landscape features to identify and name fishing areas, especially those further out to sea. The reason for this is that they are also using them to navigate by, which is what the next section will look at.

Navigation

The use of a compass or handheld GPS unit is relatively rare on Socotra, although fishermen I spoke to were aware of, or had used one (Bonfiglioli and Hariri 2004: 31). According to fishermen on Socotra, the reason that most do not have a handheld GPS unit is that they are extremely expensive, costing in the region of 50,000 Yemeni Rials (YR). To place this in context, the average monthly income for a fisherman is YR 20,260 (USD 93) a month (Hariri and Yusif 1999: 17). Consequently, fishermen on Socotra rely on more traditional forms of navigation, which are passed down from father to son. The methods used by the fishermen in navigating a vessel off Socotra's coast are dependent on whether they are fishing off the north or south coast and how far offshore they are planning to go. The different methods and techniques used to determine their course, direction and position are outlined below.

The majority of the fishermen I interviewed on Socotra and Samḥa said that they mainly use visual references to determine their position, or the course they wish to follow. This method of navigation is known as pilotage. This is an extremely effective way to determining one's position provided that one is able to correctly identify the necessary visual references. According to fishermen in Shuᶜub, Qalansiyah, Qādheb, Ḥadiboh and Erisseyl, on the north coast and Maḥfirihin, Bidōleh, Stēroh and Di-Ṣeberho on the south coast of Socotra, they primarily use landmarks, rather than seamarks as visual reference points. They said that along the north coast there are a plethora of available features. However, the primary ones they use are the peaks of the Ḥagher, low-lying foothills, coastal headlands, sand dunes, palm tree plantations, and buildings. Mosques and minarets are particularly favoured due to their white colour and height which, according to fishermen in Ḥadiboh, makes them easy to recognise. The fishermen from the north and south coast also said that along the south coast the availability of landmarks is limited to a few features, namely: the limestone escarpment that drops onto the coastal plain several kilometres inland, the headlands, sand dunes, buildings, inlets, and distinguishable breaks in the shoreline. According to fishermen in Maḥfirihin, Stēroh and Bidhōleh, the majority of these are virtually impossible to see from any great distance and this makes it difficult for them to accurately identify fishing areas that lie any distance out to sea. On Samḥa the fishermen said that they mostly use the mountains, rocks and headlands of the two islands Samḥa and Darsa; some said that they also use the headlands of the west coast of Socotra, especially when fishing to the northeast of the islands.

Position Fixing

The fishermen in the north-coast villages of Qalansiyah, Ḥadiboh, Qādheb, Ṣaqarah and Erisseyl mostly use

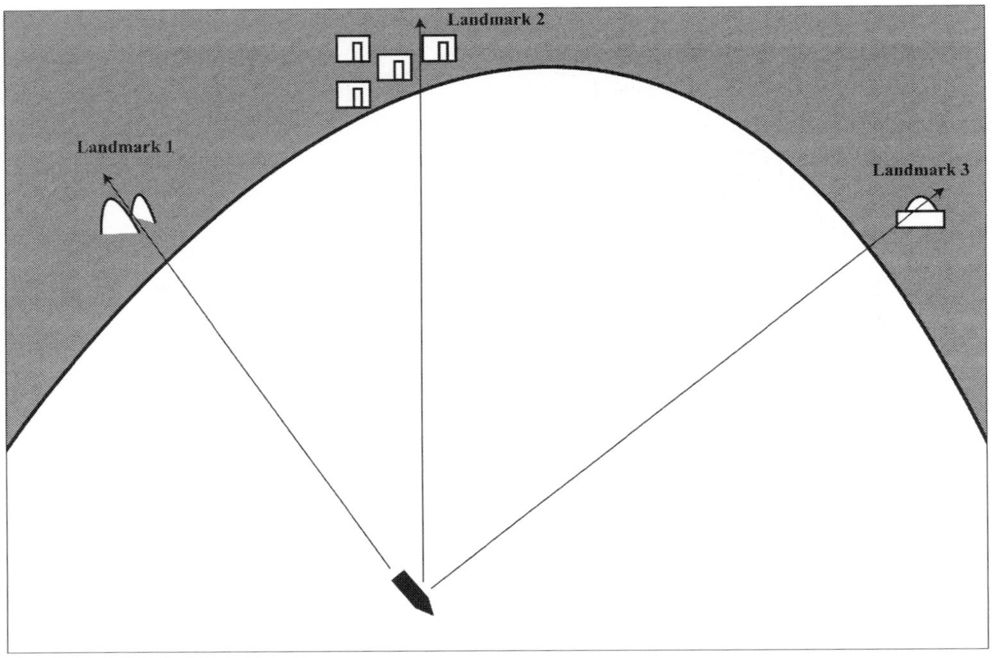

FIGURE 46. THE METHOD USED BY THE FISHERMEN TO FIND A FISHING AREA USING THREE LANDMARKS (DRAWN: AUTHOR).

between two and three landmarks to locate their fishing areas, although where the fishing area is well known, fishermen are able to use one. They mainly use a system of triangulation in which two or three landmarks are lined up at specific angles that converge at the point of observation. In Qalansiyah, fishermen said that in order to find one's position at sea it is necessary to use at least two landmarks. They also said that the best are either specific mountain peaks or headlands, although closer inshore, buildings and palm plantations can also be used. According to two experienced full-time fishermen in Qādheb,[43] it is better to use three, as it is easy to lose one if the weather changes or the sea becomes rough. In Ḥadiboh, fishermen told me that they use three landmarks, although two older experienced full-time fishermen[44] said that they could find some fishing areas by using only one. Along the south coast, fishermen in Maḥfirihin, Zaḥaq and Stēroh explained to me that they use a minimum of two landmarks. However, if they are fishing further offshore they rely on a different system of navigation that I will outline below. In Samḥa, fishermen interviewed use between one and three landmarks, depending on how close to the island they are fishing and which side of the island they are on. When fishing further offshore they use more landmarks than if fishing closer to Samḥa and Darsa, this allows them to accurately determine where they are and guard against getting lost if they lose one. However, when fishing to the west of Samḥa, because it is difficult to see Darsa, they normally only use one landmark which, according to them, cannot be lost, or they will be lost at sea.

Where a single landmark is used, the fishermen line up their vessel with that feature. They then follow an imaginary line between the boat and the feature by keeping the landmark at a specific position in relation to the boat, normally at a point on the stern, or to one side of the vessel. The fishing area is reached after a specific period of time, or when the fishermen recognise the area of sea they wish to fish in. In Ḥadiboh and Qalansiyah, fishermen said that it they knew when they had reached their fishing area by the colour of the sea and whether or not it was rocky. Where a second or third landmark is used, the fishermen head out to sea using one landmark and at a certain distance out to sea they begin to look for a second landmark. Once the second landmark has been seen they alter course to keep both landmarks at specific positions in relation to the boat. This is repeated for all consecutive landmarks until every landmark is at a specific position in relation to the boat. At this point the fishing area is reached (Figure 46). This method of locating one's position is not unique to Socotra, and has been recorded in many different areas of the world, where it still forms an important part of a mariner's navigational knowledge.

In addition to this method, the fishermen on the north coast, especially Ḥadiboh, also rely on the appearance and disappearance from view of certain mountain peaks. This method involves heading out to sea using one or more peaks as a visual reference, and when, at a certain distance from the shore, the peaks used either start to

[43] Omar Abdulla Saleh, in his 60s; Abdullah Mohammed Sallim, in his 60s, both interviewed on 8 February 2009.
[44] Khames Abdulah Salem, 75 years old; Jamen Mahafawl Saif, 70 years old, both interviewed on 22 December 2009.

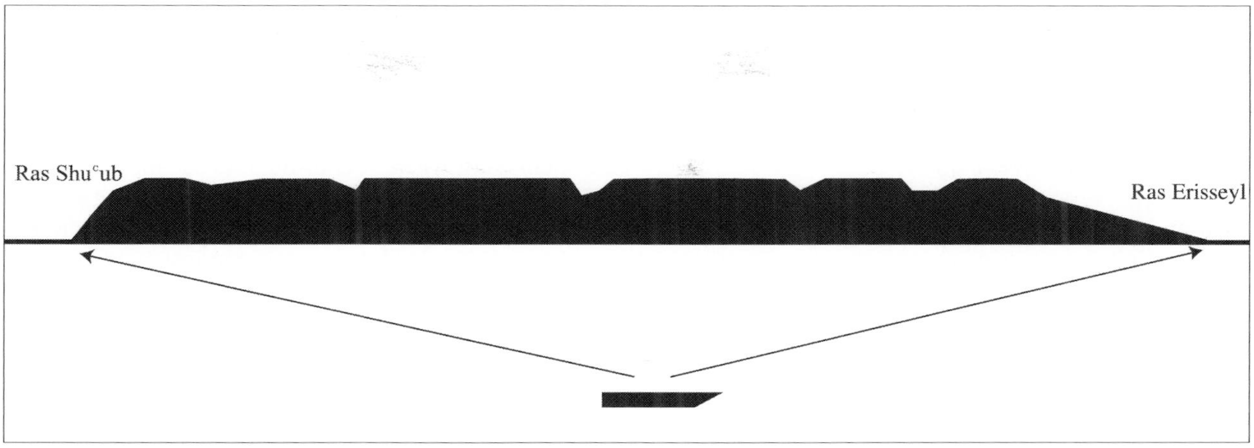

FIGURE 47. THE SILHOUETTE OF THE ISLAND AS SEEN FROM THE SOUTH COAST SHOWING THE TWO HEADLANDS THAT ARE THE LIMITS OF THE ISLAND (DRAWN: AUTHOR).

disappear behind the horizon or fade from view, knowing what peaks will take their place. The older experienced fishermen in Ḥadiboh said that they had learned to navigate out to sea using this method from their fathers, who had taught them to recognise the shape and names of each peak and in what order they appear.

On the south coast, in addition to attempting to fix a specific position using one or more landmarks the fishermen use a more generalised approach to determine their position. According to fishermen in Maḥfirihin, Stēroh, Bidhōleh and Di-Ṣeberho, when fishing offshore they are able to determine their position in relation to the shape of the silhouette of the island (Figure 47). The silhouette of the south coast comprises a number of breaks within the limestone escarpment, and it is these which the fishermen use to identify their position. They also said that the most important points to recognise are the headlands of Rās Shuᶜub and Rās Erisseyl, as if one passed these headlands one will become lost. This method of navigation is also used by the fishermen when fishing closer to the coast. Fishermen interviewed in Maḥfirihin, Stēroh, Zaḥaq and Bidhōleh told me that it is possible to recognise an area of coast according to the nature and shape of the shoreline: whether it is sand, cobbles or sheer cliff; whether there were sand dunes or palm tree plantations, which are found near specific villages; what buildings were visible, especially mosques, which are visible for some distance from the shore and occur in specific villages. The difference in this method of navigation over that used along the north coast is that the fishermen do not rely on specific landmarks to determine their position, but use their knowledge of the nature, form and shape of the island and coast. This method of using the silhouette of Socotra and relying on the appearance of the coast provides the fishermen with a surprising amount of accuracy in locating their position. However, in Bidhōleh I was told by a young and less-experienced full-time fisherman, Mohammed Hassan Eisa,[45] that he found it difficult to recognise the coast to the west and preferred to fish to the south and east of Bidhōleh, where he could recognise the landscape from the sea. The reason for this is that it had not been necessary for him to fish to the west of his village. Interestingly, he was able to identify certain features along the north coast where he had fished periodically.

In Samḥa, fishermen interviewed[46] said that the number of landmarks used to identify their position was also dependant on whether they were fishing for shark or other species. According to them, if they wanted to fish for rock fish they would need to fish in a specific fishing area and would need to use two or more landmarks. They said that the more landmarks one used the more accurate one could be, and because the fishing areas for rock fish were small, it was necessary to be very accurate. They also said that when fishing for shark further offshore it was possible to use one landmark. The reason for this is said to be that shark and other pelagic fish species are not found in very specific areas and it is only necessary to be in the vicinity of a deep area where sharks can been caught. Where only one landmark was used they said that they would know where they were by the appearance of the landmark and would adjust their position according to the shape or form it took in relation to their position. Where two landmarks were used they would normally line up on a specific landmark and follow this until the second landmark took on the correct shape. This method of using the changing shape and form of the landmark is very similar to the method used by the fishermen on the

[45] 25 years old, interviewed on 29 December 2009.
[46] The interviews conducted in Samḥa were mostly group interviews in which various topics were discussed.

south coast, albeit on a smaller scale. The method used to determine their position using two or more landmarks is much the same as that used by the fishermen on the north coast.

Determining Course to Follow

When using landmarks to determine the course to follow, the fishermen of Socotra mostly use headlands. Fishermen interviewed in Qalansiyah, Qādheb and Ḥadiboh said that they could identify several headlands along the north coast by their shape, and would use these to travel either eastward towards Erisseyl or westwards toward Samḥa. This method used to determine direction to travel is similar to the way in which the fishermen on the south coast identify their position at sea. Along the north coast the fishermen in Qalansiyah told me that when they travel westwards toward Samḥa, or the south coast, they keep the island to their left and look out for the headlands of Rās Bidoh and Rās Shuᶜub. They also said that after they pass Rās Shuᶜub it is possible to see the island of Samḥa in the distance and, if they wanted to travel to Samḥa, it was only necessary to keep the island in sight. However, if they were travelling to the south coast, they turn southeast at Rās Shuᶜub and keep heading out to sea until they can see Rās Qaṭanan. Fishermen along both the south and north coast of Socotra use this method of headland hopping when travelling along the coast, although on the south coast they use this in conjunction with the shape of the silhouette of the island. Travelling around Socotra using this method is not without its dangers, and in Qalansiyah and Ḥadiboh the fishermen told me that during certain periods they would not attempt to pass certain headlands. Fishermen on the north coast consider the most dangerous headlands to be Rās Shuᶜub and Rās Erisseyl. The reason for this is due to the strength of the current and wind in these areas, which can sweep one out to sea, or cause high waves to form and swamp vessels. They also said that the most dangerous period for passing these headlands are when the winds *ṣe̍rbihi* (Soc) or *e̍ᵓeris* (Soc) are blowing strongly. Consequently, fishermen from Ḥadiboh prefer to travel when these winds are not blowing strongly, or will travel westwards around the island, as Rās Shuᶜub is considered to be safer to pass than Rās Erisseyl.

Natural Navigational Aids

In addition to using landmarks to determine position and course to follow, the fishermen also use a number of other natural navigational aids, which are based upon their experience with the environment.

The first of these naturally occurring phenomena used in navigation are currents. Familiarity with the direction and strength of currents is important for knowing when it is safe to venture offshore, and whether it is possible to fish. However, the direction of the current is also used by fishermen along the north coast to navigate. According to fishermen in Qalansiyah, knowing the direction of the current helps if landmarks become obscured by cloud, or one is fishing out of sight of land, especially along the south coast where it is difficult to see the limestone escarpment. They said that if one were heading out to sea it is necessary to look at the direction of the current in relation to the land, because if one lost sight of land it would remind one as to the direction one needed to travel. The simplicity of this belies the actual skill which is required to take an accurate reading of the current direction, especially when using an outboard engine. Experienced older fishermen in Ḥadiboh said that knowing the direction and strength of the current was most important in the past when one was only using a paddle, as it is impossible to paddle against a strong current. They said that knowing the direction of the current allows them to plan where and when they will be able to fish and which landfall they will need to head towards. In villages along the south coast the fishermen I interviewed said that they do not use current direction to help them navigate. This is most likely due to a lack of knowledge, as on the north coast it was only the older fishermen with many years of experience who use the current direction as an aid to navigation. Notwithstanding the importance of currents, the fishermen do not rely solely on current direction to navigate.

The second natural navigational aid used by fishermen is swell direction. Several elderly fishermen I interviewed in Ḥadiboh,[47] Maḥfirihin,[48] and Stēroh[49] said that they use the direction of the swell to help them find land. According to them, it was possible to learn in which direction to find land by looking at the character and direction of the swell. The principal is based upon understanding the direction of the swell and knowing whether the swell in certain areas is closer or further apart. The fishermen said that to learn the characteristics of the swell and know how to determine ones direction based on them takes many years of experience, although it is rarely used anymore. The main reason for this is, according to those interviewed, that 'new' and younger fishermen do not want to learn about this and rely instead on landmarks.

Thirdly is the depth and colour of the sea, which is used by the fishermen to help them determine their distance out to sea. In Ḥadiboh it is also used in combination with landmarks to mark the extent of fishing areas. In

[47] Jamen Mahafawl Saif, full-time fisherman, 70 years old; Khames Abdulah Salem, full-time fisherman, 75 years old, both interviewed on 22 December 2009.

[48] Muhammad Abdulla Muhammad Dimori, full-time fisherman, 80 years old; Mohammed Ahmed, full-time fisherman, 55 years old, both interviewed on 11 February 2009.

[49] Said Salim Ahmed, full-time fisherman, in his 60s; Mounir Eissa Saleem, in his 60s; Said Saaed, full-time fisherman, in his 30s, all interviewed on 11 February 2009.

Qalansiyah several fishermen[50] said that colour is used as an additional marker for locating a specific fishing area. This is similar to what fishermen along the south coast told me. According to these fishermen, this is especially important when attempting to find a shallow water fishing area using only one landmark, as it is only the colour of the water which indicates whether one is over a favoured area. They also said that the colour of the water can also indicate to one where one is in relation to the coast, as in some areas where the wādīs flow into the sea the water changes colour.

The wind, much like the current, also plays a significant role in the lives of the fishermen, and is one of the main factors influencing when and where it is possible to fish. The fishermen recognise four main winds that are known according to the direction from which they blow. Their direction not only indicates to the fishermen what weather they are likely to expect, but also helps them determine what direction to travel. According to two elderly fishermen in Ḥadiboh,[51] when heading out to fish they keep the wind on one side of their boat and, even if they lose sight of land, they only need to ensure the wind remains on the correct side of their boat to know in which direction to find land. In Qalansiyah, fishermen said that this method was especially useful if clouds were obscuring their landmarks. However, on the south coast, Jamen Khamis Saeed Marjan Saeed[52] told me that, although his father had used this method, he did not consider it reliable as the wind direction could change during the day and it is possible to get lost if one relied on the wind. This is perhaps one of the main reasons why the fishermen interviewed said that they do not solely rely on any one natural phenomenon by which to navigate.

Celestial Navigation

According to Serjeant (1992: 172-172), in 1967 the fishermen of Qalansiyah used a 28 star calendar to differentiate between the seasons. That the fishermen were using a star calendar implies that they were able to recognise these constellations in the night sky. Consequently, I sought to discover whether the modern-day fishermen used the stars to navigate.

During interviews conducted with fishermen along Socotra's north and south coast and the island of Samḥa I found that the fishermen did not have a very good knowledge of the star calendar recorded by Serjeant, often confusing the names of the stars that appear during the seasons of *ḳeyaṭ* (Soc) and *ḥorf* (Soc). Furthermore, the use of stars to navigate was virtually unheard of, and those who fished overnight said that they would remain at sea and only come to shore during the day when they could either see the land, or the sun had risen above the horizon.

Notwithstanding this I was able to find several fishermen, who could remember how to use stars to navigate. According to Omar Abdulla Saleh,[53] in Qādheb there are two stars, *ligeʾ* (Soc), and *riḳīb* (Soc), (neither of which I have been able to identify), which he used to guide him out to sea. He also said that once one had followed these stars out it was necessary to wait at sea until sunrise to look for the land, or use the sun, to find one's way back. In Qaṭanan, Ali Jamen[54] said that he also used stars to navigate but did not know their names, and drew an image of the stars he used instead. According to the image he drew I was able to determine that he was using the constellation of Orion. He said that when he is out at sea he waits until this constellation is high in the night sky before attempting to use it. Once the constellation had reached a certain point in the night sky he would then use it to find his village by keeping the two brightest end stars, identified by me as being Rigel/β Orionis and Betelgeuse/α Orionis, to the right and left respectively (Figure 48). In Zaḥaq, Jamen Khamis[55] said that his father had taught him to use three groups of stars for navigating to his village. Using his description I have identified the groups as Pegasus, Gemini and Taurus. According to him, when out at sea he would have to wait until all three constellations came into view; once all the constellations were visible he would keep Pegasus to his right and Gemini to his left. This would place Taurus above the village and give him a course to follow. According to these fishermen, navigating using the stars is no longer practiced as few people can remember how and almost everyone waits until the sun rises. The reason for this loss of knowledge is said to be due to an upsurge in 'new' fishermen, who do not want to learn these traditions and rely instead on landmarks.

The rising of the sun provides the fishermen with another means of determining direction to travel and in villages along the north and south coast the sun is one of the main methods used to navigate. Fishermen interviewed in Ḥadiboh, Qalansiyah, Di-Ḥamari and Ṣaqarah told me that when heading out to sea in the morning it is necessary to keep the sun on one's right cheek and when returning to keep it on one's left. Conversely, on the south coast the fishermen from Maḥfirihin, Zaḥaq, Stēroh and Qaṭanan said that one needs to keep the sun on one's left cheek

[50] Ali Salim Da-Salmoho, full-time fisherman, in his 60s; Jaman Saeed Abdullah, full-time fisherman, in his 30s, both interviewed on 16 February 2009; Abaid Salem bin Awailan, full-time fisherman, in his 50s; Saeed Selem Ali, full-time fisherman, 35 years old, both interviewed on 17 December 2009.

[51] Jamen Mahafawl Saif, full-time fisherman, 70 years old; Khames Abdulah Salem, full-time fisherman, 75 years old, both interviewed on 22 December 2009.

[52] Jamen Khamis Saeed Marjan Saeed, full-time fisherman, in his 60s, 12 February 2009.

[53] Omar Abdulla Saleh, full-time fishermen, in his 60s, interviewed on 2 February 2009.

[54] Ali Jamen, full-time fisherman, in his 40s, interviewed on 28 December 2009.

[55] Jamen Khamis Saeed Marjan Saeed, full-time fisherman, in his 60s, interviewed on 12 February 2009.

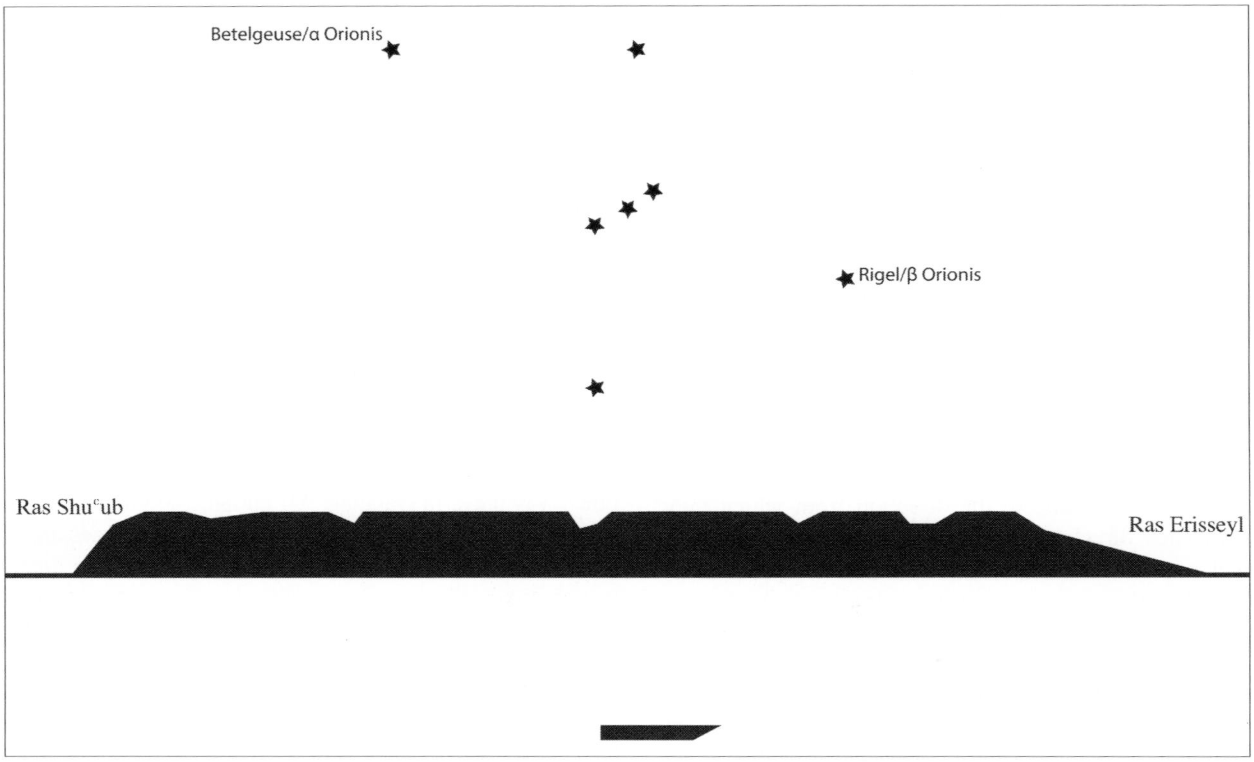

FIGURE 48. THE SILHOUETTE OF THE SOUTH COAST AND THE STARS USED TO DETERMINE THE DIRECTION TO LAND (DRAWN: AUTHOR).

going out to sea and on one's right coming home. They also said that the best time to use the sun was during the early morning when the sun was lower on the horizon and that it was the most reliable means of locating the island if one could not see land. This method is the second most common method, after landmarks, used by fishermen from all the villages I visited, and even the younger fishermen use it.

Throughout interviews concerning the way in which the fishermen navigate I was always initially told that one 'just knew' how to find a fishing area or determine the course to follow. It was not until I spent some time discussing what it was that one 'just knew' that I was able to find out about the navigational guides and directional indicators mentioned above. This, together with the secrecy surrounding favourite fishing areas, is perhaps the reason why many authors who have sought to understand how the fishermen navigate to favourite fishing areas have been so unsuccessful in getting past the phrase, 'you just know'. The way in which I have managed to get beyond this phrase has been due to my knowledge of navigation and use of participant observation. Having the opportunity to accompany the fishermen and discuss issues of navigation at sea allowed them to show and explain to me how they navigate using landmarks and various natural phenomena. During this time I was also told on successive occasions that to find your way to a fishing area, or back to the island, you needed to trust in three things, one's 'head'; one's 'heart', and God. The 'head' refers to the knowledge one has, while 'heart' refers to believing in your knowledge, in other words, to be able to navigate one must not only have knowledge, but one must believe in ones knowledge to make the right decision and God will provide.

Looking at studies of the navigational knowledge of fishermen along the South Arabian coastline and Red Sea it appears that, while the authors recognise that the fishermen were using various natural phenomena to navigate by, they were not able to describe how they were being used. According to Camelin (2006: 44-47), the fishermen in al-Shihr, Yemen, use landmarks, depth and colour of the sea, the movement of the currents, tides, birds and celestial bodies to navigate. However, other than saying the fishermen use them, she provides little information on how they did so. This is very much the same as a study in Suakin, Sudan, where Kentley (1988: 183) observes that the fishermen use the colour and depth of the sea to find favoured fishing areas, but instead of describing the method says that the fishermen 'just know' where to find specific areas.

Finally, when talking to fishermen about navigation they often referred to the dangers of being lost, especially if they were dragged out of sight of land by the wind or currents. Using the heights of the various landmarks within a formula based upon the distance to the horizon[56] I have attempted to determine the distance from which the fishermen are able to see the peaks of the Ḥagher and the outlying islands. This makes it possible to work out how far offshore they would have to be to lose sight of land. What I found was that fishermen would have to travel approximately 61Nm out to sea before they will lose sight of the highest peaks of the Ḥagher. The outlying islands and rocky outcrops further extend this visual range on the north and western side of the archipelago to approximately 73Nm out to sea. The visual range from which the various landmarks can be seen is based upon very conservative estimates that do not take into consideration various other navigational phenomena, which could further extend the visual range. Nevertheless, it is clear that fishermen would have to travel a significant distance from the shore before losing sight of land, and that the limit of *ḳeneʿiti* and the start of *al-baḥr* (Ar), would be in the region of 61Nm from land.

Conclusion

This chapter has demonstrated the diverse nature of Socotra's maritime landscape and shown how the island can be sub-divided according to the scale at which it is analysed.

The first broad-scale level of analysis in this chapter outlined the four major land and sea features which make up the maritime landscape, namely: the mountainous interior; the surrounding limestone escarpments; the coastal plains and coastline; and the submarine landscape. At this level of analysis the differences between the north and south coast of Socotra are immediately apparent. The north coast is made up of a series of well-watered verdant coastal plains, divided by limestone escarpments and headlands, and overshadowed by a mountainous interior. The south coast is made up of a long arid coastal plain that is backed by a limestone escarpment, and bordered at the eastern and western extent by sheer limestone cliffs which fall directly into the sea.

The second level of analysis looked at the fishing villages, which demonstrated the similarities and differences between areas along the north and south coast of Socotra. The importance of this is that it demonstrates the geographical variety of the terrestrial and marine landscape of fishing villages lying along the same coastal plain, and displays the differences that can be found within these villages along the same side of the island. Consequently, when comparing the village of Qalansiyah, in the northwest, with that of Ḥadiboh, in the central north, it is apparent that even though they lie on the same coastline, they are distinctly different in terms of their terrestrial and marine landscape.

Using these two levels of analysis it makes it possible to examine how the maritime landscape has affected the way in which the fishermen interact with it. Firstly, this is looked at in terms of the way in which the fishermen identify and name their fishing areas. The most apparent influence is how visual landmarks are almost directly related to the quantity of fishing areas. Evidence of this is seen in the lack of named fishing areas off the south coast, which has few distinctive landmarks and the plethora of fishing areas off the north coast, which has numerous landmarks. This correlation between the landscape and the number of fishing areas is certainly important, yet it also needs to be placed within the context of the influence of the landscape on settlement patterns. Settlement of Socotra is directly related to the availability of water and that the wetter north coast has both a longer period of settlement and is much more heavily populated. The fishermen of the north coast are also more experienced and knowledgeable, which coupled with the number of fishermen and the availability of landmarks is another reason for the high number of fishing areas off the north coast. Furthermore, the number of deep and shallow water fishing areas can also be directly related to the submarine landscape, which can differ substantially between villages with very similar topographies. This highlights the correlation between the physical landscape and the way in which it is used, understood and experienced. This is especially important when looking at how the fishermen use the maritime landscape to navigate.

The navigational methods and techniques used by the fishermen allows the cognitive aspects of the maritime landscape to be explored, as the importance attached to the landscape features is based upon the experience and knowledge of the fishermen. This is apparent when looking at the use of landmarks. Fishermen on Socotra's north and south coast and the island of Samḥa use a varying number of landmarks based not upon the availability of the landmarks, but on their knowledge and experience. This is especially relevant on the north coast where they have a number of highly visible landmarks available to them, yet many fishermen only use one. Furthermore, they also divide the maritime landscape into the way they use and experience it. This is seen in the way in which different elements of the sea are used in navigation. Finally, the incorporation of the wind, sun and to a lesser degree the stars within the maritime landscape demonstrates how it actually embodies many different aspects based upon the way in which the fishermen perceive their landscape. This is also reflected in the naming of fishing areas, many of which are named after significant landmarks in the vicinity that are also

[56] Square Root (height above surface / 6.752) = distance to horizon.

used to find them. Using the names of significant features not only helps the fishermen know which landmarks to use in order to navigate to their fishing areas, but also allows for a degree of vagueness. This vagueness is not accidental as, even though the name and landmark used may be known to many fishermen, without first-hand knowledge of the actual location of the specific fishing area it would be impossible to find. Therefore, it allows the fishermen to share their knowledge of the landmarks, yet still keep their fishing areas secret.

Having determined how the maritime landscape is used by the fishermen of Socotra to identify and navigate to their fishing areas it is now necessary to look the weather and determine what effect this has on the fishermen.

Chapter 8

The Climate

The maritime landscape does not just embody the physical aspects of land and sea, but also the climate and the way in which it is understood, engaged and experienced (Westerdahl 1992; Hunter 1994; Parker 2001; Cooney 2003; Bender 2006). Therefore, when studying the climatic conditions on Socotra it is not only important to understand how they affect fishing activities, but also how fishermen perceive and interact with them. Weather has played an important role in the lives of mariners and fishermen of the Indian Ocean for thousands of years, influencing almost all aspects of their working lives. The seasonal nature of the monsoon provides a long term rhythmic structure to the fishermen and sailors in all parts of the Indian Ocean, whilst local meteorological phenomena influence their activities in specific locales. This situation is particularly true for Socotra, whose geographical position and topography play an important role in determining the weather conditions experienced by the fishermen. This chapter explores the influence of the weather on the fishermen of Socotra by looking at how monsoon and local winds are formed, what affect they have, and how they are interpreted, using both meteorological and ethnographic information. It also analyses the formation and influence of the various currents flowing past Socotra and looks at their influence. This corpus of knowledge concerning the weather is referred to throughout the rest of this study to demonstrate the role weather and currents have on all aspects of the fisherman's life.

The Monsoon winds and their influence on Socotra

Socotra is influenced by several large-scale weather phenomena, which include the seasonally reversing monsoon winds and ocean-atmospheric interactions such as the Indian Ocean Dipole and the El Niño-Southern Oscillation (Saji *et al.* 1999; Prasad and McClean 2004; Neff *et al.* 2001). These phenomena all affect Socotra's climate, although it is the winds of the monsoon which have the greatest influence. The Indian Ocean monsoon is a seasonal wind which blows alternately from one side of the Indian Ocean to the other in a north easterly (NE) and south westerly (SW) direction. The yearly cycle of these winds has its greatest effect on those people whose lives are intimately connected to the sea, and dictates both the timing and duration of their fishing and sailing activities.

The formation of the monsoon winds over the Indian Ocean is the result of the interaction between major air masses over Asia and the Indian Ocean, the shift in latitude of the Inter-Tropical Convergence Zone (ITCZ) and the annual monsoon cycle (Fleitmann *et al.* 2004: 28-30). During the winter months (September to early March), the NE monsoon winds are generated by a pressure differentiation arising between the low pressure ITCZ, which is situated south of the equator, and a cell of high pressure, which is situated over the Eurasian continent. In spring, as the Eurasian continent begins to warm and the ITCZ starts to move northward, the pressure gradient reverses and the SW monsoon winds begin to blow across the Indian Ocean (Figure 49). During the summer months (June to August), as the ITCZ reaches its northern most point the south westerly winds reach the peak of their intensity, after which the ITCZ begins to move southward and the strength of the monsoon winds start to diminish.

The seasonal change of the winds outlined above belies the variability that can be experienced in different areas of the Indian Ocean. According to Hasse and Brown (2001: 226); Cornish and Ives (2006: 69, 71), and Frampton and Uttridge (2008: 48), the direction, timing and strength of the monsoon winds are affected by a number of meteorological and topographical phenomena, such as strong local winds and mountainous landscapes. As a result of these phenomena there are areas, such as Socotra, in which the effects of the monsoon winds are either nullified or contrary. These phenomena also affect the transition between the monsoon seasons resulting in either an abrupt change in wind direction occurring over the course of a few days, or a gradual change occurring over a period of several weeks. Furthermore, during the height of the monsoon they can also cause the winds in certain areas to undergo breaks or lulls (Schott and McCreary 2001: 6). An account by Commander Haines, a British officer who spent several years surveying the Southern Arabian coastline in the 19th century, demonstrates this variability:

> 'I would observe that the experience of several years along this coast has taught me not to place implicit confidence on the regularity of the seasons, as I have frequently during the same month, in different years, experienced exactly opposite winds' (Haines 1845:149).

Contrary to many authors, (Bowen 1951: 162; Villiers 1952: 6; McGrail 2002: 83; Agius 2005: 191) the monsoon seasons are divided into four and not two. The most important and well known are those named after the

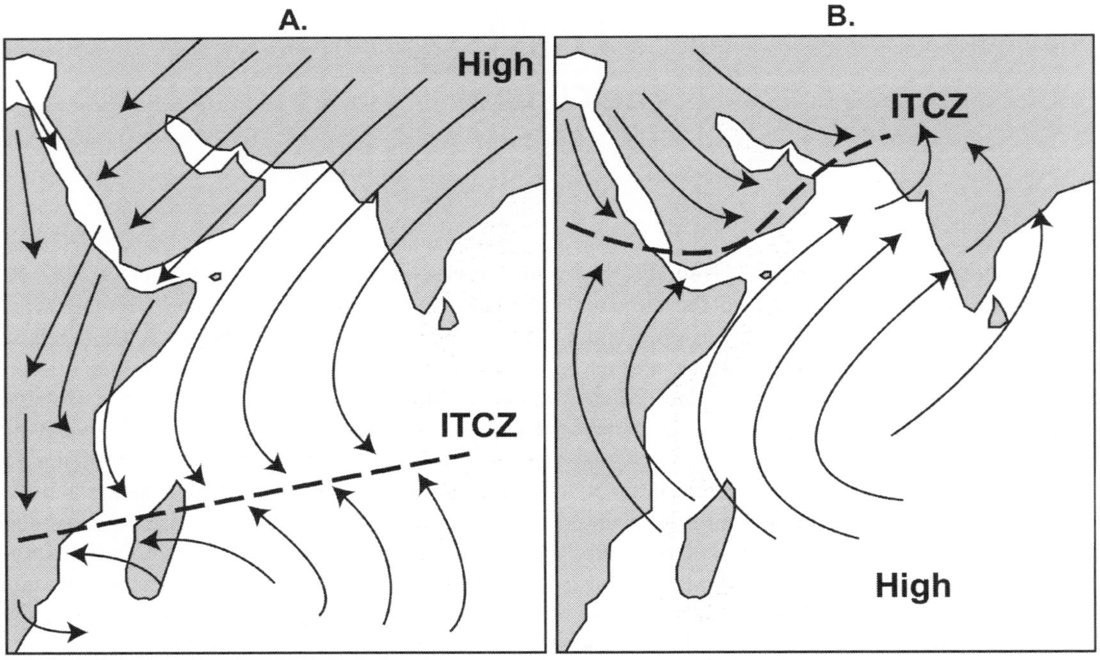

FIGURE 49. THE DIRECTIONAL FLOW OF THE MONSOON WINDS ACROSS THE INDIAN OCEAN DURING THE NE MONSOON, A AND THE SW MONSOON, B (DRAWN: AUTHOR).

predominate winds that occur during this time, namely: the south westerly and north easterly monsoon. The lesser known and often forgotten are those that fall between these two, called the inter-monsoon seasons. The north easterly monsoon occurs during the winter months, and from approximately early September they begin to blow from the Eurasian continent, passing across India and the Arabian Sea in the direction of East Africa. The winds generally begin to wane in early March, as the first inter-monsoon season begins. The weather of the NE monsoon season is generally fine with small amounts of cloud and little or no rainfall (Frampton and Uttridge 2008: 85). During the summer months, from approximately early June, the SW monsoon winds begin to blow from an area of sea off the East African coast, passing up along the African coast before traversing the Arabian Sea, in the direction of India. The SW monsoon winds generally begin to wane from early August, heralding the beginning of the second inter-monsoon season. The weather of the SW monsoon is generally cloudy and unsettled with high winds and considerable rainfall (Weller *et al.* 1998: 1961). The inter-monsoon seasons, much as their name suggests, occur between the two predominate monsoon periods, which do not abruptly shift from a north easterly to south westerly direction. Instead, there is a lull, or transitional period before the NE and SW winds begin to blow with any significant force. These periods can differ from area to area, but for the Western Indian Ocean they generally occur between March and early May, before the SW monsoon winds, and between August and early September, before the NE monsoon winds. The weather for both seasons is characterised by variable and light-to-calm winds that are eventually replaced by either the SW or NE monsoon winds (Weller *et al.* 1998: 1968). This transition does not suddenly change at a specific date, and it is not unknown for the SW or NE winds to undergo a series of 'false starts' over the course of several weeks, before they begin to blow constantly in a NE or SW direction.

Due to Socotra's unique geographical position and mountainous landscape the island is affected by the monsoon winds in a number of different ways. Firstly, the monsoon winds bring two rainy seasons to the island. The first rains occur between August and October, during the SW monsoon, and the second between April and May, during the NE monsoon. The rains of the SW monsoon tend to fall at higher elevations, particularly in mountainous south west facing areas where clouds form (Culek *et al.* 2006: 43). The rains of the NE monsoon tend to be the heaviest, as these winds blow over a large expanse of water, collecting moisture before they reach the island (Mies and Behyl 1996: 40). These two periods of rain, coupled with the mountainous topography of the island, mean that Socotra has a wetter climate and better supply of water than the low-lying neighbouring areas of Arabia and Africa. However, due to the mountainous topography of Socotra, a great deal of this rainfall occurs mainly along the northern and eastern side of the island, resulting in these being wetter than the southern and western sides (Scholte and De Geest 2010: 1507). The resulting availability of water along the northern and eastern half of the island has a direct effect on the population, and the wetter northern half has always been more densely inhabited than the more arid south. Furthermore, fishermen told me that one of their main concerns is the availability of water that, especially along the south coast, severely limits where they can settle.

The availability of water on Socotra's northern coast has been well known since at least the 1st century AD. According to the *Periplus Maris Erythraei*, (mid-1st century AD), the northern side of Socotra has two rivers ending in bays where vessels can find anchorage and water (Casson 1989: 167). The availability of water is also mentioned by Ibn al-Mujāwir (d. AD 1291), who describes the north coast of the island as an oasis that has rivers of sweet fresh water that flow from the mountains into the sea (Ibn al-Mujāwir 2008: 263). This is very similar to what can still be seen along the north coast today, which has several large lagoons, although it is only during heavy rains that the non-perennial streams flow. By the 16th and 17th centuries the availability of water on the north coast had become well known, and Socotra was frequently visited by Portuguese, English and Dutch ships seeking supplies (Kerr 1811-1894; Hawkins 1878; Purchas 1905-1907; Foster 1906-1927; Barbosa 1967: 59-63). The importance of the availability of water on Socotra is reflected in the accounts of the Portuguese who, even after they abandoned their efforts at subjugation, still called at the island to obtain supplies of water (Beckingham 1983: 177).

Secondly, due to the combination of meteorological phenomena mentioned above, the seas around Socotra are affected by strong winds and severe storms during both the SW and NE monsoon (Mies and Behyl 1996: 40; Rayner 2004: 95). A meteorological study undertaken by Jameson (1949: 113) into the storminess of the seas in the vicinity of Socotra found that it lies within an area of the Arabian Sea where winds are likely to reach over gale force for extended periods. During the NE monsoon, this area experiences winds in excess of force 7 (Beaufort Scale) for over 20% of the time, falling to 8% during the inter-monsoon period. This is in contrast to the Gulf of Aden and along the coast of Oman which, during these periods, experiences winds in excess of force 6 for less than 10% of the time (Vora and Grattan-Cooper 2007: 32). During the SW monsoon, the winds off Socotra reach in excess of force 7 for 40% of the time in June to around 85% of the time in July and August (Jameson 1949: 67-120; Vora and Grattan-Cooper 2007: 32). This is in contrast to the Gulf of Aden and coast of Oman which, during the SW monsoon, experiences winds in excess of force 7 for just 30% of the time.

The storminess of the seas in the vicinity of Socotra is attested to by many travellers, sailors and fishermen, in the past and today. The most detailed historical account is that of the navigator Ibn Mājid (fl. AD 1500). In his *Kitāb al-Fawā'id fī uṣūl al-baḥr wa'l-qawā'id'* (The Book of Benefits in the Principals of Navigation), he mentions the dangers of high winds and severe sea-state when sailing in the vicinity of Socotra, especially during the SW monsoon (Tibbetts 1981: 229-230). The dangers of these high winds and rough sea state are also referred to by numerous Portuguese and English captains during the 16th and 17th centuries, when the Portuguese and English ships travelled pass the island (Foster 1967: 30-39; Longworth Dames 1967: 59-63; Foster 1905: xxvii). In the 18th century the Franciscan missionary Václav Prutky (d. 1769) provides a vivid account of his experience of the SW monsoon winds off Socotra. According to him, when sailing past Socotra in August 1751, the seas were so terrible and frightening in the vicinity of the island that few vessels pass close to it (Arrowsmith-Brown 1991: 389). That the seas were so violent is unsurprising considering that Prutky was sailing past Socotra during the height of the SW monsoon, a feat which the sailors and fishermen I have spoken to would never contemplate.

This storminess also affects Socotra's coastline directly, by effectively cutting the island off to sea traffic for approximately four months of the year. This is a result of the strong winds and heavy surf that make the anchorages and landing conditions extremely hazardous, if not impossible. According to an early Admiralty pilot guide to the Indian Ocean, both the NE and SW monsoons are dangerous for shipping on the north coast of Socotra (Horsburgh 1841: 291). It says that during the NE monsoon the prevailing winds can blow in violent gusts, during which time it is almost impossible for ships to find anchorage. During the SW monsoon, the winds are purportedly violent and blow incessantly, making it extremely hazardous for shipping to approach or anchor. This is echoed by the modern Admiralty pilot guide, which also advises shipping to give the north eastern coast of Socotra a wide berth during the SW monsoon, as the winds and currents can drag one onto outlying reefs (Vora and Grattan-Cooper 2007: 383). On the south coast, the winds of the NE and SW monsoon are steadier and less violent, although the large swell and breaking surf still make it almost impossible to land or launch any vessels (Morris 2002: 20). According to the Admiralty guides, the safest period for shipping is during the inter-monsoon seasons, when the winds become calmer and it is possible to find safe anchorages (Horsburgh 1841: 292; Findlay 1897: 673; Vora and Grattan-Cooper 2007: 383). These guides also state that the first inter-monsoon period, between March and early May, is the season of fine weather and is the safest time to visit the island, whereas the second inter-monsoon period, between August and early September, can be difficult for smaller sailing vessels due to the strong sea and land breezes (Findlay 1897: 673). This was corroborated by my conversations with the Socotri fishermen, who referred to the difficulties of fishing during this period.

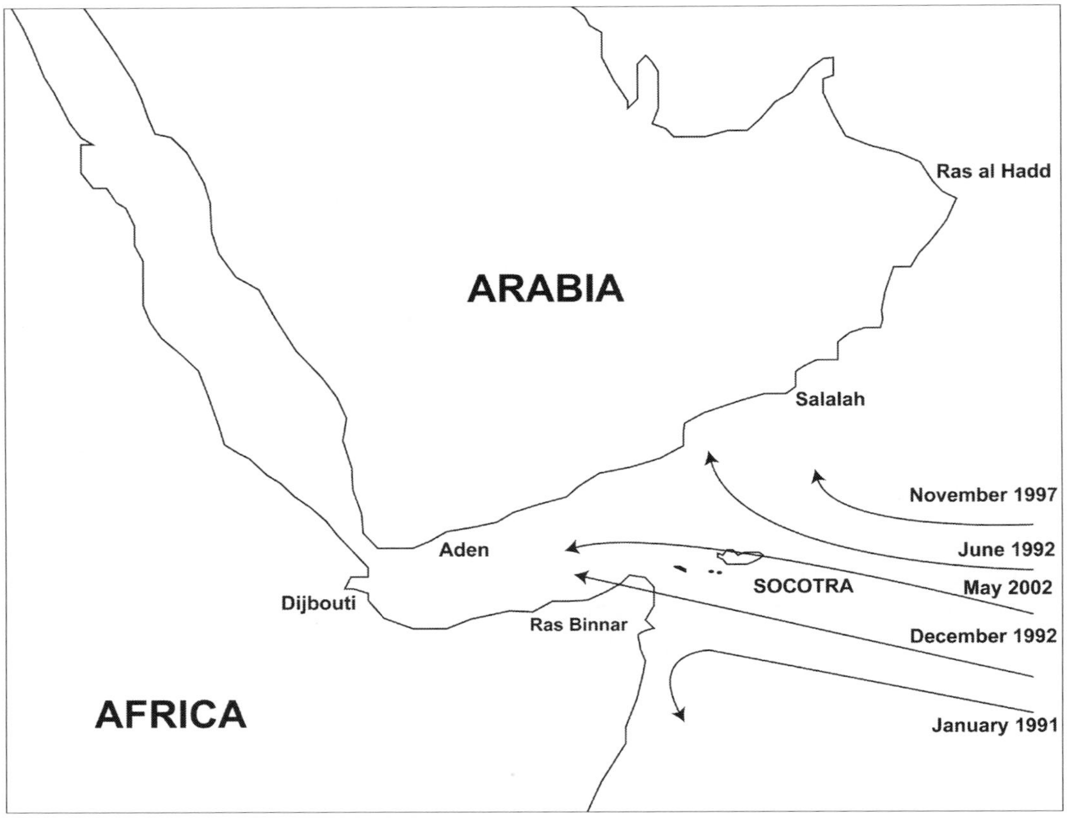

FIGURE 50. TROPICAL CYCLONE TRACKS IN THE VICINITY OF THE SOCOTRA ARCHIPELAGO (DRAWN: AUTHOR).

Historically, there are numerous accounts of the seasons in which it is possible to approach the ports of Socotra's north coast, and the difficulties faced by shipping attempting to anchor outside these periods. The first account by Ibn Mājid observed that the best season for shipping to access the ports of the island was the NE monsoon. According to him, during the SW monsoon the ports of the north coast are all closed, because of the high winds and large swell (Ibn Mājid 1981: 230). This is contrary to Horsburgh's account, but is actually a true reflection of the NE monsoon which is, according to fishermen and sailors I spoke to, actually safe. The reason for this is that the NE monsoon winds can be sporadic, rather than incessant like the SW monsoon winds, and during periods of calm it is possible to anchor, even large vessels, off the north and south coasts. This is corroborated by Portuguese, Dutch, and English accounts, which state that shipping that had missed the yearly monsoon wind for sailing to India would spend part of the NE monsoon anchored off the island (Kerr 1811-1894; Da Costa 1973). Anchoring off either coast during the NE monsoon may be possible, but it is not without its dangers. A description of Afonso Dalboquerque's brief stay on the north coast recounts how several ships of his squadron were almost lost when they were hit by violent gusts of the NE monsoon (Commentaries 1875, 1: 56).

Tropical Cyclones

The seas in the vicinity of Socotra are also subject to tropical cyclones during the NE monsoon, which are formed at sea through the combination of high sea temperatures and a low atmospheric pressure. Tropical cyclones are characterised by torrential rain and hurricane force winds that combine to create a high sea state and limited visibility (Cornish and Ives 2006: 115). The seas around Socotra are particularly prone to this phenomenon, with an average of five to six occurring a year (Rajeevan and Butala 1990: 410; Vora and Grattan-Cooper 2007: 27). They generally occur during the NE monsoon, but have also been recorded during the months of May and June (Abdulla 1996: 18; Rayner 2006: 24). Tropical cyclones, once formed, tend to track westerly from the Arabian Sea towards the Arabian coast, with many passing the Socotra archipelago (Figure 50).

The dangers of tropical cyclones are attested to in many accounts of sailing in the Indian Ocean, and according to the ship's captain Buzurg ibn Shahriyār al-Rāmhurmuzī (d. AD 1009), it was necessary to take drastic measures to survive an encounter with them (Al-Rāmhurmuzī 1981: 91). Ibn Mājid also mentions the dangers associated with encountering a tropical cyclone, and says that they

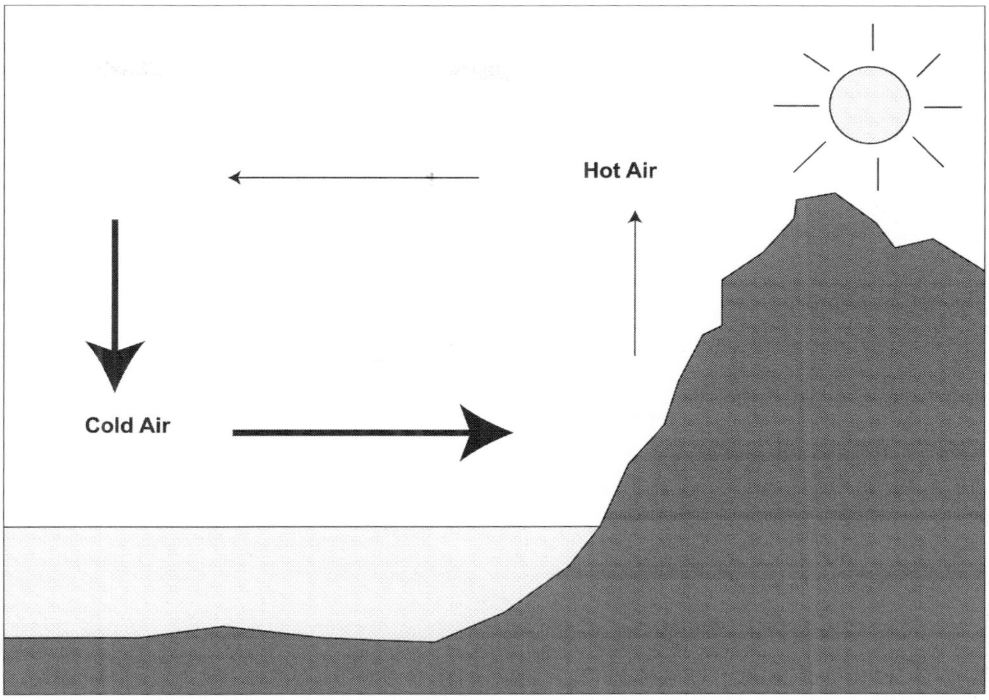

FIGURE 51. THE FORMATION OF A SEA BREEZE, ILLUSTRATING THE MOVEMENT OF THE WINDS (DRAWN: AUTHOR).

occur in the straits between Cape Guardafui and Socotra, particularly when the SW monsoon winds subside. (Ibn Mājid 1981: 196; 238).

Local winds and their influence on Socotra

The local winds of Socotra naturally play an important role in the lives of the people living on the coast and have a significant impact on their fishing. Local winds can, in certain circumstances, completely alter the effects of the prevailing monsoon winds, creating areas within which the high winds of the monsoon are cancelled out or are contrary. The local winds that affect the fishermen on Socotra are the result of a complex interplay between the temperature gradient between the land and sea at certain times of the day, and the nature of the island's coastal landscape, which is a varied mixture of steep, cliff-lined coasts, open beaches and protected bays backed by dry and barren or wet and verdant coastal plains.

The first of these winds is known as a sea breeze, as the resultant wind blows from the sea to the land. A sea breeze is formed as the air over the land is heated. This causes the air over the land to rise, creating a pressure imbalance, which results in cold air from the sea being drawn in to replace the hot air rising off the land (Figure 51). Sea breezes usually occur during the afternoon when the land has heated sufficiently to cause the air to rise. Generally, by mid-afternoon a sea breeze reaches its maximum strength, and wind speeds of force 4-6 can be encountered (Tibbs 2008: 64). According to the fishermen I spoke to, the strength of these winds can prevent fishing, especially during the hotter summer months when the differences in the temperature gradient, and consequently wind strength, are at their most extreme.

The second local wind affecting fishermen on Socotra is the land breeze, whose formation is based upon the fact that the land cools faster than the sea. Consequently, the air above the sea remains warmer than that over the land at night, causing a pressure imbalance, which results in the cold air from the land being drawn in to replace the hot air rising off the sea (Figure 52). A land breeze generally occurs during the evening, when the land has cooled sufficiently to create a pressure imbalance, and usually fades shortly after sunrise. The average wind speeds generated by a land breeze tend to be between force 3-4 (Hasse and Brown 2001: 226). These winds only affect those fishing offshore at night and can blow them further out to sea or make anchorages uncomfortable.

Land and sea breezes are further affected by topography and vegetation cover, with drier barren areas generating higher wind speeds than those having vegetation, and mountainous coasts causing winds to blow further offshore or change direction (Miao *et al*. 2003: 169). The main influences occur along Socotra's north coast that has a greater expanse of cliff lined coast than the south, which results in land breezes extending further out to sea than those blowing off the south. These cliff-lined shores also affect land and sea breezes by deflecting them,

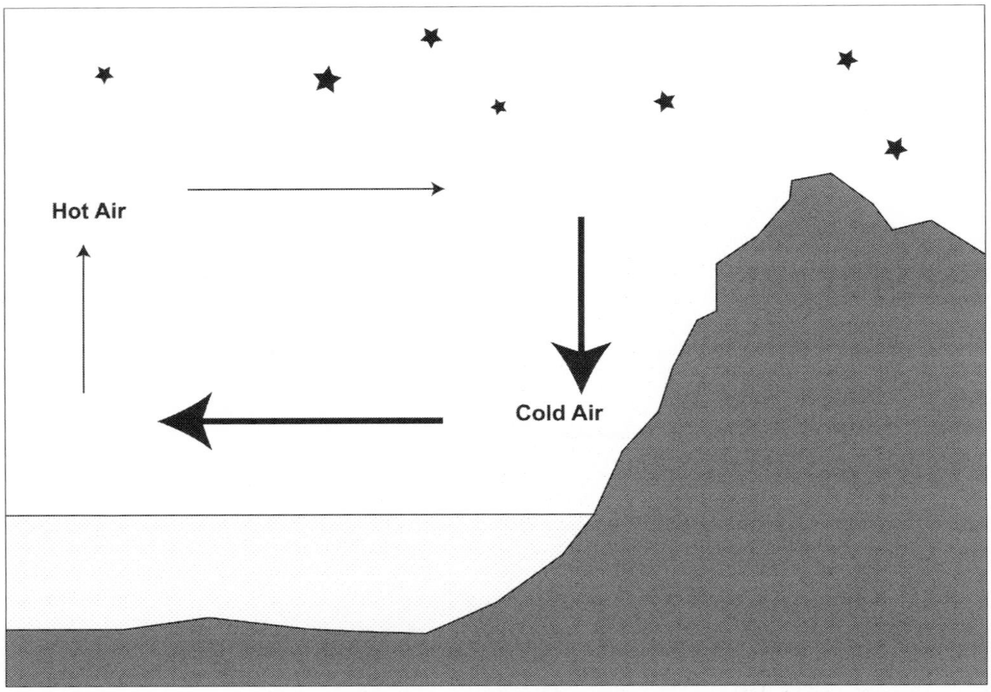

FIGURE 52. THE FORMATION OF A LAND BREEZE, ILLUSTRATING THE MOVEMENT OF THE WINDS (DRAWN: AUTHOR).

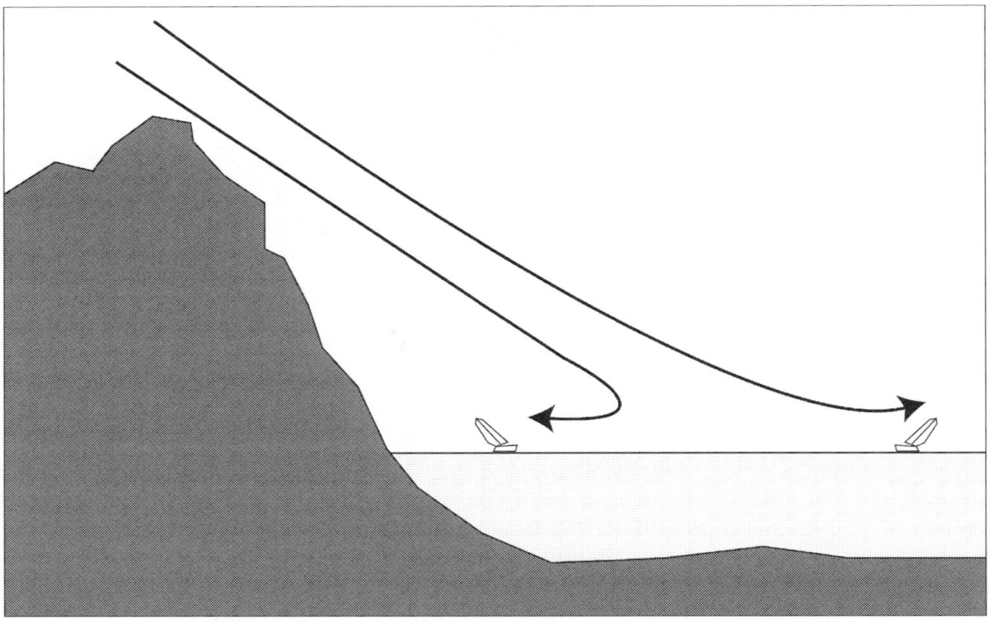

FIGURE 53. THE EFFECTS OF A LAND BREEZE COMING OFF HIGH GROUND. NOTE THE CONTRARY WIND CLOSE TO THE COAST (DRAWN: AUTHOR).

resulting in areas of calm or contrary winds. The effect of a cliff-lined shore on a land breeze is demonstrated in Figure 53. The wind generated by a land breeze coming off a steep cliff-lined coast has two components. The first is the wind close to the foot of the cliff which tends to be strong and gusty, blowing ships toward the shore, and the second is the wind further out, which is persistent and strong, blowing ships away from shore.

The cliff-lined shores of the north coast have the opposite effect on a sea breeze, and those closest to the shore deflect off the land, forming a disturbed, contrary wind close to the cliffs. This contrary wind can blow ships away from the shore, as seen in Figure 54.

Historical evidence for the effect local winds had on shipping can be found in 19th and 20th century pilot guides to the Indian Ocean, which indicate that the winds of Socotra's south coast are steadier and less violent than those on the north (Horsburgh 1841: 291-292; Findlay 1897: 673; Vora and Grattan-Cooper 2007: 383). These guides also state that the winds blowing off the mountains of the north coast tend to blow with great force, making it dangerous for ships to anchor in these areas. Conversely,

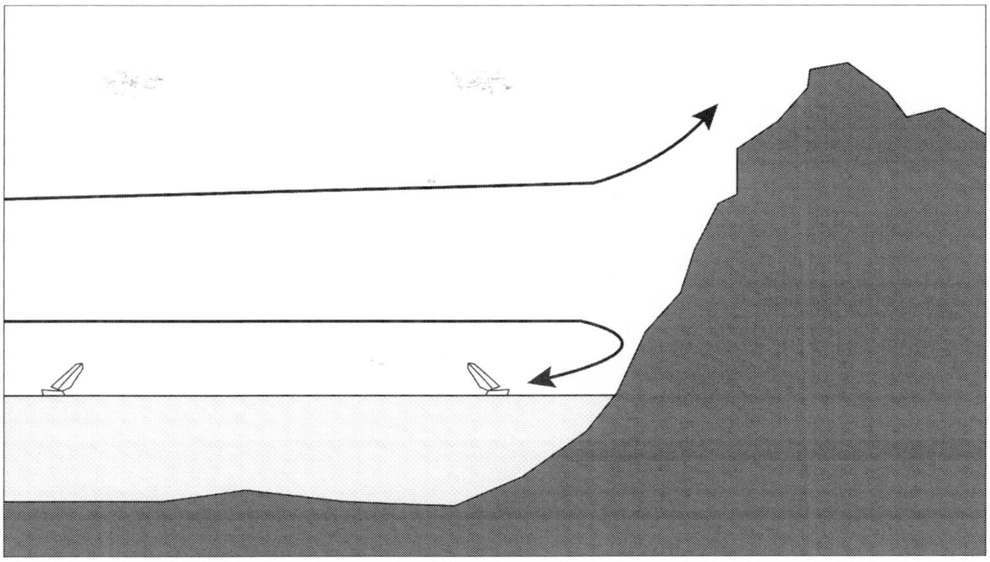

FIGURE 54. THE EFFECTS OF A SEA BREEZE BLOWING ONTO HIGH GROUND. NOTE THE CONTRARY WIND CLOSE TO THE COAST (DRAWN: AUTHOR).

the mountainous nature of the north coast can also afford shelter from the prevailing monsoon winds, effectively creating an area of calm even during the height of the SW monsoon. Evidence for this phenomenon is prevalent from the 16th century onwards, when Portuguese, Dutch and English sailors began to call at Socotra (Hagenaer 1650: 20; Foster 1878; Purchas 1905-1907; Foster 1905: 107; Barbosa 1967: 59-63). The clearest description is given by Captain David Middleton, during his visit in 1609.

> 'In the months of June and July the wind blows in this valley [The Ḥadiboh Plain] with astonishing violence; yet only a short gun-shot off towards the town of Delisha, over against the road where the ships ride, there is hardly a breath of wind' (Kerr 1824, 8: 142).

Today, Delisha or ᶜAririhun Di-Lisheh, as it is known, remains a favoured fishing area during the SW monsoon due to this phenomenon, and fishermen from surrounding areas fish there. Further evidence for the effect Socotra's mountainous topography can have on the prevailing winds is demonstrated in a study by Fett and Burk (1981: 1527-1541). This study shows that, during the SW monsoon Socotra forms a natural barrier to the prevailing wind. As a result of this barrier, the monsoon winds are deflected over an area of sea to the north of the island, resulting in an area of significantly lower wind speeds and a reduced sea state (Fett and Burk 1981: 1529).

The influence of these local winds is first alluded to in the 13th century when Marco Polo (d. AD 1324) claims the inhabitants of Socotra were sorcerers, who could raise tempests at will, and caused the winds to become calm or even change direction (Yule and Cordier 1993: 407). As demonstrated above, these events can be explained by meteorological phenomena that continue to affect shipping along Socotra's coast. However, in the Middle Ages, there was a strong belief in the power of humans to be able to control winds and raise storms (Rappoport 1971: 79). This is likely to have been one reason for Socotra's inhabitants to have become known as sorcerers. By the 16th century, although these phenomena were no longer being attributed to the inhabitants, they were not well understood and Socotra retained its aura of mystery and danger.

Currents and their influence on Socotra

Currents play a significant role in the sailing and fishing activities of the people of the North West Indian Ocean, and their effects can be felt both in the open ocean and near the shores. In Socotra, the strength and direction of the current has a significant effect on the fishing practices and the timing and direction of sea voyages. To fully understand the effects these currents have on shipping and fishing practices, it is important to understand how they are formed and what seasonal variations occur.

The formation of currents in the open ocean is the direct result of the wind on the surface (Cornish and Ives 2006: 151). The currents of the Indian Ocean are no exception, and their direction and strength are directly influenced by the monsoon winds. Consequently, the currents occur at the same time and flow in the same direction as the SW and NE monsoon winds, although much like these winds, there is some degree of variation. This variation is mainly due to bathymetry and the difference in the strength of the monsoon and local winds, especially during the inter-monsoon periods (Shankar *et al.* 2002: 66; Schott and McCreary 2001: 5). Wind strength also affects the speed of the surface currents, and during the constant high winds of the SW monsoon season, they can reach high speeds. This is particularly true for Socotra

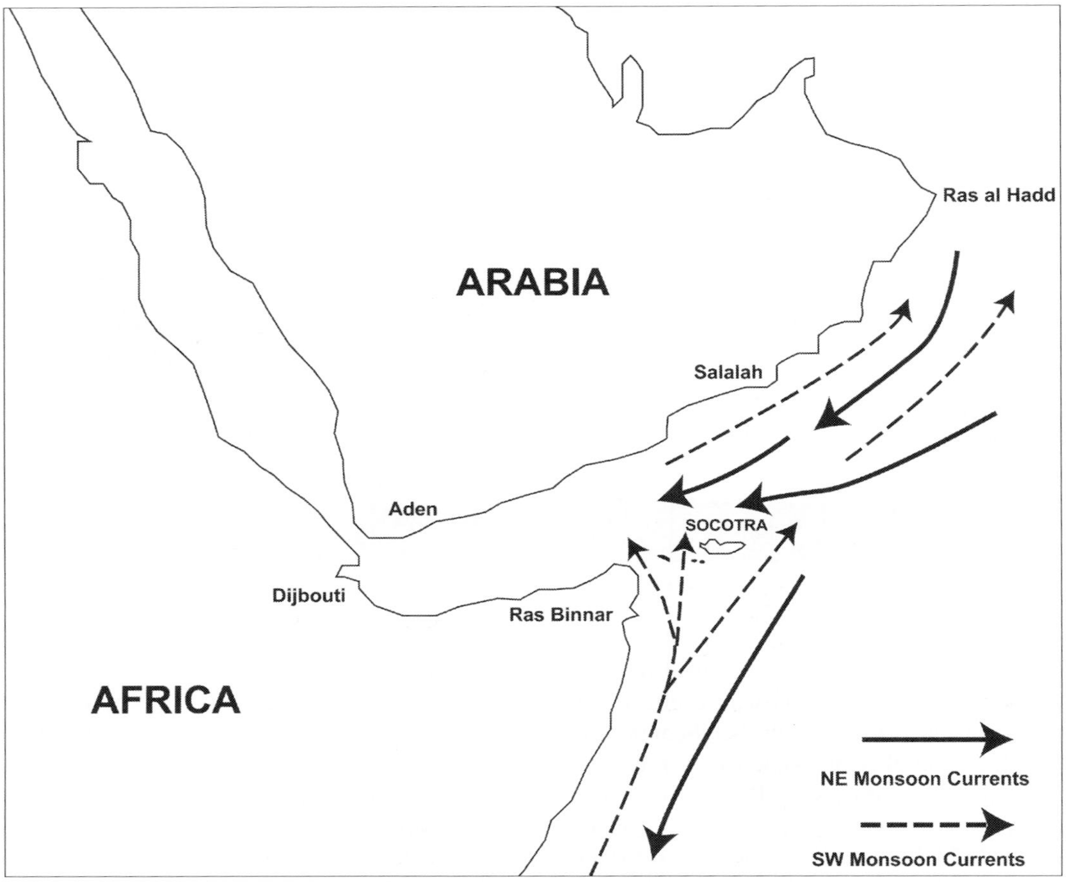

FIGURE 55. THE FLOW OF THE SOMALI CURRENT PAST SOCOTRA DURING THE NE AND SW MONSOON SEASONS (DRAWN: AUTHOR).

where, during the SW monsoon, the strongest known currents in the world occur with rates of 7-8 knots having been recorded (Cornish and Ives 2006: 153).

The dominant current affecting the region is the Somali current, which undergoes a significant change in speed and direction during the two monsoon seasons (Schott and McCreary 2001: 37-56). During the NE monsoon the Somali current travels southwards, passing to the north and east of Socotra, whilst during the SW monsoon it travels northwards, passing to the east and west of the island (Figure 55). The constant high winds of the SW monsoon make the Somali current particularly fierce during this period.

The flow pattern of the Somali current becomes more complex when it reaches the sea area of Socotra and as a result local currents are very irregular. This complexity is due to the effects of the monsoon winds, local winds and the bathymetry of the coastal areas, all of which play a significant role in the direction and strength of near-shore currents (Wirth *et al.* 2001: 1280). Whilst the strength and direction of the currents tend to be irregular, it is still possible to make some generalisations according to the season. During the NE monsoon currents tend to flow in a south-south east direction and reach speeds of around 2-3 knots, while during the SW monsoon they tend to run north westerly, reaching speeds of up to 8 knots, making it virtually impossible for vessels to make any significant headway (Cornish and Ives 2006: 153).

The currents around Socotra are further influenced by tidal streams, which tend to be very irregular, and may run for between six to 16 hours in one direction. The general direction of the tidal streams can be split between the southern and northern sides of the island. The tidal streams on the southern side tend to set westerly with the ingoing stream and easterly with the outgoing, while those of the north tend to set westerly with the outgoing and easterly with the ingoing (Vora and Grattan-Cooper 2007: 383).

The Somali current not only influences the currents around Socotra but also, due to the bathymetry, creates an area of upwelling near the coast. Upwellings occur when the surface current is drawn away from an area and the colder, nutrient rich waters of the depths rise up to take their place. This nutrient rich water creates an increase in the abundance of fish, resulting in extremely rich fishing grounds that last for the duration of the upwelling (Banaimoon 1996: 20). The upwelling that occurs off Socotra makes the fishing grounds amongst the most productive marine areas in the world (Hariri *et al.* 2002: 7).

The direction and strength of the currents passing Socotra play a vital role in marine navigation, often dictating the timing and course of the routes to be followed. Locally the strong currents can be dangerous to ships that venture too close, as they can rapidly draw them onto the shoals and reefs that surround the island. The direction and strength of the currents passing Socotra have been recorded from at least the 16th century. The earliest account is written by Ibn Mājid, who describes the seasons within which the currents can assist shipping, and the dangers of approaching Socotra during adverse currents (Ibn Mājid 1981: 230-236). Today, even ocean routing guides mention the strong currents that can be encountered off the island; the dangers of being dragged onto the shoals and reefs of the eastern side, and the best periods to undertake a voyage past the island (*Ocean passages for the world* 2004: 103).

The influence of winds and currents on Socotra's fishing communities

The fishing communities on Socotra have developed a detailed knowledge of their natural environment, and can accurately foretell the coming of seasons and their associated winds. Fishermen in villages throughout the island told me that their knowledge of the environment has been developed over several generations; passed down from father to son. Consequently, what I discovered was that the fishermen from different villages have developed their own distinct understanding of the environmental phenomena that affect their daily lives. This is in direct contradiction to my predecessors work (Serjeant1992; Naumkin 1993; Morris 2002), whose interpretations of the characteristics of the various seasons as perceived by various communities were supposed to be common throughout Socotra. While the names and general effect of the winds and currents are understood by all the fishermen and allow for some generalisations to be made, the meanings these phenomena have for individual fishing communities differed substantially. This made it apparent that Serjeant, Naumkin, and to a lesser degree Morris, had overly simplified the fishing seasons. However, before exploring the differences between the various fishing communities it is necessary to firstly look at the how the monsoon and local winds have been previously interpreted, and then to look at what similarities may exist with the data I have gathered.

Monsoon Winds

As mentioned previously, the monsoon seasons have specific characteristics for different periods of the year. While these have already been discussed, their characteristics require reiteration to help provide a comparison for the ethnographic data gathered. According to Vora and Grattan-Cooper (2007: 32), each monsoon season occurs within a specific period of time and is characterised by specific wind strength, direction and weather (Figure 56).

At this level of analysis, the direction, strength and weather of the monsoons appear to occur within very specific periods. However, as mentioned earlier, whilst the monsoon seasons affecting Socotra are the same as those affecting the entire Indian Ocean, there are some differences in their characteristics and timing.

The first ethnographic account of the monsoon seasons recognised by the fishermen of Socotra was undertaken by Serjeant in 1967 (1992: 172-173; 1995: 96-97). According to Serjeant, they recognised two monsoon seasons, namely: the NE monsoon, *azyab* (Ar), and the SW monsoon, *kōs* (Ar). Furthermore, he says that they also recognised several seasons, namely: winter, *shitāʾ* (Ar), spring, *rabīʿ* (Ar), summer, *ṣayf* (Ar), autumn, *kharīf* (Ar), and specific periods when the weather or wind changes (Figure 57).

What is apparent in this table is that there are several gaps between the various seasons, which Serjeant does

Monsoon Season	Start	Finish	Wind	Weather
NE (Winter)	September	March	NE (Force 3 to 4, rarely 7)	Few clouds, fine, little rainfall
Inter-monsoon	Late March	May	Variable (Force 0 to 4)	Variable, fair with intermittent cloud and squally winds, frequent heavy rains and thunderstorms
SW (Summer)	June	August	SW (Force 7 and above)	Cloudy, unsettled, high rainfall
Inter-monsoon	Late August	Early September	Variable (Force 0 to 4)	Variable, fair with intermittent cloud and squally winds, frequent heavy rains and thunderstorms

FIGURE 56. THE TIMING AND CHARACTERISTICS OF EACH MONSOON SEASON TAKEN FROM VORA AND GRATTAN-COOPER (2007: 32).

Monsoon Season	Start	Finish	Winds	Weather
azyab (Ar) NE monsoon	4. Oct.	6. April	NE winds begin to blow	
shitāʾ (Ar) Winter	4. Oct.	22. Dec.		Period of rain
	17. Oct.	31. Oct.		
rabīʿ (Ar) Spring	4. Jan.	23. March		
ṣayf (Ar) Summer	5. April	22. June		NE monsoon ends
kōs (Ar) SW monsoon	18. April	8. Sep.		
	1. May	8. June		*Mūsim maṭar* (Rainy season)
	27. May		Strong south westerly winds at sea	
	9. June		Strong south westerly winds on land	
kharīf (Autumn)	5. July	21. Sep.		No rainfall
	8. Sep.		The south westerly winds weaken	
	21. Sep.			Possible rainfall

FIGURE 57. THE SEASONS, WINDS AND WEATHER AS RECORDED BY SERJEANT (1992: 172-173; 1995: 96-97).

not explain. These discrepancies are one of the first indications that Serjeant's informants were probably not in agreement on the actual dates for the various seasons and this simplification of the seasons is flawed. According to Serjeant's informants, the NE monsoon lasts for seven months, beginning in October and ending in April; while the SW monsoon lasts for five months, beginning in April and ending in September. These timings are exactly the same length as given by Vora and Grattan-Cooper (2007: 32) for the NE monsoon, but for the SW monsoon, Serjeant's timing is significantly longer. In addition, according to Serjeant's informants it rains during the end of September and October, and again from May to June. Comparing this with Vora and Grattan-Cooper (2007: 32), it is clear that the rains on Socotra occur during the NE monsoon, when little rainfall is experienced elsewhere in the Indian Ocean. The reason for this is due to the vagueness of Vora and Grattan-Cooper's data, which refers to the entire Indian Ocean. What this demonstrates is the time lag between the formation and start of the winds in the Indian Ocean and how and where their effects are felt and can differ in specific areas. Finally, Serjeant states that the fishermen and sailors refer to the beginning of *azyab*, on 4 October, as the opening of the sea, *al-futūḥ* (Ar), which signifies to them the beginning of the fishing season. The beginning of *kōs*, according to Serjeant, is 5 April, although he says that it is not until 27 April that the sea is closed to shipping, *mughallaq al-baḥr* (Serjeant 1995: 96). During this period, Serjeant claims that the winds cause the sea to boil and raise clouds of dust on the beach, making it impossible to fish. What this illustrates is that the discrepancies in the timings for the SW monsoon is most likely due to Serjeant's informant's perception of the fishing seasons, and the reason that the SW monsoon is longer is that it is only considered to end when it is possible to resume fishing. These differences clearly demonstrate the dangers of using broad generalisations to understand the effects of the monsoon winds on a specific locale and how people's perceptions can affect the length and conditions of a particular season, a point I will raise again later.

The second ethnographic work to look at the seasons of the year with respect to Socotra fishermen was undertaken by the Russian ethnographer, Naumkin (1993). According to his informants, the fishing season is divided into two periods, based on the monsoon winds. The names of the seasons are *futūḥ* (Ar), for the season when there is no wind and it is possible for the fishermen to put to sea, and *qāfal* (Ar) for the rest of the year when strong winds prevent fishing. *Futūḥ* corresponds with the NE monsoon, with light winds and moderate sea state, and *qāfal* corresponds to the high winds and violent sea state of the SW monsoon (Figure 58). This division is

Monsoon Season	Start	Finish	Wind
futūḥ NE monsoon	Late October	April	No wind
qāfal SW monsoon	May	Early October	Strong wind

FIGURE 58. THE MONSOON SEASONS AND WINDS OF SOCOTRA TAKEN FROM NAUMKIN (1993: 166); NAUMKIN (1993 SUPPLEMENT: 8).

particularly interesting in that Naumkin's informant's perception of the monsoon seasons is purely based upon whether the strength of the wind makes it possible to fish or not.

The final ethnographic work to look at the monsoon seasons is that of Morris (2002), (Figure 59). This work, unlike that of Serjeant and Naumkin, focuses on the seasons recognised by the pastoralists of the interior, and does not look primarily at the fishing communities. Nevertheless, it does provide a useful comparison between the interior and coastal inhabitants and how the naming of the seasons is similar.

According to Morris, the pastoralists recognise eight seasons, which include the NE and SW monsoon. These seasons are all identified according to the winds and weather experienced, as outlined in Figure 59. The NE monsoon or winter season is known as *ṣēreb* (Soc), and begins in late October. It is characterised by heavy rains in the highlands, which gradually move toward the lowlands of the north coast during the second half of the season. This is followed by the summer, *ḳeˈyaṭ* (Soc), which is characterised by intense heat and rare showers of rain. The next season is *menḳeˈyaṭ* (Soc), in which the heat becomes even more intense and the seas are lashed by sudden fierce storms. The season before the SW monsoon is known as *dɔ̄ti* (Soc), and is characterised by high humidity, cloudy skies and occasional showers of rain. Where no rain occurs during *dɔ̄ti* it is known as *bɛ̄-dɔ̄ti* (Soc), *bɛ̄*, meaning without or lacking. Morris also says that the end of *dɔ̄ti* and the beginning of the SW monsoon is also known as *ḥal iduˈmhur* (Soc), the time when the clouds begin to gather, although it is not recognised as a season but a meteorological event. The SW monsoon, known as *ḥorf* (Soc), begins in June and is characterised by strong winds, especially in the high plateaus of the east and north, the central Ḥagher mountains, and the seaward facing coast of the north. Morris's informants said that the mildest of the SW monsoon winds are in the interior valleys, in the southern coastal plain and in the lowland grazing areas of the interior. The SW monsoon is followed by *di-ˈilɘhe* (Soc) which begins approximately in the last week of August and ends approximately in the first week of September. *ḏi-ˈilɘhe* is characterised by variable winds and unsettled weather. This is followed by *ṣereˈbhen* (Soc), which lasts until October and is characterised by variable winds and the possibility of rain. The last season is known as *gyaˈḥś* (Soc), and is characterised by a relatively constant north easterly wind and short heavy rainstorms. Morris's only mention of the monsoon seasons with respect to Socotra's fishing communities, relates that the full-time fishermen will fish year round, except during the SW monsoon, while seasonal fishermen normally only fish during *ḳeˈyaṭ* and the beginning of *dɔ̄ti* (Morris 2002: 221). Unfortunately, she does not mention whether the fishermen recognise just two seasons when they can and cannot fish, as outlined by Naumkin (1993), or whether they recognise all the seasons used by the pastoralists.

Monsoon Season	Start	Finish	Wind	Weather
ṣēreb (Soc) Winter/ NE monsoon	Late October	February	NE wind	
	Late October	15. November		Heavy rains in NE and central plateaus and highlands
	Late November	Beginning of February		Heavy rains in the lowlands
ḳeˈyaṭ (Soc) Summer	February	April		
	End of February	Beginning of March		Haziness, rare showers
menḳeˈyaṭ (Soc)	April		Little or no wind	Extremely hot, haziness, sudden fierce storms
dɔ̄ti (Soc)	15. April	Beginning of June		
	End of May	June		Possible rains, High humidity
	June		Variable	Cloudy, restless seas
ḥorf (Soc) SW monsoon	June	September	SW wind	
	June	August	Hot, dry winds	Hot, dry
	August		Winds decrease in intensity	Possible showers
di-ˤilɘhe (Soc)	End of August	September	Intermittent wind, some lulls	Unsettled
ṣereˈbhen (Soc)	September		Variable	Possible rains, Intermittent cloud
gyaˈḥś (Soc)	October		Generally NE winds	Short heavy rainstorms

FIGURE 59. THE MONSOON SEASONS, WINDS AND WEATHER OF SOCOTRA TAKEN FROM MORRIS (2002: 16-30).

Monsoon Season	Start	Finish	Wind	Weather and activities
ṣēreb (Soc)/ *azyab* (Ar) NE monsoon / Winter	November	December	Calm wind	Sea is quiet, fishing possible
ḳe̍yaṭ (Soc)/ *ṣayf* (Ar) Summer	January	March	Calm	Cloudy, fishing
dɔ̄ti (Soc) The first inter-monsoon period	April	June	Calm	Cloudy, fishing
ḥorf (Soc)/ *kōs* (Ar) SW monsoon	July	September	Strong SW winds	No fishing or maritime traffic
ṣere̍bhen (Soc) The beginning of the second inter-monsoon period	Mid-September	Beginning of October	Variable, possibly strong winds	Unsettled, fishing possible
gya̍ḥś (Soc) The second inter-monsoon period	October		Generally NE but variable	Good fishing

FIGURE 60. THE MONSOON SEASONS, WINDS, WEATHER AND THE INFLUENCE OF THESE ON FISHING ACTIVITIES AS COMPILED FROM FISHERMEN INTERVIEWED THROUGHOUT THE ISLAND BY THE AUTHOR.

The three studies outlined above demonstrate a number of differences in the amount of seasons recognised by the fishermen. Consequently, I sought to re-investigate how the fishing communities on Socotra generally perceive the monsoon seasons and what influence these have on their fishing activities. This was done by interviewing a range of fishermen in fishing villages throughout the island. The resultant data is set out in Figure 60.

Figure 60 above represents an attempt to provide some form of generalisation of the seasons recognised by the fishermen on Socotra, although it should be borne in mind that weather and people do not always conform to generalisations and that the seasons did not have the same significance for all the fishermen. Furthermore, weather conditions are not uniform throughout the island and localised changes can and do occur. According to almost all the fishermen interviewed, the beginning of the NE monsoon starts in October and ends sometime in December, although early January and even February were mentioned. The beginning of the SW monsoon tends to vary between May and July, and the end of the SW monsoon is considered to be mid-September, although several fishermen said that in some years it had only ended in October. The actual dates for the inter-monsoon periods were difficult to determine as the dates given by fishermen from different villages along the north and south coast differed by weeks. Consequently, the months of the inter-monsoon given in Figure 56 represent the nearest possible period to those told to me by the fishermen. During this attempt to provide a generalised overview of the monsoon seasons it soon became apparent that even though they used the same names to describe the different seasons, the dates and influences of each differed from one area of the island to another. What is also apparent is that the interior population's naming of the seasons was also used by the fishermen, which would appear to demonstrate a shared knowledge, reinforcing the relationship between the coastal and interior inhabitants.

Local winds

Local winds are as important to the fishermen of Socotra as the monsoon winds and have a significant influence on the timing of, and areas in which it is possible to fish. The reason for this is that they can cancel out the effects of the monsoon winds in certain areas, allowing the fishermen to fish during those periods when the prevailing monsoon winds would have made all fishing impossible. According to Serjeant (1993: 173), the fishermen recognise four local winds (Figure 61). Unfortunately, other than mentioning the direction of these winds, Serjeant gives no further explanation of how they affect the sea, weather or fishermen on Socotra.

Naumkin (1993) makes no mention of the local winds or their effects, and the only other account to mention them is Morris (2002). According to Morris (2002: 19-20), there are four winds which are named according to the direction from which they are blowing. While Morris does not look specifically at how these winds are interpreted by the fishermen of Socotra, she does provide information on the general dangers of these winds and the Socotri terminology used (Figure 62).

Wind	Direction
'Abrī	North
Ṣarbī	East
Maydih	South
Ma'ribuh	West

FIGURE 61. THE WINDS OF SOCOTRA TAKEN FROM SERJEANT (1992: 173).

Wind	Direction	Influence
ṣe̍rbihi (Soc)	North	This is the north wind of the NE monsoon and brings the winter rains. It can also occasionally cause storm conditions to develop.
e̍ˀeris (Soc)	East	This wind is very strong, especially during winter, and can cause storm conditions to develop. It can also cause a large swell to develop and commonly blows for between three and six days at a time.
me̍de (Soc)	South	This is the south wind of the SW monsoon and completely dominates the other winds during this period. It generally blows for four and a half months of the year, making fishing impossible throughout the island.
ma̍ʿaribo (Soc)	West	This wind is especially dangerous on the south coast, blowing boats out to sea and making fishing extremely hazardous.

FIGURE 62. THE LOCAL WINDS ON SOCOTRA TAKEN FROM MORRIS (2002: 19-20).

As discussed previously, local winds can change according to a number of factors that include local topography and temperature changes between the land and sea. Consequently, it is unlikely that the local winds outlined by Serjeant and Morris will have the same effect on villages throughout the island, as different areas of the coast will be affected in different ways by the same wind. However, before exploring the effect of monsoon and local winds in various fishing villages on Socotra it is necessary to look at how current affects fishing practices.

Currents

The currents around Socotra are often mentioned by sailing guides, yet Serjeant (1992; 1995); Naumkin (1993) and Morris (2002) make no mention of their effect on the fishermen of Socotra. Therefore, I sought to determine whether the fishermen had any knowledge of the currents and what, if any, influence they had on fishing activities. During the course of my interviews it soon became apparent that the fishermen were aware of the currents, and that they did have a significant impact on their fishing activities. According to fishermen in villages throughout the north and south coast and the island of Samḥa, there are four currents, *mi̍dəher* (Soc), which are named according to the direction in which they run. Furthermore, when talking about currents, they always prefixed the name of the current with *mɛ̄ˀ* (Soc), meaning towards or in the direction of. The names of the four different currents and the direction they run in are given in Figure 63.

Direction	Name
North	*shimār* (Ar)
East	*ʿālə* (Soc)
South	*sikūṭ* (Ar)
West	*le̍ḥe* (Soc)

FIGURE 63. THE DIRECTION AND NAMES OF THE CURRENTS ACCORDING TO FISHERMEN INTERVIEWED BY THE AUTHOR.

It is apparent from Figure 63 that the terminology used by the fishermen to identify the currents is divided between Socotri, for those that run east and west, and Arabic, for those that run north and south. This poses an interesting question, why are only the easterly and westerly currents given Socotri names and the northerly and southerly currents given Arabic names? The answer is surprisingly straightforward. On Socotra, the prevailing currents run in an easterly and westerly direction, and have the most significant impact on fishermen's activities. The adoption of Arabic names for the other two currents is likely to have been due to a number of different reasons, which probably includes an influx of Arabic speaking migrants and the importation and use of vessels that made it possible to fish further out to sea, where the effect of the north and south currents would have been felt. The fishermen told me that it was important for them to understand when and at what strength the currents are running. The reason for this was twofold: first, if the currents did run with any strength it would make it impossible to use a net, which would be swept to the surface. Secondly, strong currents can cause one to be dragged out to sea. This would have meant almost certain death if one was dragged out of sight of the island and became lost. The fishermen I spoke to were aware of the direct correlation between the strength and direction of the wind and current, and attributed strong currents to certain winds. In addition, due to the importance of knowing the direction and strength of the current, fishermen have devised an ingenious way in which they are able to determine current rate and flow. According to Khames Abdulah Salem,[57] a 75 year old, elderly full-time fisherman in Ḥadiboh, to determine the strength of the current before going any significant distance offshore to fish one would take a handful of ash and compact it together with water. This clumped together ash ball would then be dropped overboard when one was some distance from the shore and the resultant trail of ash, as the ball breaks up, would indicate both the direction and flow of the current. This method of determining the direction and

[57] Interviewed on 22 December 2009.

flow of the current is not mentioned elsewhere in studies of the fishermen in Al-Batinah, Oman (Donaldson 1979; Agius *pers. comm.* January 2012), the Hadhramaut, Yemen (Serjeant 1995; Bonfiglioli and Hariri 2004; Camelin 2006), or Suakin, Sudan (Kentley 1988), but was employed by the mariners of the Cormandel coast (Congreve 1850: 103). Could this be a cultural link in Socotra's past? Regrettably, there is too little information to pursue this theory. The only study along the south coast of Arabia in which the currents are referred to is in Al-Shihr, Hadhramaut (Camelin 2006). According to Camelin (2006: 116-117), the fishermen in Al-Shihr recognise four currents, which flow either north, south, east or west. The north and south currents are said to be feeble and do not affect fishing, whereas the east and west currents are considered to be strong enough to affect their fishing activities. Unfortunately, the influence these currents have on the fishermen's activities and what they do to determine the direction of these currents is not mentioned. Nevertheless, it is clear that the easterly and westerly currents along the Hadhramaut are, much like on Socotra, the most dominate currents influencing the fishermen's activities.

The Fishing Villages

Having broadly outlined the effect various winds and currents have on the fishermen on Socotra, I now look at individual fishing villages in order to determine what effect these phenomena have at specific locales and how they are interpreted. The villages used to do this are:

On the North Coast
- Shuᶜub
- Qalansiyah
- Qādheb
- Ḥadiboh
- Ṣaqarah
- Erisseyl

On the South Coast
- Maḥfirihin
- Stēroh
- Bidhōleh
- Di-Ṣeberho

On the island of Samḥa
- Khaysat ash-Shaikh

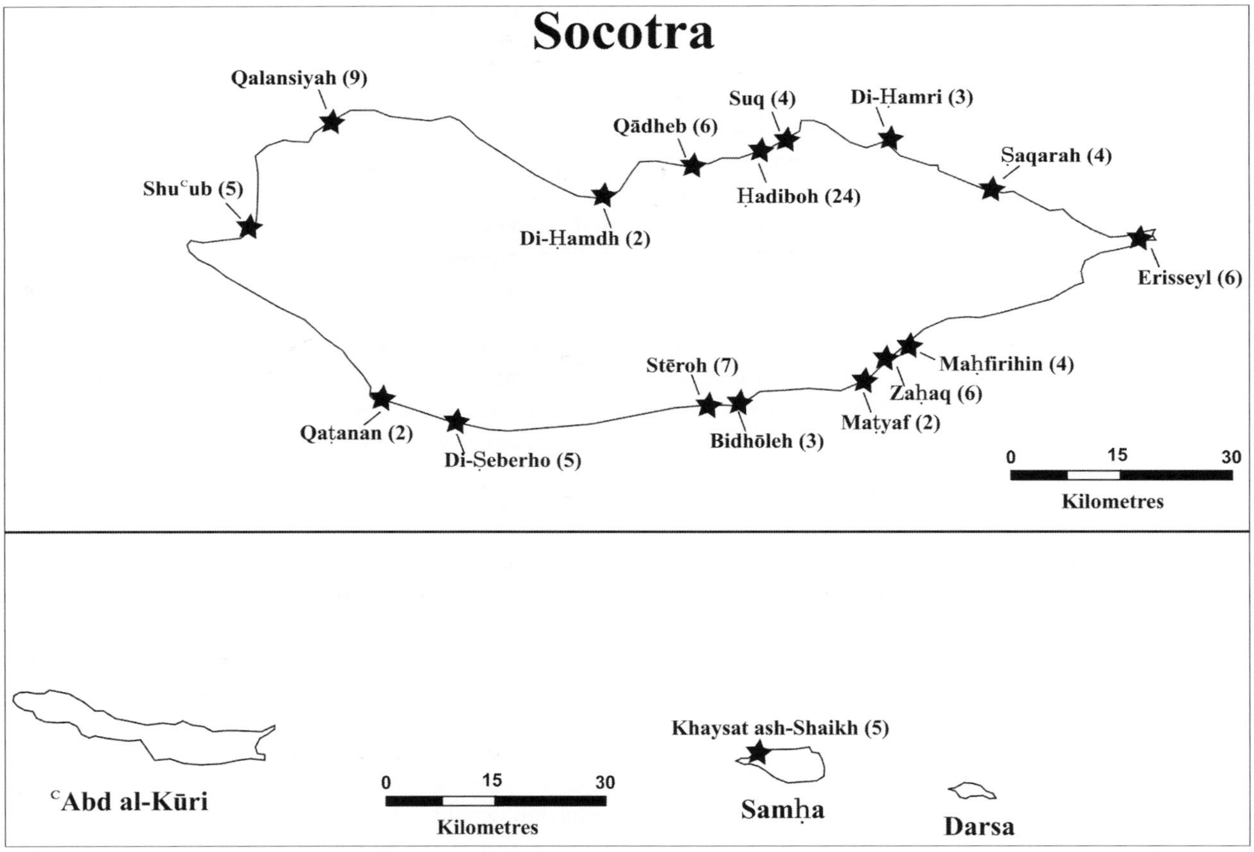

FIGURE 64. SOCOTRA AND THE OUTLYING ISLANDS OF SAMḤA, DARSA AND ᶜABD AL-KŪRI SHOWING THE FISHING VILLAGES WHERE INTERVIEWS WERE CONDUCTED. THE NUMBER OF PEOPLE INTERVIEWED IN EACH IS GIVEN IN BRACKETS.

The location of these villages and the number of fishermen interviewed in each is given in Figure 64.

The North Coast

Shuᶜub

The fishing village of Shuᶜub is mainly comprised of full-time Socotri fishermen, although there are also several resident fishermen from other areas of the Hadhramaut, Yemen. Fishermen interviewed identified two monsoon seasons, *ḥorf* (Soc) and *ṣēreb* (Soc), and whilst they recognised the seasons of *ṣerˈebhen* (Soc) and *ḳˈeyaṭ* (Soc), these had no relevance to their fishing calendar. *Ṣēreb* is the beginning of their fishing season and lasts from 1 October until 1 June, after which *ḥorf* begins. *Ḥorf* lasts for four months from June to September, during which time they said no one could fish. However, according to Adbullah Salem Saaed Abokakibak,[58] an experienced full-time fisherman, 45 years old, it is possible to fish during the beginning of June if the SW monsoon winds were late. The fishermen recognise all four local winds, and sometimes use both Socotri and Arabic terminology to describe them. According to them, the north wind is known as *ṣˈerbihi* (Soc) and it blows predominantly during the NE monsoon, bringing *dɔ̄mer* (Soc), storms, which make fishing difficult. Two very experienced full-time fishermen[59] told me that *ṣˈerbihi* is a dangerous wind as it blows vessels out to sea. They also said that this wind is especially dangerous for those who do not have an engine on their boat, as it is impossible to paddle against it. The east wind, is known as *ˈeʾeris* (Soc) and *hindī* (Ar), and is said to only blow periodically during September and October. While it can affect fishing the fishermen in Shuᶜub do not consider it to be dangerous, because it only blows for several hours at a time. The south wind is known as *mˈede* (Soc) and blows almost continuously from June to September. This is considered to be the most dangerous wind, and most fishermen leave Shuᶜub to fish elsewhere during this period. The west wind is known both as *mˈaᶜaribo* (Soc) and *kōs* (Ar) and is the predominant wind from mid-April to the end of May. Those interviewed said that fishing during this period is dangerous, especially if venturing offshore, as the westerly wind and current would drag one out to sea. In addition to the dangers posed by the westerly current, *mɛ̄ʾ ᶜālə* (Soc), the fishermen told me that if the northerly current, *shimār* (Ar), is strong it can make fishing difficult.

Qalansiyah

The village of Qalansiyah is the second largest on Socotra and hosts a range of fishermen from other villages on the island and the mainland of Yemen. The fishermen have a good understanding of the influence of the monsoon seasons in Qalansiyah and the other villages on the island. Fishermen I interviewed were full-time fishermen with many years of experience. Most had spent all of their lives in Qalansiyah, although some had worked several years overseas, either onboard fishing vessels or doing manual labour on the Arabian mainland. These fishermen were all familiar with the seasons of the year mentioned in Figure 60, although they mainly used Arabic terminology for the seasons. They said that *azyab* (Ar), the NE monsoon, begins in October and ends in May, whilst *kōs* (Ar), the SW monsoon, begins in May and ends in September. Few of them were able to agree on an exact date for the beginning or end of the NE and SW monsoon. The reason for this is that the start and end of the monsoon is dependent on the changes in the winds and weather, and only when the effect of these winds become apparent is the season considered to have started. Fishermen told me that the beginning and end of the seasons were difficult to accurately judge as each year the winds of the monsoon could differ by a couple of weeks. The fishing season in Qalansiyah is generally said to begin in October, although, according to three of the elderly full-time fishermen I interviewed,[60] it is possible to start fishing from as early as September, when the star *mˈədərək* (Soc) appears. Fishermen in Qalansiyah consider this star to be a sign that better weather can be expected, although it was only these three fishermen I spoke to who said that they fish when the star is visible. While it is not possible to fish every day, owing to the generally unsettled weather during the period in which *mˈədərək* appears, the fishermen agreed that the best part of the fishing season in Qalansiyah is the end of *ṣerˈebhen* (Soc) and the beginning of *gyˈaḥś* (Soc), when the wind and sea is calm, and everyone would fish almost continuously during this period. Fishing generally continued throughout the rest of the year until the end of *ḳˈeyaṭ* (Soc), when the weather would begin to change. Several experienced full-time fishermen[61] told me that they still fish during *dɔ̄ti* (Soc), although it is considered to be a dangerous period as the winds of the SW monsoon, *kōs* (Ar), would begin to blow. None of the fishermen I interviewed said that they fish during *kōs*, and most said that they will leave Qalansiyah to fish on the mainland of Yemen during this time. According to the fishermen in Qalanisyah the north wind is known as *ṣˈerbihi* (Soc), but they will also use the term *azyab* (Ar) to refer to this wind which blows predominately during the NE monsoon. They consider *ṣˈerbihi* to be a good wind for fishing, although as it is also said to be weak and heavily influenced by the other winds. According to four experienced full-time fisher-

[58] Interviewed on 20 December 2009.

[59] Abdulla Salem Saaed Abokakibak, 45 years old; Mohammed Malak Masham, 35 years old, both interviewed 20 December 2009.

[60] Abdullah Rahman Abod Ali Saeed, 38 years old, interviewed on 16 December 2009; Omar Saeed Abod Ali Saeed 31 years old, interviewed on 18 December 2009; Jaman Saeed Abdullah, in his 30s, interviewed on 16 December 2009.

[61] Saeed Salem Hasaan, 35 years old; Abaid Salem bin Awailan, in his 50s; both interviewed on 17 December 2009; Salam Saeed Martah, 39 years old, interviewed on 18 December 2009.

men,[62] the wind during the NE monsoon season can blow from many different directions, although it would always eventually settle back to *ṣerbihi*. The east wind is known by three different names, *eʾeris* (Soc), *hindī* (Ar) and *sharq* (Ar). This wind is regarded as dangerous during September, especially when fishing any distance from the shore. Two experienced fishermen[63] I spoke to said that during the NE monsoon it is possible for *eʾeris* to blow for several hours at a time. This makes conditions difficult for fishing at sea and most fishermen would remain on the land until it had stopped blowing. The south wind is known by the fishermen as *mede* and is the predominant wind from mid-April to the end of September. While it is possible to fish when this wind is blowing, the fishermen said that if it started to blow strongly they would stop fishing as it is too dangerous. However, according to Saeed Selem Ali,[64] during the height of *mede* it is still possible to fish in a small bay to the west of Qalansiyah, due to the protection afforded by the surrounding mountains. The west wind is known to the fishermen both as *maʿaribo* (Soc) and *kōs* (Ar) and blows from mid-April to May. The fishermen said that by May the strength of this wind will increase to such an extent that most people will stop fishing. In addition to the four winds outlined here the fishermen in Qalansiyah also recognise another wind that occurs throughout the year called *barrī* (Ar), which refers to a wind coming from the land, or a land breeze. According to the fishermen this wind was considered to be dangerous before engines were introduced to Socotra, sometime in the 1970s, as it was not possible to paddle against the force of the wind. They now say that it can cause difficulties for fishing but is not a dangerous wind. While these winds represent the general situation for the fishermen in Qalansiyah, according to an experienced full-time fisherman in his 60s, Ali Salim Da-Salmoho,[65] there were places, if one understood the winds well, where it was possible to fish almost all year round. In Qalansiyah, fishermen told me that all four currents affect their fishing. *Shimār* (Ar), *ʿālə* (Soc) and *leḥe* (Soc) are considered to be the most dangerous, especially when they run with any strength, as they can drag one out to sea. *Sikūṭ* (Ar), is not considered dangerous as it flows toward land, but it can make fishing with nets impossible.

Qādheb

The fishing village of Qādheb mainly comprises fishermen and merchants from overseas, and many of the fishermen interviewed were either second or third generation Socotris. The interviewees were all experienced full-time fishermen, who fished throughout the fishing season in Qādheb. They recognised two fishing seasons based upon the NE and SW monsoon, namely: *azyab* (Ar), the period in which it is possible to fish, and *kōs* (Ar), the period in which it is not possible to fish. According to them, *azyab* begins in October and ends in July when the monsoon winds became too strong to take a boat out, after which it is *kōs*. Fishermen use a mixture of Arabic and Socotri to describe the local winds. The north wind is known as *azyab* (Ar), and is the best wind for fishing. They said that during the north wind it is possible to fish throughout the island and even offshore. The east wind *eʾeris*, is described as the bringer of storms, making fishing difficult for several days at a time. The south wind is known as *mede*, and when it begins to blow steadily the sea is said to be *qāfal* (Ar), closed. The west wind, known as *maʿaribo* (Soc) or *kōs* (Ar) signifies, according to two experienced full-time fishermen,[66] the end of the fishing season. The fishermen also recognise the land breeze *barrī*, and consider it to be a very dangerous wind that can blow you out to sea. According to them this wind mostly occurs during January. The two currents affecting fishing in Qādheb are *ʿālə* (Soc) and *leḥe* (Soc), which is said to flow with great force when *eʾeris* or *maʿaribo* are blowing, and makes fishing offshore dangerous.

Ḥadiboh

The village of Ḥadiboh, the present day capital of Socotra, consists of a very large fishing community made up of fishermen who almost all reside there permanently. It is chiefly made up of African fishermen, who have been living there for several generations; several fishermen from the Hadhramaut and southern Oman, and those from other fishing villages on Socotra. Knowledge of winds and currents varied dramatically. The elderly Arabian and African fishermen have a good knowledge of the various differences, while others only differentiated two or three different winds and currents. The terminology used by the fishermen is generally a mixture between Arabic and Socotri, although the inter-monsoons were known by their Socotri names. Notwithstanding the terminology used, the fishermen agreed that the start of the NE monsoon in Ḥadiboh begins between the first and the 15 of October. This period of good weather is interrupted during the end of November and December when there is a short period of *dōmer* (Soc), strong winds and high seas. The exact beginning of the SW monsoon differs greatly and there was very little agreement between fishermen, although they did agree that by July the winds made it impossible to fish. The other fishing seasons recognised were, *ṣerebhen*, *gyaḥś*, *ḳeyaṭ* and *dōti*. According to the more experienced full-time fishermen, *ṣerebhen* is the period just after the SW monsoon, and heralds the

[62] Abdullah Rahman Abod Ali Saeed, 38 years old, interviewed on 16 December 2009; Omar Saeed Abod Ali Saeed, 31 years old, interviewed on 18 December 2009; Jaman Saeed Abdullah, in his 30s, interviewed on 16 February 2009; Salam Saeed Martah, 39 years old, interviewed on 18 December 2009.

[63] Abdullah Rahman Abod Ali Saeed, full time fisherman, 38 years old, interviewed on 16 December 2009; Omar Saeed Abod Ali Saeed, full time fisherman, 31 years old, interviewed on 18 December 2009.

[64] Seasonal fisherman, in his 30s, interviewed on 17 December 2009.

[65] Interviewed on 16 December 2009.

[66] Salim Games Saaed, 45 years old; Salim Saaed Atman, 55 years old, both interviewed on 2 January 2010.

beginning of the fishing season, although it is not always possible to fish as the weather remains unsettled. *ġyaḥś* takes place after *ṣerebhen* and is characterised by calm weather; for many of the less experienced fishermen it is the beginning of their fishing season. During the NE monsoon there is a period known as *ḳeyaṭ*, which is approximately three months long, from February to April. Throughout this period most of them will normally fish closer inshore as the NE winds increase in intensity, although the more experienced full-time fishermen will continue fishing offshore. The next period recognised is *dɔ̄ti*, which is approximately three months long, from mid-April to June. This period is normally the end of the fishing season for the seasonal fishermen and those who have additional forms of income, as the weather is very unsettled and fishing is said to be dangerous. In addition to these seasons I was told by Mobarik Ali Adbulla,[67] and other elderly, experienced full-time fishermen from Ḥadiboh that in January there is a period named after the star *məᶜɔ̄dif* (Soc), which means cast nets. The period during which this star is visible is recognised as a period of rough weather, when it is only possible to use cast nets from the shore. The local winds identified by the fishermen were known by their Arabic and Socotri names. The north wind is known as, *azyab* (Ar) and *ṣerbihi* (Soc), it mostly occurs during the NE monsoon. The north wind is, according to fishermen, good for fishing, and will rarely blow with any force. The east wind, *eᵓeris* (Soc)/ *hindī* (Ar), is said to be a dangerous wind for fishing. According to fishermen interviewed, the most dangerous period in which *eᵓeris* blows is during September and many fishermen are caught out by this wind, which will can begin to blow very rapidly. The south wind is known as *mede*, and the fishermen consider it to be at its most dangerous in May or September, as it can quickly become very powerful, making fishing very hazardous. The west wind, *maᶜaribo* (Soc)/ *kōs* (Ar) generally makes fishing difficult, as it sometimes brings storms and high seas. The fishermen consider the worse period for *maᶜaribo* to be in May, and will only put out to sea for a few hours in the evening when the winds are calmer. In addition to these winds the elderly fishermen also recognise *barrī* (Ar) and *mġēbīya* (Ar), which are hot dry land breezes that blow during *dɔ̄ti* and *ḳeyaṭ*. According to them, *mġēbīya* can make it difficult to fish, as it causes the sea to become very rough, although it is normally short-lived. Fishermen in Ḥadiboh know all four currents and say that they make fishing with nets impossible and can drag one offshore, if they are strong, with the exception of *sikūṭ* (Ar), which is rarely strong, and only makes fishing with nets difficult.

Ṣaqarah

The village of Ṣaqarah is relatively recently established, and is made up of Arabian and Bedouin fishermen. Fishermen I spoke to told me that there are two fishing seasons, *ṣēreb* (Soc), when it is possible to fish almost all the time, and *ḥorf* (Soc), when the winds make it impossible to fish. They said that *ṣēreb* begins in October and ends in the beginning of July, when the strong winds of *ḥorf* begin to blow. The north wind is known as *ṣerbihi* and they say it is a good wind for fishing. However, according to two relatively experienced full-time fishermen,[68] if it blows in September or October it can bring storms, making fishing difficult. The east wind is known as either *eᵓeris* (Soc) or *hindī* (Ar), and is a difficult time for fishing, due to the strength of the wind and possibility of storms. The south wind is known as *mede*, and the west wind, *maᶜaribo*. If either of these winds is blowing the fishermen said that they will not go fishing, as it is too dangerous. The only currents they knew were, *ᶜālə* (Soc) and *leḥe* (Soc), both of which are considered to be dangerous if they flow with any strength, and make net fishing impossible.

Erisseyl

The village of Erisseyl is mainly composed of full-time Bedouin fishermen from the surrounding area, with only a few fishermen from other villages coming to live there during the fishing season. Fishermen in Erisseyl only recognise two seasons, namely: *ḥorf*, a windy season when it is impossible to fish and *ṣēreb*, the fishing season. The fishing season runs from October to the beginning of June, although they did say that sometimes it is not possible to fish during May. According to two fishermen,[69] the best period to fish is between October and December, when the sea conditions were calmest. The fishermen identify the north wind as *azyab* (Ar) and *ṣerbihi* (Soc), and consider it to be a good wind for fishing. However, they say that if *ṣerbihi* blows during September or June it becomes very strong and makes it difficult for them to fish. The east wind is known as *eᵓeris* (Soc) and *hindī* (Ar), and is the most dangerous wind for fishing. Fishermen told me that if *eᵓeris* blows no vessels will go to sea or attempt to sail around Rās Erisseyl, as the sea becomes very dangerous around the offshore reefs. The south wind is known as *mede* and the west wind, *maᶜaribo* (Soc) or *kōs* (Ar). If these winds blow with any strength the fishermen say that it is impossible to fish and the sea is *qāfal* (Ar), closed. The currents, *leḥe* (Soc), *shimār* (Ar), *ᶜālə* (Soc), and *sikūṭ* (Ar) are all considered dangerous when they flow with any strength, especially near the reefs off Rās Erisseyl.

The South Coast

Maḥfirihin

The village of Maḥfirihin is the largest village on the south coast and made up of fishermen from both the

[67] Full-time fisherman, in his 60s, interviewed on 15 February 2009.

[68] Mobark Wilaal Saad, 25 years old; Salem Abdullah Saeed, 45 years old, both interviewed on 23 December 2009.

[69] Saleman Hamodi Ahmed, full-time fisherman, in his 60s, interviewed on 9 February 2009; Sindowa Ali Ahmed, full-time fisherman, in his 40s, interviewed on 23 December 2009.

north and south coast. They are experienced full-time fishermen, who spend the majority of their time fishing in Maḥfirihin. They recognise four seasons, namely: *ṣēreb*, *ḥorf*, *ḳeyaṭ* and *dōti*. According to them, *ṣēreb* is a period of calm weather during which it is possible to fish every day. By January, during *ḳeyaṭ* they limit their fishing to areas closer to the shore, as clouds obscure their landmarks and make it difficult to determine their position. Between April and June, during *dōti*, the fishermen said that it is a difficult time to fish, as the weather is very unsettled and there is a strong possibility of storms occurring. This situation gradually grows worse until the beginning of July when *ḥorf* begins, and all the fishermen would stop fishing. According to several experienced full-time fishermen,[70] the north wind, *ṣerbihi* (Soc), is only good for fishing if it does not blow strongly. The east wind, *eʾeris*, is said to be dangerous for fishing only in so far as it heralds the beginning of the stormy season and can make the landing and launching of vessels on the south coast difficult. According to Abdulla Mohammed Mobarra, a very experienced elderly full-time fishermen,[71] in his 60s, *eʾeris* only blows strongly during the day; in the evening it becomes calm, making it possible to fish a short distance from the shore. The south wind, *mede* is only considered dangerous by those fishermen who do not have an engine on their boats, as it can blow you out to sea. Fishermen in Maḥfirihin told me that, if the west wind, *maʿaribo*, starts to blow then they would stop fishing and remain at home, as it is an unpredictable and dangerous wind to be out at sea in. In addition to the winds, they also said that the currents *leḥe* (Soc), *ʿālə* (Soc), and *sikūṭ* (Ar) make fishing difficult, and if they flow strongly it is very dangerous to fish too far from the shore. *Sikūṭ* and *ʿālə*, are considered to be the most dangerous, as they can quickly drag one out of sight of land.

Stēroh

The village of Stēroh is made up of fishermen from many other fishing villages from the north and south coasts of Socotra, although most have lived in Stēroh for at least two generations. They are all full-time fishermen who spend almost all of *ṣēreb* fishing in Stēroh. They knew all the monsoon seasons in Figure 60, although only *ṣēreb*, *ḥorf*, *ḳeyaṭ*, *dōti* and *ṣerebhen* are relevant to their fishing activities. According to them, *ṣēreb* is the best period to fish due to the calm weather. The beginning of May is the start of the SW winds of *ḥorf*, and everyone will stop fishing and most move away from the coast. The two seasons, *ḳeyaṭ* and *dōti*, are both difficult for the fishermen as the weather is unsettled and short violent storms frequently occur. An experienced full-time fisherman,[72] in his 60s, Said Salim Ahmed, told me that the seasonal fishermen in Stēroh rarely fish during these seasons, and prefer to return to the hills to look after their livestock. *Ṣerebhen* is also a time of unsettled weather that makes fishing offshore difficult, although experienced fishermen said that towards the end of *ṣerebhen* it is possible to fish more frequently and many attempt to fish offshore. Fishermen use both Arabic and Socotri terminology for local winds. The north wind, known as *azyab* (Ar) or *ṣerbihi* (Soc), is good for fishing if it does not blow very strongly. However, they did say that the south wind, *mede* is the best wind for fishing, as it does not blow strongly. Fishermen refer to the west wind as, *maʿaribo* (Soc) or *kōs* (Ar), and the east wind, *eʾeris* (Soc) or *hindī* (Ar). These winds are the most dangerous winds and no-one goes fishing when they are blowing. Two currents are recognised, *leḥe* (Soc) and *ʿālə* (Soc), both of which, if flowing strongly make fishing dangerous and the use of nets impossible.

Bidhōleh

The fishermen of Bidhōleh are Arabians and seasonal Bedouin, who have been fishing there for two to three generations. They recognise two seasons, *ṣēreb* (Soc)/ *azyab* (Ar), when the winds are calm and it is possible to fish, and *ḥorf* (Soc)/ *kōs* (Ar), when high winds make it impossible to take a boat out to fish. According to fishermen I spoke to, *ṣerbihi*, *maʿaribo* and *eʾeris* all make fishing dangerous, and it is only during *mede* when they fish offshore. A few of the more experienced fishermen do fish during *ṣerbihi* or *eʾeris*, although it is risky and the fishing is not good. When *maʿaribo* blows no one goes out to sea, even with an engine, as they say it is difficult to launch or land their vessels, and fishing is bad. None of the fishermen I spoke to knew about currents.

Di-Ṣeberho

Fishermen in the village of Di-Ṣeberho have mostly come from fishing villages in the north of Socotra, although most of those I spoke to had been living there for over 30 years. They were all full-time fishermen who spent all of the fishing season living and fishing in Di-Ṣ eberho. While they did known the names of the monsoon seasons listed in Figure 60, only, *ṣēreb* and *ḥorf* had any relevance for them. They told me that *ṣēreb* is the best fishing season, as the sea and winds are calm. *Ḥorf* is considered to be the worse time of year for fishing, and during this period they would either look after their goats, repair nets and other equipment, or travel to the Hadhramaut to fish. However, an experienced full-time fisherman, in his 40s, Saeed Hamed,[73] said that he would start fishing during *ṣerebhen*, mid-September, although only late in the day or early in the morning, when the winds were not so strong. Fishermen recognised four local winds. According to them, it is not possible to fish

[70] Abdulla Mohammed Mobarra, in his 60s; Muhammed Abdulla Muhammed Dimori, 80 years old; Muslim Abdulla, in his 30s; Salim Saeed, in his 30s, all interviewed on 11 February 2009.

[71] Interviewed on 11 February 2009.

[72] Interviewed on 11 February 2009.

[73] Interviewed on 30 December 2009.

if *maʿaribo* or *ʾeris* are blowing, as the sea is very rough and it is almost impossible to launch or land their vessels. While *ṣerbihi* (Soc) can be a difficult wind during which to fish, many fishermen do. *Mede* is recognised as the best wind to fish by, as it is calm, making it possible to travel further offshore. Fishermen said that only two currents affect fishing in Di-Ṣeberho, *leḥe* (Soc) and *ʿālə* (Soc), both of which flow are strong and make fishing dangerous and the use of nets impossible.

Samḥa

Khaysat ash-Shaikh

Khaysat ash-Shaikh is the only village on the island of Samḥa and is entirely inhabited by fishermen and their families. The fishermen are all very experienced and begin fishing from a very early age. They know of, and can name all the seasons given in Figure 60, but only two have any relevance for fishing, *ṣēreb* and *ḥorf*. According to them, *ṣēreb* is the fishing season and begins in October and ends in June. The closure of the fishing season occurs during *ḥorf*, which can begin in May, but is usually in June. Fishermen told me that, during *ḥorf*, it is impossible for them to use their vessels, and they leave Samḥa, returning in October when the winds become calmer. They recognise and can name all the local winds but, other than the west wind, *maʿaribo* (Soc), none cause them to stop fishing, but only influence on what side of the island they fish. With regards the currents, I was told that even though they are aware of them, other than affecting whether they can use a net or not, currents do not stop them fishing.

The fishing seasons and influence local winds and currents have on villages along the north and south coast and island of Samḥa is summarised in Appendix 3. What this appendix clearly demonstrates is the differences and similarities between fishing villages on the northern and southern coasts of Socotra and the outlying island of Samḥa; the difficulties and dangers in attempting to provide a generalisation for the islands, and how villages in close proximity can have very different perceptions of the seasons, local winds and currents. In previous studies, fishermen on Socotra are said to have recognised between two (Naumkin 1993: 162-167), four (Morris 2002: 16-18) and six (Serjeant 1992: 172-173) different seasons. However, as I have demonstrated above, whilst the fishermen from different villages may recognise all six seasons mentioned in Figure 60, few of these seasons have any relevance to their fishing activities. Indeed, along the north and south coasts, most fishermen only differentiated between two and three different fishing seasons, and only in Ḥadiboh, Maḥfirihin and Stēroh were seven, four and five seasons regarded as being relevant. While local winds and currents are recognised as having a significant effect on fishing, the way in which they are perceived varies from village to village. What is surprising is that even villages in close proximity do not recognise the same amount of seasons, and interpret the influence of local winds and currents in very different ways. It could be argued that the larger fishing villages with a long-standing tradition of fishing would recognise more seasons than the smaller, less established villages, this does not explain why Stēroh and Maḥrifihin, both relatively 'new' fishing villages, differentiate between four and five seasons. I believe that this can be explained by a transfer of knowledge from experienced fishermen from the north who have migrated, whether temporarily or permanently, to the south. This would demonstrate that fishing seasons and the way in which local winds and currents are interpreted is a product of socially reproduced knowledge, or the lack thereof. This would also explain why the number and influence currents have in specific locales can vary so dramatically between villages in close proximity, such as Shuʿub and Qalansiyah on the north coast and Stēroh and Bidhōleh on the south coast.

These differences between fishing villages on the north and south coasts of Socotra and the outlying island of Samḥa also demonstrate the dangers of taking an overall view. While this may provide a useful introductory overview of Socotra, it tends to overshadow the differences between villages and fails to take into account those winds which occur infrequently, such as *barrī* (Ar) and *mġēbīya* (Ar). However, differentiating between the north and south coasts of Socotra can provide an insight into the way in which certain winds have an effect on fishing villages on the same side of the island. This is best demonstrated by looking at the difference in the way in which the south wind has been interpreted throughout the villages of both the north and south coast, and how the local winds affect the fishermen of Samḥa. Along the north coast the south wind is either considered to make fishing difficult or signify the end of the fishing season, whereas on the south coast it can either be good for fishing or make fishing difficult. The difference between whether a wind makes fishing difficult or not is also based upon the strength of the winds, and the fishermen often qualify statements concerning a good wind direction by saying that the wind is calm. The fishermen on Samḥa tend to view the local winds very differently and only see the wind direction as an indication as to what side of the island they will fish on. This is based upon their knowledge of the wind shadow created by Samḥa, which is how they know what winds make it possible to fish where.

Conclusion

Within this chapter it is clear that Socotra lies within an area of the western Indian Ocean that is affected by a number of powerful meteorological events that also shape the island's climate. The fishermen of Socotra find themselves in an unenviable position in which the seas and currents are at their most violent and the force of the monsoon winds is virtually unceasing. However, due to the island's topography and local conditions there are areas in which the fishermen can enjoy periods of light winds and calm seas. The actual place and time in which these periods of calm occur is dependent on several factors, which include the direction of the prevailing monsoon wind, local topography and the effect of local winds. Understanding where and when these periods of calm occur is imperative for the fisherman, who is severely restricted by these phenomena.

The importance of understanding the effect of the monsoon winds along different areas of the coast is clearly reflected in the fishermen's vocabulary and the different seasons and winds they recognise. Previous studies of the fishermen by Serjeant (1992), Naumkin (1993) and Morris (2002) have recognised the importance of the weather for fishermen, but have oversimplified their understanding by generalising the seasons they recorded. According to these studies, the fishermen are aware of only a limited number of seasons and all share the same fishing calendar. However, as I have shown the fishing seasons and the way in which they are perceived are a great deal more complex than we have been led to believe.

Firstly, fishermen recognise anything between two and seven fishing seasons. The number of seasons they recognise is based upon the village they live in and what experience and knowledge they have of these seasons. The most important two seasons are, the beginning of the fishing season, known as *ṣēreb* (Soc), *azyab* (Ar), or the period in which the sea is open, *futūḥ al-baḥr* (Ar); and the end of the fishing season, known as *ḥorf* (Soc), *kōs* (Ar), or the period in which the sea is closed, *qāfal* (Ar). The other five seasons are known as *ṣerébhen* (Soc), *gyáḥś* (Soc), *ḳéyaṭ* (Soc), *dɔ̄ti* (Soc), and in Ḥadiboh, *məᶜɔ̄dif* (Soc). The number of seasons the fishermen perceive is due in part to the experience of the fishermen who, especially in Ḥadiboh and Qalansiyah, have been fishing for several generations and have learnt to use and recognise many more of the changing seasons. Also many of the experienced fishermen often travel around the island and some have even settled along the south coast, where they have undoubtedly shared their knowledge of how to recognise the changing seasons. This is especially apparent in Maḥfirihin and Stēroh, both of which have a large population of fishermen that come from the north coast, and are the only two villages on the south coast that have more than three fishing seasons in their calendar.

Secondly, the fishing calendars used by the fishermen differ, sometimes dramatically, between villages and areas on Socotra. This is mostly due to the effect of the monsoon on a particular locale, especially on the south coast which experiences very different conditions to that of the north. These differences manifest themselves in the geographical location, and what is a period of calm in one area can be a period of unsettled weather in another. The clearest example of this is the different characteristics of *ḳéyaṭ*. Along the north coast it can vary between being a period of calm or a period of unsettled weather. Whereas on the south coast *ḳéyaṭ* is always regarded as being a period of unsettled weather, although the impact it has on fishing activities varies with each village.

Fishing seasons may have the same terminology and may even have the same characteristics, yet the impact they have on the fishing population differs a great deal. The only season in which the fishermen are severely restricted from fishing is during the SW monsoon, and even then there are fishermen who are able to fish in protected bays. During the rest of the year the way in which each season impacts upon the fishing activities is almost entirely based upon the experience of the fishermen, and those who are experienced enough know the intricacies of where and when it is possible to fish during a specific season. Furthermore, as they travel throughout the island they gather a broader knowledge, and in some cases pass this on. What this indicates is that the number of seasons recognised by the fishermen is not based upon the effects of the weather, but is based upon the fishermen's experiences, knowledge and perception of the weather. Furthermore, that these perceptions of the weather are transferred by fishermen migrating from one side of the island to another poses an even more exciting possibility. Could this transference have also taken place on a larger scale? And, is it possible that Socotra's cultural links with East Africa and the Hadhramaut have had an impact on the transference of this knowledge? These and other question can only be answered when further ethnographic work in these areas is carried out.

With regards local winds, according to Serjeant (1992) and Morris (2002), the fishermen of Socotra recognise four different winds, named according to the direction in which they blow. Morris also says that each wind has specific characteristics. However, during my research I found that whilst the names of the local winds are much the same throughout the island, their characteristics and what they meant to the fishermen differed enormously. These differences were not only apparent between the north and south coast of the island but also between villages on the same coast. This was especially noticeable with the south and east winds which differed between villages along the same coast and either represented a period of calm or a period in which the fishermen would not go fishing. Furthermore, the fishermen also differentiated between those winds that were blowing strongly and those that did not, and would qualify the direction of the wind with its strength. Thus a wind could represent both a period of calm and a period of difficulty, depending on the strength at which it blew. In addition to the four winds mentioned by Serjeant and Morris, the fishermen I interviewed identified *barrī* (Ar) and *mġēbīya* (Ar), both of which are diurnal land breezes. These two winds have no relation to the four main winds, but are still considered to be important enough to know, as they are related to specific meteorological events and periods that affected fishing activities. Furthermore, *barrī* (Ar) is also recognised by fishermen in al-Shihr (Camelin 2006: 116). This is likely to have been a word that was incorporated into the Socotri fishermen's vocabulary by the increasing amount of migrant fishermen from the Hadhramaut, and is an example of the adoption and incorporation of their traditions and knowledge. These local winds demonstrate that, much like the seasons, not only are there physical variations between different areas, but there are also variations in the fishermen's understanding and perception of the environment they work in.

Finally, that this is the first ethnographic work to look at how currents are understood by the fishermen on Socotra is surprising as the currents surrounding the island play a significant role in influencing the fishing activities undertaken and not only do they affect the type of equipment they can use, but also whether it is safe to fish offshore. Whilst the fishermen use the same names for the directional flow of the currents there is a great deal of variation in whether a current flowing in a specific direction is dangerous or not. The main agreements are that all strong currents can make fishing by net impossible and if they are flowing offshore they are dangerous. The importance of determining directional flow is therefore important and making specific attempts to know in which direction the current is flowing was imperative, although with the increasing use of engines it has become less so. Unfortunately, this means that traditional methods used to determine current direction and flow will soon be forgotten.

Part Four:
Vessels, Gear And Catch

Chapter 9

Fishing Vessels

Studying boats and the ways in which they are used and constructed provides a unique insight into the many social, technological and economic changes affecting those communities that use them. Furthermore, an understanding of the types of vessels used also offers opportunities to discover how they have affected and have been affected by the people using them. The aim of this chapter is to outline the different types of fishing vessels being used on Socotra and look at how their introduction and use has influenced the fishermen. To achieve this I analyse the historical, ethnographical and environmental evidence outlined in previous chapters to determine where these vessels came from, why they were chosen, how they are used, and what skills and knowledge is required by the fishermen to operate and maintain them.

Fishing vessels are built and used to perform an array of different functions that include hunting, locating, catching and carrying various marine species, in a wide variety of environmental conditions. In effect, they can be defined as specialised vessels designed to perform a series of well defined tasks at sea and in variable weather conditions. The types of craft that are able to operate as fishing vessels in any specific area are influenced by a number of factors which include but are not limited to the following:

- Species, location, abundance and distribution
- Fishing gear and methods
- Geographical and climatic characteristics of the fishing area
- Seaworthiness of the vessel
- Availability of finance
- Availability of boatbuilding and fishing skills
- Choice and availability of construction materials
- Economic viability

Consequently, when identifying the fishing vessel types used on Socotra these factors need to be taken into account, as they play an important role in the fishermen's preference for one vessel over another. The vessels that have been used by the fishermen of Socotra in the past and present are outlined below.

The Raft, *Ramas* (Ar) / *rēmuš* (Soc)

The earliest historically recorded vessel on Socotra and its outlying islands is a raft, which is a vessel constructed of several pieces of wood, normally logs, bound together with cord to form a floating platform. It was first described by a captain of the Dutch East India Company, Hendrik Hagenaer (*fl.* 17th century), who visited the island sometime between 1631 and 1638. During his visit he observed how, 'our people didn't see any vessels there, except for a few small rafts made of three or four pieces of timber, joined together, with which they went fishing' (Hagenaer 1650: 26). The presence of rafts is mentioned again in the late 19th century, when the English lieutenants Ormsby (d. 1857) and Wellsted (d. 1842) report seeing rafts in the north coast villages of Qalansiyah and Ḥadiboh, and along the shores of the south coast (Wellsted 1835b: 135, 161; Ormsby 1844: 363). The next person to mention this vessel is the archaeologist and traveller Theodore Bent (d. 1897), who says that in Qādheb, on the north coast, he saw a considerable number of vessels including rafts (Bent 1900: 357). The next reference, a few years later, is not on Socotra but on the island of ᶜAbd al-Kūri, which was visited by a zoological expedition led by Henry Forbes. According to Forbes (1903: xxviii), he saw a fisherman line fishing from a, 'poor raft of three narrow logs lashed together, with his legs dangling in the water, by which to paddle himself about the bay' (Forbes 1903: xxviii). Several years later, the United States Consul General to Aden, Charles Moser, not only described the raft he saw, but also photographed one being paddled by a fisherman off Ḥadiboh (Moser 1918: 268). This is the earliest image of a raft on Socotra and shows the square paddle being used and the method by which the logs were bound together. The last person to mention these vessels is Morris (2002: 224), who says that the rafts had been used extensively as lighters, for inshore fishing, and as diving platforms when diving for pearl oyster shells up until the early 20th century. She also says that they were constructed using driftwood, date palm trunks, *Sterculia* or *Ziziphus spina-christi* that were bound together with cotton rope. While these vessels are no longer in use today, I was able to interview several fishermen whose fathers had used them and gather information concerning their manufacture and use.

Several elderly full-time fishermen I interviewed in Ḥadiboh,[74] Suq,[75] and Maḥfirihin[76], said that the *rēmuš* was made from *gōdiᶜ* (Soc), the trunk of a tree. The two

[74] Esso Ibn Seyaka, in his 60s; Aneen Ibn Sankour, in his 60s; Ali Ibn Aneen, in his 60s, all interviewed on 7 February 2009.
[75] Rabain Mobarek al-Noby, in his 60s; Saaed Ahmed Nashran, in his 60s, both interviewed on 14 February 2009.
[76] Abdulla Mohammed Mobarra, in his 60s; Muhammad Abdulla Muhammad Dimori, 80 years old, both interviewed on 11 February 2009.

main tree types used in the construction of the *rēmuš* were *ˈikšə* (Soc), *Commiphora ornifolia*, and *di-ˈtimərə* (Soc), the date-palm. This is in contrast to Morris (2002: 224), who says that they would have been made from an array of different woods. The reason for this could to be due to Morris's confusion between the *rēmuš* and the *śˈerḥʌ* (Soc), a sewn vessel that was repaired using any available wood, see below. Those interviewed in Ḥadiboh and Qādheb[77] said that the reason these trees were chosen was that they were light and floated easier. The fishermen also said that they remembered that their fathers had made these by placing three or sometimes four large logs next to one another on the beach and then binding them together. Three logs were preferable to four as fewer logs made the *rēmuš* lighter and easier to carry. According to an 80 year old, full-time fisherman Muhammad Abdulla Muhammad Dimori,[78] the rafts were constructed by binding together three logs using either date-palm fibre or cotton that had been formed into a rope. The logs would be bound together by laying them together on the beach and placing a thick branch across the ends. He said that this helped hold the logs in place and made it easier to bind them. The other fishermen interviewed in villages along the north coast mostly agreed with this method, although the way in which the logs and cross branches were said to be bound together differed slightly. The main methods used to bind the logs together was either by binding the outer logs to the cross branch and then the centre log, or binding each log to the branch and then to each other.

The fishermen I interviewed in Ḥadiboh, Suq and Qādheb told me that the *rēmuš* was an extremely seaworthy vessel and could be easily landed when the surf conditions were rough, as the hard landings had little impact other than dislodging the ropes, which could then easily be retied. They also said that it was mostly propelled using a *mˈʌḳədef* (Soc)/*miqdāf* (Ar), a long paddle with either a round or square blade. The shape of the paddle had no significance for the fishermen, and the blade was made from whatever material was available. None of the nine fishermen interviewed could recall a sail having ever been used on a raft. They did say that that the rafts were mostly used to set traps, although some people had used them to handline from.

Finally two descriptions from the 19th century provide an insight into the use and importance of this vessel for fishermen. The first of these is that of the political agent and consul of Muscat, Samuel Miles (d. 1914), who said that, 'a sort of raft is used at Muscat by the Socotrians who visit that port during the fishing season; it is called Ramas and is made of three logs about six feet long, the central one being the longest and propelled by a double paddle' (Miles 1919: 2. 414). The second description to mention fishermen from Socotra fishing in Oman is the political agent for the Government of India, Percy Cox, who, in 1925, said that, 'small parties of fishermen from the island of Socotra, who camped about in the neighbouring coves made a living by fishing from their rafts, and diving for jetsam in the harbour' (Cox 1925: 195).

The presence of the Socotri fishermen and their rafts in Muscat may be explained by the itinerant nature of the fishermen on Socotra. Evidence of this is also borne out in the historical sources, which mention that they frequently used visiting shipping to travel to and from Socotra (Wellsted 1840: 323; Schweinfurth 1881: 128; Ingrams and Ingrams 1993: 190). Nevertheless, it does not explain the presence of their rafts, which are supposed to have been sailed from Socotra to Muscat in 10 to 12 days (Agius 2008: 121). That fishermen could have accomplished this feat is unlikely. First, there is no evidence on Socotra that the fishermen used sails on their rafts, and the only period in which current drift could have assisted their passage would have been during the extreme conditions of the SW monsoon season. Secondly, there are no historical accounts of them ever having made lengthy journeys and none of those interviewed said that they would take the *rēmuš* any further out than a nearby headland. Consequently, I am more inclined to believe that these Socotri fishermen in Oman would have obtained passage on passing dhows, stowing their vessels and fishing gear onboard. This practice is still evident today, although it is the fibreglass vessels that the fishermen ship to the mainland. This is mostly done just before the SW monsoon season, when the weather makes it nearly impossible to fish on Socotra.

Overall, the *rēmuš* is an exceptional vessel in terms of versatility, and it is perhaps unsurprising that on Socotra it has been in use from at least the 17th century. Furthermore, even with the introduction of a number of other fishing vessels, the *rēmuš* was still being used by a number of fishermen up until a generation ago. The popularity of this vessel is due to a multitude of factors, which include its suitability to the environmental conditions, the simplicity of its design and importantly its economic viability. This viability stems from the fact that constructing these vessels requires no major capital outlay and limited skills. In addition, they are extremely easy to repair and use. Nevertheless, as imported vessels became more affordable they were gradually replaced. Fishermen in Ḥadiboh told me that the reason the *rēmuš* was replaced was also due to it being too slow in comparison to the imported vessels and that it was difficult for them to be able to catch the high-value species, such as shark. Today there is no evidence for the *rēmuš* on Socotra, and the logs used in their manufacture are likely to have been used as fuel in lime pits, or to

[77] Salim Saeed Atman, full-time fisherman, 55 years old; Salim Games Saeed, full-time fisherman, in his 60s, both interviewed on 2 January 2010.

[78] Interviewed on 11 February 2009.

construct the boat shelters that store those vessels which eventually came to replace them.

Similarly constructed rafts have been recorded in India, Oman and Yemen (Bent 1900: 48; Hornell 1920: 25-26; Moore 1925: 138; Hornell 1970: 62-65; Prados 1996: 91). According to Bent, Moore and Prados, the rafts in Oman and Yemen were built using anything between one and 12 pieces of timber, whereas in India, the rafts recorded by Hornell (1920: 25) were all built using three logs. Furthermore, the blades of the oars used to propel the rafts in Yemen were rounded (Prados 1996: 93), whereas those in India are rectangular (Hornell 1920: 23). The similarities between the Indian and Socotri are striking, and it is possible that it could be an indication of an Indian influence. This would tie in with the historical and archaeological evidence for an Indian presence on the island, outlined in previous chapters, and emphasises the trading links which are likely to have existed.

The Date Palm-Frond Boat, *shāsha* (Ar)

The *shāsha* (pl. *shāshāt* or *shūsh*) is made from the central spines of the leaves of the date palm, which are bound together to form a flexible yet seaworthy raft. To aid buoyancy the bulbous ends of the palm branches are placed within the hull of the vessel, which is then covered by a deck also made from the date-palm spines (Figure 65). The suitability of the *shāsha* for fishing is noted by several authors, who say that because of its buoyancy and flexibility it is ideally suited to those fishermen who operate in rough seas and heavy surf (Bertram 1948: 28; Donaldson 1979: 75; Agius 2002: 122). Furthermore, this craft is said to be extremely economical, taking a skilled person only one or two days to construct using nothing but locally available material (Agius 2002: 122).

The existence of this vessel on Socotra is alluded to several times by visitors to Socotra. The earliest and most enlightening is a description by Theodore Bent who says that in Qalansiyah, 'One of our amusements was to watch boat-building accomplished by tying a bundle of bamboos together at each end and pushing them out into shape with wooden stretchers' (Bent 1900: 347). The bamboo Bent mentions is most likely to have been date palm fronds, as there are no written records of bamboo having ever grown or been imported to the island. Further westwards, in Qādheb, he says that there are a considerable number of canoes, rafts and surf-boats which are being used by the fishermen (Bent 1900: 357). These surf boats are likely to have been the same date-palm frond vessels he saw in Qalansiyah, especially as they are seen to be particularly suited to tackling the rough surf. Travelling further westward along the north coast, Bent describes how in Ḥowlef he saw, '...fishermen, who go out on little rafts made of bundles of palm-leaf ribs to drop traps for fish' (Bent 1900: 394). This description provides the most definite evidence for the existence of the *shāsha* on Socotra, and not only describes the vessel, but also how it was being

FIGURE 65. A *SHĀSHA* FROM OMAN, WHICH IS ON DISPLAY AT THE EYEMOUTH MARITIME CENTRE (PHOTO: AUTHOR).

FIGURE 66. A SEWN BOAT FOUND IN DI-ṢEBERHO (PHOTO: AUTHOR).

used. Several years later, in 1944, a British Military Intelligence report on the fisheries of Socotra said that the coastal community owned 338 canoes and six row boats (Scott *et al.* 1946: 614). I argue that these six row boats were actually the same rafts seen by Bent, 44 years previously. The evidence to support this lies in the term row boat, which signifies that they were being propelled by the use of oars, which is the method used to propel the *shāsha* (Donaldson 1979: 75). Moreover, the means of propulsion for all the other vessels found on Socotra is either paddle or sail, and it would seem unlikely that this military report would have confused the different methods of propulsion.

The only recorded use of these vessels is to deploy fish traps, although it is also possible that they were also used as a platform from which to deploy handlines and nets, as was recorded off the Al-Batinah coast in Oman (Donaldson 1979: 121). The presence of the *shāsha* on Socotra up until 1944 demonstrates that fishermen still had the necessary skills to manufacture this vessel. These skills are likely to have been brought to Socotra by fishermen from Yemen and Oman who settled on the island, or by Socotri fishermen that had learned them during their stay in these areas. The evidence for this is that, not only are there strong links between Socotra and these areas but there is also evidence to demonstrate that these vessels were being built and used along the south Arabian coastline for several decades (Haines 1845: 110; Donaldson 1979: 113). Today the *shāsha* of Socotra have all but been forgotten, and virtually no fishermen were able to recall them having existed. Were it not for an offhand comment made during a group interview with fishermen in Ṣaqarah on the types of vessels they had used, I myself would have doubted the veracity of these historical accounts. Unfortunately, during the interview[79] other than a fisherman telling me that he had seen them in use on Socotra I was not able to gather any further information concerning their local manufacture or use.

The Sewn Boat, *Śerḥʌ* (Soc)

There is no mention of any sewn boats on Socotra in the historical record. The earliest record of a sewn vessel is by Morris (2002: 224), who said that in Qaᶜarah, on the south coast, fishermen remembered a very roughly constructed vessel that was made from driftwood planking and local woods sewn together with cotton. She also said that these vessels came to the island sometime after the *rēmuš*. An elderly fisherman, Mubarak Eesa Walid,[80] said that he remembered that the *śerḥʌ* appeared after 1969 as an experiment. According to him, sewn boats were brought to the island on pearling dhows from the Gulf and sold to a few fishermen in Ḥadiboh, although they were said to be too heavy and slow to be of any use. During fieldwork I undertook in 2004, I found several sewn vessels in Di-Ṣeberho and Maḥfirihin on the south coast. These were constructed from several planks that had been caulked with date-palm fibre and fastened together with twine and treenails, wooden pegs (Figure 66). The caulking was coated with shark-liver oil. The hulls of the sewn vessels I recorded were strengthened

[79] This interview was conducted during my earlier 2004 trip to the island whilst studying the *hūrī* and I failed to understand the significance of this comment at the time and did not record the name of this fisherman.

[80] Interviewed by Miranda Morris in 2002, who kindly passed me her transcripts.

with the addition of ribs that were also sewn in place. These vessels all had a transom stern that was used to mount an outboard engine, and in Di-Ṣeberho they also had a mast step for a sail.

According to those full-time fishermen interviewed[81] in Di-Ṣeberho and Stēroh who owned the *śerḥʌ*, these had either been bought from vessels coming from Yemen or the Gulf, or directly from a boat builder in Yemen. Said Salim Ahmed,[82] a full-time fisherman 45 years old, said that he had bought his sewn vessel in Qusayᶜir, in Yemen from a boat builder. He also said that he had seen this boat in Qusayᶜir when he was working there and decided to buy it. Before buying this vessel he said that he had helped the boat builder he bought it from to make it in order to learn how to build and repair it. When the boat was finished he brought it to Socotra on a *sanbūq*. Other fishermen who owned these vessels said that they had bought them on the island or from visiting *sanbūqs*. The importance of being able to repair and sew this vessel was reflected in interviews with the other fishermen who owned them. According to Mounir Eissa Salim,[83] he had learned to sew his vessel by watching another fisherman repair his vessel and after this he had practiced the sewing technique he saw by tracing the technique he witnessed in the sand. He said that he continued to do this until he could fully understand the process and method, after which he was able to sew his own vessel. Noah Salim said that he did not know how to sew his vessel, and had always asked someone else to help him repair his vessel in exchange for fish, dates or other supplies.

These fishermen told me that they used their vessels a short distance offshore, and normally used them with one person when handlining, and two with a net. They also said that they would make use of either a sail or an outboard engine, and that they are fast and light, an important attribute when considering that they said it would have to be brought ashore every day. Furthermore, they said that they had bought their vessels before the fibreglass vessels arrived. The fibreglass vessels were first introduced to Socotra in 1967 when, under the Socialist Government, they began to be imported from Yemen. Sewn vessels recorded along the south coast appear to be very different to those of the north coast, which were, according to Mubarak Eesa Walid and Morris (2002: 224), cumbersome, badly built and slow. The reason for this difference is likely to be that the vessels brought by the Gulf pearling ships were of a different type to those bought by the fishermen along the south coast. As there is no evidence on the north coast for these sewn vessels it is difficult to tell. In 2006, I returned to undertake a detailed record of the *śerḥʌ* and found that in Di-Ṣeberho they no longer existed and in Maḥfirihin they had all been destroyed, with only a few broken sewn planks remaining. The fishermen said that the main reason they were gone was that the 2004 tsunami had destroyed them,[84] although they had been abandoned much earlier.

The methods by which the fishermen had learned to repair their vessels provide an interesting insight into the learning process, demonstrating how sewing techniques were learnt and how the characteristics of a vessel can differ from one side of the island to another. When comparing these sewn vessels with those recorded in Somalia, East Africa, Oman and Yemen there are a number of similarities in the sewing techniques used (Chittick 1980; Prados 1996, 1997; Vosmer 1997; Gilbert 1998). The closest resemblance to the *śerḥʌ* are two fishing vessels, a sewn *hūrī* recorded in al-Shihr, Yemen and a *beden* recorded in Hafun, Somalia (Chittick 1980: 301-303; Gilbert 1998: 45). These two vessels are similar in design, shape and size, and in the way they were sewn. According to Chittick (1980: 301), the treenails used to fasten the planking in the *beden* were set vertically into the adjacent planks, whereas the treenails used in the *śerḥʌ* are set at an angle, and closely resemble the fastenings used in the *sanbūqs* and sewn *hūrīs* recorded in al-Shihr, Yemen (Prados 1997: 100-102). That the sewn vessels on Socotra are similar in design to the vessels in Yemen reinforces what the fishermen said, and it is possible that the sewing tradition practiced on Socotra came from Yemen, rather than Africa.

The Dugout Canoe, *hūrī* (pl. *hawārī*) (Ar)

The *hūrī* is a dugout canoe found all along the Western Indian Ocean littoral, many having been recorded along the shores of East Africa, Arabia and West India (Moore 1920; Hornell 1946; Bowen 1952; Prados 1996, 1997, 1998; Agius 2002; Jansen van Rensburg 2010; Petersen 2010).

The first historical account of the *hūrī* on Socotra is by Theodore Bent (1900: 357), who says that amongst the variety of boats he saw along the north coast there were several canoes. He also says that the people on the island use the milky sap from the Euphorbia to coat the bottoms of their canoes (Bent 1900: 380). This seems unlikely as there are no subsequent accounts mentioning this, and none of the fishermen could ever recall anyone using the sap of a Euphorbia to coat their *hūrīs*. They said that they used shark-liver oil, which was specifically collected for this purpose. This is corroborated by Morris (2001: 223), who says that shark-liver oil is applied to the outer hull. The next description in 1966 was by the Assistant Political Advisor at Aden, G. H. H. Brown, in a report on the economic development of Socotra. Brown

[81] Noah Salim, 55 years old; Said Salim Ahmed, 45 years old, both interviewed on 14 December 2004; Mounir Eissa Salim, in his 60s, interviewed on 15 December 2004.
[82] Interviewed on 15 December 2004.
[83] Full-time fisherman, in his 60s, interviewed on 15 December 2004.
[84] See Fritz and Okal (2007) for a full account of the effects of the 2004 tsunami on Socotra.

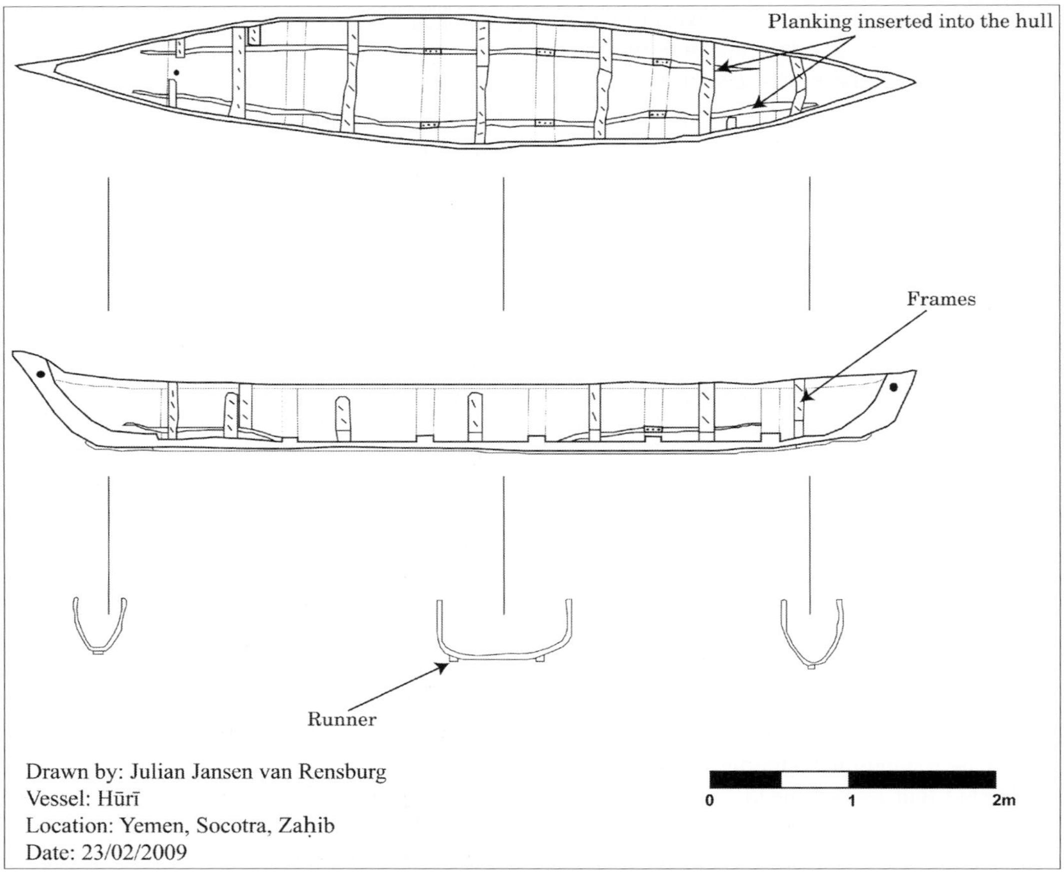

FIGURE 67. A LINE DRAWING OF A MODIFIED *HŪRĪ*. NOTE THE SPLITS IN THE HULL THAT HAVE PLANKING INSERTED INTO THEM.

(1966:28) says that *hūrī* were made from Calicut teak and cost between 550 and 800 shillings, depending on their size. He also says that due to their high cost they were either purchased by several fishermen, each of whom had a share in the boat, or by an individual, who bought it in instalments. During his survey of the north coast, he says that the *hūrī* number in their hundreds, with nearly every resident having owned at least a share in one (Brown 1966: 28). Whereas, on the south coast he records less than ten vessels, all of which he says were owned by Bedouin, who only fish during good weather. Finally, he mentions that they were mostly used for fishing, although in Ḥadiboh he remarks that African fishermen used them for pearl diving (Brown 1966: 30). Several years later, Serjeant (1992: 171), recounts that besides being used for fishing they were also used as lighters, to take goods from the shore to visiting *sanbūqs*. According to Naumkin (1993: 162-167), the *hūrīs* were used for fishing, and those fishermen who owned their own vessels had either bought them using an inheritance, were paying them off through instalments, or had inherited them through the death of a father. Morris (2002: 223) says that those fishermen who owned *hūrīs* were considered to be very fortunate. She also says that the *hūrīs* were modified locally by the fishermen, who added ribs to strengthen the hull, and runners to protect it from being damaged when it was dragged onto the beach. Furthermore, she says that they were propelled using a sail made from imported cotton, or a paddle made locally from branches of *Ziziphus spina-christi*.

The latest study of the *hūrīs* of Socotra was undertaken by this author (Jansen van Rensburg 2010). The *hūrī* I describe is a double-ended dugout canoe that is made from a single tree trunk, which may or may not have been expanded to increase the beam of the vessel. The size of the vessels I recorded varied between three to nine metres in length with a beam of one to one and a half metres. They had all been modified locally, to make them more suitable for fishing in the rough seas and heavy surf off Socotra. The modifications I recorded were all undertaken by a carpenter, who in many cases was also a fisherman. The alterations included adding washstrakes to increase the freeboard and to prevent waves from swamping the boat, and fitting ribs and crossbeams to provide additional structural reinforcement and a place to sit. In addition, I recorded several *hūrīs* whose hulls had been expanded. Where expansion of the hull did occur, two floor timbers were placed at either end of the hull and nailed in place to prevent the hull from splitting, after which two parallel gaps were cut into the hull. The *hūrī* was then filled with rocks and kept underwater in the sea or a lagoon to allow it to 'drink',[85] or become waterlogged. After several days, the *hūrī* was removed from the water and planks were fitted into the gaps, forcing the hull further apart. These planks were then caulked. Several planks were then placed across the beam to keep the sides apart, and the hull was allowed to dry slowly (Figure 67). Fishermen in Zaḥib told me that, the wider beamed *hūrīs* were less likely to overturn in rough sea conditions. Further additions included runners fitted to the outside of the hull to protect the boat when it was dragged up and down the beach, and rubbing strakes fitted to the gunwale to protect the sides from wear when line fishing (Figure 68).

Throughout Socotra, the *hūrīs* are propelled using a paddle, sail, or outboard engine, and it is possible to travel a significant distance out to sea with either. The crew size on board varies from one to three, according to the type of equipment used and a number of other socio-economic factors that were outlined earlier. In Qalansiyah[86] and Ḥadiboh[87] the fishermen said that, in calm weather, one could paddle one's *hūrī d-mʌ́ḳədef* (Soc), (*hūrī* with paddle), as far out to sea as the island of Samḥa. The only *hūrī* I saw using a sail was in Di-Ḥamari (in 2004); it was being used to take tourists out, and was not used for fishing. The owner of this *hūrī*, Abdullah Mohammed Najai,[88] a full-time fisherman in his 60s, said that he had used this sail-powered *hūrī* when fishing, but now he used a fibreglass fishing boat. He also said that sails were used by few fishermen on the island, as many people did not know how to sail. This was reiterated by fishermen in Qalansiyah and Ḥadiboh, who said that few fishermen had used sails, preferring to paddle. Several informants in Ḥadiboh said that when it became possible to buy outboard engines on Socotra, those that could afford them began to use them with their *hūrīs*, as they made their vessels faster and allowed them to travel further out to sea. According to Khamis Amer, a full-time fisherman and carpenter in his 60s,[89] if one wanted to use an engine on a *hūrī* one needed to make several modifications. These alterations included fitting additional planking to the stern to mount the outboard engine, and increasing the freeboard with extra planking to deal with the extra weight of the engine and prevent swamping in the high seas. These modifications are seen in many *hūrīs* on Socotra, along the Hadhramaut coast (Prados 1996: 94) and in Oman (Agius 2002: 119-121) (Figure 69).

FIGURE 68. A MODIFIED *HŪRĪ* IN ḤADIBOH (PHOTO: AUTHOR).

In addition to the modifications that were made to the *hūrīs*, many also required extensive repairs due to their age and the rough landings they were subject to. These repairs were carried out by those fishermen who were also carpenters, and included anything from the addition of new runners and ribs to repairing large sections of damaged hull. These areas of damage were, in some cases, so extensive that only the ends and some parts of the upper structure of the original vessel remained, with planking making up the majority of the underside of the vessel. Along the north coast there were noticeable regional differences in the type of repairs done, with damage to the hulls in Ghubbah being sewn, and those in Ṣaqarah and Ḥāllah being nailed and caulked. In Ḥadiboh and Qalansiyah the repairs were a mixture of

[85] Jamen Khamis Saeed Marjan Saeed, full-time fisherman, in his 60s, interviewed on 22 February 2009.
[86] Abdullha Rahman Abod Ali Saeed, full-time fisherman, 38 years old, interviewed on 16 December 2009; Abaid Salem bin Awailan, full-time fisherman, in his 50s; Salam Saeed Martah, full-time fisherman, 39 years old, both interviewed on 17 December 2009.
[87] Khanem Salem Mohammed, full-time fisherman, in his 40s, interviewed on 3 January 2010; Mobarik Ali Adbulla, full-time fisherman, in his 60s, interviewed on 15 February 2009; Jamen Mahafawl Saif, full-time fisherman, 70 years old, interviewed on 22 December 2009.
[88] Interviewed on 19 February 2009.
[89] Interviewed on 15 February 2009.

FIGURE 69. A *HŪRĪ* MODIFIED TO FIT AN OUTBOARD ENGINE IN QALANSIYAH. THE OWNER ABDULLHA RAHMAN ABOD ALI SAEED IS ON THE RIGHT AND MY GUIDE AHMED ABDULLA ON THE LEFT (PHOTO: AUTHOR).

both. This regional difference is likely to be due to the knowledge and skills of the fishermen in each village. I argue that the diverse population of Ḥadiboh and Qalansiyah is one of the reasons why repairs in these villages are so varied, and why those in the smaller villages of Ghubbah, Ṣaqarah and Ḥāllah tend to focus on one particular method. These repairs are likely to be influenced by the settlement of fishermen from overseas, whose skills are reflected in the types of repair practiced.

The fishermen I interviewed in Ḥadiboh, Suq, Qalansiyah and other villages on the north coast told me that, apart from the modifications and repairs needed to keep their vessels seaworthy, it was also necessary to coat the hull with shark-liver oil. This was done to prevent the *hūrī* from drying out and to stop it from being 'eaten' (being attacked by wood boring organisms), when they were used during the fishing season. According to Saad Dabowed Mousa,[90] it was necessary to coat the hull at least once a month when fishing, although when it was stored over the SW monsoon period it was not necessary to do it so frequently, as the coating was not washed off by immersion in the sea.

The methods by which the fishermen acquired their vessels differed greatly. According to a 70 year old full-time fisherman, Jamen Mahafawl Saif,[91] the *hūrīs* were first brought to Socotra by fishermen from Oman and East Africa. He also said that after this some people had bought them from *sanbūqs* coming from Africa, India and Arabia. In Qalansiyah, Abdullha Rahman Abod Ali Saeed,[92] 38 years old, said that when his father had come from Oman to settle on Socotra he had brought three *hūrīs* with him. He also said that at first his father had employed other fishermen to help him and his sons to fish, but that after a few years his father had sold two of them to other fishermen on the island. In Ṣ aqarah, Thaili Hamoadi[93] told me that when he had been working as a labourer in West India, he had bought a *hūrī* with his wages and shipped it to Socotra. In Suq, Saad Dabowed Mousa[94] said that he had ordered his *hūrī* from the *sanbūqs* that came from Africa and that his vessel was African. Several other fishermen also made this distinction between vessels coming from India, Arabia and Africa, although there is little physical difference between them. My study of wood samples taken from an array of different vessels on Socotra has also shown that they were all built from teak, which came from India (Jansen van Rensburg 2010: 101). This differs to those *hūrī* recorded in Oman, which are built from mango (Agius 2002: 119), and is likely to be demonstrative of a regional difference in *hūrīs* imported from different areas in India.

According to Miranda Morris's informant, Mubarak Eesa Walid, before a new *hūrī* is used or after substantial modifications have been made, a goat would be killed and the skin of the goat wrapped around the prow. Unfortunately, I was not able to verify this as no vessels I found had any remnants of skin, and the fishermen I interviewed did not mention this practice. Nonetheless, this form of lustration is widely recorded as having been practiced throughout Eastern Arabia, (Bowen 1955:31; Agius 2002: 111). The reason that the fishermen did not mention this ritualised practice is likely to be due to an aversion to mentioning practices which are linked to what is considered to be the era before Islam, known in Arabic as *jāhiliyyah* (Ar) (a state of ignorance, and un-Islamic practices). This is very much the same situation as that recorded by Elie (2007: 350-352), who also found that rituals of a so-called un-Islamic nature were 'conveniently forgotten' by his informants on Socotra.

In spite of the expense and numerous modifications made to the *hūrīs* brought to Socotra they remained extremely

[90] Saad Dabowed Mousa, full-time fisherman, in his 60s, interviewed on 14 February 2009.

[91] Interviewed on 22 December 2009.

[92] Full-time fisherman, interviewed on 16 December 2009.

[93] Full-time fisherman, in his 60s, interviewed on 23 December 2009.

[94] Saad Dabowed Mousa, full-time fisherman, in his 60s, interviewed on 14 February 2009.

FIGURE 70. A '*HŪRĪ* BLASTIK' MOORED OFF THE VILLAGE OF KHAYSAT ASH-SHAIKH, SAMḤA (PHOTO: AUTHOR).

popular for many years and are still used. The main reason for their popularity is that they are considered by the fishermen to be extremely effective fishing vessels, noted for their seaworthiness, durability and ability to take large loads. Fishermen on the north coast consider the *hūrīs* to be safer than other vessels when venturing further offshore as, even if they became swamped, there is no danger of them sinking. A story told to me by Abdullha Rahman Abod Ali Saeed ,[95] reinforces this point. His tale began when shark fishing near Samḥa. While attempting to bring a shark he had caught into his boat the shark struck his boat very heavily, causing it to capsize. Despite capsizing, it did not sink and he only had to turn it upright and bail it out before being able to resume fishing. The shark escaped. He said that if this had happened with his fibreglass vessel he would not be alive today as it would have sunk and he would have drowned. The few remaining *hūrīs* on Socotra are those owned by people who are either unable to afford the newer fibreglass vessels or those who wish to retain them for personal reasons. A policeman I spoke to said that he had bought a small *hūrī* to keep for fishing when he had time, while I also noticed that many children were given them by their fathers, although these were mostly used to play in rather than to fish for sustenance. Unfortunately, the majority of the remaining *hūrīs* are being used as fuel in lime pits, and each year fewer can be found.

The Fibreglass Boat

Fibreglass, or Glass reinforced plastic (GRP) boats as they are also known, were gradually introduced to Socotra from about 1979, when they began to be built in Yemen (Hariri and Yusif 1999: 3). Initially, few fishermen could afford to buy them, although this rapidly changed with the Socialist government's support for the development of the fishing sector. This support provided them with an overseas market for their fish and a guaranteed income (Elie 2007: 171-172). Consequently, they were able to save sufficient capital to buy these vessels, which gradually replaced the *hūrīs*. Fishermen along both the north and south coasts of Socotra said that the fibreglass vessels were good fishing vessels because they were large, light, fast, could carry more than the *hūrīs*, and required less maintenance. They also said that there are two types of GRP boats. The first is known by the generic name for all these boats, 'blastik' and the second is known as '*hūrī* blastik'. The 'blastik' measures approximately 7-8 metres in length and has a beam of 1.3 metres and depth of a metre. The '*hūrī* blastik' is about 9-10 metres in length and has a beam of about one metre and a depth of approximately 1.4 metres. While the major difference appears to be the length of the vessel it is the depth, which the fishermen use to separate the two. The cheaper and shallower 'blastik' boat can be found throughout Socotra, yet in Samḥa none exist. In Samḥa the fishermen only use the '*hūrī* blastik', but call it by the generic name of 'blastik'. These vessels can be seen in Figure 70 and Figure 71.

Informants in Ḥadiboh[96] said that the 'blastik' is not a reliable vessel during bad weather, as they are very unstable and are easily swamped by large waves. They

[95] Abdullha Rahman Abod Ali Saeed, full-time fisherman, 38 years old, interviewed on 16 December 2009.

[96] Khanem Salem Mohammed, full-time fisherman, in his 40s; Minathal Eisa Mobarak, full-time fisherman, 34 years old; Naeef Ghaan Ahmed, full-time fisherman, 19 years old, all interviewed on 3 January 2010.

FIGURE 71. A 'BLASTIK' FISHING VESSEL OFF ḤADIBOH (PHOTO: AUTHOR).

said that the '*hūrī* blastik' is the best vessel for Socotra, and with it one can fish throughout the open fishing season. They also said that it was necessary to have at least two people in these vessels, although normally crew sizes are between three and four. The only means of propulsion for these vessels is one or two outboard engines. The second engine is normally carried in case one fails, and even though a paddle is carried, it is only used when catching bait fish. The number of engines is based on what the fishermen can afford and even though they considered two engines to be safe, especially when fishing offshore, few can afford to buy two. According to Fouhad Nasseb Saeed,[97] there are many cases of fishermen having been lost at sea after an engine had broken down. In Ḥadiboh and Qalansiyah fishermen said that, unlike the *hūrī*, these boats were not inherently buoyant and sink if they capsize. Furthermore, they said that if one runs out of fuel or the engine breaks down it is very dangerous, as one could be swept out to sea. A 32 year old full-time fisherman, Anwar Khamis Abdul Abod Ali Saeed,[98] told me that he had once been lost at sea when his engine broke down a short distance from Qalansiyah. He said that when he tried to put the anchor down it was too deep. He then tried signalling to get somebody's attention but nobody saw him. After that the current dragged him far out to sea where he spent several days living on melted ice and fish. One night he saw some lights but the people on the vessel did not hear him, and it was only after he drifted close enough to grab onto an anchored fishing vessel that he managed to save himself. He was later found by fishermen, who took him to the shore. He could not remember the name of the village, but said that it was on the coast of the Hadhramaut. This story is not uncommon, although not many have had such a happy ending and many fishermen interviewed knew of people who have been lost at sea, either after their boat had capsized or their engine had broken down.

Fishing Dhows, *ṣə̍dʌḳ* (Soc)/ *Wārra* (Ar)

The fishermen on Socotra differentiate between two types of fishing dhows. The first is *ṣə̍dʌḳ*, which refers to a wooden sail-powered vessel and the second is *wārra*, which refers to a motorised craft. The name is taken from the whirring noise the engine makes.

According to Brown (1966: 28), fishermen on Socotra do not own dhows, although many such vessels call at the island during the NE monsoon season. This is corroborated by Serjeant (1992:163), who said that there were many dhows that visited the island, but they did not belong to the fishermen and none remained on the island year round. He also says that in 1967 the ruling Sultan ᶜIsā bin Alī bin Sālim bin Saᶜd al-Tawᶜarī Al ᶜIfrayr had shares in a dhow, which was sailed along the north coast to collect various products, including fish, to sell in Zanzibar. This is corroborated by Piggott (1961: 56), who drew an image of a '*Buti* (Sokotra type)', and said that it was seasonally visiting Zanzibar. This would probably be the first record we have of a Socotri dhow type vessel.

The first record of a dhow being owned by Socotri fishermen is by Morris (2002: 109-130), who says that

[97] Marine Fisheries Officer, 30 years old, interviewed on 22 December 2009.
[98] Interviewed on 16 February 2009.

Vessel type	Construction	Propulsion	Area of use	Fishing tackle used	Crew Size
ramas (Ar)/*rēmuš* (Soc) Raft	Built locally from logs or driftwood.	Paddle	Near-shore fishing. Throughout Socotra.	Fish traps and hand lines.	1 person
shāsha (pl. *shāshāt* or *shūsh*) (Ar) Date-palm frond boat	Built locally using date palm fronds.	Oar	Near-shore fishing. North coast.	Fish traps	1 person
śerḥʌ (pl. *śerxʌ*) (Soc) Sewn boats	Imported, but repaired locally.	Sail and outboard engine.	Near and offshore fishing. Mainly south coast, some recorded as being used on the north coast and outer islands.	Hand lines and nets.	1-2 people
hūrī (pl. *hawārī*) (Ar) Dugout canoe a. Double-ended	Imported, but modified and repaired locally.	a. Sail and Paddle b. Outboard engine and paddle.	Near and offshore fishing. Throughout Socotra and the outlying islands.	Fish traps, hand lines and nets.	1-3 people
b. Transom-stern Glass reinforced plastic (GRP) a. 'blastik' b. *'hūrī blastik'*	Imported, few modified or repaired locally.	Outboard engine	Near and offshore fishing Throughout Socotra and the outlying islands.	Fish traps, hand lines and nets.	2-4 people

FIGURE 72. FISHING VESSELS OF SOCOTRA, THOSE BELOW THE DOUBLE LINE ARE STILL IN USE, WHILE THOSE ABOVE HAVE BEEN ABANDONED.

in the 20th century several villages on Socotra and the outlying islands owned one or more wooden *sanbūqs*, which they used to fish. This would confirm earlier accounts that a Socotri type dhow did exist, although, as she does not mention whether they were built on the island, it is difficult to speculate on their origins.

The only record of a *sanbūq* having being built on Socotra is by Mubarak Eesa Walid,[99] who said that a large wooden dhow had been built on Socotra. According to him, it had been built sometime in the 1960s, when a ship carrying wood had wrecked off the east coast, near Momi. Under the orders of the Sultan the wood had been brought to ᶜAririhun Di-Lisheh, on the north coast, where the vessel was built. He said that this craft was known as *Al-ᶜIzz* (Ar) (The Mighty), and that several carpenters and blacksmiths from Ḥadiboh, Suq and Dibinih had been involved in its construction. This vessel was wrecked off the coast of Socotra several years later, and no other dhow had been built since.

The two main reasons for the lack of dhows being built on Socotra are the lack of suitable wood and the difficulties of berthing during the SW monsoon, as discussed in chapter eight. Interestingly, there are several carpenters on Socotra who have the skills to manufacture vessels. Two carpenters[100] I spoke to said that they could build a *sanbūq*, but that it would be expensive as there was insufficient wood on the island and this would have to be imported.

The descriptions of the vessels outlined above are summarised in detail in Figure 72. This outlines several aspects, namely: the type of craft being used; construction; method of propulsion; fishing tackle used, and crew size. I have omitted the large fishing dhows as they do not accurately reflect the fishing vessels in use on the island.

Conclusion

The fishing vessels outlined above are representative of the temporal social and economic changes occurring on Socotra. Furthermore, they are also representative of the constraints imposed upon fishermen by the geographical and climatic character of the fishing areas off the island; the availability of construction materials; boatbuilding skills, and importantly the availability of finance. Overall, the vessels that are used by the fishermen of Socotra are

[99] Interviewed by Miranda Morris in 2002, who kindly passed me her transcripts.

[100] Esso Ibn Seyaka, full-time fisherman and carpenter, in his 60s, interviewed on 7 February 2009; Khamis Amer, full-time fisherman and carpenter, in his 60s, interviewed on 15 February 2009.

characterised by their seaworthiness, strength, lightness, speed and cost, both in terms of capital outlay and upkeep.

The earliest and longest surviving vessel on the island is the *rēmuš*. The adoption and length of time this vessel was used is based upon several factors, the most important being that it was possible to obtain all the materials used in its construction on the island, and that constructing and repairing them required no more skill than the skills already being employed by the fishermen to make fish traps, nets and lines. Consequently, it required virtually no capital outlay and could be repaired easily, making it ideally suited to catching fish for personal consumption. The limitations of the *rēmuš* were that it was slow and cumbersome, and while it could be used to catch sufficient fish for personal consumption it could not compete with other vessels in supplying fish for a burgeoning market. As a result, the *rēmuš* was soon replaced by faster, lighter imported vessels that could catch and transport large quantities of high-value pelagic species.

Determining what role the *shāsha* had, and for how long it was being used is difficult due to the lack of direct ethnographic evidence. That it was only ever recorded on the north coast and was a popular vessel used in Oman would make it possible to argue that the vessel may have been introduced to the island by visiting Omani fishermen, although it is uncertain whether the *shāsha* was constructed on the island or brought by visiting *sanbūqs*. This vessel is ideally suited to the environmental conditions of Socotra and, much like the *rēmuš*, could have been built from locally available material at minimal cost. The reasons for the failure of this vessel to have been adopted are likely to have been due to the several factors. First, the *shāsha* is slow and cumbersome, making it little better than the *rēmuš*. Secondly, it requires specific skills in its construction, skills which would have had to have been shared. I argue that it is likely that these skills had not been shared by the Omani fishermen, who were the only ones using the *shāsha*. This would explain why it was not in use for any length of time and why fishermen I interviewed could not recall using them. Thirdly, the *shāsha* quickly becomes waterlogged and needs to be dried before it can be used again, making it necessary for fishermen to own at least two or three if they wish to fish continuously (Agius 2002: 123). This would have required a substantial investment in time and labour with little more economic benefit that that already supplied by the *rēmuš*, even though there was an abundance of raw material on Socotra.

Sewn vessels on Socotra have been both accepted and rejected on different sides of the island. How is it that the sewn vessels on the north coast were rejected, whilst those on the south coast were not only accepted, but considered ideally suited? The answer lies in the difference between the geographical and climatic conditions of the two coasts and the experience of the fishermen. The south coast is an exposed shoreline, making it necessary for vessels to be light enough to be dragged clear of the sea, whereas the north coast is relatively sheltered with shallow protected bays. Thirdly, the fishermen of the south coast mostly have limited maritime experience, whilst those on the north coast have been fishing for several generations. Consequently, those on the north coast would have been aware of the limitations and maintenance requirements of the sewn vessel and would not have needed to be concerned with dragging a heavy vessel clear of the sea, while on the south coast they would have been concerned with the lightness of the vessel, and have made more compromises with the maintenance requirements of a sewn vessel.

The *hūrī* has had a significant impact on the fishermen and fishing practices. The importation of this vessel appears to have begun with the arrival of fishermen from Arabia and Africa, who brought their boats with them. These fishermen are likely to have been at a distinct advantage over the other fishermen in that they were able to travel further out to sea and use a wider range of fishing tackle, allowing them to target a greater range of marine species. Additionally, the larger carrying capacity of the *hūrī* also meant that they would not only be able to catch and transport sufficient fish for their sustenance but could also catch and transport sufficient fish to sell. This provided the fishermen with increased economic opportunities, and soon led to a significant increase in the demand for these vessels which, even though they required a high initial capital outlay, saw them rapidly replace the other fishing vessels on the island. In spite of this, as the numerous modifications demonstrate, the *hūrī* was perhaps not ideally suited to the rigours of fishing off Socotra and were it not for the availability of carpentry skills it may not have remained such a popular choice.

The GRP vessels are the latest fishing boats to have been accepted by the fishermen of Socotra. The main reason for this acceptance is due to a mixture between economic incentives offered by the government and the advantages of this craft over the *hūrī*. The main advantages are the increased range, carrying capacity, speed and lightness of these vessels. Despite, the fact that the fishermen recognised that they were inherently more dangerous than the *hūrī*, the economic benefits appear to have outweighed the danger.

According to a recent fisheries report, the distribution of fishing vessels in 1999 remained greatest along the north coast (Hariri and Yusif 1999: 8). While this is unsurprising, the number of vessels recorded does provide an interesting insight into the changes in vessel types. According to this report, there were 350 '*hūrī blastik*' type vessels, 252 *hūrī*, 207 '*blastik*' type vessels and 34 *sanbūqs*. That the *hūrī* remains the second most popular vessel is due to a number of factors which have influenced all fishing vessels operating on Socotra. The majority of these factors have been mentioned previously, but it is worth reiterating the fact that the fishermen not only have a substantial financial investment in these vessels, but that they were ideally suited due to their seaworthiness and that they were versatile. This versatility is seen in the numerous alterations and adaptations that could be made to these vessels, such as the fitting of an outboard engine and the expansion of the beam.

Having looked at the vessels types that have been used on Socotra it is clear that there is a distinctive progressive difference between the earlier locally built craft and the later imported vessels. This change not only relates to the increased range, propulsion and carrying capacity of the imported vessels, but also to the type of fishing tackle that can be deployed and the number of people who can fish from them.

The locally built craft like the *rēmuš* and *shāsha* were initially suited to the fishermen, in so far as they provided them with an inexpensive platform from which they could access the sea with their fish traps and handlines, catching sufficient fish for their own consumption. However, the difficulties of not being able to use these vessels for several months of the year meant that, outside of this period, the fishermen on Socotra found it difficult to survive. The importation of vessels like the *hūrī* did little to change the period within which they were able to fish, but it did allow them to access richer offshore fishing grounds and use a wider range of fishing tackle. Consequently, the fishermen were able to catch larger quantities of saleable fish, which were dried and either traded with visiting dhows for supplies or kept for the leaner months when fishing by boat was mostly impossible.

The adoption of these imported vessels is not simply an economically driven change but is also a change driven by migrant fishermen, especially those that brought their vessels with them. Indeed it is possible that these migrants played an important role in the adoption of vessels. There are three examples of this. The first is the *śérḥʌ*, which was available to the fishermen on the north coast, but was only used by those on the south coast. While the environment did play a role in this, it is important to remember that these vessels were brought to the island by fishermen that had used, built and bought them in Yemen, and it was because of these fishermen and their skill and experiences that saw these vessels become established on the south coast. The second is the *hūrī* which, even with the high capital outlay required to purchase one, become the most widely spread and numerous vessel on the island. The reason is that they are exceptionally versatile craft that were proven, by those fishermen who had imported them, to be superior to the vessels previously in use on Socotra. Furthermore, the *hūrīs* were extremely resilient craft that could be maintained and modified by the fishermen to suit local conditions and take advantage of new developments, such as the introduction of the outboard engine. These attributes and the fact that many of Socotra's migrant fishermen brought their *hūrīs* with them to the island is another reason why they were so readily adopted by the local fishermen. The replacement of the *hūrī* with the GRP vessels is different, as the latter had never been seen on the island before. Consequently, the question is why they would change to a vessel type that had never been present on the island before? The answer to this lies partly in the migrant nature of the fishing community, who spend several months of the year working overseas. During this period abroad the fishermen worked aboard different fishing vessels and gained experience in their use. This would have brought them into contact with the GRP fishing vessels and allowed them to gain sufficient knowledge concerning their use. Combined with the economic incentives offered by the Socialist government it is unsurprising that a vessel unproven on Socotra was so readily adopted by the fishermen. The various factors influencing the adoption and use of fishing vessels is also reflected in the adoption and use of the fishing tackle deployed by the fishermen, which will be looked at in the next chapter.

Chapter 10

Fishing Equipment

The equipment used to capture fish is influenced by a series of interrelated factors that include the cultural background and knowledge of the fishermen, the influence of the weather and landscape, and the species being sought. These factors are especially relevant for the Socotri fishermen, who use a wide range of fishing equipment that is reflective of the diverse ethnicities of the fishing population, the social and environmental constraints in which they work, and the range of species they catch. This chapter describes and analyses the fishing tackle used by the Socotri fishermen and the relationship between the tackle used and the technological, social and environmental influences affecting its use.

In general Socotri fishermen use five fishing methods, trapping, netting, handlining, trolling and longlining. Each of these methods has its own special requirements with regards to equipment, knowledge and technique. The requirements for each method also differ substantially in terms of the material required for their manufacture, where they can be successfully deployed and what species they are most likely to catch. Consequently, I describe and analyse each of these methods separately, beginning with trapping.

Trapping

Fish Traps, *ḳerˈḳor* (Soc)

The first textual reference for fish traps on Socotra occurs in the 19th century, when the traveller and archaeologist Theodore Bent observed them lying on the beaches. According to his description, the traps were made of woven 'bamboo' matting, and resembled enormous lobster pots, 'some six to eight metres in diameter' (Bent 1900: 348). As mentioned in chapter nine, there is no evidence for bamboo on the island, and it is likely Bent confused bamboo with an endemic shrub, *Croton socotranus*. Further information on fish traps and their use comes from an account by G. H. H Brown, the resident political advisor of Aden, who in 1966 said that almost all fishing on the island was done by fish trap or line (Brown 1966: 27). Fish traps are also recorded by Naumkin (1993: 202), who says that they were made from *hefu*, a type of tree, and that they were used for shallow offshore fishing. Naumkin provides no further information on what tree species *hefu* is, although it is likely that he was talking about a small tree, known locally as *Ḥfo* (Soc), which belongs to the *Vernonia* species, and is used throughout the island for its timber (Miller and Morris 2004: 515). The most descriptive account of the traps on Socotra is given in a United Nations Development Report (UNDP) from 2002, which outlines both the type of material that was used in their manufacture and how they were deployed (Morris 2002: 225-226). It says that fish traps were made from date stalks and a number of types of local wood, namely *Croton socotranus*, *Flueggea*, *Allophylus*, and *Commiflora orniflora*.

Fishermen along the north and south coasts of Socotra said that fish traps require a specialist to make them, and only relatively few African and Arabian fishermen have the necessary specialist skills needed. In Ḥadiboh, four very experienced older full-time fishermen,[101] who still made their own fish traps told me that they make them from two plants, namely: *fɔ̄tir* (Soc), the fruiting stalk of a date palm, and *mˈitrer* (Soc), *Croton socotranus*, a widespread endemic shrub that grows abundantly on the coastal plains, that is also used for timber and fuel (Miller and Morris 2004: 546-547). Whatever the material used, the interviewees said that the process used to make a fish trap is always the same. The first step is to trim the palm branches or stalks and leave them in seawater for several days to soften. When making a trap from *mˈitrer*, the bark is then cleaned off using a piece of coral rock. The now supple branches are then split in half and the pith removed, normally using one's teeth. At this stage the branches of *mˈitrer* resemble pieces of bamboo, and it is likely that this is what Bent had seen and mistakenly identified as bamboo. Once the branches have been split they are woven together to form the walls of the fish trap (Figure 73). The fishermen said that once the first branch has been woven in, a second one is then woven in next to it to give it extra strength. The two branches are then knocked together using a small rock to ensure a tight weave. This method is almost identical to that used to make traps from *fɔ̄tir*', although these are woven onto a frame made from *mˈitrer* to keep them rigid. The walls of the traps are woven separately. Those fishermen interviewed said that the length and width of each wall is based on which element of the trap is being built and the size of the trap (Figure 74). The final stage in construction is to lay large thick branches of *mˈitrer* along the base of the trap, which act as anchors and

[101] Ali Ibn Aneen, in his 60s, interviewed on 7 February 2009; Khames Abdulah Salem, 75 years old, interviewed on 22 December 2009; Jamen Mahafawl Saif, 70 years old, interviewed on 22 December 2009; Abdullah Mohammed Hamadan, in his 60s, interviewed on 15 February 2009.

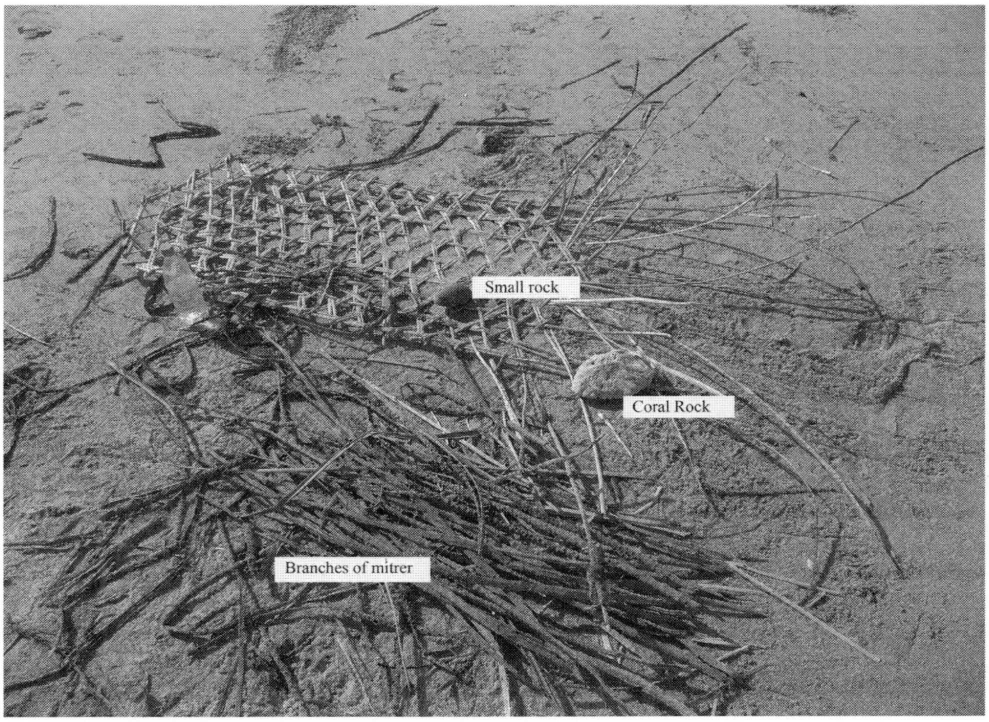

FIGURE 73. A PARTIALLY COMPLETED WALL OF A FISH TRAP IN ḤADIBOH SHOWING THE COMPONENTS AND TOOLS USED IN ITS MANUFACTURE (PHOTO: AUTHOR).

FIGURE 74. TRAVELLING ALONG THE NORTH COAST ONE OFTEN COMES ACROSS FISH TRAPS IN VARIOUS STAGES OF CONSTRUCTION. IN DI-ḤAMDH, THE TWO FISH TRAPS IN THE BACKGROUND ARE BEING LAID OUT TO DRY AFTER HAVING BEING USED FOR SEVERAL WEEKS, WHILE IN THE FOREGROUND ANOTHER ONE IS BEING CONSTRUCTED (PHOTO: AUTHOR).

keep the trap right side up. These are then tied into place using rope made from palm tree fibre or increasingly polypropylene rope (Figure 75). The fishermen told me that it is necessary for these branches to protrude beyond the base of the trap as the branches help prevent the trap from being dragged by the current. In rocky areas the protruding branches are covered with rocks to prevent the trap moving, whereas in sandy areas the branches dig themselves into the sand. They said that once the trap is finished it is then left in the sea for several days to 'darken', as when it is new, or has been left out of the sea for any length of time it is too light, and fish do not go into it. The darkening of the traps occurs due to the growth of algae, which also disguises the outline of the trap. The average length of time it takes to make an average sized trap of three metres is approximately two days, although larger traps of up to five metres can take up to four days. Once the fish trap is ready to be used it is baited and placed into the sea. According to elderly fishermen in Ḥadiboh, Qādheb and Qalansiyah, the trap

FIGURE 75. A FISH TRAP, SHOWING THE PROTRUDING BRANCHES ATTACHED TO THE BASE IN KHAYSAT ASH-SHAIKH, SAMḤA. NOTE ITS DARK COLOUR, SHOWING THAT IT HAS BEEN IN USE FOR SEVERAL WEEKS (PHOTO: AUTHOR).

is baited with either seaweed or small fish, although Morris (2002: 226), says that crab is also used. They also told me that they place marker buoys on their traps, although this is mostly during periods of bad weather or when they have been laid in deep water, when it is difficult to relocate them by sight. Traditionally the butt of a palm frond was used as a buoy, although nowadays any plastic container that floats is used.

Elderly full-time fishermen in Di-Ḥamdh, Qādheb, Ḥadiboh, Maḥfirihin and Shu^cub[102] said that fish traps are used to catch smaller inshore demersal fish, and that the catch is mostly used for personal consumption. They also said that there is no specific area in which they set their traps, although rocky areas are considered to be better than sandy. The depths at which traps are set vary according to the individual, although fishermen in Ḥadiboh said that they only set them within the sea area of *lītonten*, which lies between the shore and approximately 20 minutes out to sea, and is no more than about 10m in depth. The elderly fishermen also said that fish traps can be laid throughout the year, although if the sea becomes too rough they only lay them in sheltered areas, as rough seas can either cause them to become damaged or lost. They also claim that fish traps are increasingly being banned by the *muqaddamīn* (Ar), village leaders, as the fishermen in certain villages complain that the traps catch too many unmarketable fish that are being wasted, and that the crab or fish bait used in the traps is 'polluting' the sea. The belief that the sea can be polluted by this bait also influences the gutting of fish, which only takes place on land, as the guts are also believed to pollute the sea. According to some fishermen,[103] the real reason that fish traps are banned by some *muqaddim* is that the fishermen in those villages are jealous, as they cannot build their own traps and must buy them from those fishermen who can. While there is likely to be some truth in this, the issue of fish traps is more complex and is linked to attempts to control the catches being made by fishermen from one or other ethnic group.

The construction and use of fish traps on Socotra is similar to practices throughout Southern Arabia, the Arabian Gulf and East Africa. According to Donaldson (1979: 82-85), fish traps along the Al-Batinah coast of Oman were made by specialist trap makers, who would make them from date palm fronds, which would have been stripped and woven into various rectangular and polygonal shapes. These traps were then weighted with stones that were attached to the base of the trap and then dropped into shallow water with a buoy attached. In the Arabian Gulf fish traps were also made from date palm fronds that were similarly woven into various rectangular and polygonal shapes (LeBaron Bowen

[102] Khames Abdulah Salem, 75 years old; Jamen Mahafawl Saif, 70 years old, both interviewed on 22 December 2009; Salim Mohammed, in his 60s; Mohammed Aldolah, in his 60s; Omar Abdulla Saleh, in his 60s, all interviewed on 08 February 2009; Muhammad Abdulla Muhammad Dimori, in his 60s; Mohammed Ahmed, 55 years old, both interviewed on 11 February 2009; Saleh Ahmed Bamousa, 45 years old, interviewed on 17 December 2009.

[103] The fishermen's names have been withheld because they did not want to be named.

1951: 385-387; McIvor 1986: 56). However, according to LeBaron Bowen (1951: 386), fish traps deployed in shallow water along the east coast of the Arabian Gulf were not marked with buoys, for fear of theft. A study of the plants used by the fishermen along the East African coast, from Kenya to Mozambique, reported that the fishermen made fish traps from date-palm fronds and 'withies', a generic term used to describe thin flexible branches (Weiss 1973: 183). These traps, unlike the ones on Socotra, were made in two parts, an exterior basket made from date palm fronds and a removable interior funnel that was made solely from withies. Furthermore, they were weighted with stones or pieces of coral that were attached to the trap, similar to the practice in Al-Batinah, Oman and the Arabian Gulf, and buoyed using pieces of wood (Weis 1973: 184). The major difference from the fish traps on Socotra is that the latter do not have rocks attached to weigh them down. The reason for this is the Socotri practice of putting the traps in water to allow algae to grow on them before they are used, which would also mean that the traps would be waterlogged and heavy before they were set, making them inherently negatively buoyant. In contrast, the traditional traps of East Africa, Oman and the Arabian Gulf that are not waterlogged and would be positively buoyant, therefore they would require weighting down. The traditional fish traps that were being used in Oman, the Arabian Gulf, East Africa and along the Hadhramaut coast have almost all been replaced by wire traps (Weiss 1973: 183; Donaldson 1979: 90; Camelin 2006: 56). Today the traditional Socotri fish traps are still used throughout the island, although due to pressure from the *muqaddamīn* and the importation of wire traps they too are in decline.

Lobster Traps

The introduction of galvanised wire lobster traps began in 2003 under the auspices of the Socotra Conservation Fund which, working together with the various cooperatives, distributed several thousand traps to the fishermen. Their introduction was an attempt to limit the fishing of lobsters by net, a practice which does not allow for the effective release of under-sized or gravid female lobsters (Hariri and Abdulaziz 2006: 365-367). This project was largely successful, and galvanised wire traps are now found in villages throughout the Socotra archipelago. According to fishermen in Qalansiyah and Maḥfirihin,[104] the traps are better than nets, which are often damaged when used to catch lobster. They also said that the lobster traps, much like the fish traps, are set close to the shore, where it is rocky, as this is the best place to catch lobster. The fishermen engaged in lobster fishing told me that the best areas to catch lobsters are along the south, northeast and southeast sides of Socotra, especially in the vicinity of Maḥfirihin. Lobster traps are used throughout the open season, *futūḥ* (Ar), as they are less affected by strong currents or rocky outcrops, unlike the nets used when fishing for lobster. Galvanised lobster-traps have been introduced all along Southern Arabia, the Red Sea and Arabian Gulf, and have, in most places, almost completely replaced the use of nets for lobster fishing (Hariri *et al.* 2002: 19; Bonfiglioli and Hariri 2004: 30).

Nets

The first recorded mention of fishing nets on Socotra is from the 17th century, when Hendrick Hagenaer, a captain of the Dutch East India Company, said that the fishermen on the island were using seine nets (Hagenaer 1650: 57). The next account is not until 1967, when Serjeant (1992: 176), mentions that fishermen only use one type of net, which he calls a *ṣabb* (Ar). According to Serjeant this net is set up in a straight line, and has a double horizontal cord at the top with rocks attached to the bottom to keep it down. Furthermore, he says that the Socotri fishermen did not let fishermen from outside Socotra use any other nets on the island, as they believed that the visiting fishermen's nets gave them an unfair advantage. Several years later Naumkin (1993: 202-203), says that fishermen use three types of nets, namely: *luyuh*, a net which he does not describe; *sakka*, a seine or vertical net, and a small sinker-weighted net. Naumkin describes the seine net as having ropes, floats and hooks attached, and said that they were used to catch shark. He also said that the small sinker-weighted nets were used in shallow water in place of fish traps. The next account by Morris (2002: 224), says that the fishermen used small, circular cast nets known in Socotri as *mə́ʿadeft*, which were made locally from cotton or coarse *benj* (Soc) fibre imported from East Africa. These were of different kinds, distinguished by the size of their mesh. She also says that 'later', larger nets known as *makhwar* (Soc) were used, and that they were cast from a canoe further out to sea. In addition, she refers to an even larger net known as *maśgir* (Ar), which was laid out between the shore and the sea at right angles to the shore. This would appear to be similar to the *ṣabb* or seine net mentioned by Serjeant.

Having outlined the nets referred to in the historic accounts, I now look at the types of nets the fishermen are using today. These have been divided according to the manner in which the nets are thrown, laid or fixed in the sea. On this basis I have identified three types of nets, namely: cast nets, seine nets and drag nets.

Cast Nets

A cast net is a circular net with small weights distributed around its edge. The weights are designed to close the net as it is retrieved, thereby trapping the fish. It is

[104] Muslim Abdulla, full-time fisherman, in his 30s; Mohammed Ahmed, full-time fisherman, 55 years old, both interviewed on 11 February 2009; Salam Saeed Martah, full-time fisherman, 39 years old; Omar Saeed Abod Ali Saeed, full-time fisherman, 31 years old, both interviewed on 18 December 2009.

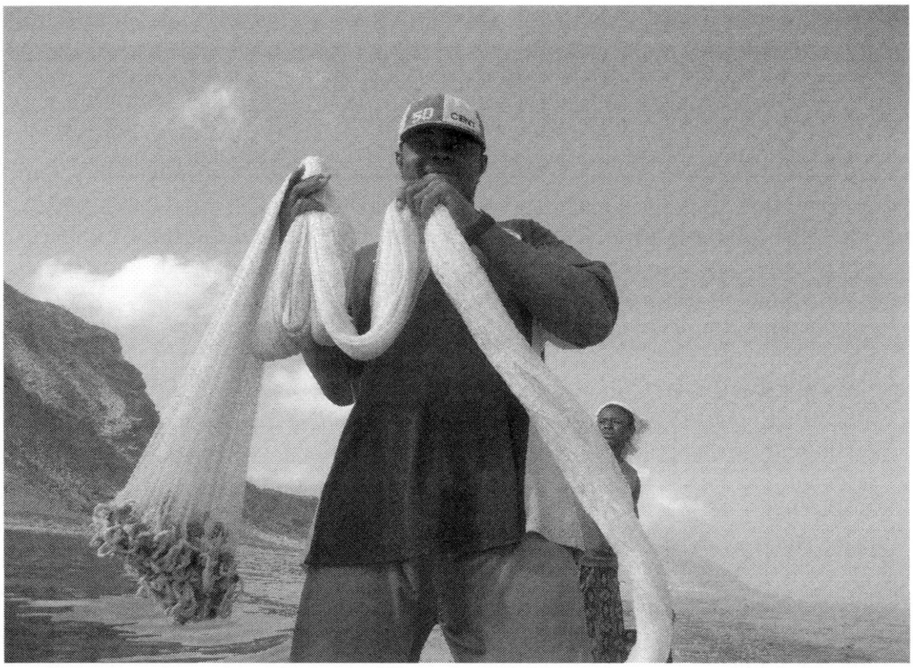

FIGURE 76. A FISHERMAN HOLDING A CAST NET ON A BOAT OFF ḤOWLEF (PHOTO: AUTHOR).

designed to be thrown into the water from the shore or from a vessel. The main use of the net on Socotra is to catch fish for bait, although it is also used periodically to catch fish for personal consumption. When the net is deployed from the shore it normally has a line attached. The fishermen wades a short distance into the water and throws it, while holding onto the line. The fisherman then pulls on the line, drawing the net closed and trapping the fish. When using a cast net to catch bait fish from a boat the procedure is different. First, the fishermen need to locate the shoal and once in range, switch the engine off. The boat is then allowed to drift toward the fish, although if they are not close enough the fishermen will paddle the boat closer. This procedure is followed as the engine noise is believed to scare the fish. The fisherman with the net then stands at the prow of the boat holding the net in his hands and draped over his arm (Figure 76). Once the boat is close enough to the shoal he casts his net. After throwing the net, the fishermen jump into the water and swim around it, in order to chase the fish into the net. This is mostly done in areas where the water is deep or the fish are especially numerous. As there is no string, the fishermen use a gaff, a metal pole with a hook at the end, to grab the middle of the net and drag it onboard. In Ḥadiboh and Suq, the fishermen go to the shallow waters off Ḥowlef to net bait fish, while in Qalansiyah, Qādheb and villages on the south coast, bait fish are either caught in sheltered areas near the shore, or directly from the shore. This method of using a cast net from a boat is almost identical to that recorded by Camelin (2006: 40) in al-Shihr in Hadhramaut and Donaldson (1979: 122), along the Al-Batinah coast, Oman. Elsewhere in the Red Sea and the Arabian Gulf cast nets are mostly recorded as being used from the shore (Kentley 1988: 182; McIvor 1993: 55; Bonfiglioli and Hariri 2004: 30).

Seine Nets

A seine net hangs vertically in the water with its bottom edge held down by weights and its top edge buoyed by floats. Seine nets can be deployed from the shore, or from a boat. There are four fixed seine-net configurations used on Socotra. The first is top-anchored, where the net is held between two anchors mid-water, the second is bottom-anchored, where the net is held with two anchors along the seafloor. The third configuration is where the net is allowed to drift around a single anchored point and the fourth is where the net is fixed to a vessel, and both net and vessel drift in the current.

On Socotra the top-anchored fixed-net method is mostly deployed using an anchored boat, which is attached to one side of the net. However, in Ḥadiboh, Qādheb and Qalansiyah, the fishermen informed me that they preferred to leave the net anchored and return to it in the morning, because it is becoming increasingly dangerous for a vessel to be anchored out at sea, as large vessels do not see them and it is possible to be run over. When this net is laid it is anchored at either end, with buoys attached to the top of the net to keep it afloat and small rocks attached to the base to keep it taut (Figure 77). The fishermen I interviewed said that this net is good for catching pelagic species, and in Ḥadiboh is normally set in the fishing area of *šiḳ* (Soc), which lies approximately

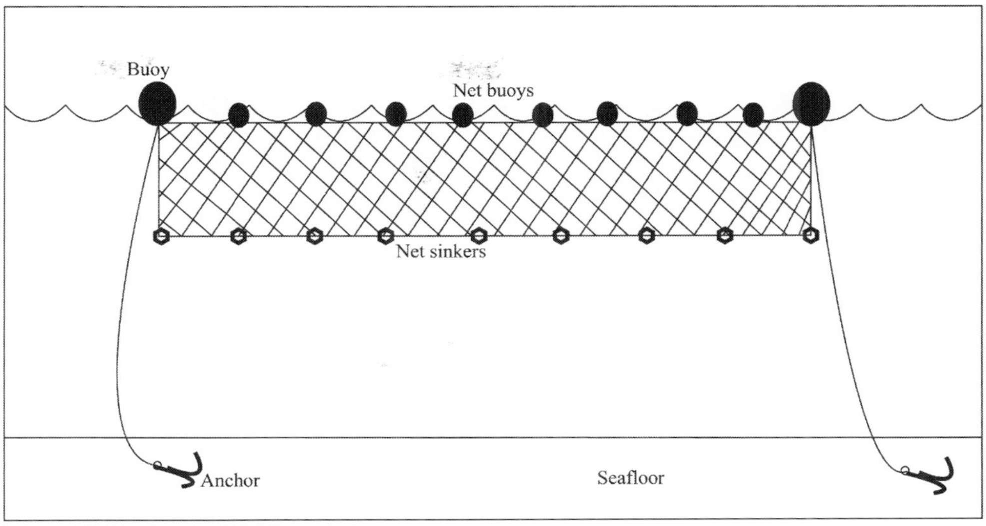

FIGURE 77. TOP-ANCHORED FIXED SEINE NET (DRAWN: AUTHOR).

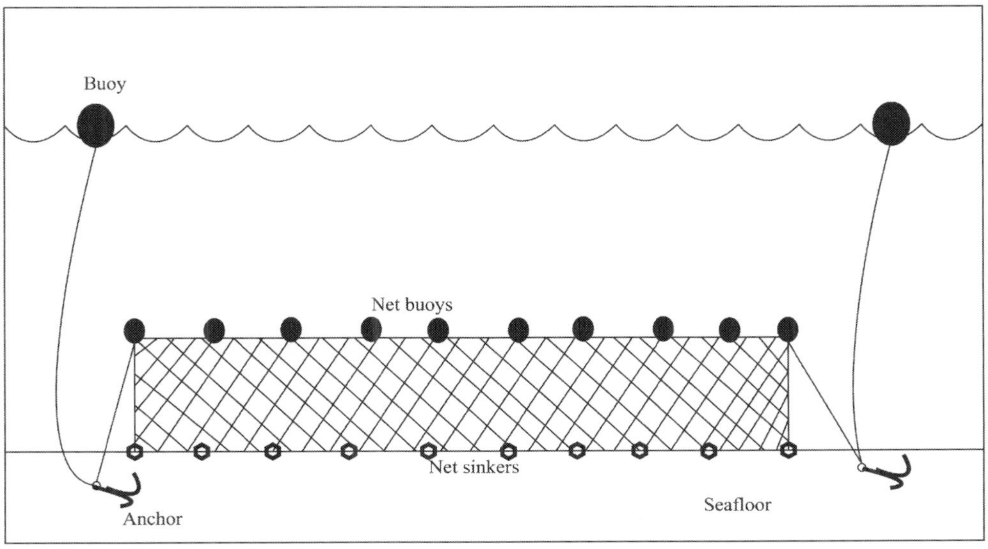

FIGURE 78. BOTTOM-ANCHORED FIXED SEINE NET (DRAWN: AUTHOR).

40 minutes to an hour from the shore. According to the fishermen I interviewed in Ḥadiboh, top-anchored nets are used in *šiḳ* and *ḳeneʿiti* (Soc) because it is the best place to catch pelagic species. According to fishermen interviewed in Ḥadiboh, Qādheb, Qalansiyah, Erisseyl, Bidōleh, Stēroh and Maḥfirihin, these nets are set once a day, unless there are vessels buying fish in which case they are set twice a day, once in the morning and once in the afternoon, around three. The fishermen also told me that this net is only used during *gyaḥś* (Soc) and *ṣēreb* (Soc), when the sea is calm, as rough weather makes it difficult to retrieve the nets.

With the bottom-anchored fixed-net method, the seine net is laid at right angles to the shore, and either end is anchored to a large rock, or increasingly an iron grapnel anchor similar to that used for anchoring vessels. The anchor points are buoyed to allow the net to be relocated. The top of the net also has several small buoys attached to keep it upright and the base has several small rocks attached to keep the net taut (Figure 78). Fishermen in Qādheb, Qalansiyah, Ḥadiboh, Stēroh and Maḥfirihin said that the bottom-anchored fixed-nets are set once a day, either in the early evening or morning and left overnight, during the fishing seasons of *gyaḥś* and *ṣēreb*, when the sea is calm. However, in Ḥadiboh, Qādheb and Maḥfirihin, fishermen said that it is also possible to set them during the beginning of *ḳeyaṭ* (Soc), if the sea is calm. They also said that these nets are set several miles out to sea, where it is just about possible to see the seafloor. In Ḥadiboh the fishermen said this net is mostly laid in rocky areas within the fishing area of *šiḳ*, as larger groupers and other demersal species are caught there. These seine nets are likely to be the same nets Hagenaer (1650: 57), Serjeant (1992: 176) and Morris (2002: 224) describe, as they remain fixed between two points and in some cases are set at right angles to the shore.

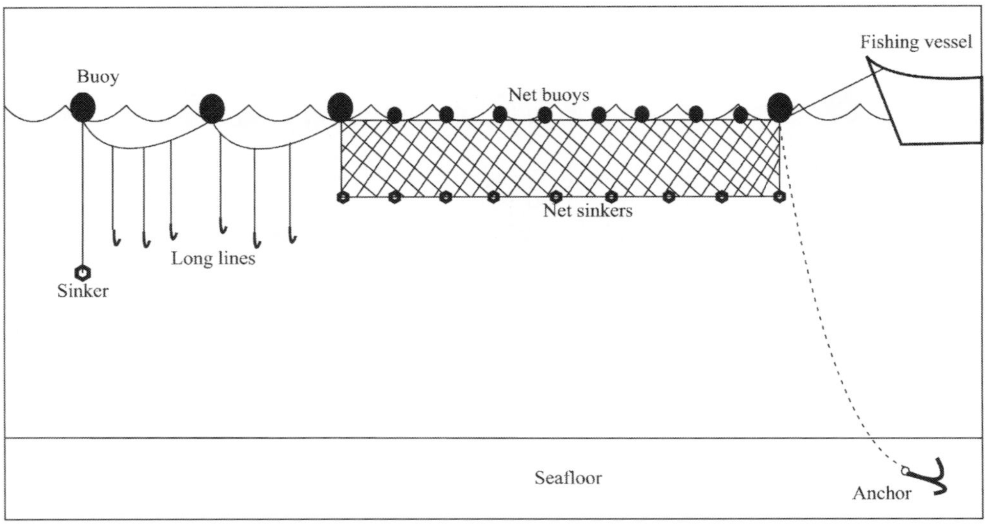

FIGURE 79. THE FIXED SINGLE-ANCHORED SEINE NET ARRANGEMENT ANCHORED TO THE SEAFLOOR (DOTTED LINE) OR TO A FISHING VESSEL (DRAWN: AUTHOR).

The configuration for the seine nets attached to a boat or to a single anchored point at sea are the same. The first element of this configuration is a seine net that has several large buoys attached along the top of the net and rocks along its base. The buoys are generally larger than the bottom and top-anchored seine nets. According to several experienced fishermen in Qādheb,[105] the buoys need to be bigger to keep the net from being dragged under when it is drifting on the surface. Furthermore, fishermen in Qādheb said that they also attach a line with several hooks to the end of the net, and at the end of the line attach a large sinker to prevent the line and net from becoming entangled and to keep the hooks submerged (Figure 79). This arrangement is then attached to the stern of the vessel and paid out until it drifts freely behind, after which it is either fastened to a fixed anchored point at sea or left to drift with the vessel. The main species targeted are shark, tuna and kingfish, although the fishermen said that any large pelagic species are welcome, as they all fetch a good price.

According to fishermen in Qalansiyah, Qādheb, Ḥadiboh, Erisseyl and Maḥfirihin, the best time for this method of netting is during the end of *gyáḥś* and the beginning of *ṣēreb*, when the sea is calm and the currents are not strong. However, in Shuᶜub, Qalansiyah, Qādheb, Erisseyl, Maḥfirhin, Zaḥaq and Stēroh, the fishermen said that it was also possible to use this method during *ḳéyaṭ*, as long as the currents are not too strong. Fishermen along the north and south coast told me that the best place to use this net is further offshore in deeper water, where shark and other larger pelagic species are found. Fishermen in Ḥadiboh said the best place is the beginning of *ḳeneᶜíti*. In Shuᶜub, Qalansiyah and Qādheb they told me that when fishing off their villages they would use this net much closer to the shore than when fishing off the south coast. The reason is that the sea off these villages is shallow for only a short distance from the shore, consequently pelagic species are found closer to the shore. Drift nets are normally set overnight and retrieved in the morning, after the fishermen have eaten their breakfast.

Drag Nets

A drag net is a net which is dragged along the sea bottom in a practice also known as trawling. Fishermen on Socotra only use this method to catch lobsters, although several shallow-water demersal fish species are often caught as bycatch. The method involves weighting the net with small rocks to keep it on the bottom and dragging it behind the vessel. This method is used throughout Socotra, but is concentrated along the northeast and southwest coasts, where lobsters are more frequent. The fishermen in Maḥfirhin, Bidhōleh, Stēroh and Shuᶜub said it is only possible to use this method in shallow water, which does not have rock or coral outcrops, and where the currents are not strong. The reason for this is that the outcroppings cause their nets to become caught and damaged, whilst strong currents cause them to lift to the surface and become entangled. They also told me that it is possible to catch lobsters throughout the open season, as long as the weather is calm and the currents not too strong. The introduction of lobster traps has reduced the amount of fishermen who use nets to catch lobsters, yet it is still practiced. According to the fishermen who still use nets, the reason they do not use the lobster traps is that they are too expensive, and that it is possible to catch more lobsters using a net. Using

[105] Salim Games Saaed, full-time fisherman, 45 years old; Salim Saaed Atman, full-time fisherman, 55 years old; Abdullah Ali Muhammed, full-time fisherman, in his 60s, all interviewed on 2 January 2010.

Mesh size Eye -ᶜ*ayn* (Ar)	Species	Market
One	Various inshore small demersal fish.	Mostly used for personal consumption or bait.
Two	Various inshore small demersal fish.	Mostly used for personal consumption or bait.
Three	Various inshore small demersal fish.	Mostly used for personal consumption or bait.
Four	Various shallow-water medium sized demersal fish.	Sold locally or to visiting vessels.
Five	Various shallow-water medium sized demersal fish and lobsters.	Sold locally or to visiting vessels.
Six	Various medium sized demersal fish, especially groupers, pelagic species, especially kingfish, small shark and lobsters.	Mostly sold to visiting vessels.
Seven	Various medium sized demersal fish, especially groupers, pelagic species, especially kingfish, small shark and lobsters.	Mostly sold to visiting vessels.
Eight	Various medium sized demersal fish, especially groupers and pelagic species, especially kingfish and small shark.	Mostly sold to visiting vessels.
Nine	Various large pelagic species, especially kingfish, small tuna and small shark.	Sold to visiting vessels
Ten	Various large pelagic species, especially tuna and shark.	Sold to visiting vessels
Eleven	Various large pelagic species, especially tuna and shark.	Sold to visiting vessels
Twelve	Favoured net for shark.	Sold to visiting vessels

FIGURE 80. THE 12 DIFFERENT MESH-SIZES; THE SPECIES EACH IS USED TO TARGET AND HOW THEY ARE MARKETED.

a drag net to catch lobsters is not unique to Socotra and has and still is being practiced by fishermen all along the south coast of the Hadhramaut from Mukalla to the border of Oman (Bonfiglioli and Hariri 2004: 36-37).

Socotri Net Classification

Notwithstanding the different netting methods used, the classification of nets on Socotra is based upon mesh size. This was first recognised by Morris (2002: 224), who said that different nets were named after the number of fingers that could be fitted inside one mesh, i.e. one-finger net. However, fishermen I spoke to on Socotra and the island of Samḥa, said that they named the nets after the mesh. According to them, the mesh of a net is known as an eye, ᶜ*ayn* (Ar), and is measured by the number of fingers you are able to fit inside. Consequently, if you are able to fit one finger into the eye, it would be a net of one eye, ᶜ*ayn wāḥid* (Ar) and not one finger. They also identified 12 net types, each of which is recognised according to the size of the mesh, or gauge. However, none of the fishermen interviewed had or used all twelve sizes. This method of classifying nets according to the mesh is similar to that recorded by Donaldson (1979: 540) in Al-Batinah, Oman, although fishermen there described the net in terms of how many meshes to the forearm or hand. Elsewhere in the Hadhramaut and the Arabian Gulf, nets are named according to the method by which they were deployed, even though mesh sizes do differ (McIvor 1986: 56; Camelin 2006: 40). That there is little similarity with the naming of nets in the Hadhramaut is surprising, especially due to the close relationship between Al-Mahrah and Socotra. The reason for this is likely to be due to the modernisation of fishing equipment and the loss of traditional practices, which along the Hadhramaut coastline occurred a lot earlier than on Socotra.

Fishermen interviewed along the north and south coasts of Socotra said that different mesh sizes were used to catch different species, although when questioned about exactly which fish were being caught with which net, it became apparent that there was a significant overlap between the different mesh sizes and the species being targeted. Using information gathered from the fishermen I interviewed, I have drawn up a table to demonstrate which species is targeted using each mesh size, what degree of overlap there is, and whether the fish caught are used locally or sold to visiting vessels (Figure 80).

During my interviews, I found that the reason for this large overlap is that fishermen rarely have more than three different types of nets. Furthermore, due to the difficulty of obtaining nets on Socotra, and their high cost, the fishermen often buy a net that can be used to catch as wide a range of species as possible. Consequently, the preferred net sizes are two, seven and 12. The reason for this is that they prefer nets which catch fish by the gills, as catching fish by the gills does not damage the fish, which would reduce its price.

Net Manufacture

Several experienced full-time fishermen in Ḥadiboh,[106] Qādheb,[107] and Qalansiyah[108] informed me that in the past nets had been made using *ˈiˀiśhur* (Soc), cotton fibre from *ˈiˀiśīrə* (Soc), the cotton bush growing on the island, or *quṭn* (Ar), imported cotton twist from East Africa. This cotton was spun into a thread by women, after which it was taken by the men to make into nets or handlines. This practice is much the same as that recorded in Al-Batinah, Oman, although there is no mention of women being involved in any stage of the net making there (Donaldson 1979: 73). In Ḥadiboh, two elderly African fishermen[109] said that they had also made nets out of the fibre taken from *di-ˈtimərə* (Soc), the date palm tree. This fibre was made into ropes and then knotted into nets. Knotting of nets, like the construction of fish traps, was a specialised task which fishermen said few people could do. Consequently, those who were able to make nets could barter for food and other supplies with those who could not. Once the net had been made it would have been put into a mixture of quicklime and water. The reaction of the slaked lime was said to 'cook' the net, and make it stronger. After the nets had been 'cooked' they would be laid out to dry. The dried nets were then either used as they were, or dyed to make them darker. According to Morris (2002: 224), the roots of two local plants *Limonium* and *Periploca* were used as a dye for the nets. The older fishermen I interviewed said that the dyed nets were used in areas where the sea was 'dark' and those not dyed in areas where the sea was 'light'. The 'dark' areas they referred to are rocky, whilst the 'light' areas are sandy.

Parallels with this method of making fish nets from cotton are found in accounts from Oman and the Arabian Gulf (LeBaron Bowen 1951: 386; Donaldson 1979: 73; McIvor 1986: 54-56). However, the use of palm-tree fibre to make nets has only ever been recorded in East Africa, where the fishermen used it to make a type of net called *juya* (Weiss 1973: 183). Could it be possible that this method of net making had been introduced to Socotra by the African slaves that were brought to the island? I argue that this is the case, as there is no record of Arabian fishermen in Socotra, Oman, or the Arabian Gulf, using palm-tree fibre to make nets. Instead the traditional fishing nets that were being used by these Arabian fishermen were all made from cotton (LeBaron Bowen 1951: 386; Donaldson 1979: 73; McIvor 1986: 54-56). Oman is the only area where the nets were recorded as being soaked in slaked quicklime, although it is possible this had been practiced elsewhere, but was not recorded. The nets on Socotra, much like elsewhere in East Africa and Arabia, have now been completely replaced with commercially made twine and nylon nets, which last longer and are more durable.

Net Restrictions

The fishermen along the north and south coasts of Socotra said that the main restrictions on using nets are to do with the weather and currents. They all said that it is only possible to use a net when the weather is calm, as strong winds and high seas made it very difficult to retrieve the nets and it is possible for the nets to become lost. Fishermen in Qalansiyah, Qādheb, Erisseyl and Maḥfirhin informed me that strong currents can also influence when it is possible to lay nets, as the current sweeps the nets to the surface and can cause them to entangle. In addition to the restrictions imposed by the weather and currents, the fishermen also need to work within the constraints imposed upon them by the *muqaddamīn* (Ar), village leaders, who decide on where and when nets can be used. The most widespread restriction imposed upon the fishermen is the ban on netting during the full-moon period. According to the Socotra Conservation Development Program (SCDP) marine officer, Fouad Naseb Saeed,[110] 30 years old, the ban on fishing during the full moon is to ensure that fish stocks are not over-exploited. The length of time this ban is enforced is based upon both the luminosity of the moon and the village's *muqaddim*. According to several elderly full-time fishermen in Ḥadiboh,[111] they are not allowed to set their nets at night for 12 days over the period in which the moon begins to wax, is full, and begins to wane. Whereas in Maṭyaf fishermen said that they are not allowed to set nets at night for 17 days over this waxing and waning phase of the moon. They also told me that even though there was a ban it made little difference, as the light of the moon makes nets visible to the fish and it is not possible to catch anything for most of this period. However, several fishermen[112] told me that it is possible to use a net during the full moon as long as you set the net in a 'dark place', where the moonlight does not shine. This practice is considered illegal, and if they are seen by other fishermen they would be reported to the *muqaddim*, who would confiscate their nets. According to them it is possible to catch significantly more fish during this period, as many fish come closer to the shore. There are virtually no parallels with the influence of the moon's luminosity on net fishing in Arabia, although it has been recorded in Brazil (Cordell 1980: 25-38). The nearest similarity in Arabia is an account by Lieutenant

[106] Khames Abdulah Salem, 75 years old; Jamen Mahafawl Saif, 70 years old, both interviewed on 22 December 2009

[107] Mohammed Aldolah, in his 60s; Abdullah Mohammed Sallim, in his 60s; Omar Abdulla Saleh, in his 60s, all interviewed on 8 February 2009.

[108] Ali Salim Da-Salmoho, in his 60s; Abdullha Rahman Abod Ali Saeed, 38 years old, both interviewed on 16 February 2009.

[109] Khames Abdulah Salem, full-time fisherman, 75 years old; Jamen Mahafawl Saif, full-time fisherman, 70 years old, both interviewed on 22 December 2009.

[110] Interviewed on 22 December 2009.

[111] Abdullah Mohammed Hamadan, in his 60s; Heni Mohammed Saeed Abdullah, in his 60s; Nasieb Saaed Khamis, in his 60s; Mobarik Ali Adbulla, in his 60s, all interviewed on 15 February 2009.

[112] I have not named these fishermen as the practice contravenes the restrictions imposed by the *muqaddim*.

McIvor, the Assistant Political Resident for the Gulf, who said that the fishermen in the Gulf used strong nets during the full moon, as sharks seeing fish in the nets frequently tore the nets apart when attempting to catch them (McIvor 1986: 56).

Fish Lines, *śˈǝ̄hor* (Soc) / *watār* (Ar)

The earliest record of line fishing on Socotra is the 17th century account of Hendrick Hagenaer, who said that the fishermen used fishing rods to catch fish (Hagenaer 1650: 57). The use of fishing rods is highly unlikely as there is no further historical or ethnographic evidence for this and it is unclear as to what is meant here. Further evidence for line fishing occurs in 1903, when an expedition lead by Forbes visited the archipelago. According to Forbes (1903: xxviii), a fisherman in ᶜAbd al-Kūri was line fishing from a catamaran, known locally as *rēmuš* (Soc). Several years later Brown (1966: 27), says that line fishing was one of the two main fishing methods employed. In 1957, Serjeant (1992: 176) says that the fishing lines being used by the fishermen were mostly made of cotton and it was only during his visit that they began to use nylon lines. Naumkin (1993: 202) makes no mention of line fishing, although does mention that hooks are used with the 'seine or vertical net', which would imply that it was similar to the fixed net method outlined above, and thus lines would have been used. According to Morris (2002: 225), the fishermen on Socotra were line fishing both from a vessel and the shore, where they used lures. She also says that the fishermen made lines from local cotton, imported cotton twist, and threads pulled from imported calico cloth.

According to elderly fishermen in Ḥadiboh, Qalansiyah and Qādheb, before it was possible to buy the nylon lines used today, fishing lines had been made by women, who spun cotton from the locally cotton bush, *ˈʔiśīrǝ* (Soc), or imported cotton twist, *quṭn* (Ar), from East Africa. In Ḥadiboh, two elderly African full-time fishermen[113] said that they had also used line made from the fibre of date-palm trees. These fishermen also told me that spun cotton was strengthened by 'cooking' it in slaked quicklime and then allowing it to dry, like the cotton nets. Many of the older fishermen remember using cotton lines for several years after it was possible to buy synthetic monofilament line, and said that this was because the latter was very expensive. While monofilament has completely replaced the cotton and date-palm fibre lines, it still remains costly for the fishermen. According to Hariri and Yusif (1999: 3), the price of fishing gear on Socotra is twice the price of that at Aden or Mukalla.

The historical and ethnographic accounts outlined above describe the types of lines being used, yet rarely identify or describe which method of line fishing is employed. In fact, each method of line fishing uses a specific technique and, in some cases, specific additional equipment. Consequently, I have divided line fishing into the three methods employed on Socotra: handlining, trolling and longlining.

Handlining

Handlining refers to fishing with a single line held in the hand. Excess line is normally spooled around a cylindrical spool. On Socotra, the shape and size of the spool varies widely, according to what is available, and it is not uncommon to see bottles, small plastic containers and pieces of wood being used. Several experienced fishermen in Qalansiyah, Qādheb, Ḥadiboh, Suq and Ṣaqarah told me that fish caught by handline is better than that caught by net as it remains fresh for longer. However, during calm weather, it is possible to catch more fish using a net, and visiting vessels buy either. They also said that handlining is mostly used when the sea becomes too rough to use a net, although in Ḥadiboh, Qalansiyah and Samḥa the fishermen said they prefer to use handlines as they can catch as many fish as netting. Furthermore, fishermen said that handlining, unlike netting, is undertaken in specific fishing areas, and that in each area it is possible to target a specific species. Broadly, the fishermen divide their handlining according to where they fish, namely: deep-water handlining, shallow-water handlining and shore handlining. The techniques and equipment each of these methods use is slightly different, as is the species targeted.

Deep-water Handlining

Deep-water handlining requires the fishermen to firstly collect the necessary cobbles, which will be used as sinkers. These are collected in sacks from areas along the shore where it is possible to find numerous large rounded cobbles (Figure 81). After they are loaded, the fishermen motor to a sheltered area where bait fish are prevalent. The fishermen I fished with in Ḥadiboh and Suq normally go to Ḥowlef, as it is a sheltered area in which large quantities of bait fish can be found. Once sufficient bait has been caught they motor out to sea following a given landmark until they reach their fishing area. Having arrived at their area the fishermen bait a single hook with fish and then wrap the line around the baited fish and a large cobble sinker (Figure 82). Once the line has been wrapped several times around the bait and the cobble, a highwayman's hitch is used to secure the line to the cobble; the cobble is then dropped overboard. The fishermen said that they will then let a specific amount of line spool out to allow the bait to reach a preferred depth. The line is then sharply tugged allowing the hitch to undo, the cobble to fall free, and the baited hook to drift loose in the current. Where the current is strong, a larger cobble sinker is used. This is allowed to drop deeper than usual before being released in order to keep

[113] Khames Abdulah Salem, 75 years old; Jamen Mahafawl Saif, 70 years old, both interviewed on 22 December 2009.

FIGURE 81. A FISHERMAN CARRYING SACKS OF COBBLES TO BE USED AS LINE FISHING WEIGHTS, WEST OF SUQ (PHOTO: AUTHOR).

FIGURE 82. A FISHERMAN WITH A BAITED HOOK WRAPPED AROUND A COBBLE SINKER READY TO BE DROPPED INTO THE WATER, OFF THE NORTH COAST (PHOTO: AUTHOR).

the baited hook under the water for as long as possible. If the fishermen get no bites they motor to a different fishing area and repeat the process, until they get a bite. When fish are biting, the fishermen let the vessel drift over the area, and only move back when the fish stop. However, if they are catching large quantities of valuable demersal species, especially grouper, they anchor in the area until the fish stop biting.

Deep-water handlining is restricted to specific deep-water areas. For example, in Ḥadiboh[114] the fishermen said that these are mostly found in the fishing area of *ḳeneʿiti* (Soc). They also said that, if the current is too

[114] Sharaf Joman Baleef, full-time fisherman, 35 years old; Salem Saeed Tamook, full-time fisherman, in his 40s; Faisal Ahmed Khalif, full-time fisherman, in his 30s, all interviewed on 1 January 2010.

strong it would be impossible to go handlining, as the hook would be dragged to the surface too quickly. During these periods they would have to find a sheltered area behind a headland where the current was not as strong, or try later in the day.

Shallow-water Handlining

Preparing for shallow-water handlining requires gathering sufficient bait beforehand. This bait is a mixture of pieces of fish, crab and shellfish. Once the fishing tackle has been stowed onboard the fishermen motor or paddle to a specific fishing area using one or more landmarks. The fishing tackle used for shallow-water handlining varies according to the village. Generally, a lead weight or holed stone is attached to the bottom of the line, after which several smaller lines with hooks are tied to the main line. The main difference between the techniques is the number of hooks used. In Qalansiyah three hooks is considered the maximum, whilst in Ḥadiboh, the fishermen use up to six. Notwithstanding the amount of hooks used, the method is the same. Firstly the hooks are baited, and then the line is lowered into the sea until it just about reaches the seafloor. Some fishermen jiggle the line to attract fish, whilst others just leave it in place. The fish targeted are large demersal species, which fetch the highest prices. They also told me that current is not normally a problem when fishing in shallow water. However, in Erisseyl the fishermen said that the current there can be very strong, making it impossible to fish in either deep or shallow areas, as the hooks are dragged up to the surface too quickly.

Shore Handlining

Fishermen throughout the north and south coast of Socotra and the island of Samḥa told me that they use handlines from the shore, especially during the SW monsoon when it is not possible to fish out at sea. They said that when handlining from the shore it is only necessary to attach a hook and lure to the line. The lure is either attached to the hook, or allowed to run freely down toward the hook, which is tied to the end of the line (Figure 83). The lure acts as a weight, making it possible to throw the line a significant distance from the shore. Once the lure hits the water it is left a few seconds before being pulled back in a tugging motion. Fishermen said that they use this tugging motion because it mimics a small fish swimming. The method used is the same throughout the island, although the type of lure differs according to the material available and skill of the fisherman, in Qalansiyah some are very elaborate. Handlining from shore is normally done during bad weather and is mostly for personal consumption. Those interviewed said that they had favoured areas on land from which they would fish. These favoured areas are where a rock extends out into the sea, or where the sea is deep and preferably rocky close to the shore. According to the fishermen interviewed in Qalansiyah, the reason for this is that it is possible to catch much larger fish in these areas.

FIGURE 83. SAAED SELEM ALI IN QALANSIYAH, SHOWING A LURE HE MADE TO CATCH FISH FROM THE SHORE (PHOTO: AUTHOR).

Handlining is one of the principal and most common methods of capturing fish throughout the Red Sea, Arabia and East Africa, although few authors differentiate between the methods used. According to a description by Kentley (1988: 186), in Suakin, Sudan, the fishermen practice a deep-water handlining method that is almost identical to that used by the fishermen of Socotra. However, in Suakin, Sudan, Al-Batinah, Oman, and the Arabian Gulf, the shallow-water handline method is predominant and, much like on Socotra, there are a wide variety of hook, lure and sinker configurations (Donaldson 1979: 128-129; McIvor 1986: 56; Kentley 1988: 184). The only description of shore handlining is by LeBaron Bowen (1951: 385), who described fishermen using handlines from the shore in Mukalla and along the eastern shores of the Arabian Gulf.

In addition to the handlining methods outlined above, fishermen on Socotra also use two other line fishing methods, both deployed from a boat. These are trolling and longlining.

Trolling

Trolling involves dragging a line carrying a lure near the surface of the water. On Socotra this line is sometimes split into two, with two lures allowed to run from one main line (Figure 84). In Qalansiyah and Ḥadiboh several

FIGURE 84. JAMEN MAHAFAWL SAIF IN ḤADIBOH, WITH HIS TROLLING LINE, HANDLINE AND LURES. NOTE THE DIFFERENT TYPES OF ARTIFICIAL LURES USED, AND HOW THE MAIN TROLL LINE IS SPLIT INTO TWO (PHOTO: AUTHOR).

experienced fishermen told me that they normally go trolling after they have set fixed nets, as they are already out at sea. They also said that they mostly troll in deeper water, which in Ḥadiboh is in the fishing area of *ḳeneʿˈiti*. The reason for this is that the deep areas are the best places to catch kingfish and tuna, the most sought-after species. The fishermen troll throughout the open fishing season, although it is almost always done after having laid fixed nets.

Longlining

Longlining takes many forms, although most are based upon the principal of a single line that has several attached branch lines called 'snoods', short lengths of line with a hook attached. On Socotra the fishermen use two methods, namely, set and drifting longlines. Fishermen from Ḥadiboh, Qādheb, Qalansiyah, Maḥfirihin, Stēroh and Zaḥaq told me that they use longlines in conjunction with fixed and drift nets to increase their chances of catching shark. However, most longlining is either bottom-set or allowed to drift. Bottom-set longlines are set by anchoring the main line to the bottom using weights spaced along the line to keep it on the seafloor. This arrangement is buoyed at either end to allow it to be relocated and retrieved. Drifting longlines are set by attaching the main line with snoods to the stern of a vessel and buoying the main line at regular intervals (Figure 85). Those fishermen said that longlines are mainly used for catching shark, although bycatches of large pelagic species like dolphin do occur. They also said that they use longlines in deep water far from the shore, as this is the best place to catch shark. In Ḥadiboh several very experienced fishermen said that they use longlines in the fishing area of *ḳeneʿˈiti* (Soc). Furthermore, they said that it is possible to use longlines throughout the open fishing season, although the best periods are between *gyˈaḥś* (Soc) and *ḳˈeyaṭ* (Soc), when the sea is calmer and it is easier to retrieve them. Trolling and longlining is practiced throughout Southern Arabia, although there is no evidence for longlines being attached to the end of fixed nets (Donaldson 1979: 539; McIvor 1986: 56; Hariri *et al.* 2002: 11-36; Beech 2004: 45).

Additional Fishing Equipment

The fishing equipment outlined above lists the main items of fishing tackle used by the fishermen. However, there are several items which have not been included and some which require additional clarification. These are as follows.

Fish Hooks, ʿˈeḳelhe (pl. ʿaḳālihe) (Soc)

According to elderly fishermen in Ḥadiboh and Qalansiyah, fish hooks were originally made by them from wood (*Ziziphus spina-christi*), shell, bone and iron, which would be made into a hook shape, *di-gīneṭ* (Soc). The best hooks were considered to be those made from iron *ḥˈʌṣihin* (Soc). These fishermen said that they had used any scraps of iron they could find, although nails were preferred, as they were easier to hammer into a hook shape. They also said that it is necessary to use the correct-sized hook for the fish you wanted to catch:

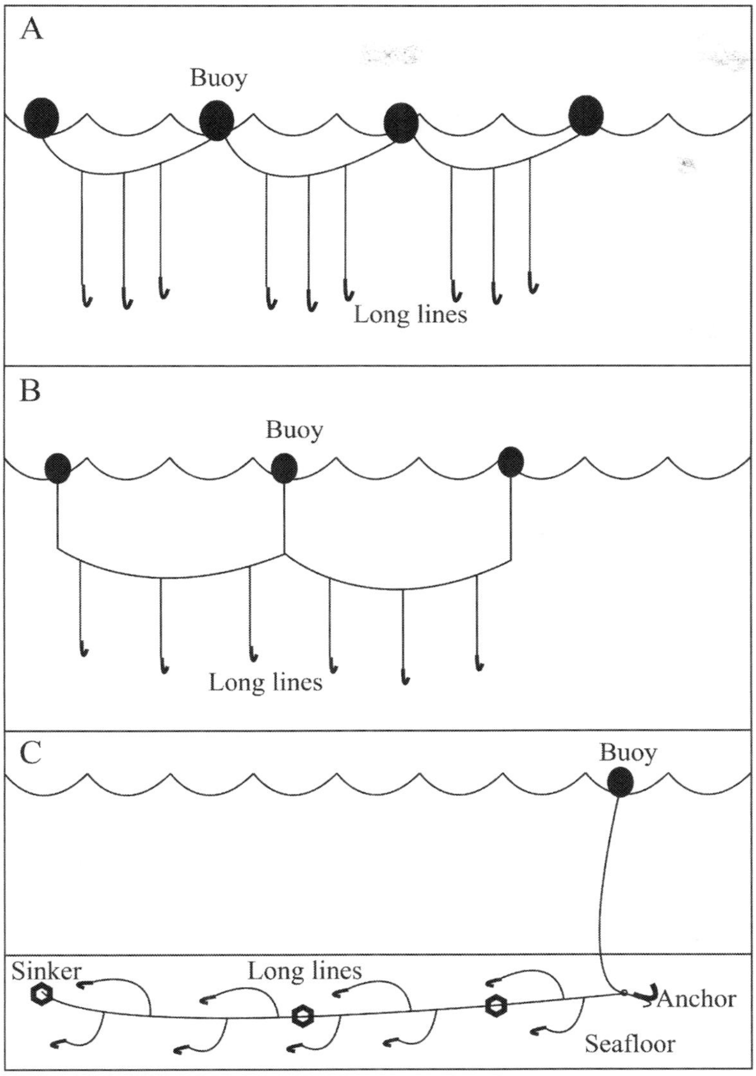

FIGURE 85. BOTTOM-SET AND DRIFTING LONG-LINES USED BY THE FISHERMEN ON SOCOTRA (DRAWN: AUTHOR).

small hooks are used to catch small fish, and large hooks for large fish. Today these traditional hooks have all been replaced by commercial stainless steel types bought from merchants in Ḥadiboh, visiting vessels or directly from the mainland. Comparable studies into the traditional fish hooks used by fishermen in Arabia are lacking, other than shell and bone fish hooks found in archaeological contexts (Beech 2004; Méry *et al.* 2008).

Fishing Lures

Fishermen in Qalansiyah, Qādheb and Ḥadiboh said that before it became possible to buy lures, they would make their own using wood, bone, stone and almost any shiny material, including glass. They also said that they would try to make the lures look like a small fish by attaching date-palm fibre to the end. This is said to mimic the tail of a small fish. Some of the fishermen still make their own fish lures from bone, date palm fibre and plastic, see Figure 83. These lures are mostly used to fish from the shore, although older fishermen said that they had used these when trolling from the boats. Today all lures used to troll from boats are commercially produced plastic and rubber equivalents that are bought from visiting vessel and merchants in Ḥadiboh. Lures for trolling and handlining in Al-Batinah, Oman and the Arabian Gulf, were also made from cloth, date palm fibre, wood and feathers, although these too have been replaced by commercially bought rubber and plastic lures (Donaldson 1979: 129; McIvor 1986: 57; Beech 2004: 45).

Fishing Sinkers

Sinkers on Socotra are either made from stone *ḥágar* (Ar/Soc) or lead *rasās* (Ar/Soc), both of which are still used today. Stone sinkers are normally untouched whole stones, although in Erisseyl the fishermen square them off to make them easier to tie to the end of a line or net. The net sinkers are normally prepared beforehand by tying string to individual rocks, and then tying them to the net (Figure 86). Fishermen in Erisseyl said that stones were only attached to the net when it was on the boat, as it made the nets easier to carry on and off the boat. In Ḥadiboh, Khames Abdulah Salem[115] told me that he also uses a holed stone, *maʿḳōmə* (Soc), which is permanently attached to a line or net. He said that this stone is used both when handlining in shallow water and as a sinker attached to the bottom of a net, although I did not find evidence for this elsewhere on the island. Fishermen on the north and south coast said that lead sinkers are only used when handlining in shallow water and are either tied to a line or bent around it. Those interviewed in Qalansiyah and Ḥadiboh said that in deep water the current is too strong to use lead, which is not heavy enough to keep the baited hook from being dragged to the surface. Stone and lead sinkers for nets and lines

[115] Full-time fisherman, 75 years old, interviewed on 22 December 2009.

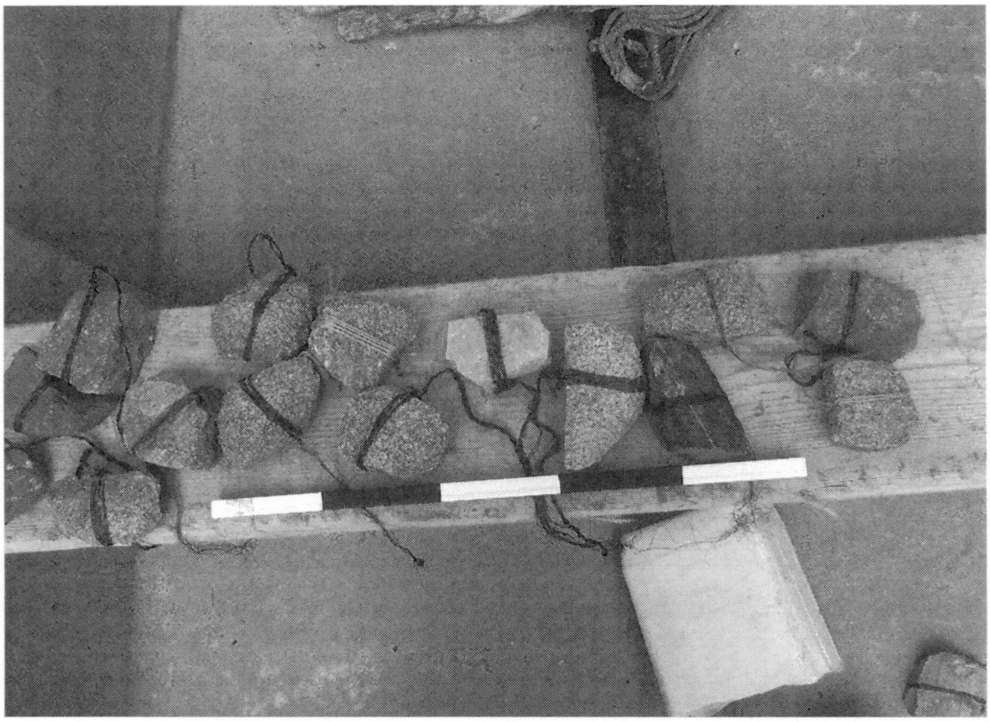

Figure 86. Stone net sinkers in Erisseyl, note how some of the rocks have been broken to make it easier to tie a line to them (Photo: author).

have been recorded in Al-Batinah; Al-Sharqiyya, Oman and the Arabian Gulf (Donaldson 1979: 129; McIvor 1986: 57; Beech 2004: 45; Agius pers. comm. 2011).

Bait, *žˈʌmdə* (Soc)

According to Morris (2002: 225) and Naumkin (1993: 202), fishermen use worms, fish, octopus, squid and crab as bait. Fishermen along the north and south coasts said that the bait they use is dependent on where they are fishing and what type of fish they wish to catch. When handlining in deep water they use whole bait fish, which is good for catching the bigger demersal and pelagic species. The bait used for shallow-water handlining is more varied, and includes crab, shellfish, and pieces of flesh cut from almost any fish. None of the fishermen said that they use worms. Baiting of longlines is normally done with whole low-value demersal or pelagic fish. However, the fishermen told me that the best bait to use when longlining for shark is dolphin meat, as sharks prefer it. The bait used elsewhere along the coasts of Southern Arabia is as varied as that used by the fishermen on Socotra, and includes all manner of marine species (Donaldson 1979: 129; McIvor 1986: 57; Kentley 1988: 184; Camelin 2006: 38).

Gaff, *mˈinzek* (Soc)

A gaff is a metal pole that has a ring in one end and is hooked at the other (Figure 87). Fishermen in Ḥadiboh and Qalansiyah said that it is mostly used to gaff large fish, such as sharks, that have been netted or handlined to help drag them into the boat. It is also used in the retrieval of cast nets. According to Morris,[116] a gaff was also used on Samḥa to catch a species of turtle known as, *ḏ-il-wāšik* (Soc). The method used is to paddle up to the turtle and, when it comes up to breathe, for the fisherman to leap upon it and gaff it in the flesh between the neck and shoulders. Depending on the size of the turtle it would either be dragged onboard or towed alongside to a beach, where it would be slaughtered. Gaffs were normally bought from vessels visiting Socotra, although the fishermen said it is now possible to buy them on the island. Gaffs are also recorded in al-Shihr, Hadhramaut, where they are used to drag larger pelagic species on board (Camelin 2006: 78).

Harpoon

The harpoon used on Socotra is made from a thick wooden branch that is whittled down to make a pole. A barbed steel head is fixed to one end and fastened in place, and a date-palm fibre rope attached (Figure 88). The rope is stored in a date palm fibre basket onboard and spooled out once a fish has been harpooned. The use of harpoons on Socotra has been recorded by several authors, the earliest being Marco Polo, who says that they were used to hunt whales (Yule and Cordier 1993:

[116] Personal Communication November 2011.

FIGURE 87. A GAFF, *MÍNZEK* (SOC), IN THE SOCOTRA FOLK MUSEUM (PHOTO: AUTHOR).

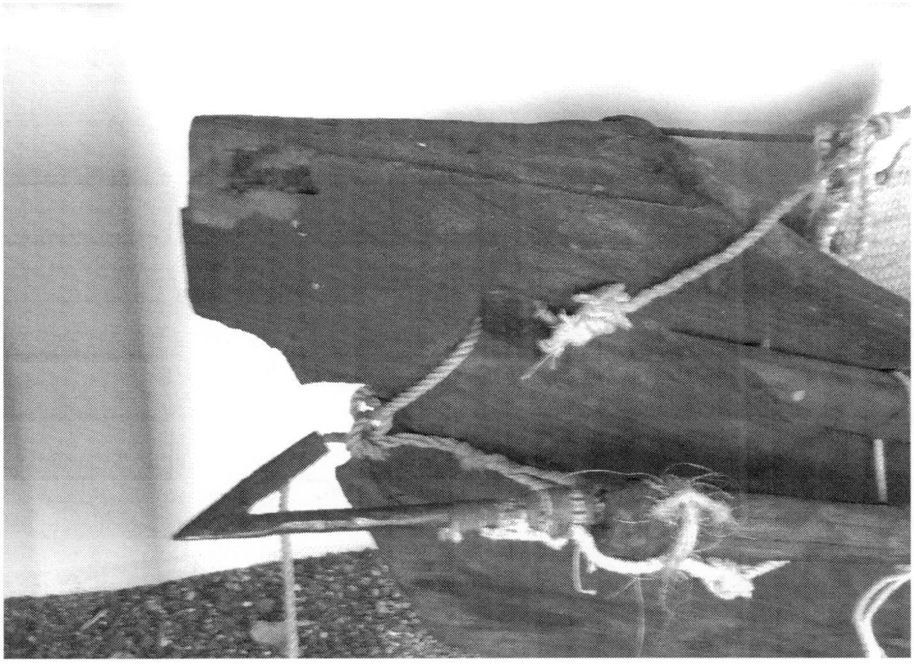

FIGURE 88. THE BARBED STEEL HEAD OF A HARPOON IN THE SOCOTRA FOLK MUSEUM (PHOTO: AUTHOR).

2.407). It is later recorded as being used to kill shark that had firstly been captured using seine nets, longlines or when handlining (Serjeant 1992: 175; Naumkin 1993: 202; Morris 2002: 224). Harpoons are rarely used today as, according to fishermen in Qalansiyah and Ḥadiboh, the sharks caught are normally retrieved dead. The use of harpoons was also recorded in the Arabian Gulf, where they were used to catch turtles, porpoises, sharks and rays (McIvor 1986: 57).

Fish Club

According to Morris (2002:202), most boats carried a stout wooden club for stunning larger fish. The fishermen told me that this club is normally shaped from a thick wooden branch made from *mítrer*, and that it is always carried onboard. However, they said that the club is only used when a large or dangerous fish has been caught and even then it would only be used if it was absolutely necessary. The reason for this is that the fishermen do not want to damage the fish, which would make it difficult to sell, and because they believe that dead fish do not stay fresh. Fishermen in Ḥadiboh said that damaged and dead fish are very difficult to sell locally. This is in contrast to fishermen in Suakin, Sudan and Al-Shihr, Hadhramaut, who club most large fish caught (Kentley 1988: 184; Camelin 2006: 76).

Remora

In addition to the fishing methods outlined here is the Socotri fishermen's practice of using remora to catch turtles (Morris 2002: 229). The remora, also known as a suckerfish, is an elongated fish with an oblong sucker on top of its head, which it uses to attach itself to ships, whales, turtles, sharks and other large fish. During a fishing trip in Ḥadiboh the fishermen I was with caught a large remora, which was brought into the boat and occasionally wetted with water to keep it alive. According to them, it would be later used to catch turtle. To do this they said that it was necessary to firstly tie a rope to the remora and then when a turtle is spotted to release it into the water. The remora would then swim and attach itself to the turtle and both could be dragged back to the boat. As we did not see a turtle that day the remora was passed to another boat. They said that if the remora could not be used, or it died, they would use it for bait. As strange as this practice may seem, in the past it has been recorded worldwide, from the Americas, East Africa and the Comoros (Hornell 1950: 35; Martin and Martin 1978: 120; Frazier 1980: 331).

The fishing tackle outlined above demonstrates the wide variety of equipment that has and is still currently being made and used on Socotra. A detailed summary of this equipment, the method of its deployment, seasons in which it is used, species targeted and the locations in which these species are targeted are outlined in Appendix 4.

Conclusion

The variety of fishing tackle being made and used on Socotra demonstrates a number of important points concerning the type of equipment used; its development and the locales in which it is mainly deployed. As mentioned in chapters seven and eight, there are distinctive differences between the north and south coast and individual villages along the same section of coast. These differences are based upon a combination of factors which include the terrestrial and marine landscape, ethnicity, knowledge and experience of fishermen. These factors also play a role in the variety of fishing tackle being made and used, and importantly provide an insight into how fishing traditions have developed.

Nets and lines have been used on Socotra from at least the 17th century and provide an interesting insight into the social, economic and environmental influences. The first is that nets and lines were and remain today the primary means of catching fish, even though only a few people had the necessary skills to make them. While it may be tempting to attribute an ethnicity to these fishermen this is fraught with problems, as experience and knowledge is likely to have played a more significant role. Consequently, it is most likely that the few fishermen who were able to make nets were experienced fishermen that had been fishing for a significant length of time. On Socotra, this would imply that they were initially East Africans, or settled fishermen from the Hadhramaut, who have been fishing on the island for several centuries.

Setting of nets relies on a number of important concerns, which include the nature of the seabed, the luminosity of the moon and the strength of the current. While these restrictions play a significant role in where and when nets can be used, it is the species sought that ultimately determines where and when they will use nets. Fishermen wishing to target high-value pelagic species need to set top-anchored or fixed single-anchored seine net, those targeting demersal species need to set bottom-anchored nets, whereas lobsters will require a drag net. These factors also influence line fishing and trapping, which also are set in such a manner as to target specific species.

Along the south coast of Socotra fishermen tend to favour netting, whereas on the north coast handlining predominates. This is also reflected in the naming of fishing areas, outlined in chapter seven, as named fishing areas tend to be specific locales where handlining for specific species is carried out. Consequently, it appears that the lack of any specific fishing areas along the south coast is also reflected in the fishing tackle deployed and that that the choice of netting over handlining is partly based upon the availability of landmarks. While it can be argued that the predominance of handlining over netting in the north coast is a major factor in the availability of landmarks, it is also necessary to look at a number of other factors. These factors include the depth of the sea in the vicinity of villages on the north and south coast, the availability of high-value pelagic species in these areas, and the short period of calm weather when it is possible to use a net. With these factors in mind it is possible to say that the choice of handlines over nets is reflective of the terrestrial and maritime landscape, and the experience and knowledge of the fishermen. Consequently, when the weather is calm it is possible for the fishermen to use traps, nets and lines to target a wide range of species at a variety of different locales for local and overseas consumption. During this period it is the demand for specific species that is the main determining factor in what tackle will be used and where it will be set, whereas when the weather deteriorates, it is the difficulties of using, locating and retrieving specific tackle that influences what will be used and why netting and trapping is often abandoned in favour of handlining. While this has a limited impact on the type of species being caught, it certainly affects the effort required to obtain the same quantities of fish that could be caught using nets. During the SW monsoon the tackle used undergoes a drastic change as fishermen are restricted to fishing in protected bays using shore handlines, cast nets and possibly traps, and their catches are almost purely for personal consumption.

The demand for specific fish species on Socotra is driven by visiting vessels, which influence both what fishing tackle will be used and where it will be deployed. Consequently, when demand for a species occurs, fishermen are required to set specific tackle in those areas where it is possible to maximise the capture of the species sought. With regards to lobsters this would entail setting lobster traps or dragging nets along the south, northeast and southeast of the island. However, when fishing for high-value demersal or pelagic species the fishermen tend to use a combination of methods, such as netting, trolling, longlining and handlining. This allows them to maximise their catch. Furthermore, this demand also influences the risks fishermen are willing to take, and it is not uncommon to hear about fishing vessels running into difficulties attempting to retrieve nets in rough weather conditions.

Finally, when comparing the fishing tackle made and used on Socotra with that in the Hadhramaut, Yemen, Al-Batinah, Oman and the Arabian Gulf it is possible to gain an insight into how fishing tackle and methods on Socotra and elsewhere have been adapted to fit specific social and environmental constraints. According to Donaldson (1979: 160-161), fishermen along the Al-Batinah coast of Oman were divided between two areas based upon whether cast nets or beach seines were predominately used. The reason for this division was said to be the distribution of fish, the difference in the depth of the sea, constraints of current and winds, and the cost of fishing tackle. Similarities with the influence of the environment and distribution of fish are also mentioned in the Hadhramaut by Camelin (2006) and Bonfiglioli and Hariri (2004). These factors are also reflected in the influences affecting the Socotri fishermen. However, the fishermen on Socotra are further constrained by the demand for fish which, unlike on the mainland, is restricted to a few months of the year. Furthermore, they are also restricted by social constraints on where and when specific gear can be used, and what species can be taken. The next chapter looks at the marine species being targeted by the fishermen and how the fisheries economy has developed and changed over time.

Chapter 11

The Fisheries Economy

To be a successful fisherman requires a specialised knowledge of the marine species one is hoping to catch. Understanding when and where specific species can be caught is one of the most important attributes for a fisherman, especially on Socotra, where the fishing season is limited to a few months of the year. Furthermore, unless catching purely for subsistence, one also requires a market for one's catch, and it is this market which can further influence what is caught and when. The aim of this chapter is to look at what marine species are being exploited by the fishermen of Socotra, where these species occur, and how the fisheries trade influences when and what is caught. To address these aims this chapter looks at the historical trade and exploitation of marine species on Socotra and traces this up to the present day, whilst also analysing the season in which they are caught and their distribution.

Historically the economy of Socotra has always been tied to products obtainable from the sea, from the time of the *Periplus Maris Erythraei*, (mid-1st century AD), in which turtle shells are listed as one of the main articles of trade up until the present day when fish is one of the island's main exports. The marine species that have been and are still exploited by fishermen for personal consumption and trade are listed below.

Demersal and pelagic fish

The seas surrounding Socotra are amongst the most productive marine areas in the world (Hariri *et al.* 2002: 7). The richness of marine species off Socotra is due to the upwelling of nutrient rich waters that occurs off the island's coastline. Today, the fishermen on Socotra tend to target a specific range of pelagic and demersal species. The main pelagic species targeted are sharks, kingfish, tuna (yellow-fin, long-tailed and others), dolphin-fish, island bonito, rainbow runner, anchovies, sardines, herrings and mackerel. The main demersal species targeted are groupers, emperors, trevallies, sweetlips, snappers and scad (Nichols 2001: 39-50). While it may not be possible to trace the exact species being targeted in the historical record, looking at the trade in fish can provide an insight into the importance of the fisheries market on Socotra.

The earliest record for the trade in fish is Marco Polo in the 14th century, who lists 'great quantities of salted fish of a large and excellent kind' amongst the main items being traded by the inhabitants of Socotra (Yule and Cordier 1993: 406). The nature and scope of this trade in salted fish is difficult to trace within the historical record, a situation not unique to Socotra, as studies for the trade in salted and dried fish are lacking for much of the Western Indian Ocean (Yajima 1976: 16). The few historical and contemporary accounts that do mention this trade cite East Africa, in particular Mombasa, as the main export market for Socotri salted and dried fish (Foster 1908: 359; Brown 1966: 27- 29; Martin and Martin 1978: 134; Serjeant 1992: 175). This is echoed by one of Morris's informants,[117] who says that during *ḳe̍yaṭ* (Soc), January to March, boats from Arabia and the Gulf going to East Africa stop at Socotra to collect salted fish. He also says that at the end of *dɔ̄ti* (Soc), April, boats from East Africa will come to Socotra to trade grain for salted fish. Further evidence for this trading link appears in the 17th century, in a letter from the son of the Sultan of the island of Pate, Lamu archipelago, Kenya, identifying vessels of the Sultan of Qishn, Al-Mahrah, and Socotra as 'allies' to whom the Portuguese were to hand *cartaze* (Barendse 2009: 74). *Cartaze* was a trading license issued by the Portuguese in an attempt to control and enforce a trading monopoly over the Indian Ocean. This letter would appear to indicate that the trade links with Socotra were of particular importance to the Sultan's son and, even though what is being supplied is not mentioned, it is most likely that it was salted and dried fish, one of Socotra's main exports to East Africa for several centuries.

The next indication of the trade in salted and dried fish is an account from the 19th century by Lieutenant Ormsby, who mentions that African slaves were used by their Arabian masters to fish, although he does not mention who they were selling their catch to (Ormsby 1844: 374). As mentioned earlier, it would appear that the Arabians were using their slaves to catch, salt and dry fish for the market in East Africa, which would have been an important source of income for them. The earliest detailed analysis of the trade in dried fish occurs in the 20th century, when the political advisor G. H. H. Brown reports on the economic conditions of Socotra. In his report Brown identifies fishing as the chief means of subsistence, and one of the most important exports of the island. According to him, dried fish was gathered into sacks and kept until dhows from East Africa and Arabia came to the island, where it was then bartered for

[117] Interviewed by Miranda Morris in 2002, who kindly passed me her transcriptions.

grain and other supplies (Brown 1966: 27- 29). These dhows only arrived during the open season, when the monsoon winds were calm, and cruised down the north coast, stopping at villages to barter for fish. He also notes that due to the lack of anchorages and difficulties of approaching the south coast it was not visited by the dhows, and that catches there were solely for local consumption. However, he does mention that the south coast was rich in fish, although the coastal settlements are only ever inhabited by a few Bedouin who come down to the coast to fish during calm weather. Brown is also the first person to identify the species of fish being caught, dried and salted (Brown 1966: 27). The pelagic species he identifies are shark and kingfish, both of which remain highly prized. The other fish species he identifies are 'whitefish', a generic term used to describe a variety of demersal species. The demersal species remain an important catch on the island today, although most are still consumed locally. Incidentally, it is perhaps not surprising that Brown and later Serjeant did not identify the local fish being caught by their names. The main reason for this is likely to have been, as I found, that the same species can be given different names from one village to another.

During the 1967 British expedition, Serjeant conducted a study into the fishing population and records that fishing was undertaken both for local consumption and export to East Arica where dried fish was exchanged for maize. According to him, the Sultan of Socotra used his slaves to catch and dry fish, after which he then sold the dried fish to passing dhows (Serjeant 1992: 175). Serjeant also says that those African and Arabian fishermen who were not slaves were generally bound by debt to shop owners, who gave advances to the fishermen, on the condition that they sell their fish to them. This normally resulted in the fishermen being debt bound to the merchants for life, a situation which was much the same along the coast of the mainland of Yemen (Serjeant 1992: 176). That the merchants were also engaged in the trade in fish would imply that fishing was an important source of income for many on the island, although the wealth appears to have remained in the hands of the merchants rather than the fishermen. These historical accounts also demonstrate that the fisheries trade is mostly with East Africa and that, much like all trade on Socotra, it is reliant on visiting vessels. Furthermore, these vessels are governed by the monsoon seasons, with vessels only arriving on the island during the NE monsoon. This trade is also shown to be concentrated along the north coast, where there is a larger fishing population, a greater number of fish and safer anchorages.

The only fish species identified by Serjeant is shark, which he says are bought by shark fishing dhows from Arabia and marketed in East Africa (Serjeant 1992:176). According to Morris (2002: 226), there was always a high demand for shark from visiting vessels, and all fishermen tried to catch them. Several full-time fishermen in Qalansiyah,[118] Qādheb[119] and Erisseyl,[120] said that it was impossible to catch enough sharks, as vessels from the mainland would buy all they could catch (Figure 89). This is reflected in a fisheries management report which estimates that an average of 7283 tons of shark a year is caught off Socotra, making it one of the most heavily fished species on the island (Saaed 2000: 123-126).

Serjeant points out that in Ḥadiboh oil is extracted from the liver of sharks and sold by the petrol can or barrel (Serjeant 1992: 176). Today it is still possible to see several barrels of shark liver oil being processed on the north coast (Figure 90). According to full-time fishermen from Ṣaqarah[121] and Erisseyl,[122] the oil is used locally to coat the hulls of the few remaining wooden vessels, but most is sold to visiting dhows, which take it to India. According to Morris, the oil and liver from some sharks is also consumed locally by Bedouin, who mix it together with cereal for themselves (Morris 2002: 226).

Up until 1967, trade in fish was almost entirely based around a system of reciprocal exchange in which fish was exchanged for various supplies (Brown 1966: 28; Serjeant 1992: 134-135). This system was partly disrupted during the Socialist period (1970-1990), when a range of new consumer goods were introduced. This led to a dramatic change in the eating habits of the population, and saw a move away from dates, fish, milk and ghee towards tinned milk, tea, rice and flour (Elie 2004: 74). This also began to change the nature of the economy from one that was exchange based to one in which cash took precedence. This cash-based economy is the norm for most villages on the island today, although in several smaller fishing villages I visited on the south coast and the outer island of Samḥa, bartering is still practiced. The fishermen interviewed at these villages said that they barter fish for supplies because fishing and other supplies are easier to obtain and cheaper when obtained from dhows than from the merchants on Socotra.

The onset of the Socialist era also heralded an increase in new equipment, motorised vessels and the setting up of fishing cooperatives and cartels (Naumkin 1993: 164). This provided the basis for the eventual commercialisation of the fisheries sector which, after 1990 and the formation of the Republic of Yemen, became better developed. As a result of this development

[118] Abdullha Rahman Abod Ali Saeed, 38 years old; Anwar Khamis Abdul Abod Ali Saeed, 38 years old, both interviewed on 16 December 2009.

[119] Salim Games Saaed, 45 years old; Salim Saaed Atman, 55 years old, both interviewed on 2 January 2010.

[120] Sindowa Ali Ahmed, in his 40s; Mohammed Selem Abo, 56 years old, both interviewed on 23 December 2009.

[121] Salem Abdullah Saeed, 45 years old; Thaili Hamoadi, in his 60s; Mobark Wilaal Saad, 25 years old; Salam Rashid Hamoadi, 25 years old, all interviewed on 23 December 2009.

[122] Fohaad Ali, in his 60s; Sindowa Ali Ahmed, in his 40s; Frzir Ahmed Hamed, 28 years old, all interviewed on 9 February 2009.

Figure 89. Fishermen in Erisseyl offloading their catch of shark (Photo: author).

Figure 90. Barrels of shark liver oil in Ṣaqarah (Photo: author).

there was a large increase in the number of Yemeni and other vessels visiting the island to buy fish. Today, 25 to 30 vessels a day visit Socotra during the fishing season (Nichols 2001: 29). The increase in demand for fish has been welcomed by most fishermen. However, many fishermen in Ḥadiboh, Qalansiyah and Qādhab told me that as more people have begun to fish it is becoming more difficult to find fish. Consequently, they now need to spend longer out at sea. Furthermore, unlike in the past, the market for dried fish is substantially less, as vessels coming to the island want to buy fresh fish, which is put on ice and taken to the mainland of Yemen. The majority of these vessels anchor near large fishing villages to buy fresh fish from the local fishermen, which unlike the dried fish needs to be caught while the vessels are anchored. Moreover, because these vessels will only purchase specific fish species and because they provide the fishermen with their only market, these vessels influence what fish species are targeted. Today the main fish species targeted are the high-value pelagic species such as kingfish, tuna, bonitos, dolphin-fish and shark, which make up the majority of the fishermen's catch

(Nichols 2001: 40-43). These species are almost all sold to visiting vessels, although some are sold locally in the fish market at Ḥadiboh where they fetch a high price. These species are all migratory, and are found at the edge of the continental shelf, where the depth of the sea drops steeply in excess of 200m (Nichols 2001: 43). According to fishermen interviewed in Qalansiyah, Qādheb and Ḥadiboh, it is possible to catch these pelagic species throughout the NE monsoon period, although the peak fishing season is between October and December. They also told me that even though these are the optimum periods, if the weather is bad it is not always possible to fish for the pelagic species, as fishing offshore can be dangerous.

In addition to the pelagic species, fishermen also target shallow-water demersal species such as groupers, emperors, trevally, snappers, and sweetlips. According to Nichols (2001: 45), these species are distributed along the shallow waters surrounding the island in depths between three and 100 metres. He also says that they migrate to the shallow inshore waters during May to October, when sea temperatures rise and when they begin to feed voraciously. According to experienced fishermen along the south coast and those in Ḥadiboh and Qalansiyah, it is possible to catch these demersal species throughout the NE monsoon, although the best period is October and December when the sea is calm. The reason this period is favoured is likely to be due to the migration of fish to shallow inshore waters and their voracious feeding habits, which would make them easier to catch. The majority of these demersal fish are sold locally or used for personal consumption, although in Ḥadiboh and Qalansiyah fishermen interviewed said that some visiting vessels will buy big groupers.

The location of visiting vessels also plays a significant role in where the fishermen catch fish. The visiting vessels rarely anchor off smaller villages, as there are fewer fishermen to buy fish from. Consequently, fishermen in these villages either fish for personal consumption, or are required to transport their catches to where these vessels are anchored. This was clearly communicated to me by fishermen in Bidhōleh and Stēroh on the south coast, and Ṣaqarah on the north coast, who told me that vessels rarely anchor near their villages. They said that if they want to sell their fish, they either transport them to where the vessels are anchored, or fish at those villages where they are anchored. This situation is different in Ḥadiboh, Suq and Qādheb as the fishermen can sell their catch to either the visiting vessels or at the large local market in Ḥadiboh. This movement of fishermen around the island is not new, having taken place over several decades. In Qalansiyah, two fishermen[123] told me that in the past they often travelled along the north coast, fishing, processing and storing dried fish in anticipation of the arrival of the dhows. This was echoed by one of Morris's informants,[124] who said that many years ago he and his brother had travelled to the south coast to catch and dry fish. These dried fish were then placed in sacks and taken to the closest anchorage, where visiting dhows bought them.

During the SW monsoon fishing becomes virtually impossible, which traditionally would mean that many fishermen would have to remain on Socotra, tending the date plantations or looking after livestock. However, fishermen in Qalansiyah and Ḥadiboh said that whilst they had done this in the past, they nowadays preferred to leave Socotra and fish off the coasts of the Arabian mainland. Several informants[125] told me that they would either attempt to find crew positions on larger fishing vessels, or ship their own vessels to the mainland of Yemen in order to fish independently.

While demersal and pelagic fish species form the largest part of the fisheries economy on Socotra, there are many other marine species that have been and are exploited by the fishermen. The influence of these other species on the economy tends to be short lived, having been driven by overseas demand. However, locally, some marine species are an important source of sustenance, especially during the SW monsoon when it is difficult to catch fish. The earliest recorded of these species to be exploited are turtles.

Turtles

The trade in turtle shell on Socotra was first recorded in the *Periplus* (mid-1st century) and again in the 13th century by the Chinese inspector of maritime trade Chau Ju-kua (d. AD 1231), who listed it as a commodity coming from Socotra (Hirth and Rockhill 1911: 130-132). While there is little more historical evidence for this trade, the exploitation of turtles can be traced up to the present day. According to Forbes (1903: xxx), fishermen on ᶜAbd al-Kūri captured large quantities of turtles, as evidenced by the large quantities of turtle shells strewn about their houses. The next account is by Morris (2002), who says that turtles were hunted on Socotra and the outlying island of ᶜAbd al-Kūri. She also mentions that they were traditionally an important source of food for all the islanders, and that most were killed when they came ashore (Morris 2002: 116, 229). According to her, the turtles would be disembowelled and the meat and fat mixed together. This would be kept in pots for periods of

[123] Abaid Salem bin Awailan, full-time fisherman, in his 60s; Ali Salim Da-Salmoho, full-time fisherman, in his 60s, both interviewed on 16 February 2009.

[124] Mubarak Eesa Walid, interviewed by Miranda Morris in 2002 who kindly passed me her transcriptions.

[125] Jaman Saeed Abdullah, full-time fisherman, in his 30s, interviewed on 16 February 2009; Omar Saeed Abod Ali Saeed, full-time fisherman, 31 years old, interviewed on 18 February 2009; Saeed Salem Hasaan, full-time fisherman, 35 years old, interviewed on 17 February 2009; Saeed Selem Ali, full-time fisherman, 35 years old, interviewed on 17 February 2009.

hunger or brought out for a favoured guest. The shells, although no longer sold, were used as covers, water troughs and serving dishes.

The killing of turtles in Yemen was made illegal in 1991, although this has done little to curb demand for turtle meat and eggs (Hariri *et al.* 2002: 92), and on Socotra there is still a thriving local market. Several people[126] I spoke to said that turtle meat is a delicacy which is good for one's health and is also used as an aphrodisiac. They said that they and others still hunt turtles, like their fathers before them, even though they know it is illegal. They also said that turtle meat can be sold for a high price as many people like it, although the ban makes it difficult to sell to fishing vessels from the mainland. Consequently, turtles are mostly consumed locally. Turtle shells are rarely used, and most are dumped along the shoreline where the turtle has been slaughtered. The main species found on Socotra are green, hawksbill and loggerhead turtles (Pilcher and Saad 2000: 83). However, according to Morris,[127] the fishermen distinguish between five different types. The first of these is known locally as, *nāmilə* (Soc), a large turtle which is only seen in deep water offshore and does not come to the shore, possibly a leatherback turtle. The second is known as *di-ᶜabdḕrihon* (Soc), a small turtle that is found out at sea and does not come ashore to lay eggs. This can be identified as a loggerhead turtle. The third turtle identified by the fishermen is *D-il-wāšik* (Soc), this is usually seen out at sea, but occasionally do come ashore to lay their eggs where they are caught, possibly an olive ridley turtle. The fourth is known as *ḳāraṭ* (Soc), which is caught when it comes ashore to lay eggs. This can be identified as a hawksbill turtle. The last turtle to be identified is known as *bḕᶜelə* (Soc), which is also caught when it comes ashore to lay its eggs. This can be identified as a green sea turtle. My informants did not distinguish between species, and considered all turtles good eating. They did say that it was best to hunt turtles when they were nesting, as one could collect the highly prized eggs as well as the turtle. They also said that the best place to catch a nesting turtle is along the northwest coast, especially on the beaches in the vicinity of Rās ᶜAbelḥen. However, this area is often patrolled by the police. Fishermen interviewed said that turtles can be caught anytime between May and July, although the best period to catch them is between June and July. Several other fishermen said that it was also possible to catch turtles at sea throughout the year, although it would then be necessary to take them to a remote beach to slaughter. This situation is not unique to Socotra, and turtles are illegally caught throughout the southern Red Sea and Gulf of Aden. Furthermore, in Sudan, Djibouti, Yemen and Somalia, fishermen still catch them on beaches, where they are slaughtered and the eggs collected (Hariri *et al.* 2002: xii).

[126] I have omitted their names and the villages I interviewed them in because of state policing.

[127] Miranda Morris personal communication October 2011.

Lobster (*Panulirus*)

The earliest mention of lobsters on Socotra is in the 16th century, when Finch records how lobsters were caught in the bay of ᶜAririhun Di-Lisheh (Purchas 1905: IV, 17-18). However, there is little further information to determine whether this was for trade or subsistence. The next account comes from Ernest Bennett, travelling companion of the Bents. He notes that, on Socotra, it was possible to buy large lobsters extremely cheaply, although he too does not elaborate on whether they were being caught for trade or subsistence (Bennett 1897: 408). The availability of lobsters is also mentioned by Brown, who says that fishermen took large amounts, but implies that they were caught for subsistence rather than trade (Brown 1966: 28). According to Morris (2002: 115; 134), on Samḥa and ᶜAbd al-Kūri lobsters were a welcome bycatch found in fish traps, although some fishermen would also actively dive for them as they were considered good eating.

Today, lobsters are commercially exploited on Socotra and they represent an important source of income for the fishermen. However, due to the lack of commercial freezing facilities, the main period in which lobster fishing takes place is during the NE monsoon, when vessels from the mainland come to the island. According to fishermen in Ḥadiboh[128] and Di-Ḥamari,[129] during the tourist season there is an increasing demand from hotels and restaurants on the island, and it is also possible to sell directly to tourists at eco-lodges. They told me that whilst this is a good source of income, they prefer to sell to visiting vessels which buy all the lobsters the fishermen can catch. However, they did say that if they were not able to sell the lobsters caught they would eat them, and that they were considered a delicacy. Fishermen in Qalansiyah[130] and Maḥfirihin[131] said that when vessels wishing to buy lobster arrive, they will concentrate on catching lobster rather than fish as lobster fetches a higher price and they are able to sell all of their catch. This situation is much the same on the mainland of Yemen, where lobster catches greatly increase the monthly earnings of fishermen (Bonfiglioli and Hariri 2004: 44).

Shells

The trade in shells provides an interesting insight into the diversity of species being exploited on Socotra. The

[128] Faisal Ahmed Khalif, full-time fisherman, in his 30s; Salem Saeed Tamook, full-time fisherman, in his 40s; Sharaf Joman Baleef, full-time fisherman, 35 years old, all interviewed on 01 January 2010.

[129] Yahya Zakria Ahmed, full-time fisherman, in his 30s; Salim Mohammed, full-time fisherman, in his 60s, both interviewed on 8 February 2009.

[130] Saeed Salem Hasaan, full-time fisherman, 35 years old, interviewed on 17 December 2009; Abaid Salem bin Awailan, full-time fisherman, in his 50s, interviewed on 17 December 2009; Salam Saeed Martah, full-time fisherman, 39 years old, interviewed on 18 December 2009

[131] Muslim Abdulla, full-time fisherman, in his 30s; Salim Saaed, full-time fisherman, in his 30s, both interviewed on 11 February 2009.

main shells traded are the cowry (*Cypraea*), pearl and pearl oyster shell (*Pinctada*), whilst many other molluscs are used locally.

Cowry shells (Cypraea)

According to the Portuguese captain Duarte Barbosa, the island of Socotra had a plentiful supply of cowry, 'of the valuable kind' (*Book of Duarte Barbosa* 1967: 63). This is interesting in that, from at least the 14th century, there was an especially large trade in cowries between the Indian Ocean and West Africa,[132] where they were used to purchase African slaves. Furthermore, at the time of Barbosa's visit, this trade must have been substantial, and while he certainly recognised the importance of these shells there is little indication in the Portuguese, English or Dutch accounts that they were being commercially exploited. The only time cowries are mentioned again is in the 20th century, when Botting (2006: n 90) observes that the West African troops attempted to take sacks of cowry shells back home with them. While it is possible that Socotra was engaged in the cowry trade, the nature and scale of this trade is difficult to determine. Today, cowries are actively collected by fishermen as ornamental shells to sell to tourists, even though the trade in them is illegal. This trade has provided the fishermen with a new market, which they have been quick to exploit. The scale of the trade in ornamental shells is substantial, and several kilogrammes have been confiscated from tourists attempting to take them off the island.[133]

Pearl shell (Pinctada)

On Socotra, the black-lip pearl shell (*Pinctada margaritifera*) is known as *mọ̍ṣəliḥ* (Soc). According to fishermen I interviewed in Ḥadiboh[134] and Qādheb,[135] this shell, unlike the pearl oyster shell, *bi̍lbil* (Soc), (*Pinctada radiate*, and others of this family), was collected for the shell, rather than the pearl, *luᵓluᵓ* (Ar). In Qādheb[136] one informant showed me several shells that he had collected in the past and said that he had been holding onto them to sell, but that there was no longer a market for them.

The first account of the trade in pearl shell is by Charles Moser, who in 1918 said that the 'Africans' dive for pearl shells, which was in high demand for its mother of pearl interior (Moser 1918: 278). This trade is also mentioned in Brown's report, which says that there is an abundant trade in cameo shell (Brown 1966: 30). According to Morris (2002: 228), the trade in cameo grew during the British occupation of Aden, and many people from Socotra, Somalia and East Africa became involved in diving for these shells. She says that the fishermen would keep the shells until trading vessels arrived (Morris 2002: 227). Furthermore, with the increased demand for the shells, people also began to eat the flesh, although it was not specifically dived for food (Morris 2002: 228). This was reiterated by an elderly full-time fisherman Jamen Mahafawl Saif,[137] 70 years old, who said that the flesh of these shells was very good eating, and was considered to be an additional bonus when diving for the shells. The trade in cameo shell appears to have almost completely died out after the British left Aden, although Wranik (1999: 171) says that there is still a limited market, driven by merchants from the Gulf. Today there is no trade in pearl shell, and other than mementos I was shown, none of the fishermen I interviewed dived for them.

According to the fishermen, pearl and pearl oyster shell can be found on the north coast, between Rās Qadamah in the east to Rās Ḥowlef in the west. However, they told me that the best areas were in Qādheb, Ḥadiboh, Suq and ᶜArirhun Di-Lisheh. They also said that it was only possible to dive for these shells during *ke̍yaṭ*, when the seas were *šwa̍r* (Soc), calm, as one was then able to see the shells from the surface.

Pearl oyster shell

Fishermen in Ḥadiboh and Qādheb[138] told me that the pearl oyster shell, *bi̍lbil* (Soc) is much smaller than the *mọ̍ṣəliḥ* (Soc), and that it is found in much shallower water. They also said that the shell of the *bi̍lbil* is not worth anything, but if one was lucky one could find a pearl and get a lot of money for it.

The pearling trade on Socotra is alluded to in several historical accounts, although it is not until 20th century that it is possible to determine the importance of this trade in the fisheries economy. According to Serjeant (1996: 177), the first reference to pearls on Socotra is by al-Kindī (d. AD 873), who says that there were pearl banks around the island. In the 17th century Finch mentions that the 'natives' dived for pearl oyster shells although he does not elaborate further (Purchas 1905: IV, 18). The next reference is by Brown, who reports on an active pearl trade. According to him, the trade was controlled by the Sultan of Socotra, who had the sole

[132] The book by Jan Hogendorn and Marion Johnson, *The Shell Money of the Slave Trade* (Cambridge: Cambridge University Press, 1986) provides a full account of the size and scope of this trade, although Socotra is not mentioned.

[133] According to Bohdana Rambouskova, the former Communication Officer for the Socotra Governance and Biodiversity Project over a hundred kilograms of shells have been confiscated from tourists (Friends of Socotra Conference, Bern, Switzerland, 23-25 September 2011).

[134] Esso Ibn Seyaka, full-time fisherman, in his 60s, interviewed on 15 February 2009; Khames Abdulah Salem, full-time fisherman, 75 years old, interviewed on 22 December 2009; Jamen Mahafawl Saif, full-time fisherman, 75 years old, interviewed on 22 December 2009.

[135] Omar Abdulla Saleh, full-time fisherman, in his 60s; Mohammed Aldolah, full-time fisherman, in his 60s; Abdullah Mohammed Sallim, full-time fisherman, in his 60s, all interviewed on 08 February 2009.

[136] Mohammed Aldolah, full-time fisherman, in his 60s, interviewed on 08 February 2009.

[137] Interviewed on 15 February 2009.

[138] These fishermen were the same as those interviewed for the pearl shell, *mọ̍ṣəliḥ*.

right to deal in pearls and that fishermen were obliged to sell through him or his agents. Due to this control, the pearl trade was not of great importance to fishermen on the island and brought them little in the way of income (Brown 1966: 30). The reason for this was that the pearling vessels coming from the Gulf mostly brought their own crews, and there was little opportunity for local fishermen to become involved. Several pearling dhows from the Gulf came to visit the island in the pearl-diving season of 1967 as recorded by Serjeant. According to him, pearling was free to all, although the trade in pearls remained under the control of the Sultan and his agents. While both 'the inhabitants' and several Somalis were apparently engaged in pearling, Serjeant does not specify whether the inhabitants were African, Arabian or Socotri pearl divers, or who the Somalis were working for (Serjeant 1996: 176-177). This observation is later elaborated upon by Morris, who says that vessels from Somalia and the Gulf and Oman would come to the island for several months to dive for pearls, and that the islanders were also engaged in diving for pearls, although most would use their own vessels rather than work for visiting pearl diving vessels (Morris 2002: 227-228). Today, there is no demand for pearl or pearl shells due to the introduction of cultured pearls in the 1920s, the Great Depression of the 1930s, and the two world wars (Carter 2005: 158).

The fishermen I interviewed, said that they remembered when they had dived for pearls there were many people on the island who had tried to get involved. However, they said that it was the African fishermen who were mostly involved in diving for pearls, as they were the best divers. This is corroborated by the historical and earlier ethnographical accounts, which refer to divers as being African (Roe 1967: 30-39; Serjeant 1996: 176; Morris 2002: 227). Furthermore, contrary to Brown's report, the fishermen I spoke to said that when they had dived for the pearl shells and pearls they could make good money in a short period of time, although this is likely to be relative to that which was made when fishing. Today, none of the fishermen dive for pearls, although I was told by one informant in Qādheb[139] that he knew where to find large areas of pearl shells, and if there was a market he and others were ready to dive for them again.

Opercula, *Ṭ̓ifher* (pl. *ṭ̓ifheriḥtin*) (Soc)

According to Brown, the opercula of 'certain species' were sometimes traded to the mainland where they were used as a drug that was believed to assist women in lactation (Brown 1966: 31). Several years later, Serjeant records a shell on Socotra called *jawḥāf* (Ar), which was sold and exported to al-Mukalla, where it was ground and used in perfume. The shell was known on the South Arabia coast as *ẓufur* (Ar) where, like on the island, the opercula was burnt, ground and mixed with oil before being put into women's hair (Serjeant 1996: 178). According to Morris, the opercula of several shells were in great demand by the sailors of Oman, where it was an important ingredient in fumigant incense mixtures (Morris 2002: 177). The fishermen I interviewed made no mention of this trade in *ṭ̓ifher*, and it would appear that it had been relatively short-lived. The reason is probably a decline in the demand from Socotra, which is likely to have been brought about by competition from places such as Sudan, where opercula are processed and marketed in large quantities (Hariri *et al.* 2002: 36).

Shellfish gathering, *Šáḥaḳ* (Soc)

Shellfish have played an important part in the lives of both coastal and mountain inhabitants, although they are not traded, but exploited directly for food. The exploitation of shellfish was first recorded by the archaeologist Shinnie, who was involved in the 1956 Oxford University expedition to Socotra. He found substantial shell-midden deposits near the fishing village of Rās Momi, on the eastern end of Socotra, and concluded that they were the result of sustained exploitation over a long period of time (Shinnie 1960: 101). The use of shellfish as sustenance is also mentioned by Boxhall (1966: 218), who says that the fishermen would eat them, and Morris (2002: 221) says that the islanders were 'assiduous shellfish gatherers'. The fishermen would also use shellfish as a means of alleviating hunger, or to change their monotonous diet of dates and fish. According to Morris, the gathering of shellfish was generally only undertaken by children and women, and in some areas it was considered to be shameful for a man to be engaged in this (Morris 2002: 229). Today, shellfish are still exploited locally by both men and women. Fishermen interviewed in Qalansiyah,[140] Di-Ḥamdh[141] and Ṣaqarah[142] told me that they would eat shellfish, but mostly during the SW monsoon season when it was difficult to catch fish, or when they were camping away from home and their supplies of food were running low. They also said that shellfish is collected for use in fish traps.

Ambergris (*Ambra grisea*)

The earliest record of ambergris on Socotra is a 10th century account by al-Hamdānī (d. AD 945), who

[139] Salim Games Saaed, full-time fisherman, 45 years old, interviewed on 2 January 2010.

[140] Ali Salim Da-Salmoho, full-time fisherman, in his 60s, interviewed on 16 February 2009; Abdullha Rahman Abod Ali Saeed, SCDP representative and full-time fisherman, 38 years old, interviewed on 16 December 2009; Saeed Selem Ali, seasonal fisherman, 35 years old, interviewed on 17 December 2009.

[141] Yahya Zakria Ahmed, full-time fisherman, in his 30s; Salim Mohammed, full-time fisherman, in his 60s, both interviewed on 8 February 2009.

[142] Thaili Hamoadi, full-time fisherman, in his 60s; Mobark Wilaal Saad, full-time fisherman, 25 years old, both interviewed on 23 December 2009.

mentions that along the shores of Socotra there were large quantities of it to be found (al-Hamdānī 1983: 93). The quantity and availability of ambergris is again mentioned by several authors from the 13th to 21st century, although there is no mention of it being traded (Forbes 1903: xxx; Purchas 1905: IV, 13; *Book of Duarte Barbosa* 1967: 62; Polo 1993: 406-407; Ibn al-Mujāwir 2008: 264). The difficulty in attempting to understand the market for ambergris is that the historical accounts do not record anything about the nature and scale of this trade. The only mention of the economic worth of this product is in the 20th and 21st centuries when we learn that it was being sold according to its weight, where the weight of one rupee would be equivalent to the same weight in ambergris (Serjeant 1992: 179; Morris 2002: 172). According to Morris (2002: 115), any ambergris found on the island belonged to the Sultan of Socotra. She also says that it is believed to be a bringer of good fortune, and was used locally for many different ailments. Morris says that the finding of ambergris is considered to be both good fortune and dangerous, and there were several rituals which needed to be followed when collecting it. These were to do with protecting oneself against bad spirits and the evil eye. She also says that it was considered to bring good luck and was much sought after for its medicinal properties; it also represented an important source of wealth and would often be sold to visiting merchants (Morris 2002: 176-177).

There are three types of ambergris recognised on Socotra: black, the poorest quality; brown, the intermediate; and white, the best. During my interviews, fishermen in Ḥadiboh[143] and in Qādheb[144] told me that ambergris could be found all along the beaches, although recently there was little to be found anywhere on the island. The truth of this is difficult to ascertain, as they said that if they did find some, and people knew, it would invoke the evil eye. However, I was told a story by Ali Salim Da-Salmoho[145] about a fisherman who found ambergris, but not knowing what it was, used it to coat the outside of his vessel, thereby wasting a rich find. This story was told to me to explain the problem with too many 'new' fishermen that had no knowledge of the sea and were wasting its gifts.

The items listed above are the main products that were and continue to be exploited by the fishermen of Socotra, although it is unlikely to be a complete picture as new demands will certainly bring about the exploitation of new species. This has been recently demonstrated with regard to the sea cucumber, which has become a commercially exploited species that is actively dived on Socotra.[146]

Sea cucumber, *ḥfōs* (Soc)

The sea cucumber has only begun to be commercially exploited on Socotra in the last five years, although the market for them remains limited (Nichols 2001: 53). The main areas within which fishermen dive for sea cucumbers are along the north coast, especially off the villages of Ḥadiboh, Di-Ḥamari, Erisseyl, Shuᶜub and Qalansiyah. According to fishermen interviewed in these villages, it is only possible to dive for sea cucumbers from December to March, and they were mostly found in about 10m of water. They also said that when they can dive is dependent on sea conditions, as during rough weather visibility is poor and it is not possible to see or catch them.

In summary, the fisheries trade on Socotra has been active for millennia, and various marine species have been targeted. While turtles are the earliest recorded species, pelagic and demersal fish species have been the main economic staple throughout Socotra's history. The trade in almost all other marine species has been relatively short-lived, although in each case fishermen have been quick to adapt to the new marketing opportunities. The most discernible short-term change was the development of the pearling industry, which provided a seasonal change to fishing and allowed fishermen to pursue an alternative source of income. Today, it is the increasing market for lobster and sea cucumber, which provides the fishermen with another source of income, although fish still remains their primary source.

Furthermore, other than a limited local demand, the main driving force behind the fisheries economy on Socotra was, and remains the market opportunities afforded by visiting trading vessels. These vessels not only provide a market for their catch, but also essential supplies of food and fishing equipment. Their reliance on these vessels also means that almost all fishing activity is dictated by when they arrive and what species they purchase, especially as local demand is relatively low. The importance attached to these vessels was demonstrated to me during interviews in Qalansiyah. According to several fishermen,[147] if a vessel wishing to buy shark comes to their village they go fishing offshore, even if the weather is dangerous. The reason is that these vessels only visit the island for a short period each year and, if they do not fish, the period of the SW monsoon will be economically difficult.

[143] Jamen Mahafawl Saif, full-time fisherman, 70 years old; Khames Abdulah Salem, full-time fisherman, full time fisherman, 75 years old, both interviewed on 15 February 2009.

[144] Omar Abdulla Saleh, full-time fisherman, in his 60s, interviewed on 08 February 2009; Abdullah Ali Muhammed, full-time fisherman, in his 60s, interviewed on 02 February 2009.

[145] Ali Salim Da-Salmoho, full-time fisherman, in his 60s, interviewed on 16 February 2009.

[146] According to a lecture given by Uwe Zajonz of the Senckenberg Research Institute, who has been actively involved in the fisheries management of the Socotra Archipelago (Friends of Socotra Conference, Bern, Switzerland, 23-25 September 2011).

[147] Saeed Salem Hasaan, full-time fisherman, 35 years old; Abaid Salem bin Awailan, full-time fisherman, in his 50s; Saeed Selem Ali, full-time fisherman, 35 years old, all interviewed on 17 December 2009.

Conclusion

Fishing on Socotra is influenced by a series of interrelated factors, which affect what, when and where fish and other marine species are caught. These factors include the practical constraints imposed by the environment, the economic influences of demand and supply, and being able to locate and capture the species sought. The environmental influences are a mixture of weather and maritime landscape, both of which impose certain constraints on when and where it is possible to fish, and dictate where species are likely to be more abundant. Climate is the most influential of these and has divided the fishing season into two very specific periods based upon access to the sea. However, as shown here and in previous chapters, the open season is subdivided by the fishermen into different periods of fishing activity, within which specific areas and species are targeted. While climate does play an important role in when it is possible to fish, it is the narrow shallow-water shelf of the north coast and wide shallow-water shelf of the south that determines where to fish. Especially as the submarine topography affects the quantity and type of demersal and pelagic fish species that occur, and the distance fishermen are required to travel to catch them.

The importance of these environmental factors cannot be overstated, however, it is the demand for fish and other marine species that ultimately determines the nature and scope of fishing activities. Locally, this demand is limited, and most of what is caught is either used for personal consumption or within *maḥrif* (Soc), a system of mutual assistance and dependency. Local demand has a limited impact on the fisheries economy, although it does impact on what species are harvested. This is especially apparent during the SW monsoon season, when the inability to catch fish can result in a demand for shellfish. While it is necessary to be aware of the influence of this local demand, the most influential economic influence is the demand coming from overseas. This overseas demand is represented by visiting vessels, which not only purchase fish but also bring essential supplies to the island. As a result of this, the fishermen are almost totally reliant on when these vessels arrive and what they purchase. This is especially apparent today where there is a greater demand for fresh fish, which needs to be caught whilst these vessels are anchored at Socotra. Furthermore, the demands of these vessels tend to be species-specific, which makes it necessary for the fishermen to target their fishing activities according to what these vessels buy. This in turn influences where the fishermen fish as specific high value species, like shark, are found in deeper offshore areas. Consequently, the fishermen target specific areas to find these species. Targeting specific species also requires the fishermen to adapt different fishing techniques and equipment and drives the fishermen to adopt specific types of tackle. With these factors in mind it is now possible to provide an overview of the fishermen's seasonal calendar and outlining the various fishing activities, species and methods used. See Figure 91, Socotra's seasonal calendar, outlining the various fishing activities, species caught and methods used.

Season	Period	Climate	Activities	Species and Methods
gyaḥś (Soc) This period is said to be the beginning of the open season, *futūḥ al-baḥr* (Ar)	*gyaḥś* lasts for most of October, although it can begin as early as mid-September.	This period is characterised by a steadier NE wind known as *ṣer̍bihi* (Soc). During the latter half of October the rains of the SE monsoon season normally begin. The sea is generally very calm. Visibility is good, although during the rain showers it decreases considerably.	This period is considered to be best for fishing, as the sea is said to have been replenished over the SW monsoon season. It is possible to fish every day. Due to the calm seas, it is possible to travel further offshore for the pelagic fish.	This is the best fishing period for shark, tuna and kingfish. Most fishing is done using nets, although some fishermen use hand lines. Fish traps are used extensively.
NE winter monsoon season *ṣēreb* (Soc)	The NE monsoon season last for approximately five months, October to February.	During this period the north wind, *ṣer̍bihi* (Soc), blows continuously.	The Bedouin migrate to the coast to fish.	Shark, tuna and kingfish are still fished.

FIGURE 91. SOCOTRA'S SEASONAL CALENDAR, OUTLINING THE VARIOUS FISHING ACTIVITIES, SPECIES CAUGHT AND METHODS USED.

Season	**Period**	**Climate**	**Activities**	**Species and Methods**
azyab (Ar) This season is also known as the winter season, *shitāʾ* (Ar). During the whole NE monsoon period the sea is said to be open, *futūḥ al-baḥr* (Ar)	The NE monsoon wind changes yearly and there can be up to a month's difference between when they begin and end.	This wind also brings storms, *dɔ̄mer* (Soc). During the first half of this period, October to January, heavy rains fall in the highlands and they are the coldest months. During January to February the rains move down to the lowlands and cloud forms over the mountains. Visibility is variable, and in the first half of this period it can be relatively good, while during the second half it normally decreases.	Vessels from overseas start to arrive. In January the mountains are covered in cloud and, without GPS, it is difficult to determine your position out at sea. The fishermen spend more time moving around the island to fish.	The fishermen will also start catching rock fish and lobsters. From January onwards fewer people on the north coast use nets and fish traps due to stormy weather. Handlining predominates Fishing on the south coast is considered to be very good, mainly nets used.
ḳeˈyaṭ (Soc) Socotris consider this the summer season. Therefore it is also known as *ṣayf* (Ar).	*ḳeˈyaṭ* is approximately three months long, from February to April. During some years *ḳeˈyaṭ* can begin in January and end in May.	The NE winds decrease in intensity, and on the north coast there are periods of calm seas known as *šwar* (Soc). Toward the end of this season the south side of the island is affected by strong westerly winds, *maˈʿaribo* (Soc). Very little rain falls during this period and it begins to become much warmer. Visibility is generally good, although by April the visibility deteriorates as a haze develops. By April the sea begins to become rough and short-lived violent storms occur. Visibility also decreases as clouds begin to gather.	Fishing during this period is divided into two periods. The first is from February to March and the second during April. The wind and sea conditions at the beginning of this season remain calm. April is characterised by frequent storms and fishing offshore becomes more dangerous. Fishing on the south coast during this period is dangerous, and few people fish offshore. Almost all the Bedouin fishermen stop fishing and return to the hills.	Diving for pearls and pearl shell was normally during this period, especially during *ḳeˈyʌṭ*. Fishing for shark, tuna, kingfish, lobster and rock fish continue throughout the first half of this season. During April, fishermen fish more for rock fish and less for the pelagic species. By April few people fish offshore, as the storms make it very dangerous. Fishing along the south coast continues throughout this period, although by April it becomes more dangerous.
dɔ̄ti (Soc)	*dɔ̄ti* is approximately three months long, from mid-April to June.	During this period the winds and sea conditions are variable.	The few remaining Bedouin fishermen stop fishing.	Fishing is mostly concentrating on rock fish, although some fishermen along the north coast go offshore to fish for shark.

FIGURE 91. CONTINUE.

Season	Period	Climate	Activities	Species and Methods
		Unpredictable rainfall falls throughout the island. The rain brings strong winds and limits visibility. Sea conditions are variable and change very quickly. Toward the end of this season the sea becomes very rough.	Fishing is extremely uncertain and very few fishermen go offshore to fish.	This is the beginning of the turtle nesting season. Where possible turtles are caught. Nets are infrequently used and handlining predominates.

FIGURE 91. CONTINUE.

Chapter 12

Conclusion

This book has been divided into four specific sections in order to study the Socotri fishermen, the environment in which they are operating within and the equipment they are using. The first section introduced the parameters of the current analysis providing a detailed summation of the diverse literature concerning the island of Socotra, and outlines the theoretical and methodological approaches I have adopted within this study. The second part examined the social and cultural diversity of the fishing communities on Socotra with particular regard to the 'ethnic' identity, or absence of, the Socotri people. These chapters also attempted to trace the presence of these distinct communities within the historical and archaeological record. The focus of the third part was the environment and landscape of Socotra, specifically the fishermen's knowledge of the environment and landscape in different areas and villages across the island. This knowledge was then analysed according to the differences and similarities in how the fishermen perceived, used and adapted to the weather and landscape. The fourth part focused on the equipment used by the fishermen and analysed the way in which they have adapted their traditions and equipment according to the influences of the environment, landscape, new technologies and changing marketing opportunities.

In this final section I will place the study of Socotra and its fishing communities within the context of Indian Ocean studies. The aim here is to demonstrate how this study can aid in our understanding of the social, cultural and political factors influencing maritime communities and port towns along the Indian Ocean littoral. Thereafter I look at the answer to the main question posed in this research: How have social, environmental and technological influences shaped the maritime traditions of the fishermen of Socotra?

Socotra in the context of Indian Ocean studies

Anthropologists, historians and archaeologists studying Indian Ocean communities and cultures have long realised that these communities are rarely isolated from wider social, political and economic changes (Ray 1994; Chaudhuri 1985; Abu-Lughod 1989; Horton and Middleton 2000; Pearson 2003; Kearney 2004; Mack 2007; Alpers 2009). Scholars are increasingly aware that developing an understanding of the connections between communities and cultures in different places involves an approach which takes into account the drivers and agents of wider changes. One that looks at the culturally nuanced and historically changing notions of place, economy and identity (Gupta and Ferguson 1992; Appadurai 1995). This is especially significant for the study of maritime societies, in particular fishing communities, whose interactions with other communities and groups may be differentially affected by social, political and economic processes on a local and global scale. Within this chapter I utilise the ethnographic and historical information presented in previous chapters to explore the significance of my study in aiding the understanding of maritime societies along the Indian Ocean and Red Sea littorals. To achieve this I draw on a range of historic, archaeological and ethnographic studies to explore issues concerning coastal communities, in particular fishermen. The main themes I plan to address are: fishing as a way of life; the relationships between communities' lives and the sea in the context of ongoing change; their role as cultural agents and the emergence of hybrid identities within these communities, and how shifting geopolitical currents play out on a local level in places where, as on Socotra, the environment has placed constraints on possible ways of life.

Over the past millennia the Indian Ocean littoral has been inhabited by a variety of communities involved in maritime activities. The earliest of these maritime communities is likely to have consisted mainly of fishermen, who were primarily engaged in the exploitation and trade of a wide range of marine resources. This is evidenced both in early sources such as, *On the Erythrean Sea* (2nd century BC); the *Periplus Maris Erythraei* (mid-1st century AD), as well as various archaeological findings in the Red Sea and Arabian Gulf (Potts 2012; Thomas 2012; Beech 2004; Rice 1994; Groom 1981). It is also argued that these communities are likely to have been responsible for the early emergence of seafaring and maritime trade (Boivin *et al.* 2009: 251-278). Subsequent developments, such as the discovery of the use of the monsoon winds; the development of seafaring and maritime trade, and the growth of ports would have led to significant changes to these maritime communities. One of the greatest impacts these developments are likely to have had is an increasing degree of occupational specialisation in maritime activities. While many of these activities would have been fulfilled by fishermen, the economic, social, cultural and political trajectories of each specialism would have changed their very nature, effectively separating fishermen from sailors and merchants. Consequently, attempting to understand fishermen, their way of life and their relationship with the maritime communities of which they form a part of, requires an understanding of the various ecological, social, economic and political interactions that have, over time shaped and re-shaped them and the maritime communities of which they form a part.

It is beyond the scope of this research to undertake a detailed analysis of the changing history of trans-oceanic connections between the Red Sea and the Indian Ocean over the course of two millennia. Instead this study shall focus on the major socio-economic and religious changes that have influenced the nature of trade between the Red Sea and Indian Ocean. To achieve this I shall be using a world-system approach (after Beaujard 2005), which looks at the global, regional and local interactions of maritime communities, and takes into account the connections between different regions and the effects they have had on the character of maritime communities in certain areas. This process not only allows one to understand the role played by the various port cities, but also provides an insight into questions concerning the ethnic and cultural diversity of maritime communities.

The world-system approach, as adopted here can be seen to have developed at a progressive rate, following economic cycles of growth and decline that largely corresponded with cycles of political and religious events. The first of these cycles of concern here are from the 1st to 6th century AD, a period marked by the interconnectedness of the Mediterranean and Indian Ocean through the Red Sea (Beujard 2005: 421). In the 1st century AD Greco-Roman sailors and merchants were actively engaged in a well-established Indian Ocean maritime trading network, which was governed by a number of political bodies, and clearly divided into a number of distinct trade routes dictated by the monsoon winds (Casson 1989). During this period it was the Red Sea ports which were the main outlet for goods coming from South Arabia, India and Africa to the Mediterranean. The nature and scale of this trans-continental trade and the socio-cultural interactions of the inhabitants at these Red Sea ports is best demonstrated by looking at the Red Sea ports of Berenike (Sidebotham 2011; Sidebotham and Wendrich 2007), and Myos Hormos (Peacock and Blue 2011; Peacock and Blue 2006), and comparing these with Socotra.

The port of Berenike was initially established in the 3rd century BC as a Ptolemaic military and administrative centre, but later evolved into an important port city within the Indian Ocean trading network (Sidebotham 2011: 7). During its peak, Berenike had a population of approximately 500 to 1000 inhabitants who, on account of the apparent dearth of burials are presumed to have comprised mainly of temporary settlers that gathered during periods in which visiting shipping created demand for labour (Sidebotham 2011: 68-69). Archaeological finds of pottery, inscriptions and faunal remains provide evidence that these settlers were of varying socio-economic statuses and came from the Mediterranean, Egypt, Africa, South Arabia and India (Sidebotham and Wendrich 2007). In addition, the archaeological evidence also demonstrates the importance of Berenike's position as a port. A position which was largely based on the overland routes to the Nile valley, and one that relied on the hinterland for supplies of water and food. Berenike's eventual demise in the 6th century AD was the result of several years of decline brought about by a number of factors that included increasing difficulties in maintaining the inland trade routes; competition from Arabian and Aksumite merchants in the southern Red Sea; the collapse of the Gupta-Vakataka Empire and Tamilakam states in India and increasing regional conflicts within the Red Sea (Power 2010: 322; Sidebotham 2011: 280-281).

The port of Myos Hormos was built in the Ptolemaic period, and is first mentioned in the 2nd century BC by Agatharchides of Cnidus (Peacock and Blue 2011: 345). By the 1st century AD it became an important trading centre on the Red Sea coast which, with its sister port Berenike, facilitated the Indo-Roman trade of luxury goods into the Mediterranean and the export of Roman fine wares and wine to southern Arabia, East Africa and India (Tomber 2008: 351). Similarly to Berenike, Myos Hormos was linked to the Nile valley by a road across the Eastern Desert, by which traded goods were distributed. Archaeological evidence for this trade is seen in large quantity of ceramics from the Mediterranean, Nile Valley, India and Yemen, as well as textiles, inscriptions and archaeobotanical remains including coconuts, peppercorns and timber (Peacock and Blue 2011; Peacock and Blue 2006; Tomber 2008; Van der Veen and Cox 2011). These remains also provide us with an insight into the inhabitants, demonstrating that the port of Myos Hormos was as multi-cultural and ethnically diverse as that of Berenike. Unlike Berenike, Myos Hormos enjoyed a relatively short period of prosperity from the 1st to 2nd century AD, and was unable to recover from the period of economic and political difficulties faced by the Roman Empire in the mid-3rd century AD (Sidebotham 2011: 354).

Berenike and Myos Hormos are particularly useful as case studies for attempting to define the characteristics of maritime communities on account of the work of Ross Thomas (2007; 2012). As demonstrated above, the archaeological and textual evidence from Berenike and Myos Hormos suggests a rich multi-cultural and ethnically diverse population at both sites. According to Thomas (2012: 180) the textual evidence has been instrumental in identifying individuals, small groups, and particularly the brief settlement of specific groups such as the Palmyrans, Nabataeans, and Gauls or Germanic peoples who were involved in various tasks within the port. However, it was through his intra and inter-site analysis of the ceramic, faunal and other material culture that Thomas was able to distinguish between areas of different consumption practices and activities within these port sites. This has allowed the identification of distinct areas within the ports in which specific ethnic groups were concentrated, and suggests that there was some form of socio-spatial differentiation. Of particular interest here is the distribution of maritime artefacts, specifically fishing and ship equipment. According to Thomas (2012: 178), maritime artefacts in Myos Hormos were common and represented in every area excavated. At Berenike, however, maritime artefacts represented only a small proportion of all artefacts, presumably because Berenike was more militarily, administratively and religiously active than Myos Hormos. Interestingly, in Myos Hormos rigging and sail elements were found solely within in the 'finer' warehouse and residential structures (Thomas 2012: 178). This division supports the notion that increasing occupational specialism of maritime activities had effectively separated 'low status' fishermen from sailors, who are likely to have had a higher status within the port. With regards to the remains of sailing vessels found within Myos Hormos and Berenike, studies have shown that the wood came predominately from an Indian source (Blue 2010: 6-7). Moreover, the sail cloth is not of local manufacture and would appear to have been sourced in India (Blue 2010: 6). The construction and rigging of these ships were, however, in the Mediterranean style: shell-first, secured by pegged mortise and tenon joints and rigged with a square sail. This has led Lucy Blue to suggest that India not only supplied the wood used to construct the vessels of Greco-Roman Indian Ocean trade, but also the boat building skills (Blue 2010: 10). The implications of this are not discussed, although it may be assumed that this would have given sailors from western India a higher status within the maritime communities at these ports, even though their social status at home was likely to have been lower (Chaudhuri 1985: 122). While Thomas has effectively established an ethnic identity for the inhabitants of Myos Hormos and Berenike, there is some disagreement as to whether some artefacts may be used to accurately shed light on the wider characterisation of the ethnicity of the port inhabitants during this period. This is particularly apparent in the case of an inscribed ostraka discovered in Myos Hormos, which refers to a request for a permit to move a fishing boat by a man who is identified as being an *Ichthyophagos* (Fish-eater). Thomas interprets the *Ichthyophagos* as that to which Ptolemy (*c.* 168 AD) distinguishes as an ethnic group of Egyptian fishermen known as the *Arabaegypti Ichthyophagi* in the northern Red Sea (2007: 149-160). Nalesini (2008: 13), however, argues that this presumption is fraught with difficulties as there are several well documented cases showing that the cultural meaning of this ethnonym in the historical sources changes considerably throughout the centuries. Thus while it is possible to assume that this man was a fisherman, there is no evidence to support that fishermen based at Myos Hormos were ethnically *Ichthyophagi*, or to assert that all fishermen belonged to a single ethnic group (Nalesini 2008: 16). It is likely that fishing was an occupation that was undertaken by a number of different ethnic groups of presumably low status. This is supported by ethnographic and historical studies throughout the Indian Ocean, especially on Socotra, where fishermen are noted as belonging to a culturally diverse group of low status (Chaudhuri 1985: 121; Camelin 2006: 16; Barendse 2009: 1.98).

Socotra's involvement in the Indo-Roman trade is attested to in the *Periplus Maris Erythraei* (32.10. 3-25), which states that the island was a major supplier of dragon's blood, aloes and turtle shells and was inhabited by merchants from India, Greece and Arabia (Casson 1989: 69). Archaeologically, the only evidence we have for Socotra participating in the Indo-Roman trade are fragments of a Roman amphora; remnants of high-quality Mediterranean glazed wares of the 1st century AD, and ceramics from the Hadhramaut, India and the Persian Gulf dated to the 1st to 4th centuries AD (Naumkin and Sedov 1993: 605). The relative dearth of material evidence is believed to be due to an embargo having being placed on Socotra by the Hadrami kings, which lasted from the 1st to 3rd centuries AD. This situation eventually changed when the Hadrami kings were defeated by the Sabaeans, and their power over Socotra diminished (Bukharin 2012: 538). Recent findings of a series of drawings and inscriptions from Hoq cave, in the north western coast of Socotra, proves that people from Western India, South Arabia, Ethiopia and Palmyra visited the island from the 2nd century BC to the 6th century AD (Strauch 2012: 540). The earlier of these inscriptions (2nd and 1st centuries BC) are predominately South Arabian, after which Greek and Palmyrian inscriptions from the 3rd and 4th century AD predominate. The Greek texts clearly point to the presence of Greek speaking seamen from Egypt, indicating a direct line of trade with Egyptian ports like Berenike and Myos Hormos at this time. Following the early 5th century AD the inscriptions are mostly Ethiopians with Christian names, which have been dated to the 6th century AD. The Indian textual evidence ranges from the 1st to 5th centuries AD and is indicative of Socotra's long-term involvement with India.

The historic, inscriptional and archaeological evidence indicates that Socotra functioned as an important entrepôt that was being run by foreign merchants. While the lack of archaeological evidence makes it difficult to determine the nature and scale of Socotra's involvement in the Indian Ocean trade at this time, the inscriptions provide a glimpse of the changing nature of Red Sea trade. What is evident is that early trade was most likely being undertaken by South Arabian merchants, probably from the Hadhramaut. This changed with the rise of ports in the northern Red Sea in the 3rd and 4th centuries AD, concurrently with the port of Berenike. Furthermore, these inscriptions also reflect the movement of trade to the southern Red Sea as Aksumite trade increases. This would appear to indicate that Socotra maintained its trading links with a range of different centres and kingdoms over the centuries, especially India, which has a long history of involvement. Indeed, it would seem that, owing to Socotra's geographical position, it was a stopping off point for numerous traders on the way to India, East Africa and the Red Sea. Consequently, it is possible that it served both as a trading emporium and as a meeting point where information concerning the best ports of trade within the Red Sea could have been exchanged.

What is evident in this brief overview is that these ports were part of a dynamic trading network, and that the merchants involved in this trade were a heterogeneous mixture of people that were likely to have been intermingling and exchanging not only goods but ideas. In Berenike and Myos Hormos the hinterland population appears to formed part of the ethnically diverse maritime community, yet the degree of their involvement and socio-economic status is difficult to establish. It is also apparent that those involved in fishing were low status individuals who were from a variety of different ethnicities. What is particularly interesting is that when we compare the distribution and social status of fishermen in Myos Hormos with the contemporary fishing communities on Socotra we can see a distinctive socio-spatial relationship not only with regards to the fishermen, merchants and interior population, but also between the fishermen themselves. This relationship is particularly evident with regards to settlement patterns and not only reinforces the findings in Myos Hormos that the fishermen settled in specific areas separated from other port inhabitants, but that there is likely to have been a spatial division between the various ethnicities within the fishing communities. Furthermore, it is possible to surmise, from the contemporary evidence on Socotra, that this division could also have extended out to sea, and that the fishing vessels and possibly the fishing areas may have been segregated into different ethnic affiliations.

The decline of Indo-Roman trade in the late 6th century AD marks an end to this cycle and the beginning of the subsequent cycle of our world-system, which is dominated by the rise of the religious and philosophical doctrines of Islam. The rise of Islam over the course of the 7th and 8th centuries AD was nothing short of meteoric, and under the Umayyads (*c.* 7th–8th centuries AD), Islamic rule extended westward across North Africa, into Spain and eastward through Persia and the Indus valley. This made it possible to unite the trans-continental trade between the Indian Ocean and Mediterranean under a single political body (Chaudhuri 1985: 45). During the Umayyad period the capital of the empire was Damascus, resulting in a distinct shift in the demand and consumption of luxury goods from India and the Mediterranean to Syria. After the Abbasid revolution (*c.* 749-750 AD), Baghdad became the capital and trade shifted from the Red Sea to the Arabian Gulf. However, due to deteriorating political and economic conditions in Iraq there was an increasingly western movement into the Red Sea in the 9th and 10th centuries (see Power 2008; 2010). These events resulted in a gradual shift in the focus of trade from the Gulf to the Red Sea that reached its peak under the Fatimids (*c.* 10th–12th centuries AD). The strong economic position of Egypt was maintained under Mamluk rule (*c.* 13th–16th centuries AD), and Indian Ocean trade continued to flourish up until the 15th century AD, after which it went into a slow decline. This decline was the result of a number of factors to do with the black plague, increasing state intervention in trade, and the arrival of Europeans into the Indian Ocean. The rise and fall of the Islamic caliphates is important in our understanding of trade in the Indian Ocean, as it formed an important part of a trade network that included China, India and Africa. Under the Islamic empire the Indian Ocean trading network became a unified space, providing a basis for the global exchange of goods and people, together with their ideas, beliefs and knowledge.

What effect this new religion had on maritime communities, why it was accepted, and how it became so widespread is particularly pertinent to this study. As we have seen, Indian Ocean maritime communities are made up of a heterogeneous and cosmopolitan group of people, many of whom have contacts with other maritime societies in other coastal areas. The expansion of trade under the Caliphates not only increased existing trading networks, but also provided an organisational framework with extensive commercial and cultural linkages under a single identity, Islam. Islam became especially attractive for Indian Ocean merchants, as it provided an organisational framework to regulate business transactions between people over very long distances, and was useful in building trade networks and getting access to credit (Sheriff 2010: 257). Islam also provided other members of the coastal population with a single unifying identity that crossed social and ethnic boundaries and gave them a sense of religious, social and cultural *communitas*. This sense of belonging was especially important for fishermen, who suffered from a depressed social, economic and political position in society (Horton and Middleton 2000: 20; Ray 2003: 48; Pearson 2003: 172; Sheriff 2010: 46). This is clearly seen on Socotra and in India, where the adoption of Islam allowed fishermen to become part of an Islamic community and adopt an identity that could help alleviate the ethnic and class bias to which they were subject (Chaudhuri 1985: 121).

Although Islam was the dominant religion within the region at this time, it is clear that not all people in the Indian Ocean became Muslims. This is evident in various written accounts that refer to the Hindu, Jewish and Christian merchants, who were actively engaged in trade in ports all along the Red Sea, Gulf, India and China (see Ray 1994; Chaudhuri 1985; Abu-Lughod 1989; Pearson 2003). Perhaps one of the clearest examples comes from Goitein and Friedman (2008), whose work has shown the major role Jewish merchants have played in the Indian Ocean trade during the 10th and 11th centuries AD. Despite this religious diversity it is clear that being Muslim afforded certain benefits, as attested by the higher taxes levied on foreign, non-Muslim, merchants in Ayyubid Aden (Smith 1995:140). The diversity of religions that seafaring societies are exposed to, does pose the question as to what aspects of these religions were important to these societies and to what degree there was a propensity for syncretism. We may examine this phenomena by looking at ceremonies and the incorporation of folk beliefs into these societies. A good example of the importance of shared ceremonies in modern fishing communities may be found in a study undertaken by Lokita Varadarajan, who observed how Hindu and Muslim sailors and fishermen in Gujerat shared certain rites to mark the beginning of the navigation and fishing season (Varadarajan 1980: 28-35). Further examples can be found in the rituals performed by sailors when passing places of danger. These are especially prevalent around Socotra, and include the giving of offerings to the sea and erecting markers to commemorate safe passage (Serjeant 1996; Strauch 2012). The incorporation of folk beliefs can still be seen today and include the killing of animals before and after a journey, the placing of animal skins on the prow, and the painting of occuli on the prow and stern. These practices are exclusively maritime in nature, and are performed specifically for safety at sea, bountiful catches and favourable wind (Hornell 1920, Vosmer 1997, Agius 2012). The sharing of these ceremonies and the incorporation of folk beliefs into religious doctrine not only demonstrates what is important to seafarers, but exemplifies the different needs of maritime communities and their close relationship with the sea.

Returning to the question of the influence Islam had on maritime communities, it is necessary to understand that Islam is essentially an urban religion that sought to absorb tribal and ethnic identities into an Islamic community, *umma* (Ar). The impact this had on maritime communities can be seen in East Africa amongst the Swahili, who represent a specialised coastal adaption of farming societies that were transformed by their adoption of Islam, and its urban ethos, and their participation in long-distant trade (Horton and Middleton 2000: 27). This transformation was instrumental in the creation of a Swahili society and culture that effectively separated them from the people of the hinterland. Notwithstanding this social separation, the Swahili remained economically tied to the hinterland, and were required to build large and complex networks of patronage. This change began in the 8th century AD, when demand for wood, ivory and slaves from East Africa led to the development of proto-urban entrepôts, and the introduction of Islam as evidenced by the construction of mosques, such as that recorded at the site of Shanga (Horton *et al.* 1996). As finds of imported glass and ceramics of Chinese, Arabian and Persian provenance found in excavations at Swahili sites such as Shanga, Kenya have shown, the Swahili were engaged in a long-distance trade from at least the 9th century AD (Horton *et al.* 1996: 317-318). The acceptance of Islam by the Swahili appears to have been widespread along the coast from the 10th century AD and it is likely that it was, in part, driven by the extensive commercial and cultural linkages Islam afforded. By the 14th century AD demand for East African resources had grown to such an extent that Swahili ports extended almost all along the East African seaboard. While their acceptance of Islam may have strengthened the Swahili's position as commercial middlemen, it was their control over the import and export of goods into East Africa that was most important. The control of long-distance exchange between the very different economies and cultures of Africa, Arabia, India and Europe was based on their ability as intercontinental cultural brokers to build relations of trust, affinity and quasi-kinship with their trading partners. This was greatly facilitated by the adoption of Islam and intermarriage between the Swahili and their African and Arab trading partners, which led to the emergence of a hybrid mix of different cultural elements. Regardless of this hybrid mix, Swahili society is defined as Muslims, who speak a dialect of Kiswahili (Horton and Middleton 2000: 15). This single entity is divided into social, cultural and class differences, which effectively separates the merchants from the fishermen and farmers. These differences are based upon Swahili self-identification, which are self-defined claims to an ethnic origin that is not defined on racial grounds but to actual or claimed places of origin (Horton and Middleton 2000: 16). They include those who can be termed indigenous and have a lower social rank and those who claim ancestral associations with immigrants from Arabia and hold a higher social and cultural rank. This social and cultural ranking system is similar to Socotra, where social, economic and cultural status is determined by one's origins. However, unlike the Swahili, on Socotra there is a distinctive racial division that exists both between the Socotri Bedouin of the interior and those settled along the coast, and between the Arabian and African fishermen. The importance of this is that it demonstrates the misconceptions of unity often assigned to Muslim maritime communities and highlights their ethnic, cultural and class diversity.

Finally, when looking at interaction between maritime communities, especially merchants, the difficulties of communication are often overlooked (Pearson 2010: 7-14). While this is likely to have been less of a problem for Muslim merchants, polyglot intermediaries would have been vital. According to Pearson (2010: 14), these intermediaries would have been made up of kin, slaves, concubines or wives. The historical evidence on Socotra supports this view, with evidence of merchants from India using Socotri women as concubines to bypass the Arabian middlemen and obtain aloes directly from the interior Bedouin. In addition, Arabian fishermen and merchants are also recorded as having marriage ties with Bedouin families in the interior. These ties were and still are used as a means of obtaining accessing goods from the interior and obtaining sustenance during periods of drought.

Throughout this section I have referred to the people living and visiting ports throughout the Indian Ocean littoral, their heterogeneity and the variety of social, religious and cultural traditions they were exposed to. Before I look at the next cycle of our world system it is necessary to address the question of what role diaspora communities played. Diaspora communities are made up of those people who, due to social, economic and environmental reasons, left their homeland. Due to the absence of nation states during this period, diaspora communities are referred to as being 'trans-local' rather than 'trans-national', a term which also reflects the flexible boundaries of space within the Indian Ocean (Freitag 2003: 3). The focus here is on the people from the Hadhramaut, many of whom migrated to various ports along the rim of the Indian Ocean, where they not only maintained strong ties to their homeland but also took an active part in the economic, religious and political life of their host communities. The expansion of trade with the rise of Islam played a crucial role in the Hadhramaut diaspora networks, as the ports along the Hadhramaut were perfectly situated in the movement of regional and overseas trade between all parts of the Indian Ocean from the early to late Islamic periods (Whitcomb 1988: 176-263). Population pressures on scarce environmental resources, ongoing tribal violence and increased economic opportunities are all cited as having played a major role in migration (Manger 2010: 48). However, there is also the religious dimension and the process of Islamisation in which religious scholars were encouraged to travel, both for reasons of trade and to spread the faith. This played an important role in the Hadrami diaspora as Islam contained political, social, and economic institutions which helped forge links between the Hadramis and their host communities. Besides religious teachings and trade many Hadramis of lower status and wealth also performed menial tasks as labourers and fishermen. Hadrami integration with their host communities was complex, as some migrants disappeared into their local communities and no longer acknowledging their Hadrami identity, while others sought to maintain their links to the homeland and other Hadramis (Freitag 2003: 50). These links were maintained through an elaborate network of social and economic connections that resulted in migrants from particular areas and families in the homeland concentrating in specific overseas locations. These connections were further reinforced by the many Hadramis in the homeland, who often depended on the migrants' remittances for their livelihood, and also became part of these 'dispersed, but highly interrelated communities' (Freitag 2003: 3). Notwithstanding these close links to the homeland and other migrants, many Hadrami married into their host societies, hastening their integration and assimilation. The consequences of this were that these communities often held multiple identities linking them to both their place of origin and their present residence. This creolised identity underwent a number of changes that were shaped over time and in differing geographical contexts. Evidence for this can be seen in the term *muwallad*, which signifies someone of mixed origin and does not necessarily carry any particular stigma or negative inference outside of the Hadhramaut, whereas it holds strong and negative connotations in the homeland where it is directed at 'African' Hadramis from the Swahili coast and Somalia (Manger 2010: 10). The changing nature of diaspora identity is also evident in East Africa, where having an Arabian identity denotes higher social status and along the coast of Malabar in India where those who intermarry with the local communities are given the honorific title Mappila or 'sons-in law', highlighting not only their difference but also their social integration (Sheriff 2010: 280).

During the early period of Islamic hegemony in the Indian Ocean, trade was mainly dominated by Muslim Arabs from the Red Sea and Egypt. This situation gradually changed as local converts, such as the Swahili, and Middle Eastern Muslim migrants, much like the Hadrami, took control of the trade (Pearson 2003: 95). The reason that Hadrami merchants played such an important role is in part due to the presence of Hadrami in ports throughout the Indian Ocean. This presence is mostly to do with the Hadrami diaspora, and provided Hadrami merchants with social, cultural and economic brokers, usually kin, in most major trading centres. These brokers, with their knowledge of local languages and customs, were not only able to supply information on the markets and act as mediators, but could also hold onto goods until market prices were higher. This allowed these merchants a great deal more bargaining power than those who were reliant on employing a local broker and would have to leave at a set time in order to catch the monsoon wind home. The use of brokers would have also been relevant to fishermen, who could have used the diaspora network to assist them in finding areas in which there were rich fishing grounds, and to successfully compete against local fishermen, both in terms of local knowledge and the market for their catch.

According to Muslim chroniclers, Socotra remained a Christian enclave well into the 16th century AD, however the reality of this Christian dominance can be questioned. While Christian inhabitants formed a substantial part of the Socotri population, they were mostly living in the interior. The coastal community appears to have been Muslims who, much to the disappointment of the Portuguese, were actively engaged in converting women and children from at least the 16th century, but probably earlier (Commentaries 1884: 1.53; Brásio 1943: 12; *The Book of Duarte Barbosa* 1967: 1.62). That the coastal community were Muslims is not surprising, but that there was a substantial Christian population in the very heartland of Islam certainly deserves further study. At present there is little information available for such an analysis, although comparison with the Swahili coast-hinterland relationship can help. The Muslim merchants on Socotra were mainly trading in dried fish, exploited by the mixed slave population, and aloes and ghee that would have had to have been procured from the interior Christian inhabitants. The trade of these goods was based on a number of merchants vying for limited resources, and although this was not on the same scale as the Swahili, it is clear that that the religious differences on Socotri played no significant role in the trade. Conversely, it is likely that the Christian inhabitants were reliant on their Arab brokers as, much like today, there would have been social and cultural barriers such as language. Moreover, it is also likely that, like the Hadramis, many of the Arab brokers had kinship ties with the mainland and could arrange collection on a less sporadic basis. This is especially apparent when looking at the historical kinship ties between the Arab coastal community on Socotra and the Mahrah tribes along the Hadhramaut and Dhofar littoral. The Mahri diaspora, unlike the Hadrami was less widespread, and yet they played an important role on Socotra, facilitating trade and intermarrying locally. Throughout Socotra's history the Mahri have been acting as social, economic and cultural brokers with both the coastal and interior inhabitants. This involvement has several parallels with the Hadrami diaspora in that, during the 10th century, while most of the Mahri retained links with the homeland and their identity as Mahrah, many others converted to Christianity and severed their links with the homeland. This resulted in a loss of their original identity and their absorption into an interior Christian Socotri identity. Of particular significance here is that the two groups of Mahri took converging courses that led to the formation of two very separate identities. Finally, with regards the intermarrying of the Mahri amongst the fishermen, it is clear that even though there was a great deal of Arab African interaction the racial prejudices of the homeland remained. The evidence for which is seen in the contemporary racial divisions seen in the spatial organisation of housing and that those of African descent are still referred to by the derogatory term *muwallad*.

The final cycle in the world-system I will be examining starts with the arrival of the Portuguese and the beginning of European hegemony over Indian Ocean trade. Initially the Portuguese were assimilated into existing networks of trade, being no different than the variety of African, Arabian, Persian and other merchants' involvement in the Indian Ocean. This situation soon changed as the Portuguese identified and conquered the main choke points and strategic places around the Indian Ocean littoral, in an attempt to undermine Muslim dominance and gain control over the Indian Ocean spice trade. The Portuguese were soon followed by other European nations, who sought to control both inter-regional and the long-distant oceanic trade by controlling various port cities. This situation gradually changed in the 17th to 18th centuries as these nations, especially the British, also began to assert their dominance over the hinterland stifling trade to those port cities, such as Surat, that were not under their control (Das Gupta 1979). These processes eventually led to the decline of Asian and Muslim trade, and by the 19th century the British dominated Indian Ocean trade leaving local merchants to compete for niche, small-scale areas of operation.

Despite the attempts of the Portuguese to dominate trade and establish themselves as major traders they were quickly assimilated into the polyglot and heterogeneous port cities at this time. The reason for this is due in part to their propensity for intermarriage. An interesting parallel with the Hadramis can be made here, as this intermingling also resulted in hierarchical discrimination between the 'pure' Portuguese, those of mixed Asian and Portuguese descent and those of mixed Portuguese and African descent (Pearson 2003: 154). During the Portuguese occupation of Socotra it is believed that they intermingled with a tribe of the interior, many of whom today have blue eyes. While this is unsubstantiated it has remained a popular myth, which is often used by the coastal community to subvert the claims of the interior Bedouin as being 'true' Socotri. The Portuguese arrival in East Africa resulted in a significant change to the role played by the Swahili, who were effectively marginalised, first along the southern and later along the northern coastline. This situation was exacerbated with the establishment of the colonial Omani Sultanate of Zanzibar in 1829, whose commercial enterprise exerted a powerful control over both the coast and interior, forcing the Swahili into an even more marginalised position. The marginalisation of the Swahili was further hastened under the colonial administration of the British, who assumed political monopoly over most of the coast until the independence of Kenya and Tanzania in the 1960s. As a result of which, even though Swahili is widely spoken throughout most of East Africa, the term has come to refer to a marginalised and internally divided category of people without any obvious sense of political identity (Horton and Middleton 2000: 14). Conversely, after the benign neglect that characterised British involvement with Socotra there was an active Russian Socialist policy of interference which, even after Yemeni independence, has affected the socio-economic and cultural structure of its inhabitants. This has led to wide ranging socio-economic differences that have also influenced social hierarchies and spatial division as well as generating large scale changes to the coastal population. This was mostly due to investment in the fishing industry, which not only economically empowered African fishermen, but also led to an influx of Arabian migrant fishermen and large scale settlement along the coasts of Socotra.

Throughout this section I have taken a broad brush approach to historical events, highlighting specific periods, people, areas and events in an attempt to tease out the major themes in the history of the maritime communities of the Indian Ocean trade and the role Socotra has taken. The next section tackles the ethnographic data gathered during my study of the fishermen of Socotra in the context of other maritime ethnographies. The aim here is to look at the emergence of hybrid identities within maritime communities and their role as cultural brokers.

The fishermen of Socotra are made up of a diverse social and cultural mixture of people from parts of Africa and Arabia. However, even amongst this hybrid community there are ethnic differences, many of which relate to origins and race. This is specifically seen in the emergence of two groups of people, the Socotri/ Africans and the Socotri/ Arabs. The emergence of these creole identities stems from wider social and political influences, and is used by these groups as a means of self-identification and social status. Membership within these two groups is based primarily on race and, with regards the Socotri/ Arabs, social links between families on Socotra and those on the Arabian mainland. The links to mainland Arabia form part of an elaborate social hierarchy amongst the Socotri/ Arabs, in which higher status individuals are those with links to specific Mahri or Hadrami families. Studies of contemporary maritime societies along the East African coastline, notably Lamu and Mafia Island, and India's west coast, notably Kerala, provide further insight into the development of creole identities. According to the Dutch ethnographer Adriaan Prins, in Lamu the coastal people, Swahili, are defined by long-distance relationships of trade, shipping and fishing. The Swahili are divided into three components: those of so-called Arab descent; the peasant-like Bajun, and the African Swahili (Prins 1965: 56). These three groups form a distinctive social structure which is based on actual or claimed place of origin and of descent which, unlike on Socotra, is not based on race. Notwithstanding this division, the social structure within which each group operates is generally open, and allows for greater freedom in changing group-affiliation in crews, settlements and mosque communities. This has facilitated the acceptance of strangers and allowed for shipwrecked mariners to be accepted into society on an equal footing, provided they accept Islam (Prins 1965: 173). Consequently, when looking at a so-called Swahili identity it is apparent that it has emerged from a complex interplay between different groups with many different identities. As such, the term Swahili refers to a range of different identities, each of which has differing economic, political and cultural characteristics. The next group we look at here are the residents of Mafia Island, who have strong historical and cultural links with the Swahili. According to Walley (2004: 110-112), the communities on Mafia are divided between, the *jamaa*, those people with kinship ties to families on the island; the *wageni*, those who are seen as being guests, visitors, strangers or outsiders, and the *mwenyeji*, those who are assimilated into the coastal society by virtue of kinship ties and long-term residency. Similarly to the Swahili, these groups on Mafia are not racially or ethnically divided, but are formed out of kinship networks, both within their own communities and other distant coastal areas. This is in contrast to studies in Kerala where, even with varying religious affiliations, divisions within maritime societies are based upon one's caste. Consequently, the caste system determines one's position within society, even amongst the heterogeneous Mappila Muslims that have settled in Kerala (Hoeppe 2007: 113). Furthermore, unlike the maritime societies in East Africa, there is little possibility for people from a particular caste to gain acceptance, whether through religious affiliation, long-term residency or kinship. The importance of understanding the formation of a creole identity amongst maritime communities lies in understanding a society's maritime culture. Within this book I have outlined the diversity of the ethnic groups involved in fishing and their influence in the formation of a maritime culture. What I have shown is that the so-called Socotri maritime traditions are actually an amalgamation of a various different traditions that have been shaped and formed by various ethnicities over the course of time. The transformation of maritime traditions was also recognised on Mafia Island which, in spite of a long history of Swahili maritime cultural influence, underwent a series of independent transformations. The most important transformation was the development of the local fisheries economy from one that was subsistence based and virtually non-existent to one that was cash based. This transformation resulted in many Mafia Island residents learning to fish not only from the Swahili, with whom they had close kinship ties, but also from immigrants from southern Tanzania (Walley 2004: 146). The importance of this is that it contradicts many assumptions that traditions are bounded by, and passed on within, particular cultural groups. Instead individual traditions, much like the various individual ethnicities that constitute the heterogeneous coastal communities of the Indian Ocean, are amalgamated into broader traditions based upon the constraints of the locale in which they are practised. However, for these traditions to be accepted it is necessary for there to be an acceptance that will actually bring about this change, no small feat within the conservative world of fishermen. Within my research I have shown that the acceptance of new technologies, vessels and practices has been a direct result of second or third generation immigrants that have married locally yet retained strong ties to fishing communities on the mainland. These immigrants act as cultural brokers, by mediating between different cultural groups and instigating change through their acceptance and use of these new technologies, vessels and practices. On Mafia and in Madagascar this situation is similar insofar as cultural brokers tend to be accepted within these societies by virtue of their kinship ties or long-term residency (Walley 2004: 111-145; Mack 2007: 9-10). Moreover, many of these cultural brokers are also engaged in the facilitation of goods and services between the interior and coastal inhabitants and merchants. This role is based primarily on the establishment of social or religious ties, much like the early Swahili merchants outlined above and the fishermen on Socotra, whose established ties with the interior inhabitants is essential for their livelihood.

Within the final section of this conclusion I explore the social and economic changes taking place in the Red Sea in the context of changing geopolitical events and how these have affected the fortunes of various ports. In addition, I look at how Socotra's island community could be used as a case study for exploring issues relating to social, economic and political connectivity, colonisation, abandonment, cultural interaction and isolation.

The starting point for this discussion is Rome's annexation of Egypt in 30 BC, and its control of the Eastern desert, renowned for its gold and emerald mines, quarries and Red Sea ports. The two most important ports at this period were those of Berenike and Myos Hormos in the northern Red Sea, which facilitated trade between the Indian Ocean and the Mediterranean. Following the annexation of Egypt, the political situation remained relatively stable up until the 3rd century AD, when large areas of the Eastern Desert were acquired by a kingdom of the nomadic Blemmyes, resulting in the abandonment of Myos Hormos (Thomas 2010: 142). The port of Berenike, as previously mentioned, managed to remain an important link in this trade up until the 6th century AD (Sidebotham 2011: 280-281). The written evidence demonstrates that these Roman ports were in fact inhabited by a wide range of different ethnicities from an array of socio-economic backgrounds. Moreover, the archaeological evidence demonstrates that these ethnicities were grouped into specific areas, and performed specific activities within these port sites (Thomas 2010: 172). This would appear to show that each ethnic group had a specific socio-economic position within the port, although how this was affected by the geopolitical changes that influenced the prosperity and decline of these ports remains a mystery. Perhaps, much like on Socotra, following the decline of the incense trade many of the migrants and local farmers either immigrated to other areas or turned to fishing and animal husbandry for their livelihood (Doe 1992: 41; Naumkin 1993: 364).

By the 7th century AD ports and societies in the Red Sea were in terminal decline and virtually all the major ports that once supplied the Indo-Roman trade were abandoned. Indeed it was not until the mid-9th century AD, two centuries after Muslim hegemony, that an economic revival in the Red Sea was felt (Power 2009: 111). This economic revival was the result of numerous factors, including: the expansion of the Cholas dynasty in India (*c.* 848-1279 BC); the Song dynasty in China (*c.* 960-1279 BC); an increase in the trade with the Mediterranean, and the gradual decline of the Abbasid Caliphate in the Gulf. The economic revival of the Red Sea was also based upon the emergence of independent Muslim emirates that included the Tulunids of Egypt and Ziyadids of Yemen, whose shared unitary commercial practices and culture is seen as having being conducive to mercantile activity (Power 2010: 299). The economic revival these Muslim dynasties brought about reached its zenith under the Fatimid Caliphate (*c.* 969-1171 BC), which together with the Cholas and Song dynasties dominated Indian Ocean trade. During the 12th century AD, however, the Red Sea dynasties that had been instrumental in economic growth began fragmenting into economically unviable smaller polities that became involved in an internecine conflict. This increasing conflict led to the establishment of a form of military feudalism which, together with a decline in trade, saw the abandonment of several Red Sea ports between the mid-11th and mid-13th centuries AD (Power 2012: 143). Nevertheless, the strong economic position of Egypt was maintained by the successors to the Fatimid Caliphate, the Mamluks (*c.* 1250-1517 BC), who undertook intensive development of the Red Sea ports (Chaudhuri 1985: 60). This brief synopsis of the geopolitical situation in the Red Sea provides a suitable backdrop from which to explore how these events are reflected in the ports along the South Arabian littoral.

The first of these ports is Qana, situated on the southern coast of Yemen. According to historical and archaeological evidence the founding and development of Qana in the 1st century AD was the result of the involvement of the Hadhramaut kingdom in the Indo-Roman trade (Sedov 1996: 23-24). During the so-called 'lower period', dated between the early 1st and the first half of the 2nd centuries AD, Qana is believed to have functioned as a collection and distribution port for frankincense collected throughout the Hadhramaut kingdom. However, it is not until the 'middle' and 'late' periods, dated between the late 2nd and early 7th centuries AD that Qana reached its zenith. During the early part of this period, the 2nd to 3rd centuries AD, it was transformed from a transit point for vessels between Egypt and India and warehouse for frankincense to an extensive port city (Sedov 1992: 127). These changes are believed to have been due to a change in the nature of trade, as commerce began to be concentrated in the hands of Hadrami middlemen and/or foreign merchants. This also resulted in a reorientation in the trading links, which saw trade with India and the eastern Mediterranean decrease in importance, and that with North and Northeast Africa increase. Interestingly, Mediterranean pottery from this 'middle period' was also found in Hajrya, the earliest settlement on Socotra, which is situated on the northern coast of the island (Naumkin and Sedov 1993: 600-605). This would imply that there was a trading link between these two ports, which ties in with Socotra having been under the rule of the Hadrami kingdom at this time. The trading links between Qana and Northeast Africa appear to have remained strong throughout the 7th century AD when Qana was finally abandoned. It is also worth noting the presence of what is believed to have been an early Christian building that later was converted into a synagogue (Sedov 1996: 27). While the identification of the underlying building as Christian is disputed, (Bukharin 2012: 536), the presence of a synagogue attests to a large Jewish community that was either part of the local population or constituted a large part of the foreign merchants who visited Qana.

The port of Al-Shihr, just east of Qana, is one the most important Islamic coastal sites of Hadhramaut, and is well-attested to in the literary sources, where it was known as the gateway to the Hadhramaut, and together with Aden controlled the road to India (Hardy-Guilbert 2001: 69). According to both the archaeological and historical evidence, Al-Shihr retained its importance as a harbour throughout the many changing facets of the Indian Ocean trade, from the beginning of the Islamic period (*c.* 7th century AD) to the 19th century. Throughout this period it was involved in a maritime network of exchange that spread across Arabia, Africa, India and China. The main resources of Al-Shihr came from both its hinterland and the sea and included fish, incense, amber, ambergris and dates, although it also traded in and produced spices, textiles, ceramics, and silver (Hardy-Guilbert 2005: 74). Archaeological evidence from Al-Shihr predates the literary evidence for its role in the Indian Ocean trade, with finds of Samarra pottery demonstrating trade with the Gulf took place as early as the Abbasid period. In addition the archaeological evidence demonstrates that it was also engaged in trade with East Africa from the 11th rather than the 15th century AD, when Al-Shihr is mentioned in the navigational texts as the departure point for Socotra on route to Africa (Tibbetts 1981: 230). The decline of Al-Shihr at the end of the 19th century was the result of the establishment of a modern port in Mukalla.

The final port is that of Sharma, situated 50km east of Al-Shihr. This port was a well-fortified entrepôt founded in the 10th century. The main function of Sharma appears to have been as a transit outpost, as there is little evidence for any structures, such as kilns, where goods would have been manufactured. (Rougelle 2005: 287). The founding of Sharma is attributed to merchants from the Gulf, who dominated the trading routes of the Indian Ocean during the 9th to 10th centuries AD. The founding of Sharma by these merchants is likely to have been due to the political upheavals brought about by the fall of the Buyid dynasty (*c.* 934-1055 AD) and the decline of the major ports in the Gulf. The role of Sharma as a transit emporium is underlined by its natural position which completely isolates it from the hinterland. This isolation from the hinterland was enhanced by the construction of several fortifications that were built to provide protection for the warehouses and the small number of inhabitants (Rougelle 2003: 296). The extensive trading network these merchants were involved in is attested to in the ceramic assemblage, which includes a rich corpus of imports from China, East Africa and Arabia. The dominance of imported East African wares of the Tana tradition, known at 10th to 12th century AD African coastal sites, such as Shanga, Manda, Kilwa, Lamu, attest to the strong links Sharma must have had with the coastal settlements in East Africa. The relevance of this is that this trade occurred during the rise of the large trading cities and the expansion of Islam in East Africa. This not only provided an attractive market for these merchants, but also saw many Gulf traders immigrate to East Africa. Sharma also seems to have played an important role in the changing geopolitical situation of this period. This is seen in the rise of the Fatimid dynasty when Egyptian merchants were organising their own commercial networks, based on the port of Aden, and were in direct conflict with Gulf traders in the Red Sea. It is argued that Sharma was on the very edge of the Egyptian economic sphere of influence in Yemen and the last port of call for Gulf vessels on the southern coast of Arabia (Rougelle 1999: 134). This precarious position not only explains the fortifications at Sharma, but also lends credence to it having been destroyed because of an Egyptian attack, a theory that fits in with the tense geopolitical situation at this time (Rougelle 2005: 223).

These ports reflect some of the complexities of the geopolitical situation of the Red Sea during the Islamic period, and how their foundation and decline is intimately linked with the vicissitudes of the transit trade that typifies this period. They also demonstrate how geopolitical events in other areas of the Indian Ocean, such as Africa, can have an effect on the fortunes of ports in Arabia. Moreover, these ports show the intimate links they have with the hinterland, where local goods for export and markets for the trade in luxury goods were found. However, they provide little more than snapshots of the specific periods within which they were founded and declined. Taken together they can provide a glimpse into the effects of the changing geopolitical situation in the Red Sea, yet we are still not able to gather a complete picture of how these events affected the social and economic lives of the inhabitants in any one place. I would suggest that this task could be fulfilled by Socotra, which could act as laboratory within which it would be possible to gain an insight into how the complex series of events occurring in the Red Sea, and possibly elsewhere, are enacted locally. However in order for this to be possible we need to re-evaluate our misconceptions that islands are isolated enclaves with insular human societies, who are dissimilar from those on the mainland. Instead we need to understand that island communities in the Indian Ocean, much like those in the Mediterranean (Horden and Purcell 2000: 345) and the Pacific (Terrell *et al.* 1997: 155), had an all-round connectivity. This does not imply that islands, such as Socotra, were not at some stage in time isolated, but rather that they underwent a series of changes between isolation and connectivity. These changes has been attributed to a range of internal and external social, economic and political processes, which can increase or decrease an island's isolation through time. This is clearly seen in studies of island societies in the Pacific which have undergone a series of changes that began with widespread expansion and inter-island communication and trade, and gave way to a rapid retraction where island societies once more became isolated. The reasons for these changes have been attributed to a range of factors which include exchange system contraction, specialisation, and socio-political transformation which, in the last 100 years, underwent a further cycle of island interconnectivity as full-scale farming came about (Kirch 1986: 33; Gosden and Pavlides 1994: 169; Spriggs 1997:152-162). Returning to Socotra, it is clear from the historical evidence outlined in previous chapters that Socotra functioned as an important entrepôt in the Indian Ocean Trade that was intimately linked to the Hadhramaut, which exerted economic and political power over the island. Consequently, the changing geopolitical events that affected the Hadrami had a direct bearing over their control of Socotra and its isolation or incorporation into trading networks. The evidence for this is seen in the 1st to 3rd centuries AD when the Hadrami placed a trade embargo on Socotra, restricting its direct involvement in the Indo-Roman trade. The lifting of this embargo resulted in an influx of foreign traders coming to Socotra and its inclusion in the long-distant trading networks between Africa, Arabia, India and China. Unfortunately, due to the collapse of the incense trade and with increasing military conflict between the Gulf and Red Sea this prosperity was short-lived. Nonetheless, Socotra remained an important part of the Indian Ocean trading network throughout the next centuries with links to Arabia, Africa and India. Indeed, when the Portuguese enter the Indian Ocean in the 15th century they were quick to grasp the island's geostrategic significance. It is also important to remind ourselves that Socotra's geographical position also played an important role in its connectivity and its isolation, and it not only holds a geostrategic position at the entrance to the Red Sea, but is also in a sea area subject to fierce storms that restrict access to the island. Understanding this cyclical change between isolation and integration on Socotra not only allows us an insight into other island societies, but also those ports along the mainland. Ports, such as those mentioned above, which in many respects are both geographically isolated, as enclaves sited along the littoral, and connected by the transient trade and merchant communities which they rely on. The isolation and connectivity of port towns also has a bearing on the social, cultural and ethnic makeup of the population. This is clearly evident in the coastal communities which are a diverse mix of people from different areas. What makes Socotra important is that this diversity lies within a defined geographical space that is influenced by both internal and external social, economic and political events. This situation is similar to many other island communities in the Pacific Ocean where researchers have examined how socio-economic and political events have influenced the linguistic, ethnic and racial makeup of the population, their social and cultural hierarchy, and the socio-economic roles they perform (Kaye 1997; Shnukal *et al.* 2004; Flett and Haberle 2008). What these studies have shown is that these communities form complex and dynamic political, economic, social and cultural relationships and connections, even between islands having linguistic and ethnic differences (Kirch and Rallu 2007; Battersby 2004: 13-33). This is especially apparent in the Torres Strait where these relationships and connections were related to the economic and environmental differences between islands, where either fishing or farming predominated (Shnukal *et al.* 2004: 11). This not only provides insights into the how communities constrained by the environment were able to thrive, but also into the fluidity and flexibility of the boundaries between social, cultural, ethnic and linguistically different people. However, this provides only a partial picture as external administrative and legislative controls by colonial powers have a significant role to play in local economic, social and cultural relationships. This is evident in both the Torres Strait and amongst the Tlingit communities in Alaska, where these colonial controls and prejudices have also led to social and economic separation (Emmons and De Laguna 1991; Scott and Mulrennan 1991; Arthur 2001). The themes outlined above demonstrate the importance of islands for exploring the social, economic and political connectivity, colonisation, abandonment, cultural interaction and isolation. In the context of the western Indian Ocean trading networks this analysis also demonstrates the role Socotra can play in unravelling the historical and geopolitical complexities of ports. Moreover, an island like Socotra provides an insight into the role of the environment and how populations have to adapt to the constraints imposed. This is particularly relevant to Indian Ocean studies where monsoon winds and the barrenness of the hinterland limit activities. Indeed, as I have shown in this research the environment has played a fundamental role in the division between the interior and coastal population and their dependency on each other in times of drought and adverse weather conditions.

Throughout this chapter I have placed Socotra and its maritime community within the context of other historical, archaeological and ethnographic studies in the Indian Ocean. This has played a fundamental part in answering some of the wider research questions asked by scholars of the Indian Ocean studies. Firstly, maritime communities have been engaged in an extensive trans-oceanic network of contact and interaction with a range of different ethnicities and cultures involved in the Indian Ocean trade. What this study has shown is that this movement of people has been instrumental in the formation and reformation of the multicultural character and ethnic identities of these communities. On Socotra, I have also shown how changing social, economic and political power structures within the fishing community have been influential in the formation of hybrid identities. The importance of this is twofold. Firstly it provides evidence for the social, economic and political factors that have influenced the formation of hybrid identities in other maritime communities, such as the Mappila in India. Secondly, it offers an insight into the role of cultural brokers as conveyors of social, economic and religious change and how the social and kinship ties of these brokers have been instrumental in bringing about change within maritime communities. The next point raised is how understanding the environmental, social, economic, religious and political influences affecting the maritime traditions of the Socotri fishermen can help in our understanding of the traditions practiced elsewhere in the Indian Ocean, owing to the commonalities in practices, socio-economic organisation and worldview. These commonalities can be used to enhance our understanding of those communities in the past and present for which we have little information. This is especially relevant when looking at the rituals and ceremonies enacted by maritime societies, but can equally be applied to fishing equipment, vessels and traditional practices. Thirdly, when looking at the questions regarding the relationship between the hinterland and coastal communities, this study has made it apparent that it is dynamic and constantly changing. The dynamism between the coastal and interior inhabitants on Socotra is particularly significant in that it allows us understand how changes in social, economic and political power structures are played out, and provided an insight into these relationships in the archaeological record. Finally, I examined how island societies, such as Socotra, can assist in our understanding of the social, economic and geopolitical complexities of the Red Sea and Indian Ocean. Such an analysis demonstrates that on Socotra, like many other islands, the social and economic lives of the inhabitants are influenced by an array of internal and external forces. The external forces include the changing geopolitical and economic fortunes of the various countries that are involved in this trade. This not only affects the socio-economic lives of the inhabitants of the state ports but also has a direct bearing on those trading with them. Whereas, the internal forces are those relating to the ecological constraints within which changing social, cultural, economic and political factors are enacted, and which has a direct bearing on the degree of cultural variation. The social, economic, political and environmental influences affecting island societies are enacted within a spatial boundary that can be analysed as an individual unit. This unit can be used as a model whereby it will be possible to gain a holistic understanding of the processes involved in cultural variation in other areas and amongst other maritime societies due in part to the commonalities they share.

Answering the question, how have social, environmental and technological influences shaped the maritime traditions of the fishermen of Socotra has demonstrated two important points. Firstly, treating the fishing communities on Socotra as a single group of people is fundamentally flawed. The reason for this not only lies within the variety of ethnic differences found within these communities, but also the differences in their involvement, experience and perception of their environment. Secondly, when looking at a Socotri maritime tradition it is essential to bear in mind the variety of environmental, social and ethnic influences present, and when attempting generalisations one needs to include the caveat that there are significant regional variations. As a result, in order to attempt to provide a truly holistic picture of the fishermen and their traditions and answer the question I have posed it was necessary to adopt a transdisciplinary approach. The reason for this is, as I have shown, due to the interconnectivity between the physical aspects of landscape and climate, and the cognitive aspects of knowledge and experience.

What I have revealed is that the maritime traditions of Socotra have been formed and shaped by successive generations of fishermen, who have brought with them different traditions that have either been adopted or discarded. The reasons for the adoption or abandonment of traditions on Socotra are based upon a complex interplay between the social, economic and environmental constraints imposed upon the fishermen and their experience and knowledge. Therefore, even though some similarities exist, a Socotri maritime tradition can be seen to be as nuanced and varied as the fishermen and the locales within which they fish.

Further research

Due to the lack of scholarly research into the fishing communities on Socotra and other fishing communities along the African, Arabian and Red Sea littorals there are many avenues for additional research. What my research has shown is that fishermen have a rich maritime tradition and heritage which is in urgent need of even more in-depth studies. Analysis is needed in many areas of the Indian Ocean, where it would be possible to gain an in-depth view into the differences or similarities between the maritime traditions of fishermen from different social, cultural and ethnic backgrounds. Furthermore, it would also be useful to look at the archaeological, historical and ethnohistorical background of the fishermen in these areas. This would help to determine what and where their maritime traditions may have originated from and how they have adapted to the environmental conditions in a specific locale. Further research into the intangible maritime traditions of the fishermen is also required. The importance of this is twofold. Firstly, as most fishermen are illiterate there are no written records of their traditions, and with the rapidly changing fisheries sector many of them are in danger of being lost. Secondly, there is a real need to record the rich tapestry of poetry, songs and stories of the elderly fishermen, before they too are lost. The importance of recording the variety of traditions is not only to preserve a record of these traditions, but also to provide a body of information that would allow for comparisons to be made between different areas and fishing communities. This body of evidence would serve ethnographers, archaeologists and fisheries officers by providing a dataset that would be able to demonstrate how social, environmental and economic changes have affected the fishermen and the fisheries sector over time.

Appendices

Appendix 1. The fishermen interviewed.

Number	Name	Age	Occupation	Date interviewed	Village from
1	Esso Ibn Seyaka	60s	Fulltime Fisherman	7.2.2009	Ḥadiboh
2	Ali Ibn Aneen	60s	Fulltime Fisherman	7.2.2009	Ḥadiboh
3	Aneen Ibn Sankour	60s	Fulltime Fisherman	7.2.2009	Ḥadiboh
4	Mohammed Aldolah	60s	Seasonal Fisherman	8.2.2009	Qādheb
5	Omar Abdulla Saleh	60s	Fulltime Fisherman	8.2.2009	Qādheb
6	Abdullah Mohammed Sallim	60s	Fulltime Fisherman	8.2.2009	Qādheb
7	Yahya Zakria Ahmed	30s	Fulltime Fisherman	8.2.2009	Di-Ḥamdh
8	Salim Mohammed	60s	Fulltime Fisherman	8.2.2009	Di-Ḥamdh
9	Abdullah Mohammed Najai	60s	Fulltime Fisherman	9.2.2009	Di-Ḥamari
10	Saleman Hamodi Ahmed	60s	Fulltime Fisherman	9.2.2009	Erisseyl
11	Ahmed Mohammed Saaed	60s	Fulltime Fisherman	9.2.2009	Erisseyl
12	Fohaad Ali	60s	Fulltime Fisherman	9.2.2009	Erisseyl
13	Noah Salim	30s	Fulltime Fisherman	11.2.2009	Di-Ṣeberho
14	Said Saaed	30s	Seasonal Fisherman	11.2.2009	Stēroh
15	Said Salim Ahmed	60s	Fulltime Fisherman	11.2.2009	Stēroh
16	Mounir Eissa Saleem	60s	Fulltime Fisherman	11.2.2009	Stēroh
17	Abdulla Mohammed Mobarra	60s	Fulltime Fisherman	11.2.2009	Maḫfirihin
18	Muhammad Abdulla Muhammad Dimori	80	Fulltime Fisherman	11.2.2009	Maḫfirihin
19	Muslim Abdulla	30s	Fulltime Fisherman	11.2.2009	Maḫfirihin
20	Salim Saaed	30s	Fulltime Fisherman	11.2.2009	Maḫfirihin
21	Jamen Khamis Saeed Marjan Saeed	60s	Fulltime Fisherman	12.2.2009	Zaḫaq
22	Mohammed Atman Talab	30s	Fulltime Fisherman	14.2.2009	Suq
23	Rabain Mobarek al-Noby	60s	Fulltime Fisherman	14.2.2009	Suq
24	Saaed Ahmed Nashran	60s	Fulltime Fisherman	14.2.2009	Suq
25	Saad Dabowed Mousa	60s	Fulltime Fisherman	14.2.2009	Suq
26	Abdullah Mohammed Hamadan	60s	Fulltime Fisherman	15.2.2009	Ḥadiboh
27	Heni Mohammed Saeed Abdullah	60s	Fulltime Fisherman	15.2.2009	Ḥadiboh
28	Ashish Hazeem Hilaal	30s	Fulltime Fisherman	15.2.2009	Ḥadiboh
29	Nasieb Saaed Khamis	60s	Fulltime Fisherman	15.2.2009	Ḥadiboh
30	Khamis Amer	60s	Fulltime Fisherman	15.2.2009	Ḥadiboh
31	Mobarik Ali Adbulla	60s	Fulltime Fisherman	15.2.2009	Ḥadiboh
32	Jaman Saeed Abdullah	30s	Fulltime Fisherman	16.2.2009	Qalansiyah
33	Ali Salim Da-Salmoho	60s	Fulltime Fisherman	16.2.2009	Qalansiyah
34	Abdullha Rahman Abod Ali Saeed	38	Fulltime Fisherman	16.12.2009	Qalansiyah
35	Anwar Khamis Abdul Abod Ali Saeed	32	Fulltime Fisherman	16.12.2009	Qalansiyah
36	Saeed Salem Hasaan	35	Fulltime Fisherman	17.12.2009	Qalansiyah
37	Saleh Ahmed Bamousa	45	Fulltime Fisherman	17.12.2009	Shuᶜub
38	Mohammed Mouslam Ahmed	30s	Fulltime Fisherman	17.12.2009	Shuᶜub
39	Abaid Salem bin Awailan	50s	Fulltime Fisherman	17.12.2009	Qalansiyah
40	Saeed Selem Ali	35	Seasonal Fisherman	17.12.2009	Qalansiyah
41	Salam Saeed Martah	39	Fulltime Fisherman	18.12.2009	Qalansiyah
42	Omar Saeed Abod Ali Saeed	31	Fulltime Fisherman	18.12.2009	Qalansiyah
43	Saeed Masour Ahmed	60s	Fulltime Fisherman	19.12.2009	Samḫa
44	Mohammed Ali Saliman	35	Fulltime Fisherman	19.12.2009	Samḫa
45	Mohammed Sabhan Mohammed	45	Fulltime Fisherman	19.12.2009	Samḫa
46	Abdullah Ali Saeed	35	Fulltime Fisherman	19.12.2009	Samḫa
47	Khald Hlaal Saeed	20	Fulltime Fisherman	19.12.2009	Samḫa

Number	Name	Age	Occupation	Date interviewed	Village from
48	Abdullah Salem Saaed Abokakibak	45	Fulltime Fisherman	20.12.2009	Shuᶜub
49	Mohammed Malak Masham	35	Fulltime Fisherman	20.12.2009	Shuᶜub
50	Kamis Jaman Hamond	30s	Fulltime Fisherman	20.12.2009	Shuᶜub
51	Khames Abdulah Salem	75	Fulltime Fisherman	22.12.2009	Ḥadiboh
52	Jamen Mahafawl Saif	70	Fulltime Fisherman	22.12.2009	Ḥadiboh
53	Fouad Naseb Saeed	30	Head of Fisheries	22.12.2009	Ḥadiboh
54	Mohammed Selem Abo	56	Fulltime Fisherman	23.12.2009	Erisseyl
55	Sindowa Ali Ahmed	40s	Fulltime Fisherman	23.12.2009	Erisseyl
56	Frzir Ahmed Hamed	28	Fulltime Fisherman	23.12.2009	Erisseyl
57	Salem Abdullah Saeed	45	Fulltime Fisherman	23.12.2009	Ṣaqarah
58	Thaili Hamoadi	60s	Fulltime Fisherman	23.12.2009	Ṣaqarah
59	Mobark Wilaal Saad	25	Fulltime Fisherman	23.12.2009	Ṣaqarah
60	Salam Rashid Hamoadi	25	Fulltime Fisherman	23.12.2009	Ṣaqarah
61	Ali Omar	48	Seasonal Fisherman	23.12.2009	Di-Ḥamari
62	Eisa Atman Salem	18	Fulltime Fisherman	25.12.2009	Ḥadiboh
63	Ahmed Eisa Abdullah	18	Fulltime Fisherman	26.12.2009	Ḥadiboh
64	Hamed Saeed Ahmed	17	Fulltime Fisherman	26.12.2009	Ḥadiboh
65	Omar Amrin	52	Fulltime Fisherman	27.12.2009	Di-Ḥamari
66	Abdullah Ali	17	Fulltime Fisherman	28.12.2009	Zaḥaq
67	Abdullah Saeed	25	Fulltime Fisherman	28.12.2009	Zaḥaq
68	Ali Jamen	40s	Fulltime Fisherman	28.12.2009	Qaṭanan
69	Jamen Ahmed Salem	40s	Fulltime Fisherman	28.12.2009	Zaḥaq
70	Ali Saeed	60s	Fulltime Fisherman	29.12.2009	Zaḥaq
71	Mohammed Ahmed	55	Fulltime Fisherman	11.2.2009	Maḥfirihin
72	Omar Omaar	22	Fulltime Fisherman	29.12.2009	Qaṭanan
73	Samenta Ahis	60s	Fulltime Fisherman	29.12.2009	Maṭyaf
74	Sareed Saeed Saad	35	Fulltime Fisherman	29.12.2009	Maṭyaf
75	Mohammed Saeed Mohammed	33	Fulltime Fisherman	29.12.2009	Bidhōleh
76	Hadad Eisa Mohammed	45	Fulltime Fisherman	29.12.2009	Bidhōleh
77	Mohammed Hassan Eisa	25	Fulltime Fisherman	29.12.2009	Bidhōleh
78	Abdullah Eisa Ahmed	50s	Fulltime Fisherman	30.12.2009	Di-Ṣeberho
79	Saeed Hamed Ahmed	40s	Fulltime Fisherman	30.12.2009	Di-Ṣeberho
80	Hazmahan Abdulah	40s	Fulltime Fisherman	30.12.2009	Di-Ṣeberho
81	Salem Abdullah Sebrehe	30s	Fulltime Fisherman	30.12.2009	Di-Ṣeberho
82	Mohammed Abdullah Ahmed	35	Fulltime Fisherman	30.12.2009	Stēroh
83	Ali Eisa Abdullah	30s	Fulltime Fisherman	30.12.2009	Stēroh
84	Saeed Mohammed Abdullah	27	Fulltime Fisherman	30.12.2009	Stēroh
85	Ali Abdullah Ahmed	40s	Fulltime Fisherman	30.12.2009	Stēroh
86	Amar Abdullah Mobarak	35	Fulltime Fisherman	1.1.2010	Ḥadiboh
87	Faisal Ahmed Khalif	30s	Fulltime Fisherman	1.1.2010	Ḥadiboh
88	Salem Saeed Tamook	40s	Fulltime Fisherman	1.1.2010	Ḥadiboh
89	Sharaf Joman Baleef	35	Fulltime Fisherman	1.1.2010	Ḥadiboh
90	Salim Games Saaed	45	Fulltime Fisherman	2.1.2010	Qādheb
91	Salim Saaed Atman	55	Fulltime Fisherman	2.1.2010	Qādheb
92	Abdullah Ali Muhammed	60s	Fulltime Fisherman	2.1.2010	Qādheb
93	Naeef Ghaan Ahmed	19	Fulltime Fisherman	3.1.2010	Ḥadiboh
94	Minathal Eisa Mobarak	34	Fulltime Fisherman	3.1.2010	Ḥadiboh
95	Khanem Salem Mohammed	40s	Fulltime Fisherman	3.1.2010	Ḥadiboh
96	Selemann Safi Abeed	45	Fulltime Fisherman	3.1.2010	Ḥadiboh
97	Salem Ahmed Khamis	50s	Fulltime Fisherman	3.1.2010	Ḥadiboh

Appendix 2. Sample interview questions in English and Arabic.

Weather

1. What are the best times for fishing here, and in (other town)?
2. How do you know when the best time is for fishing?
3. Can you fish during other times? Why not? Where?
4. What is the name that you would give for the best time for fishing?
5. What do you call the times that you can fish in and for the other parts of the year?
6. What winds would be dangerous for fishing? Which direction do they come?
7. Can you fish on the south side of the island during these winds, what about the north?
8. Are there any areas which it is possible to fish from when the winds are strong?
9. What seasons do you fish in? How do know when these seasons start, finish?
10. Do you have a name for the different winds? How do you name these winds?

Settlement

1. When was it that this village first settled? By whom?
2. How big was it initially?
3. Did the coastline, anchorage / landing facilities influence the position of the village?
4. What other things influenced the position of the village?
5. Do you remain here all year round?
6. Where do you go if you don't stay at the village?
7. What changes to the villages around this coastline have you noticed, bigger, more people?
8. Did your grandfather / father live here, where did he stay?

Fishing Practices

1. How long have you been fishing for?
2. What fish do you prefer to catch, why?
3. Do you have a particular area where you would chose to catch certain fish or fish in?
4. Do you have a name for these areas?
5. Would people from one side of the island be able to fish at another side of the island?
6. When is the best time for fishing?
7. When would you use a net and when would you use a hand line?
8. What do you do with your catch?
9. How long would you stay out at sea fishing?
10. What do you do when you cannot fish anymore due to the weather?

Navigation

1. When you go fishing how do you know where the best places to go are?
2. How far out to sea do you go, can you still see the land?
3. How do you find your way back to the village? (Without Magellan)
4. What happens at night, how do you get back to your village?
5. Which stars would you use, how?
6. When you fish on the (north / south) side of the island how you do know where you are?
7. When and how do you travel by sea to the other parts of the island?
8. Would you go east or west around the island? Which would you choose to do (safer)?
9. Do you fish at the islands (Samha, Darsa, Abd al-Kuri)?
10. When and how do you get to them? How long does it take, and before engines how would you have got to the islands?
11. What landmarks would you use to identify fishing areas?
12. At sea how would you identify your position?

Origins

1. How long have you been on the island?
2. Did your father come from Socotra, and his father?
3. Do you know whether people came from Africa / Arabia?
4. Do you know when they came here?
5. Do you remember what they did when they were here? Did they stay in this village or move away?
6. Were they fishermen, sailors?
7. How did they come to the island?
8. Did they bring anything with them?

Appendix 3. The fishing seasons and influence local winds and currents have on villages along the north and south coast and island of Samḥa.

Villages on Socotra's North coast

Village	Seasons	Local winds	Currents
Shuᶜub	*ṣēreb* (Soc), fishing season from 1 October until 1 June. *Ḥorf (Soc), closed season from June to September.*	*ṣe̍rbihi* (Soc), fishing can be difficult due to storms. *e̍ˀeris* (Soc)/ *hindī* (Ar), good wind for fishing. *me̍de* (Soc), makes fishing impossible. *ma̍ˁaribo* (Soc)/ *kōs* (Ar), makes fishing difficult if blowing strongly.	*ˁālə* (Soc), a dangerous current that can drag one out to sea. *shimār* (Ar), can make fishing difficult if it is strong.
Qalansiyah	*azyab* (Ar), fishing season from October to May *kōs* (Ar), closed season from May to September *ṣere̍bhen* (Soc), mid-September and *gyaḥś* (Soc), October, are the best fishing periods as the sea is calm.	*ṣe̍rbihi* (Soc)/ *azyab* (Ar), good wind for fishing. *e̍ˀeris* (Soc), *hindī* (Ar) and *sharq* (Ar), are dangerous winds for fishing. *me̍de* (Soc), makes fishing impossible. *ma̍ˁaribo* (Soc)/ *kōs* (Ar), makes fishing very difficult; if it blows strongly it is impossible to fish. *barrī* (Ar), a land breeze that can make fishing difficult	*ˁālə* (Soc), a dangerous current that can drag one out to sea. *shimār* (Ar), a dangerous current that can drag one out to sea. *le̍ḥe* (Soc), a dangerous current that can drag one out to sea. *sikūṭ* (Ar), can make fishing difficult if it is strong.
Qādheb	*azyab* (Ar), fishing season from October to the beginning of July. *kōs* (Ar), closed season from mid-July to September.	*azyab* (Ar), good wind for fishing. *e̍ˀeris* (Soc), bringer of storms, can make fishing difficult. *me̍de* (Soc), makes fishing impossible. *ma̍ˁaribo* (Soc)/ *kōs* (Ar), makes fishing impossible; signifies the end of the fishing season. *barrī* (Ar), a land breeze that makes fishing dangerous.	*ˁālə* (Soc), a dangerous current that can drag one out to sea. *le̍ḥe* (Soc), a dangerous current that can drag one out to sea. Both currents make it impossible to use a net.
Ḥadiboh	*ṣēreb* (Soc)/ *azyab* (Ar), fishing season from 1-15 October to the beginning of July. *ṣere̍bhen* (Soc), beginning of the fishing season for experienced fisherman. *gya̍ḥś* (Soc), beginning of the fishing season for less experienced fishermen. *məˁōdif* (Soc), January, a period of rough weather in which it is only possible to use cast nets from the shore. *ḳe̍yaṭ* (Soc), February to April, a period of unsettled weather that makes fishing dangerous. *dōti* (Soc), mid-April to the beginning of July, seasonal fishermen stop fishing, very difficult to fish. *Ḥorf* (Soc)/ *kōs* (Ar), closed season from mid-July to September.	*azyab* (Ar)/ *ṣe̍rbihi* (Soc), a good wind for fishing. *e̍ˀeris* (Soc)/ *hindī* (Ar), a dangerous wind for fishing, especially in September. *me̍de* (Soc), a dangerous wind for fishing, especially if it blows in May or September. *ma̍ˁaribo* (Soc)/ *kōs* (Ar), bringer of storms, can make fishing difficult, especially in May. *barrī* (Ar) and *mġēbīya* (Ar), land breezes that make fishing dangerous, mostly occur during *dōti* and *ḳe̍yaṭ*	*ˁālə* (Soc), a dangerous current that can drag one out to sea. *shimār* (Ar), a dangerous current that can drag one out to sea. *le̍ḥe* (Soc), a dangerous current that can drag one out to sea. *sikūṭ* (Ar), can make fishing difficult if it is strong.

Villages on the South coast

Village	Seasons	Local winds	Currents
Ṣaqarah	*ṣēreb* (Soc), fishing season from October to the beginning of July. *Ḥorf* (Soc), closed season from mid-July to September.	*ṣe̍rbihi* (Soc), a good wind for fishing, except in September or October when it can bring storms and make fishing difficult. *e̍ʾeris* (Soc)/ *hindī* (Ar), can make fishing difficult, especially when it brings storms. *me̍de* (Soc), a dangerous wind for fishing. *ma̍ʿaribo*, a dangerous wind for fishing.	*ʿālə* (Soc), a dangerous current that can drag one out to sea. *le̍ḥe* (Soc), a dangerous current that can drag one out to sea. Both currents make using a net impossible.
Erisseyl	*ṣēreb* (Soc), fishing season from October to the beginning of June. The months of October and December are considered as the best fishing period. *Ḥorf* (Soc), closed season from mid-June to September.	*azyab* (Ar)/ *ṣe̍rbihi* (Soc), a good wind for fishing, except in September or June, when it makes fishing difficult. *e̍ʾeris* (Soc)/ *hindī* (Ar), a dangerous wind for fishing. *me̍de* (Soc), a dangerous wind for fishing. *ma̍ʿaribo*, a dangerous wind for fishing.	*ʿālə* (Soc), a dangerous current that can drag one onto the reefs. *le̍ḥe* (Soc), a dangerous current that can drag one onto the reefs. *shimār* (Ar), a dangerous current that can drag one onto the reefs. *sikūṭ* (Ar), a dangerous current that can drag one onto the reefs.
Maḥfirihin	*ṣēreb* (Soc), fishing season from November to December. *ḳe̍yaṭ* (Soc), fishing becomes more difficult, from January to March. *dɔ̄ti* (Soc), fishing possible but limited due to storms, from April to June. *Ḥorf* (Soc), closed season from July to October.	*ṣe̍rbihi* (Soc), a good wind for fishing, if it does not blow strongly. *e̍ʾeris* (Soc), brings storms that make fishing dangerous. *me̍de* (Soc), a dangerous wind for fishing. *ma̍ʿaribo*, a dangerous wind, no fishing undertaken.	*ʿālə* (Soc), a very dangerous current that can drag one out to sea. *le̍ḥe* (Soc), a dangerous current that can drag one out to sea. *shimār* (Ar), a dangerous current that can drag one out to sea. *sikūṭ* (Ar), a very dangerous current that can drag one out to sea.
Stēroh	*ṣēreb* (Soc), fishing season from November to December. *ḳe̍yaṭ* (Soc), fishing becomes more difficult due to storms, from January to April. Seasonal fishermen return to the hills. *dɔ̄ti* (Soc), fishing possible but difficult due to storms, from May to June. *Ḥorf* (Soc), closed season from July to September. *Ṣere̍bhen* (Soc), fishing possible but difficult due to storms, from September to October, when fishing becomes easier.	*azyab* (Ar)/ *ṣe̍rbihi* (Soc), a good wind for fishing, if it does not blow strongly. *e̍ʾeris* (Soc), fishing dangerous, few go fishing. *me̍de* (Soc), a good wind for fishing. *ma̍ʿaribo*, fishing dangerous, few go fishing.	*ʿālə* (Soc), a very dangerous current that can drag one out to sea. *le̍ḥe* (Soc), a dangerous current that can drag one out to sea. Both currents make using a net impossible.
Bidhōleh	*ṣēreb* (Soc), fishing season from October to June. *Ḥorf* (Soc), closed season from July to September.	*ṣe̍rbihi* (Soc), fishing dangerous, few go fishing. *e̍ʾeris* (Soc), fishing dangerous, few go fishing. *me̍de* (Soc), fishing is good. *ma̍ʿaribo*, fishing dangerous, nobody goes fishing.	None recognised.

Di-Ṣeberho	*ṣēreb* (Soc), fishing season from October to June. *ṣerebhen* (Soc), limited fishing near-shore, mid-September. *Ḥorf* (Soc), closed season from July to September.	*ṣerbihi* (Soc), fishing difficult. *eʾeris* (Soc), fishing dangerous, nobody goes fishing. *mede* (Soc), fishing is good. *maʿaribo*, fishing dangerous, nobody goes fishing.	*ʿālə* (Soc), a very dangerous current that can drag one out to sea. *leḥe* (Soc), a dangerous current that can drag one out to sea. Both currents make using a net impossible.

The island of Samḥa

Village	Seasons	Local winds	Currents
Khaysat ash-Shaikh	*ṣēreb* (Soc), fishing season from October to May/ June. *Ḥorf* (Soc), closed season from May/ June to September.	*ṣerbihi* (Soc), fishing possible. *eʾeris* (Soc), fishing possible. *mede* (Soc), fishing possible. *maʿaribo*, fishing possible.	*ʿālə* (Soc), fishing possible. *leḥe* (Soc), fishing possible. *shimār* (Ar), fishing possible. *sikūṭ* (Ar), fishing possible.

Appendix 4. The fishing tackle used by the fishermen, the method of its deployment, seasons in which it is used, species targeted and the locations in which these species are targeted.

Fishing Tackle

Equipment	**Method**	**Season**	**Species**	**Location**	**Use**
Fish traps *ḳe̍rḳor* (Soc)	Deployed from a boat or by wading into the shallows, buoyed during rough weather.	Throughout the year. During the SW monsoon season their use is limited to several protected bays.	Shallow-water demersal species, sometimes lobster	Used throughout Socotra and Samḥa. Deployed in various shallow water areas. In Ḥadiboh the fishing area of *līṫonten*	Personal consumption
Lobster traps	Deployed from boats, buoyed.	During the open fishing season.	Lobster	Mostly along the south coast. Preferred areas are along the northeast and southeast coast. Deployed in rocky shallow water areas.	Overseas market. Limited local market, normally only during the tourist season.
Cast nets *ma̍ʿadeft* (Soc) a. Line attached b. Without line	a. Cast from the shore, retrieved with attached line. b. Cast from a boat, retrieved using a gaff.	a. Throughout the year. b. Throughout the open fishing season.	Shallow-water demersal species.	Used throughout Socotra and Samḥa. a. Shallow-water areas. b. Mainly in shallow-water areas where shoaling bait fish are prevalent.	a. Personal consumption and for bait. b. Bait
Fixed seine nets a. Bottom-anchored net b. Top-anchored net	a. Deployed by boat, usually left at sea using anchors and buoys to secure it to the seabed. b. Deployed by boat, usually left at sea using an anchor and buoys, sometimes long lines attached. Can be anchored to a boat.	a. During the fishing seasons of *gyaḥś* and *ṣēreb*, when the sea is calm. Sometimes during *ḳe̍yaṭ*. b. During the fishing seasons of *gyaḥś* and *ṣēreb*.	a. Large demersal species. b. Medium and large pelagic species.	Used throughout Socotra and Samḥa. a. Set in no specific deep water area. a. In Ḥadiboh the fishing area of *šiḳ*. b. Set in no specific deep water area. b. In Ḥadiboh the fishing area of *šiḳ*, and the beginning of *ḳeneʿi̍ti*.	a. Mainly for the overseas market, some sold locally. b. Mainly for the overseas market, some sold locally.

Equipment	Method	Season	Species	Location	Use
c. Single-anchored net	c. Deployed by boat, either left attached to a single buoy or the stern of a vessel.	c. During the end of *gyaḥś* and beginning of *ṣẽreb*. Sometimes during *ḳeyaṭ* when the sea is calm and the currents are not strong.	c. Medium and large pelagic species.	c. Set in no specific deep water area. c. In Ḥadiboh the beginning of *ḳeneʿiti*.	c. Mainly for the overseas market, some sold locally.
Drift Nets	Deployed by attaching to a boat and allowing it to drift with the boat. Normally with long lines attached to the end.	During the end of *gyaḥś* and the beginning of *ṣẽreb*, when the sea was calm and the currents are not strong. Possible during the beginning of *ḳeyaṭ*.	Large and medium pelagic species. Sometimes turtle are caught as a bycatch.	Various deep water areas, over an hour from the shore. In Ḥadiboh the fishing area of *ḳeneʿiti*.	Mainly for the overseas market, some sold locally.
Drag Nets	Attached to a boat and dragged across the seabed.	During the open fishing season. Restricted to days in which the sea is calm and currents are not strong.	Lobster	Mostly deployed along the south, northeast and southeast coast. Deployed in shallow areas with few undersea outcroppings.	Overseas market.
Fish lines *śoʾhor* (Soc)/*watār* (Ar) Hand lines				Throughout the north and south coast of Socotra and Samḥa.	
a. Deep-water handlining	a. A single line deployed from a boat.	a. /b. Throughout the open fishing season. Usually not during *gyaḥś* or *ṣẽreb*, when netting.	a. /b. Medium and large pelagic and demersal species.	a. Specific deep water sites several miles from the coast. In Ḥadiboh theses sites lie in the fishing area of *ḳeneʿiti*.	a. /b. Mainly for the overseas market, some sold locally.
b. Shallow-water handlining	b. A single line deployed from a boat.			b. Specific shallow water sites close to the shore. In Ḥadiboh these sites mostly lie in the fishing area of *šiḳ*.	

Equipment	Method	Season	Species	Location	Use
c. Shore handlining	c. A single line deployed from the shore.	c. Mainly during the SW monsoon period when the sea is said to be closed, *qāfal* (Ar).	c. Shallow water demersal species.	c. Various specific areas throughout Socotra. Preferences are for projecting rocky areas with deep water.	c. Personal consumption.
Troll lines	A single line with up to two snoods attached. Trailed behind a boat. Usually deployed after having set nets.	Throughout the open fishing season. Mostly during *gyaḥś* or *ṣēreb*, when netting.	Various large and medium pelagic species.	Throughout the north and south coast of Socotra and Samḥa. No specific areas, as long as it is deep water. In Ḥadiboh the fishing area of *ḳeneᶜiti*.	Mainly for the overseas market, some sold locally.
Long lines			Various large and medium pelagic species.		Mainly for the overseas market, some sold locally.
a. Bottom set	a. A single line with several snoods attached. Anchored to the seafloor. Deployed from a boat and left overnight.	a. Throughout the open fishing season.		a. /b. Throughout the north and south coast of Socotra and Samḥa. No specific areas, as long as it is deep water.	
b. Drifting	b. A single line with several snoods attached. Allowed to drift behind a boat. Also used in conjunction with fixed and drift nets.	b. Throughout the open fishing season. However the best period is between *gyaḥś* and *ḳeyaṭ*.		a. /b. In Ḥadiboh the fishing area of *ḳeneᶜiti*, although when used in conjunction with nets also in *šiḳ*.	

Bibliography

Primary Sources

Agatharchides of Cnidus on the Erythraen Sea. 1989. Translated and edited by S. M. Burstein. London, The Hakluyt Society.

Akhbār al-Ṣīn wa-l-Hind (Relation de la Chine et de l-Inde). 1948. Translated and edited by J. Sauvaget. Paris, Belles Lettres.

Barros, João de. 1945. *Décadas, selecção, profácio e notas de António Baião*. (3 vols.). Lisboa, Livraría Sá da Costa.

Al-Bīrūnī, Muḥammad b. Aḥmad. 1983. *The Chronology of Ancient Nations: An English version of the Arabic text of the Athār-ul-Bākiya of Albīrūnī*. Translated and edited with notes and index by C. E. Sachau. Lahore, Hijra International Publishers.

The Book of Curiosities: A Critical Edition. eds. Emily Savage-Smith and Yossef Rapoport. World-Wide-Web Publication. (www.bodley.ox.ac.uk/bookofcuriosities) (March 2007). Chapter 2.15, fol. 37b, lines 21-24. [Accessed 15 October 2009].

The Book of Duarte Barbosa. 1967. Translated by M. Longworth Dames. (2 vols.). London, The Hakluyt Society.

Chau Ju-Kua, his work on the Chinese and Arab Trade in the Twelfth and Thirteenth Centuries, entitled 'Chu-fan-chï'. 1911. Translated from Chinese and annotated by F. Hirth, and W. Rockhill. St. Petersburg, Imperial Academy of Sciences.

The Commentaries of the Great Afonso Dalboquerque. 1884. Translated from the Portuguese edition of 1774 by W. De Grey Birch. London, The Hakluyt Society.

Cosmas Indicopleustes. 1896. *The Christian Topography of Cosmas, an Egyptian monk*. Translated from the Greek and edited with notes and introduction by J. W. McCrindle. London, The Hakluyt Society.

Diodorus Siculus. 1933-1967. *Bibliotheca Historica*. Translated and edited by C. H. Oldfather, C. L. Sherman, C. Bradford Welles, R. M. Greer, and F. R. Walton. (12 vols.). London, Heinemann.

The Embassy of Sir Thomas Roe to India, 1615-1619. 1967. ed. W. Foster. (2 vols.). London, The Hakluyt Society.

Finley, A. G. 1897. *Indian Ocean Directory*. London, Richard Holmes Laurie, 4th edition.

Foster, W. 1906-1925. *The English Factories in India 1665-1667*. (12 vols.). Oxford, Clarendon Press.

Hagenaer, H. 1650. *Verhael van de Reyze gedaan in de Meeste Deelen van de Oost-Indien : Uyt Gevaeren Inden Jaere 1631, en Weder Gekeert Ao. 1638: met een besondere beschrijvinge eeniger Indiaensche Coninckrijcken en de Landen*. At: Amsterdam, KIT Library. S1, s.n.

Al-Hamdānī, al-Ḥasan ibn Aḥmad and Müller, D. H. 1968. *Hamdānī's Geographie der arabischen Halbinsel: nach den Handschriften von Berlin, Constantinopel, London, Paris und Strassburg*. Leiden, Brill.

The Hawkins' voyages during the reigns of Henry VIII, Queen Elizabeth and James I. 1878. ed. C. R. Markham. London, The Hakluyt Society.

Herodotus. 1920-1957. *The Histories*. Translated by A. D. Godley. (4 vols.). London, Heinemann.

Horsburgh, J. 1841. *The India Directory, or, Directions for Sailing to and from the East Indies, China, Australia, and the Interjacent Ports of Africa and South America: Compiled chiefly from Original Journals of the Honourable Company's Ships, and from Observations and Remarks, Resulting from the Experience of twenty-one years in the Navigation of those Seas, 5th edition*. (2 vols.). London, W. H. Allen and Co.

Ibn Baṭṭūṭa, Abū 'Abd Allāh Muḥammad. 1956. *The Travels of Ibn Baṭṭūṭa, A.D.1325-1354. Volume 1*. Translated with revisions and notes from the Arabic text edited by C. Defrémery, B. R. Sanguinetti, and H. A. R. Gibb; translation completed with annotations by C. F. Beckingham, and index compiled by A. D. H. Bivar. London, The Hakluyt Society.

Al-Idrīsī, Abū 'Abd Allāh Muḥammad al-Sharīf. 1836-1840. *Nuzhat al-mushtāq fi ikhtirāq al-āfāq (Géographie)*. Translated with notes by P. A. Jaubert. (2 vols.). Paris, Imprimerie Royale.

Ibn Khurradādhbih, 'Ubayd Allāh ibn 'Abd Allāh. 1889. *Kitāb al-masālik wa l-mamālik*. ed. M. J. de Goeje. [Bibliotheca Geographorum Arabicorum, 6]. Leiden, E. J. Brill.

Ibn al-Mujāwir, Jamāl al-Dīn b. Muḥammad al-Shaybānī. 1954. *Ṣifat bilād al-Yaman wa-Makka wa-baʿd al-Ḥijāz al-musammā tārīkh al-mustabṣir (Descriptio Arabiae Meridionalis)*. ed. O. Löfgren. (2 vols.). Leiden, E. J. Brill.

Ibn al-Mujāwir. 2008. *A Traveller in Thirteenth-century Arabia, Ibn al-Mujāwir's Tārīkh al-Mustabṣir*. Translated from Oscar Löfgren's Arabic text and edited with revisions and annotations by G. Rex Smith. London, The Hakluyt Society.

The Journal of John Jourdain 1608-1617, describing his experiences in Arabia, India, and the Malay Archipelago. 1905. ed. W. Foster. London, The Hakluyt Society.

Kerr, R. 1811-1894. *A General History and Collection of Voyages and Travels*. (18 vols.). Edinburgh, George Ramsay and Company.

Al-Muqaddasī, Muḥammad b. Aḥmad. 2001. *The Best Division for Knowledge of the Regions*. Translated by B. A. Collins and M. H. al-Tai. Reading, Garnet.

Ormsby, H. A. 1844. 'Island of Sokotra', in *Arabian South and East Coasts*, S. B. Haines. Taunton, United Kingdom Hydrographic Office. OD 357.

The Periplus of the Erythraean Sea. 1912. Translated by W. H. Schoff. New York, Longman, Green and Co.

The Periplus of the Erythraean Sea. 1980. Translated and edited by G. W. B. Huntingford. London, The Hakluyt Society.

The Periplus of the Erythraean Sea. 1989. Text with introduction, translation, and commentary by L. Casson. Princeton, Princeton University Press.

Pliny the Elder. 1940-1963. *Natural History*. Books 1-19 (vols. 1-5) translated by H. Rackham; Books 20-32 (vols. 6-8) translated by W. H. S. Jones; Books 33-35 (vol. 9) translated by H. Rackham; Books 36-37 (vol. 10) translated by D. E. Eichholz. (10 vols.). London, Heinemann.

Prutky's travels to Ethiopia and other countries. 1991. Translated and edited by J. H. Arrowsmith-Brown and annotated by R. Pankhurst. London, The Hakluyt Society.

Ptolemy. 1990. *Claudii Ptolemaei Geographia*. Translated and edited by K. F. A. Nobbe with an introduction by A. Diller. (3 vols.). Hildesheim, Olms.

Purchas, Samuel. 1905-1907. *Hakluytus Posthumus*. (20 vols.). Glasgow, MacLehose.

Qazvīnī, Ḥamd Allāh Mustawfī. 1970. *Ḥudūd al-'ālam (The Regions of the World) A Persian Geography 372 A.H. – 982 A.D.* Translated from the Russian and with additional material by V. Minorsky, with a preface by V. V. Barthold, edited by C. E. Bosworth. [E. J. W. Gibb Memorial Series, 11]. Leiden, E. J. Brill; London, Luzac and Company.

Al-Rāmhurmuzī, Buzurg ibn Shahriyār. 1966. *Kitāb ʿadjā'ib al-Hind: Barruhu wa-baḥruhu wa-jazā'iruh*. Arabic text with French translation and notes by P. A. Van der Lith and L. M. Devic. Tehran, M. H. Asadi.

The Suma Oriental of Tomé Pires and the Book of Francisco Rodrigues. 1944. Translated and edited by A. Cortesão. (2 vols.). London, The Hakluyt Society.

Theophrastus, Enquiry into Plants and Minor Works on Odours and Weather Signs. 1916. Translated by A. Hort. (2 vols.). London, Heinemann.

The Travels of Nicolò dè Conti in the East in the Early Part of the Fifteenth Century. 1857. Translated from the original of Poggio Bracciolini, with Notes, by J. Winter Jones, Esq., F.S.A., Keeper of the Printed Books, British Museum, in *India in the Fifteenth Century, Being a Collection of Narratives of Voyages to India, in the Century Preceding the Portuguese Discovery of the Cape of Good Hope, from Latin, Persian, Russian, and Italian Sources*. Translated into English and edited by R. H. Major: 3-39. London, The Hakluyt Society.

The Voyage of John Huyghen van Linschoten to the East Indies: from the old English translation of 1598: the first book, containing his description of the East. 1885. eds. A. C. Burnell, and P. A. Tiele (2 vols.). London, The Hakluyt Society.

Yāqūt bin, 'Abd Allāh al-Rūmī. 1866-1873. *Jacut's Geographisches Wörterbuch (Kitāb mu'jam al-buldān)*. ed. F. Wüstenfeld. (6 vols.). Leipzig, F.A. Brockhaus.

Secondary sources

Abdulla, M. N. 1996. Tropical Cyclones and Monsoon Winds which affect Socotra Island. In H. J. Dumont (ed.), *Proceedings of the First International Symposium on Socotra Island Present and Future, Aden, 24-28 March, 1996. Vol. 2, Natural Resources and Environmental Protection*: 9-24. Aden, University of Aden Printing and Publishing House.

Abu-Lughod, J. 1989. *Before European Hegemony. The World System A.D. 1250-1350.* Oxford, Oxford University Press.

Acheson, J. M. 1981. Anthropology of Fishing. *Annual Review of Anthropology*. 10: 275-316.

Agius, D. A. 2002. *In the wake of the dhow: The Arabian Gulf and Oman*. Reading, Ithaca Press.

Agius, D. A. 2005. *Seafaring in the Arabian Gulf and Oman: People of the Dhow*. London, Routledge.

Agius, D. A. 2008. *Classic Ships of Islam: From Mesopotamia to the Indian Ocean*. Leiden, Brill.

Agius, D. A. 2012. The Rashayda: Ethnic Identity and Dhow Activity in Suakin on the Red Sea Coast. *Northeast African Studies*. 12.1:169-216.

Alpers, E. A. 2009. *East Africa and the Indian Ocean*. Princeton, Markus Wiener Publishers.

Anscuetz, K. F., Wilshusen, R. H. and Scheick, C. L. 2001. An Archaeology of Landscapes: Perspectives and Directions. *Journal of Archaeological Research*. 9.2: 157-211.

Appadurai, A. 1995. The Production of Locality. In R. Fardon (ed.), *Counterworks: Managing the Diversity of Knowledge*: 204-225. London, Routledge.

Arthur, W. S. 2001. Autonomy and Identity in Torres Strait, a Borderline Case? *The Journal of Pacific History*. 36.2: 215-224.

Banaimoon, S. A. 1996. The Biological Events Associated with the Upwelling on the Arabian Sea. In H. J. Dumont (ed.), *Proceedings of the First International Symposium on Socotra Island Present and Future, Aden, 24-28 March, 1996. Vol. 3, Agricultural and Marine Sciences*: 19-32. Aden, University of Aden Printing and Publishing House.

Barendse, R. J. 2009. *Arabian Seas 1700-1763. Volume 1: The Western Indian Ocean in the Eighteenth Century*. Leiden, Brill.

Balfour, I. B. 1888. The Botany of Socotra. *The Transactions of the Royal Society of Edinburgh, 31*. Edinburgh, Robert Grant and Son.

Battersby, P. 2004. Mapping Australasia: Reflections on the Permeability of Australia's Northern Maritime Borders. In A. Shnukal, Y. Nagata and G. Ramsay (eds), *Navigating Boundaries the Asian diaspora in Torres Strait*: 13-32. Canberra, Pandanus Books.

Beaujard, P. 2005. The Indian Ocean in Eurasian and African World-Systems before the Sixteenth Century. *Journal of World History*. 16.4: 411-465.

Beckingham, C. F. 1949. Some Early Travels in Arabia. *Journal of the Royal Asiatic Society of Great Britain and Ireland*. 2: 155-176.

Beckingham, C. F. 1951. Dutch Travellers in Arabia in the Seventeenth Century. *Journal of the Royal Asiatic Society of Great Britain and Ireland*. 1/2: 64-81.

Beckingham, C. F. 1983. Some notes on the history of Socotra. In G. R. Smith and R. Bidwell (eds), *Arabian and Islamic studies: Articles presented to R.B. Serjeant on the occasion of his retirement from the Sir Thomas Adams' Chair of Arabic at the University of Cambridge*: 172-181. London, Longman.

Beech, M. J. 2004. *In the land of the Ichthyophagi: Modelling fish exploitation in the Arabian Gulf and Gulf of Oman from the 5th millennium BC to the Late Islamic period*. Oxford, Archaeopress.

Bender, B. 2002. Time and Landscape. *Current Anthropology: Supplement*. 43: 103-112.

Bender, B. 2006. Place and Landscape. In C. Tilley, W. Keane, S. Kuechler, M. Rowlands and P. Spyer (eds), *Handbook of Material Culture*: 303-314. London, Sage.

Bent, T. 1897. The Island of Socotra. *The Nineteenth Century and After: A Monthly Review*. 41. 244: 975-992.

Bent, T. and Bent, M. 1900. *Southern Arabia*. London, Smith, Elder and Co.

Bennett, E. N. 1897. Two Months in Sokotra. *Longman's Magazine*. 30. 179: 405-413.

Bertram, G. C. L. 1948. *The Fisheries of the Sultanate of Muscat and Oman*. Muscat, The Sultanate of Muscat.

Beydoun, Z. R. and Bichan, H. R. 1970. The Geology of Socotra, Gulf of Aden. *Quarterly Journal of the Geological Society of London*. 125: 413-446.

Beyhl, F. E. 1998. Anmerkungen zum Drachenblut und zu den Namen der Insel Soqotra. *Zeitschrift der Deutschen Morgenländischen Gesellschaft*. 148: 35-82.

Biedermann, Z. 2006. *Soqotra Geschichte einer Christlichen Insel im Indischen Ozean vom Altertum bus zur frühen Neuzeit*. (Maritime Asia 17). Wiesbaden, Harrassowitz.

Birse, A. C. R., Bott, W. F., Morrison, J. and Samuel, M. A. 1997. The Mesozoic and Early Tertiary Tectonic Evolution of the Socotra area, eastern Gulf of Aden, Yemen. *Marine and Petroleum Geology*. 14. 6: 675-684.

Blommaert, J. and Jie, D. 2010. *Ethnographic Fieldwork: A Beginner's Guide*. Bristol, Multilingual Matters.

Blue, L. K. 2010. Boats, Routes and Sailing Conditions of Indo-Roman Trade. In R. Tomber, L. K. Blue and S. Abraham (eds), *Migration, Trade and Peoples: Indian Ocean Commerce and the Archaeology of Western India*: 3-13. London, The British Academy.

Boivin, N., Blench, R. and Fuller, D. Q. 2009. Archaeological, Linguistic and Historical Sources on Ancient Seafaring: A Multidisciplinary Approach to the Study of Early Maritime Contact and Exchange in the Arabian Peninsula. In M. D. Petraglia and J. I. Rose (eds), *The Evolution of Human Populations in Arabia Paleoenvironments, Prehistory and Genetics*: 251-278. Dordrecht, Springer.

Bonfiglioli, A. and Hariri, K. I. 2004. *Small Scale Fisheries in Yemen: Social Assessment and Development Prospects*. Food and Agricultural Organisation and the World Bank.

Botting, D. 1958. The Oxford University Expedition to Socotra. *The Geographical Journal*. 124. 2: 200-207.

Botting, D. 2006. *Island of the Dragon's Blood*. London, Steve Savage.

Bourdieu, P. 1977. *Outline of a Theory of Practice*. Cambridge, Cambridge University Press.

Bowen, R. LeBaron. 1951. The Dhow Sailor. *The American Neptune*. 11. 4: 161-202.

Bowen, R. LeBaron. 1952. Primitive Watercraft of Arabia. *The American Neptune*. 12. 3: 186-221.

Bowen, R. LeBaron. 1955. Maritime superstitions of the Arabs. *The American Neptune*. 15. 1: 5-48.

Boxhall, P. G. 1966. Socotra – Island of Bliss. *The Geographical Journal*. 132. 2: 213-222.

Brásio, A. 1943. *Missões Portuguesas de Socotorá*. Lisbon, Agéncia Geral das Colónias.

Braudel, F. 1972. *The Mediterranean and the Mediterranean World in the Age of Phillip II*. Translated by S. Reynolds. (2 vols.). London, Harper and Row.

Bray, Z. 2008. Ethnographical approaches. In D. Della Porta and M. Keating (eds), *Approaches and Methodologies in the Social Sciences: A Pluralist Perspective*: 296-315. Cambridge, Cambridge University Press.

Brown, G. H. H. 1966. *Social and Economic Conditions and Possible Development of Socotra*. Unpublished report.

Bukharin, M. D. 2012. The Greek inscriptions at Hoq. In I. Strauch (ed.), *Foreign Sailors on Socotra. The inscriptions and drawings from the cave Hoq*: 494-500. Bremen, Hempen Verlag.

Camelin, S. 2006. *Pêcheurs du Yémen: Organisation et Transformation d'une communauté de Pêcheurs de la côte de l'Océan Indien*. Paris, Maisonneuve and Larose.

Carter, J. 1976. Tribal Structures in Oman. *Proceedings of the Seminar for Arabian Studies*. 7: 11-68.

Carter, R. 2005. The History and Prehistory of Pearling in the Persian Gulf. *Journal of the Economic and Social History of the Orient*. 48. 2: 139-209.

Černý, V. L., Pereira, M., Kujanova, A., Vaoikova, M., Hajek, M., Morris, M. and Mulligan, C. 2009. Out of Arabia-The Settlement of Island Soqotra as Revealed by Mitochondrial and Y Chromosome Genetic Diversity. *American Journal of Physical Anthropology*. 138. 4: 439-447.

Chaudhuri, K. N. 1985. *Trade and Civilisation in the Indian Ocean: An Economic History from the Rise of Islam to 1750*. Cambridge, University Press.

Cheung, C., Devantier, L. and Damme, K. V. (eds) 2006. *Socotra: A Natural History of the Islands and their People*. Hong Kong: Odyssey.

Chittick, N. 1980. Sewn Boats in the Western Indian Ocean and a survival in Somalia. *The International Journal of Nautical Archaeology*. 9. 4: 297-309.

Congreve, H. 1850. A brief notice of some contrivances practiced by the Native Mariners of the Coromandel Coast in Navigating, Sailing and Repairing their Vessels. *Madras Journal of Literature and Science*. 14: 101-104.

Cooney, G. 2003. Introduction: Seeing Land from the Sea. *World Archaeology*. 35. 3: 323-328.

Cordell, J. 1980. The Lunar-Tide Fishing Cycle in Northeastern Brazil. In A. Spoehr (ed.), *Maritime Adaptations: Essays on Contemporary Fishing Communities*: 25-38. Pittsburgh, Universiy of Pittsburgh Press.

Cornish, M. M. and Ives, E. E. 2006. *Reed's Maritime Meteorology, 3rd edition*. London Adlard Coles Nautical.

Cox, P. Some Excursions in Oman. *The Geographical Journal*. 66. 3: 193-221.

Culek, M., Kral, K., Habrova, H., Adolt, R., Pavli, J. and Madera, P. 2006. Socotra's annual weather pattern. In C. Cheung, L. Devantier and K. Van Damme (eds), *Socotra: A Natural History of the Islands and their People*: 42-45. Hong Kong, Odyssey.

Da Costa, J. P. 1973. *Socotora' e o Domínio Português no Oriente*. San Salvador, Coimbra.

Das Gupta, A. 1979. *Indian Merchants and the Decline of Surat: c.1700-1750*. Wiesbaden, Steiner.

Dannenfeldt, K. H. 1982. Ambergris: The Search for its Origin. *Isis*. 73. 3: 382-397.

De Geest, P. 2006. *Soqotra Karst Project (Yemen), 2000-2004*. Berlin, Speläoclub.

Dewalt, K. M. and Dewalt, B. R. 2002. *Participant Observation: A Guide for Fieldworkers*. Maryland, AltaMira Press.

Doe, D. B. 1970. *Socotra: An Archaeological Reconnaissance in 1967*. Miami Florida, Coconut Grove.

Doe, D. B. 1992. *Socotra Island of Tranquillity*. London, Immel.

Donaldson, W. J. 1979. Fishing and fish marketing in Northern Oman a case study of artisanal fisheries development. Unpublished Ph.D. thesis, University of Durham.

Dridi, H. 2002. Indiens et Proche-Orientaux dans une grotte de Suqutra (Yémén). *Journal Asiatique*. 290. 2: 565-610.

Dridi, H. and Gorea, M. 2003. Le voyage d'Abgar à Suqutra. *Archéologia*. 396: 48-57.

Dumont, H. J. 1998. *Proceedings of the first International Symposium on Soqotra Island: Present and Future. Aden, 24-28 March 1996*. New York, United Nations Publications.

Dumont, H. J. 1998. *Proceedings of the first International Symposium on Soqotra Island: Present and Future. Soqotra Technical Series: 1- 4. Aden, 24-28 March 1996*. Aden, Aden University Press.

Edgell, H. S. 2006. *Arabian Deserts Nature, Origin and Revolution*. Dordrecht, Springer.

Elie, S. D. 2004. Hadiboh: From Peripheral Village to Emerging City. *Chroniques Yémenites*. 12: 53-80.

Elie, S. D. 2007. *The Waning of a Pastoralist Community: An Ethnographic Exploration of Soqotra as a Transitional Social Formation*. Unpublished Ph.D. thesis, University of Sussex.

Elie, S. D. 2008. The waning of Soqotra's pastoral community: Political incorporation as social transformation. *Human Organization*. 67. 3: 335-345.

Elie, S. D. 2009. State-Community Relations in Yemen: Soqotra's Historical Formation as a Sub-National Polity. *History and Anthropology*. 20 .4: 363-393.

Emmons, G. T. and De Laguna, F. 1991. *The Tlingit Indians*. Seattle, University of Washington Press.

Esenkov, O. E. and Olson, D. B. 2002. A Numerical Study of the Somali Coastal Undercurrents. *Deep-Sea Research*. 49. 7-8: 1253-1277.

The Food and Agriculture Organization of the United Nations. 2005-2011. *World inventory of fisheries. Change in species abundance and distribution. Issues Fact Sheets*. Text by John Everett. In: The Food and Agriculture Organization of the United Nations Fisheries and Aquaculture Department [online]. Rome. Updated 27 May 2005. http://www.fao.org/fishery/topic/14780/en. [Accessed 29 October 2011].

Feld, S. and Basso, K. H. (eds) 1996. *Senses of Place*. Santa Fe, School of American Research Press.

Fett, R. W. and Burk, S. D. Island Barrier Effects as Observed by Satellite and Instrumented Aircraft, and Simulated by a Numerical Model. *Monthly Weather Review*. 109. 7: 1527-1541.

Fleitmann, D., Matter, A., Burns, S. J., Al-Subbary, A. and Al-Aowah, A. 2004. Geology and Quaternary climate of Socotra. *Fauna of Arabia*. 20: 27-43.

Flett, I. and Haberle, S. 2008. East of Easter: Traces of human impact in the far-eastern Pacific. In A. Anderson, G. R. Clark, F. Leach and S. O'Connor (eds), *Islands of Inquiry: Colonisation, Seafaring and the Archaeology of Maritime Landscapes*: 281-300. Canberra, ANUE Press.

Fontoura da Costa, A. 1940. *Roteiros de D. João de Castro III. Roteiro de Goa a Suez ou do Mar Roxo*

(1541). Album de Tavoas. Segunda edição prefaciada e anotada por A. Fontoura da Costa. Lisboa, Agéncia Geral de Colónias.

Forbes, H. O. 1899. The English Expedition to Sokotra. *The Geographical Journal*. 13. 6: 633-637.

Forbes, H. O. 1903. The Natural History of Sokotra and Abd-el-Kuri. *Special Bulletin of the Liverpool Museums*. London, R. H. Porter.

Frampton, R. M. and Uttridge, P. A. 2008. *Meteorology for seafarers, 3rd edition*. Glasgow, Brown.

Frazier, J. 1980. Exploitation of Marine Turtles in the Indian Ocean. *Human Ecology*. 8. 4: 329-370.

Freitag, U. 2003. *Indian Ocean Migrants and State Formation in Hadhramaut reforming the Homeland*. Leiden, Brill.

Fritz, M. H. and Okal, E. A. 2007. Socotra Island, Yemen: field survey of the 2004 Indian Ocean tsunami. *Natural Hazards*. 46: 107-117.

Gavin, R. J. 1975. *Aden under British Rule, 1839-1967*. London, C. Hurst and Co.

Geddes, C. L. 1964. An Account of Socotra in the early 17th Century. *University of Colorado Studies in History*. 3: 70-77.

Geertz, C. 2000. *The Interpretation of Cultures: Selected Essays*. New York, Basic Books.

Gilbert, E. 1998. The Mtepe: Regional Trade and the Late Survival of Sewn Ships in East African waters. *The International Journal of Nautical Archaeology*. 27. 1: 43-50.

Goitein, S. D. and Friedman, M. A. 2008. *India Traders of the Middle Ages Documents from the Cairo Geniza: India Book*. Leiden, Brill.

Gosden, C. and Pavlides, C. 1994. Are Islands Insular? Landscape vs. Seascape in the Case of the Arawe Islands, Papua New Guinea. *Archaeology in Oceania*. 29.3: 162-171.

Grandidier, A., Charles-Roux, J., Delhorbe, C., Froidevaux, H. and Grandidier, G. 1903. *Collection des ouvrages anciens concernant Madagascar*. Paris, Comité de Madagascar.

Groom, N. 1981. *Frankincense and Myrrh: A study of the Arabian Incense Trade*. London: Longman.

Gupta, A. and Ferguson, J. 1992. Beyond 'Culture': Space, Identity and the Politics of Difference. *Cultural Anthropology*. 7.1: 6-23.

Haines, R. B. 1845. Memoir of the South and East Coasts of Arabia. Part II. *Journal of the Royal Geographical Society of London*. 15: 104-160.

Hardy-Guilbert, C. 2001. Archaeological Research at al-Shiḥr, the Islamic Port of Ḥaḍramawt, Yemen (1996-1999). *Proceedings of the Seminar for Arabian Studies*. 31:69-79.

Hardy-Guilbert, C. 2005. The Harbour of al-Shiḥr, Ḥaḍramawt, Yemen: Sources and Archaeological Data on Trade. *Proceedings of the Seminar for Arabian Studies*. 35: 71-85.

Hariri, K. and Abdulaziz, M. 2006. Case Study 5. Fisheries Management: Integrating Planning and Practice. In C. Cheung, L. Devantier and K. Van Damme (eds), *Socotra: A Natural History of the Islands and their People*: 356-357. Hong Kong, Odyssey.

Hariri, K., and Yusif, M. D. 1999. *Fishing communities and status of the fisheries sector in the Socotra Archipelago*. Unpublished report.

Hariri, K. I., Nichols, P. V., Krupp, F., Mishrigi, S., Barrania, A., Ali, F. A. and Kedidi, S. M. 2002. *Status of the Living Marine Resources in the Red Sea and Gulf of Aden and Their Management prepared for the Regional Organization for the Conservation of the Environment of the Red Sea and Gulf of Aden (PERSGA)*. Washington.

Hasse, L. and Brown, R. A. 2001. The Influence of Mesoscale Atmospheric Processes. In I. S. F. Jones and Y. Toba (eds), *Wind stress over the Ocean*: 218-231. Cambridge, Cambridge University Press.

Hasslöf, O. 1966. Sources of Maritime History and Methods of Research. *The Mariner's Mirror*. 52. 2: 127-144.

Hasslöf, O. 1972. The Concept of Living Tradition. In O. Hasslöf, H. Henniingsen and A. E. Christensen (eds), *Ships and shipyards, sailors and fishermen. Introduction to Maritime Ethnology*: 20-26. Copenhagen, Copenhagen University Press.

Hoeppe, G. 2007. *Conversations on the Beach. Fishermen's knowledge, Metaphor and Environmental Change in South India*. New York, Berghahn Books

Horden, P. and Purcell, N. 2000. *The Corrupting Sea: A Study of Mediterranean History*. Oxford, Blackwell.

Hornell, J. 1920. *The Origins and Ethnological Significance of Indian Boat Designs*. Calcutta, Asiatic Society.

Hornell, J. 1950. *Fishing in Many Waters*. Cambridge, Cambridge University Press.

Hornell, J. 1970. *Water transport: Origins and Early Evolution*. Newton Abbot, David and Charles.

Horton, M., Brown, H. W. and Mudida, N. 1996. *Shanga: The Archaeology of a Muslim Trading Community on the Coast of East Africa*. London, British Institute in Eastern Africa.

Horton, M., Brown, H. W. and Mudida, N. 1996. *Shanga: The Archaeology of a Muslim Trading Community on the Coast of East Africa*. London, British Institute in Eastern Africa.

Hulton, J. 2003. *South Arabia: The 'Palinurus' Journals*. Edited by W.A. Hulton, Newly reset with new and original maps and illustration and a new introduction by Carl Phillips. Cambridge, Oleander

Hunter, F. M. and Sealey, C. W. H. 1986. *An Account of the Arab tribes in the vicinity of Aden*. London, Darf Publishers.

Hunter, J. R. 1994. Maritime Culture: Notes from the Land. *The International Journal of Nautical Archaeology*. 23. 4: 261-264.

Ingrams, D. and Ingrams, L. 1993. *Records of Yemen: 1798-1960*. Farnham Common, Archive Editions.

Jameson, H. 1949. Storminess near Socotra at the beginning of the South-West Monsoon. *The Marine Observer: A Quarterly Journal of Maritime Meteorology*. 19: 67-120.

Jansen van Rensburg, J. 2010. The Hawārī of Socotra, Yemen. *The International Journal of Nautical Archaeology*. 39. 1: 99-109.

Jansen van Rensburg, J. 2012. Appendix II: Inscribed stones from Delisha in the journal of Ormsby. In I. Strauch (ed.), *Foreign Sailors on Socotra. The inscriptions and drawings from the cave Hoq*: 433-437. Bremen, Hempen Verlag.

Jasinski, M. E. 1994. Maritime cultural landscape-archaeological perspective. *Archaeologia Polski*. 38. 1: 7-21.

Kammerer, A. 1936. *Les routiers de Dom Joam de Castro: l'exploration de la mer Rouge par les Portugais en 1541*. Paris, Paul Gueuthner.

Kaye, S. B. 1997. *The Torres Strait*. The Hague, M. Nijhoff Publishers.

Kearney, M. 2004. *The Indian Ocean in World History*. London, Routledge.

Kentley, E. B. 1988. *Suakin and its Fishermen: A Study of Economic Activities and Ethnic Groupings in a Sudanese Port*. Unpublished Ph.D. thesis, University of Hull.

King, N. and Horrocks, C. 2010. *Interviews in Qualitative Research*. London, Sage Publications.

Kirch, P. V. 1986. Exchange Systems and Inter-island contact in the Transformation of an Island Society: The Tikopia Case. In P. V. Kirch (ed.), *Island Societies: Archaeological Approaches in Evolution and Transformation*: 33-41. Cambridge, Cambridge University Press.

Kirch, P. V. and Rallu, J. L. 2007. *The Growth and Collapse of Pacific Island Societies Archaeological and Demographic Perspectives*. Honolulu, University of Hawaii Press.

Klaus, R., Turner, J. and West, F. 2002. *Conservation and Sustainable Use of Biodiversity of Socotra Archipelago. Marine Habitat, Biodiversity and Fisheries Surveys and Management Sublittoral and littoral biotope manual for the Socotra Archipelago. UNOPS (United Nations Office of Project Services) Division for Environmental Programmes Project YEM/96/ G32*. Frankfurt, Senckenberg Research Institute.

Lai, C. 2000. Braudel's Concepts and Methodology Reconsidered. *The European Legacy*. 5. 1: 6586.

LeBaron Bowen, R. 1951. Marine Industries of Eastern Arabia. *Geographical Review*. 41. 3: 384-400.

Leroy, S., Gente, P., Fournier, M., d'Acremont, E., Patriat, P., Beslier, M., Bellahsen, N., Maia, M., Blais, A., Perrot, J., Al-Kathiri, A., Merkouriev, S., Fleury, J., Ruellan, P., Lepvrier, C. and Huchon, P. 2004. From Rifting to Spreading in the Eastern Gulf of Aden: A Geophysical Survey of a Young Ocean Basin from Margin to Margin. *Terra Nova*. 16. 4: 185-192.

Leslau, W. 1938. *Lexique Soqotri (sudarabique moderne) avec comparaisons et explications étymologiques*. Paris, Klincksieck.

Lonnet, A. 1998. The Soqotri language: Past, Present and Future. In H. J. Dumont (ed.), *Proceedings of the first International Symposium on Soqotra Island: Present and Future. Soqotra Technical Series: 1-4. Aden, 24-28 March 1996*: 297-308. Aden, Aden University Press.

Luigi Bricchetti Robecchi's Journeys in the Somali Country. 1893. *The Geographical Journal*. 2. 4: 359-362.

Mack, J. 2007. The Land viewed from the Sea. *Azania*. 42: 1-14.

Manger, L. O. 2010. *The Hadrami Diaspora: Community-building on the Indian Ocean rim*. New York, Berghahn Books.

Martin, E. B. and Martin, C. P. 1978. *Cargoes of the East*. London, Elm Tree Books.

McGrail, S. 2002. *Boats of the World: from the Stone Age to Medieval times*. Oxford, Oxford University Press.

McIvor, I. 1986. Notes on fishing in the Persian Gulf with list of fish found in the Persian Gulf and Oman water. *The Persian Gulf administration reports: 1873-1947*: 54-79. Gerrards Cross, Archive Editions.

Méryl, S., Charpentier, V. and Beech, M. 2008. First evidence of shell fish-hook technology in the Gulf. *Arabian Archaeology and Epigraphy*. 19. 1: 15-21.

Miao, J. F., Kroon, L. J. M. and Vila'-Guerau de Arellano, J. 2003. Impacts of Topography and Land Degradation on the Sea Breeze over Eastern Spain. *Meteorology and Atmospheric Physics*. 84. 3-4: 157-170.

Mies, B. A. and Beyhl, F. E. 1996. The Vegetation Ecology of Soqotra. In H. J. Dumont (ed.), *Proceedings of the First International Symposium on Soqotra Island: Present and Future, Aden 1996. Conservation and Sustainable Use of Biodiversity of Soqotra Archipelago, Technical Series, Volume 1*: 35-81. New York, United Nations Publication.

Miles, S. B. 1919. *The Countries and Tribes of the Persian Gulf.* (2 vols.). London, Harrison and Sons.

Miller, A. G. and Morris, M. 2004. *Ethnoflora of the Soqotra Archipelago*. The Royal Botanical Garden, Edinburgh.

Moore, A. 1920. The Craft of the Red Sea and the Gulf of Aden. *The Mariner's Mirror*. 6. 1-2: 73-136.

Moore, A. H. 1925. *Last days of Mast and Sail: An Essay in Nautical Comparative Anatomy*. Oxford, Clarendon Press.

Moser, C. K. 1918. The Isle of Frankincense. *The National Geographical Magazine*. 33. 3: 267-278.

Morgan, D. L. 1997. *Focus Groups as Qualitative Research, Qualitative Research Methods.* (Series 16). London, Sage Publications.

Morris, M. 2002. *Manual of Traditional land use in the Soqotrian Archipelago, for G.E.F. (Global*

Environmental Facility) Project YEM/96/G32. Edinburgh.

Muir, R. 1999. *Approaches to Landscape*. London, Macmillan Press.

Müller, W. W. 2001. Anitke und Mittelalterliche Quellen als Zeugnisse über Soqotra, eine einstmals Christliche Insel. *Oriens Christianus*. 85: 139-161.

Murphy, E. and Dingwall, R. 2001. The Ethics of Ethnography. In P. Atkinson, A., Coffey, S., Delamont, J., Lofland and L. Lofland (eds), *Handbook of Ethnography*: 339-351. London, Sage Publications.

Murray, D. H. 1987. *Pirates of the South China Coast 1790-1810*. California, Stanford University Press.

Nalesini, O. 2009. History and Use of an Ethnonym: Ichthyophagoi. In L. K. Blue, J. P. Cooper, J. Whitewright and R. Thomas (eds), *Connected Hinterlands: Proceedings of Red Sea Project IV held at the University of Southampton, September 2008*: 9-18. Oxford, Archaeopress.

Naumkin, V. V. 1993. *Island of the Phoenix: An Ethnographic Study of the People of Socotra*. Translated by V. A. Epstein. Reading, Ithaca.

Naumkin, V. V. and Sedov, A. V. 1993. Monuments of Socotra. *Topoi*. 70. 3. 2: 569-623.

Neff, U., Burns, S. J., Mangini, A., Mudelsee, M., Fleitmann, D. and Matter, A. 2001. Strong coherence between solar variability and the monsoon in Oman between 9 and 6 kyr ago. *Nature*. 411: 290-293.

Nichols, P. V. 2001. *Fisheries Management Plan for the Socotra Island Group, UNOPS (United Nations Office of Project Services) Division for Environmental Programmes Project YEM/96/G32*. Frankfurt, Senckenberg Research Institute.

Ocean Passages of the World, 5th Edition. 2004. Taunton, United Kingdom Hydrographic Office.

Othman, W. A. 1996. Hydrological Conditions of Socotra. In H. J. Dumont (ed.), *Proceedings of the First International Symposium on Socotra Island Present and Future, Aden, 24-28 March, 1996. Vol. 2, Natural Resources and Environmental Protection*: 203-218. Aden, University of Aden Printing and Publishing House.

Al-Oufi, H. S. 1999. *Social and economic factors influencing the emergence of collective action in a traditional fishery of Oman: an empirical assessment of three coastal fishing towns in south Al-Batinah*. Unpublished Ph.D. thesis, University of Hull.

Parker, A. J. 2001. Maritime Landscapes. *Landscapes*. 1: 22-41.

Pearson, M. N. 2003. *The Indian Ocean*. London, Routledge.

Pearson, M. N. 2010. The Idea of the Ocean. In P. Gupta, I. Hofmeyr and M. N. Pearson (eds), *Eyes across the Water: Navigating the Indian Ocean*: 7-14. Pretoria, Unisa Press.

Peacock, D. P. S. and Blue, L. K. (eds) 2006. *Myos Hormos – Quseir al-Qadim: Roman and Islamic ports on the Red Sea 1: Survey and excavations 1999-2003*. Oxford, Archaeopress.

Peacock, D. P. S. and Blue, L. K. (eds) 2011. *Myos Hormos – Quseir al-Qadim: Roman and Islamic ports on the Red Sea. Vol. 2*. Oxford, Archaeopress.

Petersen, R. K. 2010. A Clench-Fastened Boat in Kerala, Indian. *The International Journal of Nautical Archaeology*. 39.1: 110-115.

Peterson, J. E. 1985. The Islands of Arabia: Their Recent History and Strategic Importance. *Arabian Studies*. 7: 23-35.

Peucke. 1899 The Austrian Expedition to Southern Arabia and Sokotra. *The Geographical Journal*. 13. 6: 638-640.

Pilcher, N., and Saad, M. A. 2000. Sea Turtle Survey. In K. I. Hariri and F. Krupp (eds), *Conservation and Sustainable Use of Biodiversity of Socotra Archipelago, Marine Habitat, Biodiversity and Fisheries Surveys and Management, UNOPS (United Nations Office of Project Services) Division for Environmental Programmes Project YEM/96/G32. Report of Phase II*: 83-96. Frankfurt, Senckenberg Research Institute.

Popov, G. B. 1957. The Vegetation of Socotra. *Journal of the Linnean Society of London, (Botany)*. 55. 362: 706-717.

Power, T. 2009. The Expansion of Muslim Commerce in the Red Sea Basin, c. AD 833-969. In L. K. Blue, J. P. Cooper, J. Whitewright and R. Thomas (eds), *Connected Hinterlands: Proceedings of Red Sea Project IV held at the University of Southampton, September 2008*: 111-118. Oxford, Archaeopress.

Power, T. C. 2010. *The Red Sea during the Long Late Antiquity (AD 500-1000)*. Unpublished DPhil thesis, University of Oxford.

Power, T. 2012. Trade Cycles and Settlement Patterns in the Red Sea Region (C. AD 1050-1250). In A. A. Agius, J. P. Cooper, A. Trakadas and C. Zazzaro (eds), *Navigated spaces, connected places: proceedings of Red Sea Project V: held at the University of Exeter, 16-19 September 2010*: 137- 146. Oxford, Archaeopress.

Prados, E. 1996. Huris, Sanbuqs, and the Boatbuilders of Yemen. *Wooden Boat*. 131: 50-56.

Prados, E. 1997. Indian Ocean Littoral Maritime Evolution: The case of the Huri and Sanbuq. *The Mariner's Mirror*. 83. 2: 185-198.

Prados, E. 1998. Wooden Boats of the Yemeni Tihamah. *Nautical Research Journal*. 43. 4: 195-209.

Prasad, T. G. and McClean, J. L. 2004. Mechanisms for anomalous warming in the western Indian Ocean during dipole mode events. *Journal of Geophysical Research*. 109: 123-137.

Prins, A. H. J. 1965. *Sailing from Lamu: A Study of Maritime Culture in Islamic East Africa*. Assen, Van Gorcum.

Piggott, R. J. 1961. *A School Geography of Zanzibar*. London, Macmillan.

Rajeevan, M. and Butala, P. P. 1990. A Preliminary Study on the Variability of Post Monsoon Tropical Cyclone Activity over the North Indian Ocean. *Mausam*. 41. 3: 409-414.

Rappoport. A. S. 1971. *Superstitions of Sailors*. Michigan, Ann Arbor.

Ray, H. P. 1994. *The Winds of Change: Buddhism and the Maritime Links of Early South Asia*. Oxford, Oxford University Press.

Ray, H. P. 2003. *The Archaeology of Seafaring in Ancient South Asia*. Cambridge, Cambridge University Press.

Rayner, G. H. 2006. *Africa Pilot. Volume III, South and east coasts of Africa from Cape Agulhas to Raas Binna, including the islands of Zanzibar and Pemba, 14th edition*. Taunton, United Kingdom Hydrographic Office.

Robin, C. and Gorea, M. 2002. Les véstiges antiques de la grotte de Hôq (Suqutra, Yemen). *Académie des Inscriptions et Belles-Lettres. Comptes Rendus des Séances de l'annee*: 409-445.

Rougelle, A. 1999. Coastal Settlements in Southern Yemen: the 1996-1997 Survey Expeditions on the Ḥaḍramawtand Mahra coasts. *Proceedings of the Seminar for Arabian Studies*. 29: 123-136.

Rougelle, A. 2003. Excavations at Sharmah, Ḥaḍramawt: the 2001 and 2002 seasons. *Proceedings of the Seminar for Arabian Studies*. 33: 287-307.

Rougelle, A. 2005. The Sharma Horizon: Sgraffiato Wares and other glazed ceramics of the Indian Ocean trade (c.AD 980-1140). *Proceedings of the Seminar for Arabian Studies*. 35: 223-246.

Saeed, S. 2000. Preliminary survey on the status of shark stocks in Socotra. In K. I. Hariri and F. Krupp (eds), *Conservation and Sustainable Use of Biodiversity of Socotra Archipelago, Marine Habitat, Biodiversity and Fisheries Surveys and Management, UNOPS (United Nations Office of Project Services) Division for Environmental Programmes Project YEM/96/ G32. Report of Phase II*: 123-128. Frankfurt, Senckenberg Research Institute.

Saji, N. H., Goswami, B. N., Vinayachandran, P. N. and Yamagata, T. 1999. A dipole mode in the tropical Indian Ocean. *Nature*. 401: 360-363.

Schensul, S. L., Schensul, J. J. and LeCompte, M. D. 1999. *Essential Ethnographic Methods: Observations, Interviews, and Questionnaires*. California, AltaMira Press.

Scholte, P., and De Geest, P. 2010. The climate of Socotra Island (Yemen): A first-time assessment of the timing of the monsoon wind reversal and its influence on precipitation and vegetation patterns. *Journal of Arid Environments*. 74: 1507-1515.

Schott, F. A. and McCreary, J. P. 2001. The Monsoon Circulation of the Indian Ocean. *Progress in Oceanography*. 51: 1-123.

Schweinfurth, G. A. 1881. Visit to the island of Socotra. *The Anti-Slavery Reporter*. 1. 8: 127-129.

Schweinfurth, G. A. 1993. Recollections of a Voyage to Socotra. In D. Ingrams and L. Ingrams (eds), *Records of Yemen: 1798-1960*: 189-204. Farnham Common, Archive Editions.

Scott, C. and Mulrennan, M. 1999. Land and Sea Tenure at Erub, Torres Strait: Property, Sovereignty and the Adjudication of Cultural Continuity. *Oceania*. 70.2: 146-176.

Scott, H., Mason, K. and Marshall, M. 1946. *Western Arabia and the Red Sea*. Oxford, Naval Intelligence Division.

Sedov, A. 1992. New Archaeological and Epigraphical Material from Qana' (South Arabia). *Arabian Archaeology and Epigraphy*. 3.2:110-137.

Sedov, A. 1994. Qana (Yemen) and the Indian Ocean: The Archaeological Evidence. In H. P. Ray and J. F. Salles (eds), *Tradition and Archaeology. Early Maritime contacts in the Indian Ocean*: 11-36. New Delhi, Ajay Kumar Jain.

Sedov, A. V., Naumkin, V. V., Vinogradov, Y. A., Zhukov, V. A., Vinogradova, E. M., Kurkina, E. A. and Sarabjev, A. V. 2009. *Preliminary Report of the Russian Interdisciplinary Mission to the Republic of Yemen, submitted to the general organization of antiquities and museums (G.O.A.M.)*. Moscow.

Serjeant, R. B. 1963. *The Portuguese off the South Arabian Coast*. Oxford, Clarendon Press.

Serjeant, R. B. 1992. The Coastal Population. In D. B. Doe (ed.), *Socotra Island of Tranquility*: 133-180. London, Immel.

Serjeant, R. B. 1995. A Socotran star calendar. In R. B. Serjeant, and G. R. Smith (eds), *Farmers and fishermen in Arabia: Studies in Customary Law and Practice*: 94-100. Aldershot, Variorum.

Serjeant, R. B. 1996. The Coastal Population of Socotra. In R. B. Serjeant and G. R. Smith (eds), Society and Trade in Southern Arabia: 133-180. Aldershot, Variorum.

Shankar, D., Vinayachandran, P. N. and Unnikrishnan, A. S. 2002. The Monsoon Currents in the North Indian Ocean. *Progress in Oceanography*. 52: 63-120.

Shelat, B. 2012. Appendix I: The Gujarati stone inscriptions from Rās Ḥowlef (Socotra). In I. Strauch (ed), *Foreign Sailors on Socotra. The inscriptions and drawings from the cave Hoq*: 407-432. Bremen, Hempen Verlag.

Sherman Heyl, B. 2001. Ethnographic Interviewing. In P. Atkinson, A. Coffey, S. Delamont, J. Lofland and L. Lofland (eds), *Handbook of Ethnography*: 369-383. London, Sage Publications.

Sheriff, A. 2010. *Dhow cultures of the Indian Ocean: Cosmopolitanism, Commerce and Islam*. New York, Columbia University Press.

Shinnie, P. L. 1960. Socotra. *Antiquity*. 34. 134: 100-110.

Shnukal, A., Nagata, Y., and Ramsay, G. 2004. *Navigating boundaries the Asian diaspora in Torres Strait*. Canberra, Pandanus Books.

Sidebotham, S. E., and Wendrich, W. Z. 2007. *Berenike 1999/2000, Report on the Excavations at Berenike, including Excavations in Wadi Kalalat and Siket and the Survey of the Mons Smaragdus Region.* California, University of California Press.

Sidebotham, S. E. 2011. *Berenike and the Ancient Maritime Spice Route.* California, University of California Press.

Simonelle-Senelle, M. C. 1997. The Modern South Arabian Languages. In R. Hetzron (ed.), *The Semantic Languages*: 378-423. London, Routledge.

Simonelle-Senelle, M. C. 1998. The Soqotri language. In H. J. Dumont (ed.), *Proceedings of the first International Symposium on Soqotra Island: Present and Future. Soqotra Technical Series: 1- 4. Aden, 24-28 March 1996*: 309-326. Aden, Aden University Press.

Smith, G. R. 1985. Ibn al-Mujāwir on Dohfar and Socotra. *Proceedings of the Seminar for Arabian Studies.* 15: 79-92.

Smith G. R. 1995. Have you Anything to Declare? Maritime Trade and Commerce in Ayyubid Aden: Practices and Taxes. *Proceedings of the Seminar for Arabian Studies.* 25: 127-140.

Spradley, J. P. 1979. *The Ethnographic Interview.* Belmont, California, Wadsworth, Thomson Learning.

Spriggs, M. 1997. *The Island Melanesians.* Oxford, Blackwell.

Strauch, I. 2012. *Foreign Sailors on Socotra: The inscriptions and drawings from the cave Hoq.* Bremen, Hempen Verlag.

Strauch, I. and Bukharin, M. D. 2004. Indian Inscriptions from the Cave Ḥoq on Suquṭrā (Yemen). *Annali.* 64: 121-138.

Terrell, J. E., Hunt, T. L. and Gosden, C. 1997. The Dimensions of Social Life in the Pacific: Human Diversity and the myth of the primitive isolate. *Current Anthropology.* 38: 155-196.

Thomas, R. I. 2010. Fishing Equipment from Myos Hormos and Fishing Techniques on the Red Sea in the Roman period. In T. Bekker-Nielsen and D. Casasola (eds), *Ancient nets and fishing gear: proceedings of the International Workshop on 'Nets and Fishing Gear in Classical Antiquity: A First Approach', Cádiz, November 15-17, 2007*: 139-160. Cádiz, Servicio de Publicaciones de la Universidad de Cádiz.

Thomas, R. I. 2012. Port communities and the Erythraean Sea trade. *British Museum Studies in Ancient Egypt and Sudan* 18: 169-199.

Tibbs, C. 2008. *On-Board Weather Handbook.* London, McGraw-Hill Professional Publishing.

Tibbetts, G. R. 1981. *Arab navigation in the Indian Ocean before the coming of the Portuguese: being a translation of Kitāb al-Fawā'id fī uṣūl al-baḥr wa l-qawā'id' of Aḥmad b. Mājid al-Najdī.* London, Royal Asiatic Society.

Tilley, C. 2006. Introduction: Identity, Place, Landscape and Heritage. *Journal of Material Culture.* 11 (1/2): 7-32.

Tomber, R. 2008. *Indo-Roman trade: from Pots to Pepper.* London, Duckworth.

Ubaydli, A. 1989. The population of Sūqutrā in the Early Arabic Sources. *Proceedings of the Seminar for Arabian Studies.* 19: 137-154.

Van der Veen, M. and Cox, A. 2011. *Consumption, trade and innovation: Exploring the botanical remains from the Roman and Islamic ports at Quseir al-Qadim, Egypt.* Frankfurt, Africa Magna Verlag.

Varadarajan, L. 1980. Traditions of Indigenous Navigation in Gujarat. *South Asia* 3: 28-35.

Varisco, D. 1994. Socotra Comes to Light. *Yemen Update.* 34: 40-41.

Vayda, A. P. and McCay, B. J. 1975. New Directions in Ecology and Ecological Anthropology. *Annual Review of Anthropology.* 4: 293-306.

Villiers, A. 1952. *Monsoon Seas: The story of the Indian Ocean.* New York, McGraw-Hill.

Vora, H. and Grattan-Cooper, A. C. 2007. *Red Sea and Gulf of Aden Pilot: Suez Canal, Gulf of Suez and Gulf of `Aqaba, Red Sea, Gulf of Aden, South-east coast of Arabia – Ra's Fartak to Ra's al Junayz, coast of Africa – Raas Caseyr to Raas Binna, Suqutrá and adjacent islands. 15th edition.* Taunton, United Kingdom Hydrographic Office.

Vosmer, T. 1997. Indigenous Fishing Craft of Oman. *The International Journal of Nautical Archaeology.* 26. 3: 217-235.

Wagenaar, A. and D'Haese, M. 2007. Development of small-scale fisheries in Yemen: An exploration. *Marine Policy.* 31: 266-275.

Walley, C. 2004. *Rough Waters: Nature and Development in an East African Marine Park.* Princeton, Princeton University Press.

Warren, B. A. 1987. Ancient and Medieval Records of the Monsoon Winds and Currents of the Indian Ocean. In J. S. Fein and P. L. Stephens (eds), *Monsoons*: 137-158. New York, John Wiley & Sons.

Weeks, L., Morris, M., McCall, B. and Al-Zubairy, K. 2002. A Recent Archaeological Survey on Soqotra. Report on the Preliminary Expedition Season, January 5th-February 2nd 2001. *Arabian Archaeology and Epigraphy.* 13. 1: 95-125.

Weir, S. 1994. Island of the Phoenix: Book Review. *British-Yemeni Society Newsletter.*

Weiss, E. A. 1973. Some Indigenous Trees and Shrubs Used by Local Fishermen on the East African Coast. *Economic Botany.* 27. 2: 174-192.

Weller, R. A., Baumgartner, M. F., Josey, S. A., Fischer, A. S. and Kindle, J. C. 1998. Atmospheric Forcing in the Arabian Sea during 1994-1995: Observations and Comparisons with Climatology and Models. *Deep Sea Research II: Topical Studies in Oceanography.* 45: 1961-1999.

Wellsted, J. R. 1835a. Memoir on the Island of Socotra. *Journal of the Royal Geographical Society*. 5: 129-229.

Wellsted, J. R. 1835b. Report on the island of Socotra. *Journal of the Asiatic Society of Bengal*. 4: 138-165.

Wellsted, J. R. 1840. *Travels to the City of the Caliphs along the shores of the Persian Gulf and the Mediterranean: including a Voyage to the coast of Arabia, and a Tour on the Island of Socotra*. (2 vols.). London, Henry Colburn.

Westerdahl, C. 1992. The Maritime Cultural Landscape. *The International Journal of Nautical Archaeology*. 21. 1: 5-14.

Westerdahl, C. 2008. Fish and Ships. Towards a theory of maritime culture. *Deutches Schiffahrtsarchiv Wissenschaftliches Jahrbuch des Deutchen Schiffahrtsmuseums*. 30: 191-236.

Whitcomb, D. S. 1988. Islamic Archaeology in Aden and the Hadhramaut. In D. T. Potts (ed.), *Araby the Blest: Studies in Arabian Archaeology*: 176-263. Copenhagen, Carsten Niehbuhr Institute.

Wilkinson, S. 2006. Focus Group Research. In E. Silverman (ed.), *Qualitative Research: Theory, Method and Practice. Second Edition*: 177-199. London, Sage Publications.

Wirth, A., Willebrand, J. and Schott, F. 2002. Variability of the Great Whirl from Observations and Models. *Deep Sea Research II*. 49: 1279-1295.

Wranik, W. 1999. *Sokotra: Mensch und Natur*. Wiesbaden, Reichert.

W. S. Atkins International. 2001. *Socotra Archipelago Master Plan (SAMP). Phase I Final Reports. EU Project. YEM/B7/3000/IB/97/0787*. Sana'a, Yemen.

Wynne-Jones, S. 2007. It's what you do with it that counts: performed identities in the East African coastal landscape. *Journal of Social Archaeology*. 7. 3: 325-345.

Yajima, H. 1976. *The Arab Dhow Trade in the Indian Ocean*. Tokyo, Institute for the Study of Languages and Cultures of Asia and Africa.

Young, A. J. 2007. *Contemporary Maritime Piracy in Southeast Asia: History, Causes, and Remedies*. Institute of South East Asian studies, Singapore.

Yule, H. and Cordier, H. 1993. *The travels of Marco Polo: the complete Yule-Cordier edition: including the unabridged third edition (1903) of Henry Yule's annotated translation, as revised by Henri Cordier, together with Cordier's later volume of notes and addenda (1920)*. New York-London, Dover Publications-Constable.

Zajonz, U., Khalaf, M. and Krupp, F. 2000. Coastal fish assemblages of the Socotra Archipelago. In *Conservation and Sustainable Use of Biodiversity of Socotra Archipelago. Marine Habitat, Biodiversity and Fisheries Surveys and Management Sublittoral and littoral biotope manual for the Socotra Archipelago Report Phase 3. UNOPS (United Nations Office of Project Services) Division for Environmental Programmes Project YEM/96/G32*. Frankfurt, Senckenberg Research Institute.

Zajonz, U. and Khalaf, M. 2002. Inshore fishes of the Socotra Archipelago: diversity and community structure. In *Conservation and Sustainable Use of Biodiversity of Socotra Archipelago. Marine Habitat, Biodiversity and Fisheries Surveys and Management Sublittoral and littoral biotope manual for the Socotra Archipelago Report Phase 3. UNOPS (United Nations Office of Project Services) Division for Environmental Programmes Project YEM/96/G32*. Frankfurt, Senckenberg Research Institute.